SARGON II, KING OF ASSYRIA

ARCHAEOLOGY AND BIBLICAL STUDIES

Brian B. Schmidt, General Editor

Editorial Board:
Aaron Brody
Annie Caubet
Billie Jean Collins
Israel Finkelstein
André Lemaire
Amihai Mazar
Herbert Niehr
Christoph Uehlinger

Number 22

SARGON II, KING OF ASSYRIA

Josette Elayi

SBL PRESS

Atlanta

Copyright © 2017 by Josette Elayi

All rights reserved. No part of this work may be reproduced or transmitted in any form or by any means, electronic or mechanical, including photocopying and recording, or by means of any information storage or retrieval system, except as may be expressly permitted by the 1976 Copyright Act or in writing from the publisher. Requests for permission should be addressed in writing to the Rights and Permissions Office, SBL Press, 825 Houston Mill Road, Atlanta, GA 30329 USA.

Library of Congress Cataloging-in-Publication Data

Names: Elayi, Josette, author.
Title: Sargon II, King of Assyria / by Josette Elayi.
Description: Atlanta : SBL Press, 2017. | Series: Archaeology and biblical studies ; number 22 | Includes bibliographical references and index.
Identifiers: LCCN 2017009197 (print) | LCCN 2017012087 (ebook) | ISBN 9780884142232 (ebook) | ISBN 9780884142249 (hardcover : alk. paper) | ISBN 9781628371772 (pbk. : alk. paper)
Subjects: LCSH: Sargon II, King of Assyria, –705 B.C. | Assyria—History. | Assyria—History, Military.
Classification: LCC DS73.8 (ebook) | LCC DS73.8 .E43 2017 (print) | DDC 935/.03092 [B] —dc23
LC record available at https://lccn.loc.gov/2017009197

Printed on acid-free paper.

Contents

Author's Note vii
Abbreviations ix

Introduction 1

1. Portrait of Sargon 11
2. Sargon's Ascent to the Throne 25
3. Heir to the Assyrian Empire 33
4. The Conquest of the West 45
   - Palestine — 45
   - Syria — 61
   - Phoenicia — 67
   - Cyprus — 72
   - Egypt — 78
5. The Northwest of the Empire 85
   - Mushki/Phrygia — 87
   - Que, Hilakku, Samal — 90
   - Tabal, Bit-Purutash — 98
   - Gurgum — 103
   - Kummuhu — 106
   - Kammanu/Melid — 109
6. The Wars in the North of the Empire 115
   - Shubria, Amidi, Tushhan — 115
   - Ukku, Kumme — 122
   - The Mashennu and Rab-Shaqe Provinces — 126

	Mannea	129
	Urartu	136
	Hubushkia, Musasir	143
7.	Neutralization of the Eastern States	153
	Central Zagros	155
	Media	163
	Ellipi	169
	Elam	171
8.	Recurring Problems in the South	177
	Aramean and Chaldean Tribes	177
	Babylonia	182
	Dilmun	190
	Arab Tribes	194
9.	End of Reign	201
	The Inauguration of Khorsabad/Dûr-Sharrukîn	201
	The Suspicious Death of Sargon	210
	The "Sin" of Sargon	213
10.	Chronological Synthesis of Sargon's Reign	219

Conclusion: Assessment of Sargon's Reign 245

Selected Bibliography 257
Index of Ancient Sources 267
Index of Modern Authors 268
Index of Personal Names 275

Author's Note

Because my book was completed before the publication of Sarah C. Melville's *The Campaigns of Sargon II, King of Assyria 721–705 B.C.* (Campaigns and Commanders 55, [Norman: University of Oklahoma Press, 2016]), I was unable to consult it.

Abbreviations

AAE	*Arabian Archaeology and Epigraphy*
AANEA	Archaeopress Ancient Near Eastern Archaeology
ABS	Archaeology and Biblical Studies
ACFP	*Atti del Congresso Internazionale di Studi Fenici e Punice*
AchHist	Achaemenid History
ActAnt	*Acta Antiqua Academiae Scientiarum Hungaricae*
ADPV	Abhandlungen des Deutschen Palästina-Vereins
AeL	*Ägypten und Levante*
AfO	*Altorientalische Forschungen*
AfOB	Altorientalische Forschungen Beiheft
A.J.	Josephus *Antiquitates judaicae*
AJA	*American Journal of Archaeology*
ALASP	Abhandlungen zur Literatur Alt-Syrien-Palästinas und Mesopotamiens
AMI	*Archäologische Mitteilungen aus Iran*
AMIT	*Archäologische Mitteilungen aus Iran und Turan*
AncCiv	*Ancient Civilizations from Scythia to Siberia*
ANESSup	Ancient Near Eastern Studies Supplement Series
ann.	annals
AnOr	Analecta Orientalia
AnSt	*Anatolian Studies*
AntSem	Antiquités Sémitiques
AO	Louvre Museum acquisition number
AoF	*Altorientalische Forschungen*
AOS	American Oriental Series
ARAB	Luckenbill, Daniel David. *Ancient Records of Assyria and Babylonia*. 2 vols. Chicago: University of Chicago Press, 1926–1927. Repr., New York: Greenwood, 1968.
ARRIM	*Annual Review of the Royal Inscriptions of Mesopotamia Project*

ARTA	*Achaemenid Research on Texts and Archaeology*
ASSF	Acta Societatis Scientiarum Fennicae
Atiqot	*'Atiqot*
AUU	Acta Universitatis Upsaliensis
AW	*Antike Welt*
AYBRL	Anchor Yale Bible Reference Library
BA	*Biblical Archaeologist*
BaghM	*Baghdader Mitteilungen*
BASOR	*Bulletin of the American Schools of Oriental Research*
BBVO	Berliner Beiträge zum Vorderen Orient
BES	*Bulletin of the Egyptological Seminar*
Bib	*Biblica*
BibOr	Biblica et Orientalia
BiE	Biblische Enzyklopädie
BiOr	*Bibliotheca Orientalis*
BM	tablets in the collections of the British Museum
BMes	Bibliotheca Mesopotamia
BMRP	British Museum Research Publication
BN	*Biblische Notizen*
BO	*Bibliotheca Orientalis*
BCSMS	*Bulletin of the Canadian Society for Mesopotamian Studies*
bull	inscription on a bull colossus at Khorsabad
CAD	*The Assyrian Dictionary of the Oriental Institute of the University of Chicago.* Chicago: The Oriental Institute of the University of Chicago, 1956–2006.
CAH	Cambridge Ancient History
CahRB	Cahiers de la Revue biblique
CANE	Sasson, Jack M., ed. *Civilizations of the Ancient Near East.* 4 vols. New York: 1995. Repr. in 2 vols. Peabody, MA: Hendrickson, 2000.
CBQ	*Catholic Biblical Quarterly*
CHANE	Culture and History of the Ancient Near East
chr.	chronicle
CNIP	Carsten Niebuhr Institute Publications
CRIR	Culture and Religion in International Relations
CSSH	*Comparative Studies in Society and History: An International Quarterly*
CTN	Cuneiform Texts from Nimrud
CWA	*Current World Archaeology*

CWA	Cambridge World Archaeology
DASOR	Dissertation Series of the American Schools of Oriental Research
DHA	*Dialogues d'Histoire Ancienne*
DoArch	*Dossiers d'Archéologie*
ErIs	*Eretz-Israel*
FO	*Folia Orientalia*
GAT	Grundrisse zum Alten Testament
GBLC	Guide Belles Lettres des Civilisations
GG	Groundwork Guides
GM	*Göttinger Miszellen*
HANE/M	History of the Ancient Near East/Monographs
HANE/S	History of the Ancient Near East/Studies
HEO	Hautes Études Orientales
HiMA	*Revue Internationale d'Histoire Militaire Ancienne*
Hist.	Herodotus *Historiae*
HSAO	Heidelberger Studien zum Alten Orient
HW	History of Warfare
IEJ	*Israel Exploration Journal*
inscr.	inscription
IOUsm	Istituto Universitario Orientale, Seminario di Studi Asiatici, Series Minor
Iran	*Iran: Journal of the British Institute of Persian Studies*
IrAnt	*Iranica Antiqua*
JA	*Journal Asiatique*
JAAS	*Journal of Assyrian Academic Studies*
JAH	*Journal of Ancient History*
JAOS	*Journal of the American Oriental Society*
JARCE	*Journal of the American Research Center in Egypt*
JBQ	*Jewish Bible Quarterly*
JCS	*Journal of Cuneiform Studies*
JEgH	*Journal of Egyptian History*
JEOL	*Jaarbericht van het Voorazjatisch-Egytisch Gezelschap (Genootschap) Ex oriente lux*
JFA	*Journal of Field Archaeology*
JHebS	*Journal of Hebrew Scriptures*
JHS	*Journal of Hellenic Studies*
JNES	*Journal of Near Eastern Studies*
JSOT	*Journal for the Study of the Old Testament*

JSOTSup	Journal for the Study of the Old Testament Supplement Series
JSSSup	Journal of Semitic Studies Supplement Series
K.	tablet in the Kouyunjik collection of the British Museum
KAI	Donner, Herbert, and Wolfgang Röllig. *Kanaanäische und aramäische Inschriften*. 2nd ed. Wiesbaden: Harrassowitz, 1966–1969.
KAW	Kulturgeschichte der antiken Welt
Kemet	*Kemet: Die Zeitschrift für Ägyptenfreunde*
l(l).	line(s)
LAOS	Leipziger altorientalistische Studien
MC	Mesopotamian Civilizations
MemPhil	Memoirs of the American Philosophical Society
Mesopotamia	Mesopotamia: Copenhagen Studies in Assyriology
MSym	Melammu Symposia
NABU	*Nouvelles Assyriologiques Brèves et Utilitaires*
ND	field numbers of tablets excavated at Nimrud (Kalḫu)
NEA	Near Eastern Archaeology
NEAEHL	Stern, Ephraim, ed. *The New Encyclopedia of Archaeological Excavations in the Holy Land*. 5 vols. Jerusalem: Israel Exploration Society, 1993–2008.
NeHeT	*Revue numérique d'Égyptologie*
no(s).	number(s)
NS	new series
OAC	Orientis Antiqui Collectio
OBO	Orbis Biblicus et Orientalis
OeO	Oriens et Occidens
OLA	Orientalia Lovaniensia Analecta
OLP	*Orientalia Lovaniensia Periodica*
OPSNKF	Occasional Publications of the Samuel Noah Kramer Fund
Or	*Orientalia* NS
OrAnt	Oriens Antiquus
OSEE	Oxford Studies in Early Empire
PA	Památky Archeologické
PapyVind	*Papyrologia Vindobonensia*
PEFR	Publications de l'École Française de Rome
PIHANS	Publications de l'Institut Historique-Archéologique Neéerlandais de Stamboul

pl(s).	plate(s)
PNA	Baker, Heather, and Karen Radner, eds. *The Prosopography of the Neo-Assyrian Empire*. Helsinki: Neo-Assyrian Text Corpus Project, 1998–.
PPP	Peshdar Plain Project Publications
pr.	prism
QGS	Quaderni di geografia storica
Qad	*Qadmoniot: A Journal for the Antiquities of Eretz-Israel and Bible Lands*
RA	*Revue d'Assyriologie et d'archéologie orientale*
RAI	Rencontres Assyriologiques Internationales
RB	*Revue Biblique*
REA	*Revue des Études Anciennes*
REG	*Revue des Études Grecques*
ResAnt	*Res Antiquae*
RGTC	Répertoire Géographique des Textes Cunéiformes
RIMA	Royal Inscriptions of Mesopotamia, Assyrian Period
RIMA 1	Grayson, Albert Kirk, Grant Frame, Douglas Frayne, and M. P. Maidman, eds. *Assyrian Rulers of the Third and Second Millennia BC (to 1115 BC)*. RIMA 1. Toronto: University of Toronto Press, 1987.
RIMA 2	Grayson, Albert Kirk, ed. *Assyrian Rulers of the Early First Millennium BC I (1114–859 BC)*. RIMA 2. Toronto: University of Toronto Press, 1991.
RIMB	Royal Inscriptions of Mesopotamia, Babylonian Period
RIMB 2	Frame, Grant, ed. *Rulers of Babylonia: From the Second Dynasty of Isin to the End of Assyrian Domination (1157–612 BC)*. RIMB 2. Toronto: University of Toronto Press, 1995.
RINAP	Royal Inscriptions of the Neo-Assyrian Period
RINAP 1	Tadmor, Hayim, and Shigeo Yamada, ed. *The Royal Inscriptions of Tiglath-Pileser III (744–727 BC) and Shalmaneser V (726–722 BC), Kings of Assyria*. RINAP 1. Winona Lake, IN: Eisenbrauns, 2011.
RINAP 3	Grayson, Albert Kirk, and Jamie Novotny, eds. *The Royal Inscriptions of Sennacherib, King of Assyria (704–681 BC)*. 2 vols. RINAP 3. Winona Lake, IN: Eisenbrauns, 2012–2014.
RlA	Ebeling, Erich, et al., eds. *Reallexicon der Assyriologie*. Berlin: de Gruyter, 1928–.

ROMOP	Royal Ontario Museum Occasional Papers
RSF	*Rivista di Studi Fenici*
SAA	State Archives of Assyria
SAA 1	Parpola, Simo. *The Correspondence of Sargon II, Part I.* SAA 1. Helsinki: Helsinki University Press, 1987.
SAA 4	Starr, Ivan. *Queries to the Sungod.* SAA 4. Helsinki: Helsinki University Press, 1990.
SAA 5	Lanfranchi, Giovanni Battista, and Simo Parpola. *The Correspondence of Sargon II, Part II.* SAA 5. Helsinki: Helsinki University Press, 1990.
SAA 6	Kwasman, Theodore, and Simo Parpola. *Legal Transactions of the Royal Court of Nineveh Part I: Tiglath-pileser III through Esarhaddon.* SAA 6. Helsinki: Helsinki University Press, 1991.
SAA 7	Fales, Frederick Mario, and John Nicholas Postgate. *Imperial Administrative Records, Part I: Palace and Temple Administration.* SAA 7. Helsinki: Helsinki University Press, 1992.
SAA 11	Fales, Frederick Mario, and John Nicholas Postgate. *Imperial Administrative Records, Part II.* SAA 11. Helsinki: Helsinki University Press, 1995.
SAA 12	Kataja, Laura, and Robert Whiting. *Grants, Decrees and Gifts of the Neo-Assyrian Period.* SAA 12. Helsinki: Helsinki University Press, 1995.
SAA 15	Fuchs, Andreas, and Simo Parpola. *The Neo-Babylonian Correspondence of Sargon II, Part III: Letters from Babylonia and the Eastern Provinces.* SAA 15. Helsinki: Helsinki University Press, 2001.
SAA 17	Dietrich, Manfried. *The Neo-Babylonian Correspondence of Sargon and Sennacherib.* SAA 17. Helsinki: Helsinki University Press, 2003.
SAA 19	Luukko, Mikko. *The Correspondence of Tiglath-pileser III and Sargon II from Calah/Nimrud.* SAA 19. Helsinki: Neo-Assryian Text Corpus Project, 2012.
SAAB	*State Archives of Assyria Bulletin*
SAAS	State Archives of Assyria Studies
SAAS 2	Millard, Alan. *The Eponyms of the Assyrian Empire: 910–612 BC.* SAAS 2. Helsinki: Neo-Assyrian Text Corpus Project, 1994.

SAAS 3	De Odorico, Marco. *The Use of Numbers and Quantifications in the Assyrian Royal Inscriptions*. SAAS 3. Helsinki: Neo-Assyrian Text Corpus Project, 1995.
SAAS 6	Radner, Karen. *Die neuassyrischen Privatrechtsurkunden als Quelle für Mensch und Umwelt*. SAAS 6. Helsinki: Neo-Assyrian Text Corpus Project, 1997.
SAAS 8	Fuchs, Anreas. *Die Archives des Jahres 711 v. Chr. nach Prismenfragmenten aus Ninive und Assur*. SAAS 8. Helsinki: Neo-Assyrian Text Corpus Project, 1998.
SAAS 11	Mattila, Raija. *The King's Magnates: A Study of the Highest Officials in the Neo-Assyrian Empire*. SAAS 11. Helsinki: Neo-Assyrian Text Corpus Project, 2000.
SAAS 23	Svärd, Saana. *Women and Power in the Neo-Assyrian Palaces*. SAAS 23. Helsinki: Neo-Assyrian Text Corpus Project, 2015.
SAOC	Studies in Ancient Oriental Civilizations
SciAnt	*Scienze dell'Antichita: Storia, archeologia, antropologia*
ScrHier	Scripta Hierosolymitana
Sem	*Semitica*
SHANE	Studies in the History of the Ancient Near East
Skyllis	*Skyllis: Zeitschrift für Unterwasserarchäologie*
Sm.	tablet in British Museum, excavated by George Smith at Kouyunjik (Nineveh)
SMEA	*Studi Micenei ed Egeo-Anatolica*
SSN	Studia Semitica Neerlandica
StMes	*Studia Mesopotamica*
StOr	Studia Orientalia
StPohlSM	Studia Pohl Series Maior
TA	*Tel Aviv*
TAVO	Tübinger Atlas des Vorderen Orients
TCL	Textes cunéiformes. Musée du Louvre
TMO	Travaux de la Maison de l'Orient
Trans	*Transeuphratène*
TransSup	Transeuphratène Supplement
UISK	Untersuchungen zur indogermanischen Sprach- und Kulturwissenschaft
VA	Vorderasiatisches Museum
VDI	*Vestnik Drevney Istorii* [*Journal of Ancient History*]
VT	*Vetus Testamentum*

VTSup	Supplements to Vetus Testamentum
WA	*World Archaeology*
WBJb	*Jahrbuch: Wissenschaftskolleg zu Berlin*
WZKM/S	Wiener Zeitschrift für die Kunde des Morgenlandes Sonderband
ZA	*Zeitschrift für Assyriologie*
ZÄS	*Zeitschrift für Ägyptische Sprache und Altertumskunde*
ZDMG	*Zeitschrift der Deutschen Morgenländischen Gesellschaft*
ZDPG	*Zeitschrift des Deutschen Palästina-Vereins*

Key to Transliterated Words

kibrāt	Akkadian words are indicated by italics.
DINGIR	Sumerian word signs are indicated by capital letters

Explanation of Symbols

[ ]	single brackets enclose restorations.
⌐ ¬	raised brackets indicate partially visible signs.
( )	parentheses enclose additions in the English translation.
...	a row of dots indicates gaps in the text or untranslatable words.

Introduction

The imperialism of the great states of the Near East began to manifest itself in the third millennium BCE, with King Sargon of Akkad or Agade, who built the Sumerian-Akkadian Empire and was the precursor and model of the Assyrian kings.[1] In the second millennium, it was the Hittite Empire that extended over part of Turkey and northern Syria.[2] Samsî-Addu (Shamshi Adad I), king of Ekallatum, conquered the entire upper Mesopotamia and proclaimed himself "king of the world" (šàr kiššáti).[3] However, the action of these kings was still limited to the conquest of regional hegemonies, and the conquered territories did not on the whole recognize the authority of a central government.[4] Although Naram-Sîn of Akkad, the grandson of Sargon, asserted his claims to sovereignty over the five parts of the earth (the center: Agade, and four peripheral countries), the desire for universal domination essentially characterized the first millennium. It was especially formalized in the Assyrian inscriptions of King Ashurnasirpal II (883–859), with the excesses of an over-reaching pride—yet he

---

1. Joan Goodnick Westenholz, *Legends of the Kings of Akkade*, MC 7 (Winona Lake, IN: Eisenbrauns, 1997); Aage Westenholz, "The Old Akkadian Period: History and Culture," in *Akkade-Zeit und Ur III-Zeit*, ed. Walther Sallaberger and Aage Westenholz, OBO 160.3 (Göttingen: Vandenhoeck & Ruprecht; Fribourg: Presses Universitaires, 1999), 17–117.

2. Billie Jean Collins, *The Hittites and their World*, ABS 7 (Atlanta: Society of Biblical Literature, 2007).

3. RIMA 1:47–76; Pierre Villard, "Shamshi-Adad and Sons: the Rise and Fall of an Upper Mesopotamian Empire," *CANE* 2:873–83. On royal epithets, see, e.g., Marie Joseph Seux, *Épithètes royales akkadiennes et sumériennes* (Paris: Letouzey et Ané, 1967), 13–14.

4. Some scholars consider Akkad as the first known world empire: Mario Liverani, *Akkad, the First World Empire: Structure, Ideology, Traditions*, HANE/S 5 (Padova: Sargon, 1993). Other scholars prefer to speak of imperialism, not of empire, e.g., Jean-Jacques Glassner, *La Mésopotamie*, GBLC (Paris: Belles Lettres, 2002), 29–32.

contributed no more than his predecessors to the rise of Assyria.⁵ The true founder of the Assyrian Empire was King Tiglath-pileser III, who reigned from 744 to 727.⁶ Upon his accession to the throne, he initiated a series of military operations to conquer a vast continental territory with ocean access. This action consisted of more than merely episodic raids to bring in booty; he actually created a genuine imperialist-dependent system, a strong and effective source of considerable wealth. The Assyrian Empire was the first known "universal" empire of ancient times, in other words, large, centralized, and structured. Although it is sometimes said that the first universal empire was the Persian Empire or the empire of Alexander, this can only be said through ignorance of the Assyrian Empire. Its inevitable evolution, in an agonistic conception of sovereignty, was, first, the ongoing mechanism of conquests to annex "the four regions (of the world)" (*kibrāt arba'i*), and, second, the growing weight of the Assyrian administration which oppressed the conquered states, providing a land base for the political system.

The term *empire* is used for convenience by modern historians as the Assyrians called their country the "land of Assyria" (*māt Aššur*). This term comes from the German *Reich* and was born in the context of nineteenth century Prussia, based on the concept of the Holy Roman German Empire, with an emperor appointed by God, the supreme and almighty legislator.⁷ As defined by James Laxer, a Canadian specialist in political economy, "An empire exists when one nation, tribe or society exercises long-term domination over one or more nations, tribes or external societies.... The ability of the empire to determine what happens, the outcomes in the societies under its control, is what distinguishes an empire from

---

5. Albert Kirk Grayson, "Studies in Neo-Assyrian History," *BO* 33 (1976): 134–45; RIMA 2:189–393.

6. Paul Garelli, "The Achievement of Tiglath-pileser III: Novelty or Continuity?," in *Ah, Assyria...: Studies in Assyrian History and Ancient Near Eastern Historiography Presented to Hayim Tadmor*, ed. Mordechai Cogan and Israel Eph'al, ScrHier (Jerusalem: Magnes, 1991), 46–57. However, John Nicholas Postgate considered that there was continuity between the Medio-Assyrian and Neo-Assyrian periods; John Nicholas Postgate, *The Land of Assur and the Yoke of Assur: Studies on Assyria 1971–2005* (Oxford: Oxbow, 2007).

7. Christian Karl Josias von Bunsen, a Prussian diplomat and scholar, seems to have been the first to use it for the history of ancient Egypt; see *Ägyptens Stelle in der Weltgeschichte*, 5 vols. (Berlin: Gotha, 1844–1857).

other forms of political organization."[8] This definition of the concept of empire may be applied to the Assyrian state from the moment it was large enough and characterized by a programmatic supremacy, continuing hegemonic expansion, and a solid state-structure. These conditions were only met for the Assyrian state under Tiglath-pileser III. The history of the Assyrian Empire thus extends from 744 to 610 BCE, that is, a little less than a century and a half. After Tiglath-pileser III, his successors Shalmaneser V, Sargon II, and the Sargonids (Sennacherib, Esarhaddon, and Ashurbanipal) consolidated the Assyrian Empire. At the end of its history, it included the entire Near East, Elam, the Zagros, Turkey including Cappadocia, Cyprus, and Egypt.

The Assyrians had a deplorable reputation for ferocity. The Bible is mostly responsible for this reputation; it considered the Assyrian king as the armed wing of Yahweh, who destroyed the kingdom of Israel as punishment for its idolatrous behavior, beginning with the reign of King Jeroboam. An oracle of Isaiah also announced his action against the kingdom of Judah: "The Lord will raise against them the powerful and abundant waters of the River—the king of Assyria and all his army. It will rise everywhere above its bed, it will cross all its banks, it will invade Judah" (Isa 8:7–8).[9] The reputation for ferocity was amplified with the discovery of archaeological remains and texts in Iraq during the nineteenth century. They contain vivid descriptions of brutality, such as those of Ashurnasirpal II's campaigns, who boasted of having "dyed the mountain as red wool with the blood of slain enemies." "I have impaled them on stakes," he wrote, "I have skinned them and I have spread their skins on the walls of their cities," or "I sliced their hands, their fingers, their noses, their ears, I tore out their eyes, I cut their heads and I stacked them to form pillars."[10] In fact, the Assyrian civilization has been reduced to these acts of sadism through the dreadful vision that Europe had of the fading Ottoman Empire.[11] The modern judgment about this civilization was all the more unfavorable as it was compared with the "Greek miracle" of Hellenic-centric thinking. The Assyrians even gained a reputation for lacking an artistic and intellectual impulse and were viewed

---

8. James Laxer, *Empire*, GG (New York: Groundwood, 2006), 9.
9. Unless otherwise noted, this and all translations are mine.
10. RIMA 2:216–21, A.0.101.1, i.52–53, 87–89, 117–118.
11. Frederick Mario Fales, *Guerre et paix en Assyrie: Religion et impérialisme* (Paris: Cerf, 2010), 44; Francis Joannès, "Assyriens, Babyloniens, Perses achéménides: la matrice impériale," *DHA* Suppl. 5 (2011): 28–29.

as incapable of abstraction. For example, the monstrous winged bulls of Khorsabad (Dûr-Sharrukîn), the capital of Sargon, were compared with the delicate Greek statues of Phidias. The Assyrian mathematical texts have long been considered as disparate and approximate recipe lists without demonstration and symbolism because they were evaluated in comparison with the Greek models. However, recent studies have shown their specificity and importance, specifically by the operations, the global algorithmic level, the solution strategy, and the calculation technique (base 6). Even if the calculation in base 10, a system emanating from Indian mathematicians, has become widespread today, base 6 has not completely disappeared (60 seconds in a minute, 60 minutes in an hour, and 360 degrees in a circle). The science of numbers, arithmetic and algebra, was founded by the Sumerians and brilliantly developed by the Assyrians.[12]

It was King Sargon II (Šarru-kîn) who played an important and prestigious role in the history of the Assyrian Empire, providing its driving force at the peak of its renown. Three kings named Sargon existed in Mesopotamia. Sargon I, king of Assyria around 1920–1881 BCE, is little known.[13] Sargon, king of Akkad or Agade, around 2335–2279 according to the middle chronology, was so famous in the ancient world that he became legendary. Finally, Sargon II, who ruled from 722 to 705 and who bore the same name as his illustrious ancestor, is now the best known.[14]

It has often been said that a historian depends on his or her sources; this is especially true in ancient history, where they are often very lacunar and irregular. The historian of the Assyrian Empire, especially of Sargon's reign, is fortunate to have extensive documentation, sometimes even an overabundance. Without having performed a precise count of the Akkadian tablets that were found, they are estimated at half a million, and their number has increased with more recent discoveries. "Yet we have not found and exploited only a fraction, perhaps digitally huge but proportionally ridiculous," wrote Jean Bottéro.[15] Indeed, Sargon, like all Assyrian

---

12. See, e.g., Igor Mikhailovich Diakonoff, "Some Reflections on Numerals in Sumerian towards a History of Mathematical Speculation," *JAOS* 103 (1983): 83–93.

13. RIMA 1:45–46.

14. I shall specifically write Sargon II only when there might be confusion with Sargon I or Sargon of Agade. Some scholars date the beginning of Sargon's reign in 721, his first full year; I prefer to date it in 722, his accession year, even though it is an incomplete year.

15. Jean Bottéro, *L'écriture, la raison et les dieux* (Paris: Gallimard, 1987), 35:

kings, was anxious to leave to posterity the glory of his reign, in a spirit of emulation, striving to outdo the exploits of his predecessors. He had very detailed annals written, and all kinds of royal inscriptions on stone or metal material bear witness to his actions.[16] Stelae and rock reliefs were

---

"dans un sous-sol inépuisable, une gigantesque bibliothèque d'un demi-million de pièces pour le moins."

16. Official inscriptions: David Gordon Lyon, *Keilschrifttexte Sargons: König von Assyrien (722-705 v. Chr.)* (Leipzig: Heinrich, 1883); Hugo Winckler, *Die Keilschrifttexte Sargons*, vols. 1-2 (Leipzig: Pfeiffer, 1889); Franz Heinrich Weissbach, "Zu den Inschriften der Säle im Palaste Sargon's II. von Assyrien," *ZDMG* 72 (1918): 161-85; François Thureau-Dangin, "Les annales de la salle II du palais de Khorsabad, révision du texte d'après les estampages de Botta," *RA* 24 (1927): 75-84; *ARAB* 2.1-230; Arthur Gotfred Lie, *The Inscriptions of Sargon II, King of Assyria: Part I; The Annals* (Paris: Geuthner, 1929); Andreas Fuchs, *Die Inschriften Sargons II. aus Khorsabad* (Göttingen: Cuvillier, 1993); SAAS 8; RIMB 2:143-52; Grant Frame, *The Royal Inscriptions of Sargon II, King of Assyria (721-705 BC)*, RINAP (Winona Lake, IN: Eisenbrauns, forthcoming); Karen Radner, *State Correspondence in the Ancient World: From New Kingdom Egypt to the Roman Empire*, OSEE (Oxford: Oxford University Press, 2014), 64-93.

Other inscriptions: Cyril John Gadd, "Inscribed Prisms of Sargon II from Nimrud," *Iraq* 16 (1954): 173-201; Hayim Tadmor, "Fragments of an Assyrian Stele of Sargon II," *Atiqot* English Series 9-10 (1971): 192-97; Louis D. Levine, *Two Neo-Assyrian Stelae from Iran*, ROMOP 23 (Toronto: Royal Ontario Museum, 1972), 38-39; Giorgio Raffaele Castellino, "Il frammento degli Annali di Sargon II," in *Malatya III: Rapporto preliminare delle campagne 1963-1968, il livello eteo imperiale e quelli neoetei*, ed. Paolo Emilio Pecorella and Giorgio Raffaele Castellino, OAC 12 (Rome: Centro per le antichita e la storia dell'arte del Vicino Oriente, 1975), 69-73; Henry William Frederick Saggs, "Historical Texts and Fragments of Sargon II of Assyria. 1: The 'Aššur Charter,'" *Iraq* 37 (1975): 11-20; Zdzislaw Jan Kapera, "The Ashdod Stele of Sargon II," *FO* 17 (1976): 87-99; SAA 6; Grant Frame, "The Inscription of Sargon II at Tang-i Var," *Or* 68 (1999): 31-57; John David Hawkins, "The New Sargon Stele from Hama," in *From the Upper Sea to the Lower Sea: Studies on the History of Assyria and Babylonia in Honour of A. K. Grayson*, ed. Grant Frame and Linda Wilding, PIHANS 101 (Leiden: Nederlands Instituut voor het Nabije Oosten, 2004), 151-64; Grant Frame, "The Tell Acharneh Stela of Sargon II of Assyria," in *Tell Acharneh 1998-2004: Rapports préliminaires sur les campagnes de fouilles et saison d'études*, ed. Michel Fortin, Subartu 18 (Turnhout: Brepols, 2004), 49-68; Kathleen Abraham and Jacob Klein, "A New Sargon II Cylinder Fragment from an Unknown Provenance," *ZA* 97 (2007): 252-61; Grant Frame, "A New Cylinder Inscription of Sargon II of Assyria from Melid," in *Of God(s), Trees, Kings, and Scholars: Neo-Assyrian and Related Studies in Honour of Simo Parpola*, ed. Mikko Luukko, Saana Svärd, and Raija Mattila, StOr 106 (Helsinki: Finnish Oriental Society, 2009), 65-82.

intended to testify to the conquests and to mark the limits of the Assyrian Empire. Two unusual official inscriptions are the Letter to Assur and the Assur Charter. On the walls of his palace, representations were made of his conquests with spectacular actions in reliefs, sometimes accompanied by an epigraph, which prefigured our modern comics.[17]

To these numerous documents are added thousands of clay tablets, remarkably preserved in the arid soil of the Iraqi desert: letters and legal and economic documents. These clay tablets are written in cuneiform characters in the Neo-Assyrian dialect of the Akkadian language. Between 1,155 and 1,300 letters and fragments of letters are attributed to Sargon's reign, but only some of them are authored by Sargon.[18] In contrast to the royal inscriptions, they report daily events aimed at informing the Assyrian king, and they lack explanations of the context. Therefore, they are difficult to interpret, but they are the only sources for some regions. In fact, the Assyrian scribes also wrote on boards of wood covered with wax, or exceptionally of ivory. These boards were lighter; bound together by hinges like books, they were easier to read and store, and they were reusable. Scribes also wrote with ink on sheets of papyrus and parchment scrolls. These categories of material were not very suitable for the cut reeds used on clay tablets. A bas-relief depicts two scribes in the process of recording spoils of war: one was writing on a hinged writing-board, probably in Akkadian, the other on a papyrus or parchment scroll, possibly in Aramaic.[19] However, the passage of time has been disastrous for fragile wooden, papyrus, and leather material; they have all disappeared, except for a few wooden boards, for example, discovered in Nimrud (Kalhu).[20] Only the stone, metal, and clay inscriptions remain today. A question arises: What

---

17. Paul-Émile Botta, *Monuments de Ninive*, vols. 3–4 (Paris: Imprimerie Nationale, 1849); Pauline Albenda, *The Palace of Sargon King of Assyria: Monumental Wall Reliefs at Dur-Sharrukin, from Original Drawings Made at the Time of Their Discovery in 1843–1844 by Botta and Flandin*, Synthèse 22 (Paris: Recherches sur les Civilisations, 1986).

18. SAA 1:xi (1,300 letters); SAA 5; SAA 15; Bradley J. Parker, *The Mechanics of Empire: The Northern Frontier of Assyria as a Base of Imperial Dynamics* (Helsinki: Neo-Assyrian Text Corpus Project, 2001), 84; Natalie Naomi May, "Administrative and Other Reforms of Sargon II and Tiglath-pileser III," *SAAB* 21 (2015): 93–94 (1,155 letters).

19. SAA 1:103, fig. 28 (BM 124955); see SAA 17:2.

20. Laurie E. Pearce, "The Scribes and Scholars of Ancient Mesopotamia," *CANE* 4:2265–78.

proportion of perishable texts have we lost compared with the preserved texts? It is impossible to know. The history of Sargon can only be written using the existing documentation. There are also external sources, such as Babylonian, Urartian, Egyptian, biblical, and Greek.

The nonwritten documentation is important, too. Little evidence survives from the renovation by Sargon of Ashurnasirpal's palace in Nimrud, where he resided at the beginning of his reign. The main information is provided by the palace of Khorsabad, first excavated by Paul-Émile Botta and V. Place.[21] This discovery was made quite by chance. Indeed, Botta was excavating a site which he had not identified and which did not deliver immediate results; he did not know that it was in fact the prestigious city of Nineveh (Mosul). Losing patience, in 1843 he moved his excavation site to Khorsabad, where he made the first soundings. He was lucky to discover in this new site a part of the palace of Sargon. Place excavated almost all the royal palace, as well as urban doors, walls of the lower town and of the acropolis, and part of "Palace F." In the twentieth century, in the 1930s, American surveys aimed to verify Place's results; the conclusion was that the excavations had been well conducted, relative to that period, and that corrections to be made were marginal.[22] An Iraqi Mission in 1993 resumed the excavations of the palace, about which we lack details.[23] Some reliefs from the palace, associated with four campaigns, are now in the Iraq Museum, the Louvre Museum, and the Oriental Institute of the University of Chicago. A large number of reliefs were lost in a ship that sank in the Tigris while transporting them; however, they do survive in drawings made during the excavations.[24]

The purpose of this book is to study the history of Sargon's reign, which was fertile in events in all its aspects, but mainly political, economic, social,

---

21. Nicole Chevalier, "L'activité archéologique des consuls de France au XIXe siècle en Assyrie," in *Khorsabad, le palais de Sargon II, roi d'Assyrie*, ed. Annie Caubet (Paris: Documentation française, 1995), 79–106.

22. Gordon Loud, *Khorsabad: Part I; Excavations in the Palace and at a City Gate*, OIP 38 (Chicago: University of Chicago Press, 1936); Gordon Loud and Charles B. Altman, *Khorsabad: Part II; The Citadel and the Town*, OIP 40 (Chicago: University of Chicago Press, 1938); Karen L. Wilson, "Oriental Institute Discoveries at Khorsabad (1929–1935)," in Caubet, *Khorsabad, le palais de Sargon II*, 107–31; Pauline Albenda, "Dur-Sharrukin, the Royal City of Sargon II, King of Assyria," BCSMS 38 (2003): 5–13.

23. Francis Joannès, *Dictionnaire de la civilisation mésopotamienne* (Paris: Laffont, 2001), 249.

24. Albenda, *Palace of Sargon*.

military, and religious. This study will enable the course of his reign to be understood in relation to the context of its time and his personal choices. To what extent did relationships between the different areas and events affect Sargon's decision making? What did he attempt to achieve, and how did he go about fulfilling his objectives? As a matter of fact, the history of Sargon's reign coincides with his personal history, for apart from his filiation nothing is known of his life prior to his ascent to the throne. Several issues emerge and, wherever possible, are answered: Did he have a clear plan or program at the beginning of his reign? Or did he respond to various challenges in different areas as and when they arose? What can be said of his evolution during his reign? How did he manage to lead the Assyrian Empire at the peak of its power? Was it by consolidating and expanding it through successive conquests? What can be said about Sargon himself? What were his qualities and skills? What were his shortcomings? To what extent and in what fields was he a conservative or an innovator? In what matters can it be said that he succeeded or failed?

My methodology is adapted to the specific topic of this book and to the available sources.[25] The approach is multidisciplinary: political, geographic, ethnographic, strategic, economic, along with textual studies, onomastic analyses, and other related disciplines. My historical approach is not immediately theoretical but primarily "down-to-earth," that is to say, very close to the documents. After their analysis, it is possible to move on to a historical synthesis, with a partial synthesis at the end of each chapter. Synopses reflecting the beginning and end of his reign will enable the reader to measure changes, gradual or sudden, and their results. The limited framework of a book constantly forced me to select from a mass of overabundant data, accompanied by a consistent series of comments, which impressed me as fundamentally essential. Some facts and minor features were sacrificed through necessity. This is especially true with the letters; where there are several unsolved problems of reading, attribution, dating, and interpretation, I have selected and analyzed only those letters relevant for the topic at hand. The book's format and progression are centered on decisive events, the determining facts, and the interpretations that seemed to me the most plausible given the current state of research. Other proposed interpretations are presented in

---

25. For my conception of history, see Josette Elayi, "Être historienne de la Phénicie ici et maintenant," *Trans* 31 (2006): 41–54.

footnotes; sometimes I concluded that it was impossible for me to choose between several hypotheses.

Chapter 1 ("Portrait of Sargon") strives to encompass the character of the king before putting him into action. Through his official inscriptions and through his representations on the walls of his palace, Sargon wished to convey a specific image of himself. After having analyzed all his conquests and the achievements of his reign, it will be possible to determine to what extent this image is true or distorted by propaganda. Chapter 2 ("Sargon's Ascent to the Throne") explains the basis on which he managed to establish his empire. His ascent to the throne is far from clear, and several problems are posed: Did he choose his name himself? Was he or was he not a usurper? Why did he have to face such massive opposition? Chapter 3 ("Heir to the Assyrian Empire") presents the state of the Assyrian Empire when Sargon inherited it. It is important to assess its extent, as well as the changes and innovations accomplished during his reign. After this, the book follows a geographical progression; even though the Annals are chronological, their chronology is often questionable. Further, all the other inscriptions are based on a geographical order; however, in the study of each area (starting from west and moving counterclockwise until finally reaching the south), the decisive chronological stages of his reign have been highlighted: chapters 4 ("The Conquest of the West"), 5 ("The Northwest of the Empire"), 6 ("The Wars in the North of the Empire"), 7 ("Neutralization of the Eastern States"), and 8 ("Recurring Problems in the South").[26] The purpose of these chapters is not to analyze itineraries or military strategy, but mainly to place the campaigns in a geopolitical frame. What was Sargon's purpose in each campaign? What was the economic and strategic potential of the different areas? How did actions in one part of the Near East affect what happened elsewhere? How did the result of each campaign contribute to the building of the empire? Chapter 9 ("End of Reign") focuses on the last three years of Sargon's reign, with the inauguration of the palace of Khorsabad, at a time when he was at the height of his glory, power, and wealth. This chapter is also devoted to unsolved questions: How can the king's death be explained? What was the so-called sin of Sargon? Chapter 10 ("Chronological Synthesis of Sargon's Reign") provides, as far as possible, a chronological frame for the events

---

26. This order seems to me more logical than the order of the summary inscriptions of the bulls, starting from east counterclockwise to Babylonia: Fuchs, *Inschriften Sargons II*, Stier 1–106.

of Sargon's reign. It proposes a synthesis of his motivations and strategy during the different periods of his reign, and the steps and reasons of his evolution. Finally, the book concludes with an assessment of Sargon's contributions to the evolution of the empire ("Conclusion: Assessment of Sargon's Reign"). Research sources are available to readers at the end of the book, in line with the publishing requirements: a selected bibliography for each chapter; an index of ancient texts used; an index of the personal names cited, with brief comments and dates for situating them both in a diachronic and synchronic perspective, and finally, an index of modern authors cited.

1
Portrait of Sargon

Is it possible to have an idea of the physical portrait of Sargon? Several representations of Sargon exist, mainly in his palace of Khorsabad/Dûr-Sharrukîn, where he is the principal subject of the wall reliefs. The king is represented in various attitudes and contexts: fighting, hunting in the royal park, receiving Assyrian officials, foreign tributaries, foreign captives, and banqueting.[1] He is depicted standing, and in his chariot, fighting or hunting. He raises his hand in salutation or he shouts, waving a bow and arrow. He holds a long staff, a spear, or a flower. The king's costume is always the same: it consists of a long dress reaching down to the ankles, ornamented with rosettes and a band of rosettes inscribed in squares at the bottom. Over this long dress, the king wears a large mantle with its outer edge embroidered and fringed. On his feet, he wears sandals. His weapon consists of a long sword in its scabbard fixed at the waist, the lower end extending behind him. The facial features are modeled with precision: thick raised eyebrows, heavy lids, and delineated iris. Above the gracefully shaped full lips is a small moustache. The hairdo of his beard and hair is very sophisticated, combining ringlets and curls. He wears very fine jewelry. His headdress consists of a tall cap, flat at the top and surmounted by a large conical tip and decorated with bands of rosettes and long ribbons: this headdress makes him recognizable as being the king. Sargon is always represented taller than the others, thanks to his high cap.[2] It is not a realistic portrait, but the conventional image of an Assyrian king; it resembles other portraits of Ashurnasirpal II or Sennacherib, for example. However, he can be recognized without any doubt

---

1. Albenda, *Palace of Sargon*, 223–57.
2. Ibid., 94 and pl. 44; Guillaume Sence, "Dur-Sharrukin: Le portrait de Sargon II; Essai d'analyse structuraliste des bas-reliefs du palais découvert à Khorsabad," *REA* 109 (2007): 436–39.

because of the place where he is represented: his palace of Khorsabad. In fact, his representation, decided by himself, was intended to give an idealized image of how he wanted to be seen and not of how he actually was in reality—something we shall never know.

The name of Sargon has been much debated. This is not a debate devoid of importance because the naming of an individual in Mesopotamia was not accidental. It was always an important act that contributed to the identity of the individual; thus, in the substitution ritual, to transfer the name amounted to a transfer of identity.[3] On several occasions Sargon himself gave his own interpretation of his name in connection with justice: "In accordance with the name which the great gods have given me—to maintain justice [*kittu*] and right [*mīšaru*], to give guidance to those who are not strong, not to injure the weak—the price of the fields of that town (Khorsabad) I paid back to their owners...,"[4] or in a royal decree: "The just king [*šarru kīnu*] [...] whose lordship the goddess Ninmena[nna ha]s magnified, to protect the feeble from mistreatment and to give guidance to the weak."[5] He also established a curious correspondence of his name with a measuring length, used for the walls of Khorsabad: "I made the circumference of its wall 16,283 cubits, corresponding to my name [*nibīt šumīya*], and established the foundation platform upon the bedrock of the high mountain."[6] None of the interpretation attempts has solved this riddle.[7]

---

3. Marc van de Mieroop, "Literature and Political Discourse in Ancient Mesopotamia: Sargon II of Assyria and Sargon of Agade," in *Munuscula Mesopotamica: Festschrift für Johannes Renger*, ed. Barbara Böck, Eva Cancik-Kirschbaum, and Thomas Richter, AOAT 267 (Münster: Ugarit-Verlag, 1999), 329.

4. *ARAB* 2.120; Andreas Fuchs, *Die Inschriften Sargons II. aus Khorsabad* (Göttingen: Cuvillier, 1993), 39–40, 293.

5. SAA 12:20, 19.5'-6'.

6. *ARAB* 2.121; Fuchs, *Inschriften Sargons II*, 42, l. 65.

7. Wolfram von Soden (*Aus Sprache, Geschichte und Religion Babyloniens: Gesammelte Aufsätze*, ed. Luigi Cagni and Hans-Peter Müller [Naples: Istituto universitario orientale, 1989], 334–35) has suggested that the number represented the number of days Sargon had lived before the measurements of the city wall were fixed. Eckhart Frahm ("Observations on the Name and Age of Sargon II and on Some Patterns of Assyrian Royal Onomastics," *NABU* 2 [2005]: 48, no. 44) proposed to interpret the name as "Assyrian hieroglyphs," a pictographic writing of a lion and a bird. See also Laurie E. Pearce, "Number-Syllabary Texts," *JAOS* 116 (1996): 462; Laura Battini, "Les portes urbaines de la capitale de Sargon II: Étude sur la propagande royale à travers les données archéologiques et textuelles," in *Intellectual Life in the Ancient Near East:*

In fact, his name is written *Šarru-ukīn* or *Šarru-kēn(u)*, with several variants.⁸ It has to be noticed that spellings for rendering the name as *Šarru-ukīn* are attested only in less important royal inscriptions, that is, in letters and documents. Therefore Fuchs suggested that *Šarru-ukīn* was Sargon's original name and that he reinterpreted it as *Šarru-kēn(u)*.⁹ The biblical spelling of Sargon's name, *srgwn*, attested in Isa 20:1, probably forms the basis for its modern conventional rendering. Most scholars interpret Sargon's name as "the faithful king," in the sense of "right and just," precisely the way in which Sargon himself interpreted it.¹⁰ However, Novotny proposed a different interpretation, conjectural but which makes more sense according to her: *Šarru-ukīn* would have been a birth name, with the meaning "the king (Tiglath-pileser) has established stability/justice."¹¹ It would mean that Sargon was born in 745 BCE and received his name in honor of the new era his father was about to inaugurate. This interpretation is unlikely because the name is typologically unusual and this birth date is impossible.¹² According to Vera Chamaza, Sargon's name was a phonetic reproduction of the contracted pronunciation of *Šarru-ukīn* to *Šarrukīn*, so that it should be interpreted as "the king has obtained/established order," chosen because of his political program.¹³ In this hypothesis, does it mean he rescued the country from a state of disorder provoked by his brother, or was this disorder created by his own attempt to seize power? A related question is whether Sargon's name was a birth name, a throne name, a profession-related name, or something else.¹⁴ It is

---

Papers Presented at the Forty-Third Rencontre assyriologique internationale, Prague, July 1–5, 1996, ed. Jiri Prosecký, RAI 43 (Prague: Oriental Institute, 1998), 50–51.

8. Fuchs, *Inschriften Sargons II*, 414–15; Frahm, "Observations on the Name," 46–47; *PNA* 3.2:1239–40.

9. Fuchs, cited in Frahm, "Observations on the Name," 50 n. 29.

10. See, e.g., Hayim Tadmor, "Sennacherib, King of Justice," in *Sefer Moshe: The Moshe Weinfeld Jubilee Volume*, ed. Chaim Cohen, Avi Hurwitz, and Shalom Paul (Winona Lake, IN: Eisenbrauns, 2004), 386; according to him, Sennacherib characterized himself by ethical values in order to stress that they were real, and not only nominal as in the case of his father.

11. Jamie R. Novotny, review of *The Neo-Babylonian Correspondence of Sargon and Sennacherib*, by Manfred Dietrich, *BiOr* 62 (2005): 84–86.

12. Frahm, "Observations on the Name," 46–47; see below, ch. 2.

13. Galo W. Vera Chamaza, "Sargon II's Ascent to the Throne: The Political Situation," *SAAB* 6 (1992): 32.

14. Walter Mayer, *Politik und Kriegskunst der Assyrer*, ALASP 9 (Münster: Ugarit-

interesting to note that the reign of Sargon was the turning point between two very different patterns of royal name-giving: previously, the names given had already been carried by ruler models; later kings carried new royal names, possibly because they had confidence in the greatness of their achievement.[15]

Sargon II seemed to enjoy playing with his name's meaning, and as he was convinced that his name reflected his royal role, he probably chose his name as a throne name because he emulated the famous Sargon of Akkad, the king par excellence.[16] In particular, such a choice can best be understood when he ascended the throne, in difficult circumstances. Sargon II never mentioned the great king of Akkad explicitly, but he was sometimes called "the second Sargon" (Šarru-ukīn/kīn(u) arkû), an epithet which is preserved in a much later source, the so-called Ptolemaic canon.[17] In literary texts from the late Assyrian period, the name of Sargon of Akkad is written LUGAL-gin or LUGAL-gi-na, as is the name of Sargon II. We should not consider the adoption of an existing name as something with merely a superficial meaning; by using this name, Sargon II must have been attempting to adopt certain characteristics of his illustrious predecessor. The name chosen, meaning that the king is legitimate, could be taken as a sign that both men were usurpers. Sargon of Akkad seems to have seized power from his master Ur-Zababa, governor (ENSÍ) of Kish, while Sargon II appears to have come to the throne during a rebellion of the citi-

---

Verlag, 1995), 319; Dietz Otto Edzard, "Name, Namengebung.B," *RlA* 9:109, §5.1; "Thronnamen?," *RlA* 9:109. An official of the reign of Ashurbanipal had the same name: SAA 4:285–86, no. 305, r., l. 6, which indicates that this name was rarely used but was not restricted to ruling kings.

15. Frahm, "Observations on the Name," 47–48.

16. See, e.g., Albert Kirk Grayson, "The Empire of Sargon of Akkad," *AfO* 25 (1974–1977): 56–64; Brian Lewis, *The Sargon Legend: A Study of the Akkadian Text and the Tale of the Hero Who Was Exposed at Birth*, DASOR 4 (Cambridge: American Schools of Oriental Research, 1980); Jerrold S. Cooper and Wolfgang Heimpel, "The Sumerian Sargon Legend," *JAOS* 103 (1984): 67–82; Westenholz, *Legends of the Kings of Akkade*; May, "Administrative and Other Reforms," 79–80.

17. Hannes D. Galter, "Sargon der Zweite: Über die Wiederinszenierung von Geschichte," in *Altertum und Mittelmeerraum: Die antike Welt diesseits und jenseits der Levante; Festschrift für Peter W. Haider*, ed. Robert Rollinger and Brigitte Truschnegg, OeO 12 (Stuttgart: Steiner, 2006), 279–302; May, "Administrative and Other Reforms," 103–4 (with bibliography).

zens of Assur against the king Shalmaneser V.[18] The military greatness of the man who founded the Akkadian Empire that dominated Mesopotamia in the twenty-fourth century could have seemed a model to follow. The ancient Sargon was present in the legendary tradition as the conqueror of the entire world, although the exact extent of his conquests was unknown. In the period of Sargon II, interest in the ancient Sargon flourished, as is visible in the large number of chronicles, omens, and epics.[19] It has been suggested that a text now referred to as The Sargon Geography and the so-called Weidner Chronicle could be late Sargonid texts that made more sense in the reign of Sargon II than in other reigns.[20] In any case, the legendary tradition of Sargon of Akkad was still sufficiently alive to encourage Sargon II to adopt his name as a throne name following his prestigious model. However, if this hypothesis is correct, it is unclear what his original name was.

The personality of Sargon II explains why he probably took Sargon of Akkad as a model by adopting his name. First, he believed that he had been endowed by the gods with an exceptional intelligence: "my all-embracing wisdom and the fertile planning of my brain, which thinking Ea and Bêlit-ilâni had made to surpass all of the kings, my fathers."[21] At first sight, this statement appears in contradiction with the fact of having chosen a model. At the same time, he was certain of being able to surpass this due to his intelligence, superior to that of the previous kings, including the famous Sargon of Akkad himself. In many of his inscriptions and figurative representations, he displayed an excessive pride and dedicated a cult to himself, putting his name forward: "Assur, Nabû, and Marduk have entrusted me an unrivaled kingdom and have caused my gracious name to attain the highest (renown)" (*zi-kir šumī*(mu)-*i*[*a dam*]-*qu ú-še-ṣu-ú*).[22] He detailed with pleasure the qualities associated with his intelligence:

---

18. Knut Leonard Tallqvist, *Assyrian Personal Names*, ASSF 43.1 (Hildesheim: Olms, 1994), 217–18; *PNA* 3.2:1239, considers that it is rather unlikely that Sargon II chose his name deliberately in allusion to his illustrious namesake given the fact that his inscriptions never refer to him.

19. Albert Kirk Grayson, "Assyria: Tiglath-pileser III to Sargon II (744–705 B.C.)," in *The Assyrian and Babylonian Empires and Other States of the Near East, from the Eighth to the Sixth Centuries B.C.*, ed., John Boardman et al., 2nd ed., CAH 3.2 (Cambridge: Cambridge University Press 1991), 88.

20. Van de Miroop, "Literature and Political Discourse," 317–39.

21. *ARAB* 2.105.

22. *ARAB* 2.77; Fuchs, *Inschriften Sargons II*, 75, XIV, l. 2.

"The king endowed with clear understanding, sharp of eye, in all matters the equal of the Sage (*šin-na-at apkalli*) (Adapu), who waxed great in wisdom and insight and grew old in understanding."[23] The cult of his image prompted him to be represented at different places throughout his empire. This is one of the reasons why he had carved stelae made, bearing his image as a majestic and all-powerful king during his campaigns, in conspicuous places and along passageways. Sometimes, he mentioned them in his inscriptions. Some of them have been discovered: those of Ashdod, Larnaka, Hamath, Tell Acharneh, Nadjafehabad, Tang-i Var, and perhaps Samaria.[24] He also had himself represented on the reliefs of the palace of Khorsabad.[25] He was convinced that his name would attain the highest reputation.

Sargon II was primarily a warrior king who personally led numerous military campaigns. He was a megalomaniac conqueror who dreamed of conquering the world in the footsteps of his distant predecessor Sargon of Akkad. He decorated himself with titles signifying that he had reached his goal: "king of the universe" (*šàr kiššati*), "king of the four quarters (of the world)" (*šàr kib-rāt arba'i*). He always put forward his greatness and power: "the great king" (*šarru rabû*), "the mighty king" (*šarru dannu*).[26] He liked to describe himself as a formidable and invincible warlord: "mighty hero, clothed with terror, who sends forth his weapon to bring low the foe, brave warrior, since the day of whose (accession) to rulership, there has been no prince equal to him, who has been without conqueror or rival."[27] However, leading every single attack in person, omnipresent, throwing himself happily into battle, smashing, destroying, killing, cutting down, defeating, and capturing: that is how Sargon wanted to be seen by his contemporaries and remembered by future generations. If all this was true, he would have

---

23. *ARAB* 2.119; Fuchs, *Inschriften Sargons II*, 37, Zyl. 38; *PNA* 1.1:43.

24. Florian Janoscha Kreppner, "Public Space in Nature: the Case of Neo-Assyrian Reliefs," *AfO* 29 (2002): 367–83; Hannes D. Galter, "Sargon II. und die Eroberung der Welt," in *Krieg und Frieden im Alten Vorderasien: 52e Rencontre Assyriologique Internationale, International Congress of Assyriology and Near Eastern Archaeology, Münster, 17.–21. Juli 2006*, ed. Hans Neumann et al., RAI 52; AOAT 401 (Münster: Ugarit-Verlag, 2014), 329–43; Katsuji Sano, "Die Repräsentation der Königsherrschaft in neuassyrischer Zeit: Ideologie, Propaganda und Adressaten der Königsinschrifte," *StMes* 3 (2016): 215–36.

25. See below, ch. 8.

26. Fuchs, *Inschriften Sargons II*, 32, Zyl. 2.

27. *ARAB* 2.137.

jeopardized the whole empire because he would probably have been killed on the battlefield at the beginning of his reign. As a matter of fact, he was killed on the battlefield, but after seventeen years of campaigns. The reality was different. We have the confirmation from a message of admonition written by a courtier or magnate to Esarhaddon, but which also referred to his predecessors: "Of course, the king, my lord, should not go to the midst of battle! Just as the kings, your ancestors have done, take position on a hill, and let your magnates do the fighting!"[28] Even though Sargon was much more invested in the military campaigns than his successors, he sometimes delegated the command of an expedition to one of his generals, contrary to what is written. For example, it was probably the commander-in-chief who led the campaign of Ashdod in 711, although he claimed to have conducted it himself.[29]

Sargon, just like the other Assyrian kings, was convinced that his gods approved his policies. He was a king of justice, and, therefore, his wars were just. When he was fighting against his enemies, he was entitled to punish and mistreat them as criminals who did not fear the names of the gods, and to do so with unrestrained brutality. Therefore, it was natural for him to describe the atrocities as normal episodes in battle descriptions. The descriptions of atrocities in Sargon's inscriptions do not appear to express acts of sadism, as was the case in Ashurnasirpal II's inscriptions. However, they do mention the main types of atrocities described by his predecessors. The severed head is a topic that has always attracted attention, and it was an indispensable element in Assyrian warfare. The taking and counting of head trophies were traditionally described in Assyrian annals and represented on reliefs. However, the severed heads were not individually named before the reign of Esarhaddon. Sargon followed the customary Assyrian practice in warfare of cutting off the heads of enemies for "statistical" purposes because large numbers were always impressive. Decapitated heads were considered important war trophies, and scribes elaborated a record-keeping system where they tallied the number of slain enemies.[30] During his eighth campaign against Rusâ of Urartu, Sargon

---

28. SAA 16:74, no. 77, r., ll. 3–8 (according to Fuchs's translation).

29. Jeffrey A. Blakely and James W. Hardin, "Southwestern Judah in the Late Eighth Century B.C.E.," *BASOR* 326 (2002): 51.

30. Dominik Bonatz, "Ashurbanipal's Headhunt: An Anthropological Perspective," *Iraq* 66 (2004): 93–101; Theodore J. Lewis, "You Have Heard What the Kings of Assyria Have Done: Disarmament Passages vis-à-vis Assyrian Rhetoric of Intimida-

killed large numbers of soldiers, filling the mountain valleys with them. Cutting off their heads was only part of the slaughter.[31] He also used to pile up the enemies' corpses, either on the ground or at the bottom of the sea (Persian/Arabian Gulf).[32] Several scenes of his palace in Khorsabad depict naked bodies, most of them decapitated, covering the terrain of the battlefield.[33] Another scene shows an Assyrian soldier cutting the throat of a fallen foe.[34] The description of the carnage sometimes used poetic images: "I made the blood flow like river water in ravines and precipices, dyeing lowlands, foothills, and highlands red as if with anemone-flowers."[35] He also boasted of having dyed the skin of his enemy Iaûbidî of Hamath red like an *illūru*-plant, possibly because he had flayed him.[36] Flaying the skin was another usual atrocity that he inflicted on Bag-dâti of Uishdish, as well as burning, scalding, piercing the hand, throwing into iron fetters.[37] The worst treatment was inflicted on Amitashshi's sons: "the two sons whom he had begotten, I [skinned] alive [and boiled their bodies] together with the fat of Amitashshi."[38] Although royal scribes accompanied the king on every military campaign and probably collected raw data in the field, the composers of the heroic inscriptions did not put realism and accuracy among their top priorities. To what degree such depictions of atrocities reflect reality remains an open question due to the one-sided nature of our primary sources. It is difficult to distinguish the reality from the rhetoric of intimidation expressed in the inscriptions and figurative representations.

---

tion," in *Isaiah's Vision of Peace in Biblical and Modern International Relations: Swords into Plowshares*, ed. Raymond Cohen and Raymond Westbrook, CRIR (New York: Palgrave Macmillan, 2008), 79–80; Rita Dolce, "'Losing One's Head': Some Hints on Procedures and Meanings of Decapitation in the Ancient Near East," in *Making Pictures of War: Realia et Imaginaria in the Iconology of the Ancient Near East*, ed. Laura Battini, AANEA 1 (Oxford: Archaeopress, 2016), 45–56; Ariel M. Bagg, "Where Is the Public? A New Look at the Brutality Scenes in Neo-Assyrian Royal Inscriptions and Art," in Battini, *Making Pictures of War*, 57–82.

31. *ARAB* 2.154.
32. *ARAB* 2.92.
33. Albenda, *Palace of Sargon*, pls. 119–23.
34. Ibid, pl. 136.
35. *ARAB* 2.154; Benjamin R. Foster, *Before the Muses: An Anthology of Akkadian Literature*, 3rd ed. (Bethesda: CDL, 2005), 798.
36. *ARAB* 2.118; Abraham and Klein, "New Sargon II Cylinder Fragment," 256, ll. 10′–11a′; *PNA* 2.1:497.
37. *ARAB* 2.10, 118; *PNA* 1.2:251.
38. Winckler, *Keilschrifttexte Sargons*, 1:146, ll. 9–11; *PNA* 1.1:102.

The intent of such rhetoric was called "deterrent propaganda." Whenever possible, Sargon used intimidation tactics, a kind of psychological warfare in the modern sense of the term.[39] He had inherited this from Tiglath-pileser III who was a master in the art of psychological warfare through display tactics. To demoralize the inhabitants of the city that he wanted to conquer, he would display atrocities such as decapitated or flayed victims.

However, even though psychological war was an intrinsic part of warfare in order to intimidate the enemy into not fighting, Sargon primarily depended on classic warfare, just like the other Assyrian kings. He was highly effective in terms of military intelligence and strategy in his quest for victory.[40] While he was crown prince, Sennacherib summarized for his father the intelligence reports coming from the northern frontiers. Sargon had an efficient spy system, and during the campaigns, he had reconnaissance scouts with skills superior to those of the enemy's. Surrounded by enemies on all sides of his empire, Sargon had to concentrate in each campaign on just one foe alone. Any attempt to redirect the army to another region once it was on the move would have had disastrous results. Therefore he had to choose the target wisely before the beginning of each campaigning season. He knew how to mislead his enemy, for instance, by lulling it into a false sense of security; in 714, instead of taking a mountain gorge route, he unexpectedly advanced over the snow-and ice-covered ridge, descended the other side, and deployed in the valley. Or he secretly led a detachment of select troops along difficult and rarely used mountain paths to take the city of Musasir by surprise.[41]

What kind of relations did he have with his troops? Sargon was not a charismatic leader, like Alexander the Great, for example. He seems to have been just as terrifying to his own troops as he was to his enemies,

---

39. Lewis, "You Have Heard," 88–89.

40. Andreas Fuchs, "Assyria At War: Strategy and Conduct." in *Oxford Handbook of Cuneiform Culture*, ed. Karen Radner and Eleanor Robson (Oxford: Oxford University Press, 2011), 392–93; Peter Dubovský, "King's Direct Control: Neo-Assyrian *Qepu* Officials," in *Organization, Representation, and Symbols of Power in the Ancient Near East*, ed. Gernot Wilhelm, RAI 54 (Winona Lake, IN: Eisenbrauns, 2012), 449–60; Pierre Villard, "Quelques aspects du renseignement militaire dans l'empire néo-assyrien," *HiMA* 3 (2016): 87–97.

41. Fuchs, "Assyria at War," 392–95; Brian T. Carey, "Assyrian King Sargon II's Urartu Campaign of 714 BC Was as Sensible as It Was Ruthless," *Military History* (September 2005): 64, 70–71.

holding them with an iron hand. A royal letter of convocation to his cavalry gives a clear idea of his handling of the army:

> This is a royal order of great emergency! Assemble the commanders and the horsemen of your cavalry unit immediately! Whoever is late will be impaled in the middle of his own house, and his sons and daughters too will be slaughtered, which will then be the fault of his own! Don't delay! Drop everything and come straight away![42]

According to this letter, Sargon treated his soldiers like his worst enemies in order to reinforce obedience and discipline. Yet, as he often made displays of barbaric treatment and slaughter of his enemies and their families, but never of his soldiers, one is inclined to think that this royal letter contained mere threatening words in order to be obeyed—and they were probably sufficient because his soldiers had themselves attended and actively participated in violent scenes of this type. Moreover, he did not have to fear the fate of several Roman emperors due to the occurrence of revolts in his own army. Except for the core of the "royal contingent," an elite unit led by members of the royal family, the Assyrian army was a heterogeneous, colorful, multiethnic entity. It was made up of provincial troops, armies of vassal kings, prisoners of war, and various auxiliaries, according to the principle of divide and rule. As a result, the constituent parts of the "huge hosts of Assur" could not plot and form an alliance against Sargon. Instead, they probably competed to obtain the king's favor. In return for their services, most soldiers probably received a piece of land. Mercenaries and auxiliaries possibly received some form of payment. However, as in most armies, the main incentive to fight must have been the share of expected spoils of war, which were frequent because the Assyrians invariably emerged victorious. Sargon paid particular attention to the plundering carried out by his "brave warriors": "I let my fierce troops into his (Rusâ) splendid garden, one of the attractions of his city, which was ornamented with fruit and vines…. They picked his countless fruit and left no pleasure for the weary of heart for many years to come."[43]

---

42. SAA 1:22, text 22; Fuchs, "Assyria at War," 396. He thinks that the Assyrians used the same methods with their enemies and their own troops.

43. Foster, *Before the Muses*, 803; Tamás Dezső, "A Reconstruction of the Army of Sargon II (721–705 BC) Based on the Nimrud Horse Lists," *SAAB* 15 (2006): 93–140; John Nicholas Postgate, "The Invisible Hierarchy: Assyrian Military and Civilian

His policy of conquest did not exclude economic objectives.[44] The conquest took on very different forms depending on where it was conducted. Just like the other Assyrian kings, Sargon knew which were the most productive lands and the richest territories, as can be seen from the fact that he often described their abundance and wealth in great detail, for example, in the area of Ulhu, Rusâ's resort town. He knew how to exploit the resources of these territories, but without causing their ruin. Paradoxically in some places, the Assyrian pressure contributed to the development of production activities, for example, in Ekron (Israel) with the installation of genuine industrial oil factories. The military campaigns in unknown regions, such as Urartu with its agricultural and mining resources, were carefully prepared in order to obtain the best political and economic benefit. Conversely, regions that offered no economic interest, such as the mountains of eastern Anatolia or the rebellious regions of Chaldea, were subjected to a merciless policy of terror.

Following Assyrian tradition, Sargon extolled the role played by his gods. He made extensive use of all possible religious means to guarantee supernatural support for his dangerous expeditions. Most of his inscriptions started with the mention of his gods: mainly Assur, "father of the gods," Nabû and Marduk, the great gods of whom he was the favorite.[45] He was "prefect of Enlil," "priest of Assur," and "elect of Anu and Dagan."[46] In the Cyprus stela, he also invoked other gods such as Sîn, Shamash, Adad, and Ishtar.[47] He started his campaigns at the command of Assur, trusting in his support. Several times during his campaigns, "he lifted up his hands to Assur, his lord," who helped him; he succeeded "with the help

---

Administration in the Eighth and Seventh Centuries BC," in *The Land of Assur and the Yoke of Assur: Studies on Assyria: 1971–2005* (Oxford: Oxbow, 2007), 331–60; Fuchs, "Assyria at War," 386–88.

44. Fales, *Guerre et paix en Assyrie*; Joannès, "Assyriens, Babyloniens, Perses achéménides," 32–33.

45. Grant Frame, "The God Aššur in Babylonia," in *Assyria 1995: Proceedings of the Tenth Anniversary Symposium of the Neo-Assyrian Text Corpus Project, Helsinki, Sept. 7–11, 1995*, ed. Simo Parpola and Robert M. Whiting (Helsinki: Neo-Assyrian Text Corpus Project, 1997), 55–64; Vladimir Sazonov, "Some Remarks Concerning the Development of the Theology of War in Ancient Mesopotamia," in *The Religious Aspects of War in the Ancient Near East, Greece, and Rome*, ed. Krzysztof Ulanowski, CHANE 84 (Leiden: Brill, 2016), 36–43.

46. *ARAB* 2.104, 117, 180; Fuchs, *Inschriften Sargons II*, 31.

47. Lie, *Inscriptions of Sargon II*, 43.

of the great gods, his lords."[48] In his famous Letter to Assur, he recounted in detail the events of the eighth campaign.[49] Every stage of a campaign was accompanied by rituals and sacrifices in order to please the gods and to obtain victories. Standards showing images of the gods, probably mounted on chariots, accompanied the soldiers during their march. They were visible to all during the battles. No doubt the religious rituals calmed fears, convinced the soldiers that they were fighting for a just cause, and helped them in the most desperate situations. As Sargon knew the importance of the gods at war, they were permanently present in all his campaigns. He offered them several precious gifts, for example, to Marduk in Babylon, he gave gold, silver, bronze, iron, lapis lazuli, woolen and linen garments, boxwood, cedar, cypress; similarly to Bêl, Sarpanit, Nabû, and Tashmet, gods of the cities of Sumer and Akkad. It has been noticed that gods were much less represented in the palace of Khorsabad than in the palaces of previous kings, but it would be risky to interpret the religious beliefs of Sargon because we lack personal elements of information.

Another traditional characteristic of Sargon was that he was a "builder king." First, this consisted of restoring the palaces of the previous kings and the temples of the gods, in particular in Nimrud, Nineveh, Babylon, and Uruk. He also built a new palace: the so-called burnt palace, near the temple of Nabû, in the southwestern part of Nimrud. His major work was the building of his new capital of Khorsabad.[50] All these magnificent monuments were conceived as prestigious works. They were built for his glory and were intended to preserve the memory of his greatness for future generations. After the usual malediction to those that would destroy his inscription and name, he addressed future kings who would honor his memory: "In days to come, let the future prince, among the kings, my sons, restore the ruins of that palace, let him look upon my memorial stela, let him anoint it with oil, offer sacrifices and restore it to its place."[51] Last but not least, Sargon needed large palatial structures to store the huge amount of booty that he systematically brought back from all his numerous campaigns. Most of his booty was made up of luxury items, sometimes cumbersome, such as furniture inlaid with ivory. He did not want to pile

---

48. Ibid., 65, l. 25.
49. *ARAB* 2.140–78.
50. See below, ch. 8.
51. *ARAB* 2.90.

it all up, but to display at least some of it for his pleasure and the pleasure of his visitors.

Sargon was basically a warlord who learned the art of warfare, but was he also a cultivated man like Ashurbanipal, for example, whose education is known? We lack sources on Sargon's education because we know nothing of his life before he ascended to the throne of Assyria. It is clear that he was an aesthete with very good artistic and eclectic taste for several branches of the arts, as illustrated in his palace of Khorsabad. His education was probably not as complete as that of Ashurbanipal, who boasted of being the only king of the dynasty to know how to write. However, Sargon appears to have been interested in education, as is shown by the education he gave to Sennacherib and to the inhabitants of his new capital Khorsabad, who had various cultures and languages.[52] He probably received the usual Assyrian education, that is, the education of a scribe: languages (Sumerian and Babylonian) and some elements of arithmetic. However, it is uncertain whether he followed the "second cycle" of studies, such as the art of divination and literature. In his Letter to Assur, he explains that he left Nimrud to embark on his eighth campaign, at the date "written in an ancient tablet," but we do not know who had read this tablet, Sargon himself or a scribe. The royal libraries of Nimrud, Nineveh, and Khorsabad were constituted on kings' initiatives, and Sargon necessarily participated in their enrichment. It has been suggested that he himself directed the edition of various texts covering the exploits of his possible model Sargon of Akkad, with particular attention being devoted to geographical details, useful for choosing military routes.[53]

In short, Sargon wanted to project an image of justice, piety, energy, strength, ability, and intelligence. It now has to be checked, through the analysis of his accession to the throne, his conquests, and the achievements of his reign, to what extent this image is distorted by propaganda.

---

52. *ARAB* 2.86, 93; Fuchs, *Inschriften Sargons II*, 72, ll. 92–95.

53. Sidney Smith, "The Supremacy of Assyria," in *The Assyrian Empire*, ed. J. B. Bury, S. A. Cook, and F. E. Adcock, CAH 3 (Cambridge: Cambridge University Press, 1925), 60.

2

Sargon's Ascent to the Throne

According to the Babylonian Chronicle, King Shalmaneser V died in the month of Tebet (the tenth month of the Assyrian calendar, January) in 722 BCE, and Sargon succeeded him on the throne of Assyria on the twelfth of Tebet.[1] Shalmaneser V was the legitimate heir of his father Tiglath-pileser III, as can be seen in the letters written to his father when he was crown prince, under his birth name Ulûlâyu, which means "born in Elul" (ca. August–September, the sixth month). The name Shalmaneser means "the god Salmanu is foremost." Few official documents commissioned by him during his short reign (727–722 BCE) survive.[2] He was living in Nimrud, where some weights bearing his name have been found. Little is known about his political, military, and building accomplishments because of the lack of documents. He continued the subjugation of the west initiated by his father. According to the Babylonian Chronicle, he conquered (or devastated) Samaria. The conquest of Samaria is also mentioned in the Bible (2 Kgs 17:3–6; 18:9–11) and Josephus (*A.J.* 9.283–287). Three campaigns are recorded in the Eponym Lists in 725 (year 2), 724 (year 3), and 723 (year 4), but the names of the places concerned are broken. As Samal appears to be a province in the reign of Sargon, and not in the reign of Tiglath-pileser III, it is likely that it was annexed by Shalmaneser V. The Bît-Adini seems to have been devastated by him. However, the five-year

---

1. Albert Kirk Grayson, *Assyrian and Babylonian Chronicles* (Winona Lake, IN: Eisenbrauns, 2000), 73, chr. 1, ll. 29–31.

2. John A. Brinkman, *A Political History of Post-Kassite Babylonia 1158–722 B.C.*, AnOr 43 (Rome: Biblical Institute Press, 1968), 243–45, 360; *PNA* 3.1:1077; Karen Radner, "Shalmaneser V. in den *Nimrud Letters*," *AfO* 50 (2003–2004): 95–104; John A. Brinkman, "A Legal Text from Babylon Dated in the Reign of Shalmaneser V," *NABU* 1 (2008): 11–13, no. 8; RINAP 1.

siege of Tyre mentioned by Josephus is more probably to be ascribed to Sargon than to Shalmaneser V.³

The sources are silent concerning the cause of Shalmaneser V's death after only five years of reign. Did he meet his death in the struggle for the kingship of Assyria? It seems, especially from the use of a euphemism for "he died" (*šīmāti*.MEŠ), that his death was the result of natural causes.⁴ However, the succession was awkward, as is indicated by the fact that Sargon's numerous inscriptions contain only one reference to his predecessor. Sargon provided an explanation, not of his death but of the interruption of his reign, in the so-called Assur Charter (K. 1349). The god Assur punished him for a grave fault he had made:

> Shalmaneser, who did not fear the king of the world, whose hands have brought sacrilege in this city (Assur), pu[t on...] on his people, [he] impo[sed] the compulsory work and a heavy corvée, paid them like a working class [...]. The Illil of the gods, in the wrath of his heart, overthrew [hi]s rule, and [appointed] me, Sargon, as king [of Assyria]. He raised my head; he let [me] take hold of the scepter, the throne (and) the tiara [...].⁵

The purpose of Sargon's explanation was less to explain the end of Shalmaneser V's reign as having been deposed because he had robbed the city of Assur of its traditional privileges, than to justify his own ascent to the throne. He did not believe that his predecessor was responsible for this problem of taxation, as is shown in another inscription: "I restored the exemption from taxation in the cities of Assur and Harrân, which had fallen from distant past in oblivion, and their privileges which had been cast aside."⁶ It has also been stated that these compulsory works were not

---

3. Josette Elayi, *Histoire de la Phénicie*, Pour l'histoire (Paris: Perrin, 2013), 166–74; see below, ch. 4.

4. Gerd Steiner, "Das Bedeutungs feld 'Tod' in den Sprachen des Alten orients," *Or* 51 (1952): 242–43; Nadav Na'aman, "The Historical Background to the Conquest of Samaria (720 BCE)," *Bib* 71 (1990): 218 n. 37; Bob Becking, *The Fall of Samaria: An Historical and Archaeological Study*, SHANE 4 (Leiden: Brill, 1992), 22 n. 6; Vera Chamaza, "Sargon II's Ascent," 21–33; K. Lawson Younger, "The Fall of Samaria in Light of Recent Research," *CBQ* 61 (1999): 461–82.

5. Saggs, "Historical Texts and Fragments," 14–15, ll. 31–35; Vera Chamaza, "Sargon II's Ascent," 24–25.

6. Weissbach, "Zu den Inschriften der Säle," 176.

performed by Shalmaneser V, but by Tiglath-pileser III. This would have prompted the opposition from the priesthoods and notables of Assur and Harrân, deprived of power, and ended later with the assassination of Shalmaneser V.[7] However, this hypothesis is groundless. In fact, Shalmaneser V, contrary to the hopes of the priests, probably maintained the existing situation, which was only changed by Sargon.

The question as to whether Sargon II was a usurper or not has long been debated. The opinion in favor of usurpation is mainly based on the meaning of his name and on the silence of the sources over his origin.[8] If the name *Šarru-kīn* means "the faithful king," it would be a means to legitimate his accession, as in the case of Sargon of Akkad who certainly was a usurper. The fact that Sargon II was closely connected to Harrân has been interpreted as though he was coming from a collateral royal branch starting with Tiglath-pileser III.[9] In fact, the absence of the patronymic in Sargon's inscriptions was also a feature of Tiglath-pileser III's and of Sennacherib's inscriptions. Sennacherib, Sargon's son, was totally silent concerning his origin in his official annals. Currently the opinion that Sargon was not a usurper is better supported. In fact, the filiation is indicated in two Sargon inscriptions where he was clearly presented as the son of Tiglath-pileser III, king of Assyria.[10] He also referred to his "royal fathers" in the so-called Borowski Stela, probably originating from Hamath.[11] Sargon was not the only king to be silent on his origin: just like Tiglath-pileser III his father, and Sennacherib his son, it could be a sign that he wanted to begin a new period, with a new political program, or that he was actually in conflict with his dynasty. Two brothers of Sargon are known: Shalmaneser V, his predecessor, and Sîn-ahu-usur, who in 714 was in command of the

---

7. Harmut Schmökel, *Keilschriftforschung und alte Geschichte Vorderasiens*, HdO 2/3 (Leiden: Brill, 1957), 265; Herbert Donner, *Geschichte des Volkes Israel und seiner Nachbarn in Grundzügen*, GAT 4/2 (Göttingen: Vandenhoeck & Ruprecht, 1986), 316.

8. See above, ch. 1; A. T. Olmstead, *Western Asia in the Days of Sargon of Assyria, 722–705 B.C.: A Study in Oriental History* (New York: Holt, 1908): 33; Bruno Meissner, *Könige Babyloniens und Assyriens* (Leipzig: Quelle & Meyer, 1926), 174; Wolfram von Soden, *Herrscher im Alten Orient* (Berlin: Springer, 1954), 94–95; Donner, *Geschichte des Volkes Israel*, 316–17; Glassner, *Mésopotamie*, 313.

9. May, "Administrative and Other Reforms," 87–90.

10. Felix Thomas, "Sargon II., der Sohn Tiglat-pilesers III.," in *Mesopotamica-Ugaritica-Biblica: Festschrift für Kurt Bergerhof*, ed. Manfred Dietrich and Oswalt Loretz, AOAT 232 (Neukirchen-Vluyn: Neukirchener Verlag, 1993), 465–70.

11. Hawkins, "New Sargon Stele," 160, l. 10.

royal cavalry guard and who had his own residence in Khorsabad.[12] Atalia was Sargon's wife, but who was his mother? It may have been Tiglath-pileser III's wife Iabâ. As a matter of fact, there is a mystery concerning her identity because only two bodies were found in a burial site in Nimrud, containing inscriptions of three queens: Iabâ, Banîtu, and Atalia.[13] The following hypothesis was proposed: Iabâ could have been one and the same person as Banîtu, Shalmaneser V's wife, if Shamaneser had married his father's widow, another wife rather than his mother. It was an old strategy to further secure the succession. As a son of Tiglath-pileser III, we might expect to find Sargon attested in a prominent military or administrative role in the archives dated to his father's reign, but the name by which he was known before he became king has not yet been identified. We also lack information on the role and office of Sargon during Shalmaneser V's reign; this could be explained by the scarcity of sources. The hypothesis that he had been the governor of Assur during this reign has no documentary basis.[14] It has also been suggested that he carried out some kind of priestly function or that he was active in this area, because of his affection for this institution, or that he held the office of "vizier" (*sukkallu*) at Harrân.[15] If Sargon was, as it seems, a son of Tiglath-pileser III and a brother of Shalmaneser V, correspondingly, he would not have been the founder of a new dynasty. This would mean that for a long time before the end of the Assyrian Empire the same dynasty was on the throne of Assyria.[16] Yet, whatever his reasons, Sargon wanted to stand aloof from his dynasty.

How old was he when he came to power? We know that his son Sennacherib, who ruled from 705 to 681 BCE, had a son named Ashur-nâdin-

---

12. *ARAB* 2.154, 177; SAA 1:43–69; *PNA* 3.2:1344–46; H. D. Baker, "Salmanassar V," *RlA* 11:585–87; Radner, "Salmanassar V. in den Nimrud Letters," 95–104; Shalmaneser V could also be his half-brother.

13. *PNA* 1.2:265, 2.1:485; Stephanie Dalley, "The Identity of the Princesses in Tomb II and a New Analysis of Events in 701 BC," in *New Light on Nimrud, Proceedings of the Nimrud Conference Eleventh–Thirteenth March 2002*, ed. John E. Curtis et al. (London: British Institute for the Study of Iraq, 2008), 171–75.

14. R. Campbell Thompson, "An Assyrian Parallel to an Incident in the Story of Semiramis," *Iraq* 4 (1937): 42.

15. Vera Chamaza, "Sargon II's Ascent," 33; May, "Administrative and Other Reforms," 89.

16. Ernst Friedrich Weidner, "Kleine Mitteilungen," *AfO* 9 (1933–34): 79; Vera Chamaza, "Sargon II's Ascent," 32.

shumi, who became king of Babylon in 700.[17] Ashur-nâdin-shumi was then at least twenty years old, which means that he was born around 720 at the latest. Sennacherib was not Sargon's first child if we consider the meaning of his name "Sîn has replaced the brothers." Assyrian men generally would marry when they were between twenty-six and thirty-two years old, but members of the royal family could possibly marry earlier.[18] Therefore, it seems reasonable to assume that Sennacherib was born around 745 (or at the latest 740) and Sargon around 770 (or at the latest 760).[19] Sargon was already middle-aged when he came to power; he must have been between forty and fifty years old. His adult son Sennacherib assisted him in running the empire as crown prince. He was probably designated as crown prince as early as the time of his father's accession to the throne; he was living in the *bīt ridûti*, "residence of the crown prince."

In what circumstances did Sargon ascend the throne? It is commonly assumed that he became king in violent circumstances, however, that is not completely clear.[20] On the one hand, neither the Eponym Lists nor the Assur Charter describing the outcome of the first two regnal years of Sargon reported disturbances in the region in relation to the seizure of power.[21] This should therefore allow for the supposition that the new king did not emerge through major internal difficulties.[22] On the other hand, the quasi-absence of references to his predecessor in the voluminous body of his royal inscriptions and his accusation against Shalmaneser V of having robbed the city of Assur of its traditional privileges seem to indicate an awkward succession. Moreover, some political decisions of

---

17. *PNA*, 3.1:1113–15 (with references), 1.1:202–3.

18. SAAS 6:157; Martha Roth, "Age at Marriage and the Household: A Study of Neo-Babylonian and Neo-Assyrian Forms," *CSSH* 29 (1987): 737.

19. Around 765, according to Frahm, "Observations on the Name," 47.

20. E.g., Glassner, *Mésopotamie*, 55, 313; Sence, "Dur-Sharrukin," 430: Eckhart Frahm, *Einleitung in die Sanherib-Inschriften*, AfOB 26 (Vienna: Institut für Orientalistik der Universität Wien, 1997), 1–2. It is unproven that he had ousted his brother Shalmaneser V from the Assyrian throne, as stated by Karen Radner, "The Ashur-Nineveh-Arbela Triangle: Central Assyria in the Neo-Assyrian Period," in *Between the Cultures: The Central Tigris Region from the Third to the First millennium BC*, ed. Peter A. Miglus and Simone Mühl, HSAO 14 (Heidelberg: Heidelberger Orient-Verlag, 2011), 323.

21. Saggs, "Historical Texts and Fragments," 1–20.

22. Donner, *Geschichte des Volkes Israel*, 317; Vera Chamaza, "Sargon II's Ascent," 25.

Shalmaneser V were changed or revoked by Sargon. For example, Hullî, king of Tabal, who had been deported, was reinstalled; Gunzinânu was replaced by Tarhun-azi as the head of the vassal-state Kammanu. In addition, he probably canceled an administrative measure of his predecessor by reopening the sealed emporium of Egypt and encouraged trade.[23]

Sargon seems to have met immediately with massive opposition in the Assyrian heartland as well as in other parts of the empire. His "accession year" (*rēš-šarrūti*) was the part of the year between his actual accession to the throne and his first official year of reign starting with the following month of Nisan; it lasted three months from Tebet 722 to Nisan 721. During his accession year and his entire first year (721), he was busy securing his throne because no military endeavor can be attributed to this period. He was not even able to prevent Babylonia from being seized by Marduk-apla-iddina II (Merodach-baladan in the Bible). Two independent sources show that Sargon did not conduct any military expedition during the first year of his reign: the Babylonian Chronicle and the Assur Charter; both sources date the battle with Humban-nikash I the Elamite near Dêr to year 2 (in the Babylonian Chronicle) and to his second *palû* (in the Assur Charter), that is, in 720. For as proud and valorous warrior king as he claimed to be, this one year and three month period of inactivity, without carrying out any expedition, was difficult to justify, which is why he had the chronology of his campaigns falsified. The Prisms dated his campaigns one *palû* ("year") earlier than the Annals from Khorsabad. The initial discrepancy of the chronology between the four groups of texts of Sargon has been a headache for Assyriologists for a long time. For example, Olmstead doubted the authenticity of the historical data in the Annals and preferred the Prisms.[24] Weidner assumed that the *palû* in the Prisms carried a different connotation from that in the Annals: it would have been used only for those years in which Sargon in person led his army in war.[25] Tadmor seems to have better understood the chronological problem.[26] He classified the texts of Sargon in four groups, following a decreasing order

---

23. *PNA* 1.2:431, 2.1:476–77, 3.2:1243, 1315–16.

24. Olmstead, *Western Asia in the Days of Sargon*, 8–11.

25. Ernst F. Weidner, "Šilkan(ḫe)ni, König von Muṣri, ein Zeitgenosse Sargons II: Nach einem neuen Bruchstück der Prisma-Inschrift des assyrischen Königs," *AfO* 14 (1941–44): 40–53.

26. Hayim Tadmor, "The Campaigns of Sargon II of Assur: A Chronological-Historical Study," *JCS* 12 (1958): 22–40.

2. SARGON'S ASCENT TO THE THRONE

of reliability: the Eponym Lists, the Assur Charter, the Prisms, and the Annals from Khorsabad. In the Eponym Lists and the Assur Charter, the beginning of military campaigns was ascribed to the second *palû* (year 2), as indicated in the Babylonian Chronicle. The first *palû* in the Prisms was not counted from Sargon's year 1 (721), but from his first campaign, which took place in the second year of his reign, after Nisan 720. In the Annals, the first campaign was dated to year 1 or maybe even to the accession year, although the fragmentary state of the first lines means that it cannot be determined with any degree of accuracy.[27] The method of referring to every year of the king's reign as relating to a *palû* presupposed the existence of yearly campaigns. Even if the king stayed in Assyria as mentioned in the Eponym Lists (*ina māti*), the Khorsabad Annals recorded a military expedition.[28]

Three different methods were used by the scribes in Sargon's inscriptions: the first and most reliable method, reflected in the Assur Charter and used in the early years of the reign, involved dating the beginning of military campaigns from the second *palû* (year 2). The second method used in the Prisms dated the campaigns of year 2 in the first *palû*; this was a later attempt to suppress the fact that Sargon did not go to war before his second regnal year. The final edition of the Khorsabad Annals tried to normalize the chronology and to glorify Sargon's reign by beginning them with an account of victories. The same attempt is apparent in the Display Inscription from Khorsabad where Sargon's conquests start in his accession year: "From the year of my accession to the fifteenth year of my reign, I brought about the defeat of Humban-nikash, the Elamite, in the plain of Dêr."[29] As a consequence of this deliberate discrepancy in the chronology of Sargon's campaigns, it is difficult to establish an accurate dating of all of them, which is why the study of the campaigns has to be based on a geographical and, whenever possible, chronological framework.

What was the state of the Assyrian Empire that Sargon inherited in 722? It had not significantly changed during the short reign of Shalmaneser V,

---

27. William W. Hallo, "From Qarqar to Carchemish: Assyria and Israel in the Light of New Discoveries," *BA* 23 (1960): 52–57, 33; Fuchs, *Inschriften Sargons II*, 86–89; 313–14; Nadav Na'aman, "Sargon's Second *palû* according to the Khorsabad Annals," *TA* 34 (2007): 165–70.

28. E.g., in year 10: Eponym Chronicle Rm 2.97 (Arthur Ungnad, "Eponymen," *RlA* 2:433), and Annals: Fuchs, *Inschriften Sargons II*, 125–26, 324–25.

29. *ARAB* 2.55; Fuchs, *Inschriften Sargons II*, 196, 344.

who had continued his father's policy: consolidating it by military campaigns, collecting the tribute, and realizing some building works. As a matter of fact, Tiglath-pileser III was considered as the true founder of the Assyrian Empire. He passed from selective and limited raids to the conquest of new territories in order to extend the limits of the empire in all directions.[30] In 729, he conquered Babylonia. However, he made the wise decision not to turn this prestigious region into an Assyrian province. Instead, in 728 he cleverly asked to be crowned as king of Babylonia under the name Pulû. Thus, all the middle-eastern regions were unified under a double Assyrian-Babylonian kingship. The military successes of Tiglath-pileser III were made possible as a result of political and administrative innovations. For example, in order to ensure the stability of the empire during his campaigns, he instituted the regency of the crown prince. He reorganized the army and improved his soldiers' weapons and equipment. He inaugurated a systematic policy of deportations to exercise tighter control over populations. Besides vassal-states, he created new provinces, but not too large, so as to prevent their governors from becoming overly powerful. He installed an administrative and military coverage and developed the road network throughout the whole empire. However, this new imperial system had to be consolidated and optimized, in particular by overcoming the hubs of local resistance.

In short, the ascent to the throne of Sargon, already middle-aged, is far from clear. He was apparently not a usurper because he was a son of Tiglath-pileser III and a brother of Shalmaneser V. It follows that he was not the founder of a new dynasty but wanted to stand aloof from this dynasty. For reasons unknown, he faced massive opposition in Assyria, which obliged him to secure his throne during his accession year (722) and his first year (721). In order to conceal this period of inactivity, he had the chronology of his campaigns falsified by the scribes.

---

30. Josette Elayi, "Les cités phéniciennes entre liberté et sujétion," *DHA* 16 (1990): 93–113; Garelli, "Achievement of Tiglath-pileser III," 46–51; RINAP 1; Elayi, *Histoire de la Phénicie*, 156–66.

3
Heir to the Assyrian Empire

In 722 BCE, Sargon inherited an empire where he traditionally exerted absolute power on his subjects. He was obliged to do better than his predecessors and to leave a durable memory for future generations, thanks to his military feats, as well as his restoration and building of palaces and sanctuaries. The only limit to his absolute power was religious: he had to recognize the primacy of the gods, to attend all the religious ceremonies and to respect the exemptions of the cities that had a major sanctuary.[1] The relations of the Assyrian king with his subjects were not based on social hierarchy: each of them, eminent or humble, was his servant (*urdu*), a word which also designated a slave. His subjects had to be exclusively in the king's service and "to mount guard" for him (*maṣṣartu naṣâru*), with an absolute devotion for the "royal orders" (*abat šarri*); this obligation was expressed by taking the "oath of allegiance" to the king (*adê*), an Aramaic word.[2] Those who broke this oath by treason, rebellion, conspiracy, or non-denunciation of bad actions were sentenced to death. The consequence of this system was the development of suspicion, denunciation, and search for protectors. A significant part of the correspondence addressed to the

---

1. René Labat, *Le caractère religieux de la royauté assyro-babylonienne* (Paris: Adrien-Maisonneuve, 1939); Mario Liverani, "The Ideology of the Assyrian Empire," in *Power and Propaganda. A Symposium on Ancient Empires*, ed. Mogens Trolle Larsen, Mesopotamia 7 (Copenhagen: Akademisk Forlag, 1979), 297–317; Karen Radner, "Running the Empire: Assyrian Governance," http://tinyurl.com/SBL1722a.

2. Paul Garelli, "Le roi d'Assyrie et son peuple," *SciAnt* 1 (1987): 513–24; Simonetta Ponchia, "The Neo-Assyrian Adê Protocol and the Administration of the Empire," in *From Source to History: Studies in Ancient Near Eastern Worlds and Beyond Dedicated to Giovanni Battista Lanfranchi on the Occasion of His 65th Birthday on June 23, 2014*, ed. Salvatore Gaspa et al., AOAT 412 (Münster: Ugarit-Verlag, 2014), 501–26.

king consisted of declarations of loyalty, protestations against false accusations, and denunciations of some colleague or neighbor.

In contrast, loyal subjects were rewarded by royal favor, which could, for example, consist of the conferral of an estate.[3] The Assyrian king owed them protection, and not simply formally; he could intervene militarily, for example, by helping a vassal king against external enemies or internal factions. Sargon was concerned to protect his vassal against possible incursions by great neighboring powers such as Egypt, Phrygia, Urartu, or Elam. In return for his protection, the vassal had to send him gifts (*nâmurtu, tâmartu*) and pay tribute (*maddattu*), a symbol of his submission. In order to confirm his goodwill, he could send one or several of his sons to the royal palace to receive an Assyrian education. Interruption of the payment of tribute was interpreted as an act of rebellion and was punished as such.

The Assyrian king presented himself in his official inscriptions as the sole creator and maintainer of the empire. However, other documents such as letters, reports, and administrative records show that he was supported in governing Assyria by administrative, military, and cultural elites.[4] A small group of seven high officials with traditional titles constituted the main body of Assyrian state officials. As a representative of the king, the "treasurer" (*mašennu*) supervised the construction work in the empire; in particular, he administered the transport and use of precious metals and stones. It is uncertain whether the evidence for his administrative role was limited to the reign of Sargon or whether Sargon's correspondence alone can provide us with this type of data. He was the most important official under Sargon, as he was the only one to be in the Eponym Lists with the governors of the main provinces.[5] The "commander-in-chief" (*turtānu*) was the most frequently attested in royal inscriptions. His role as the commander of a strong army in the west and as the supreme commander of the Assyrian army is well documented. He led the provincial governors and other magnates in campaigns, especially in the absence of the king.[6] The office of the "palace herald" (*nāgir ekalli*) is difficult to define, possibly spokesman and commander of the north-

---

3. Francis Joannès, *The Age of Empires: Mesopotamia in the First Millennium BC*, trans. Antonia Nevill (Edinburgh: Edinburgh University Press, 2004), 87.
4. Postgate, "Invisible Hierarchy," 331–60; Radner, "Running the Empire."
5. SAAS 2:61; SAAS 11:161–62.
6. SAAS 11:165.

eastern army during Sargon's reign.⁷ The office of the "chief cupbearer" (*rab šāqê*) is also far from being clear, possibly cupbearer of the king and commander of the northern army; the commander-in-chief and the chief cupbearer were both the most senior Assyrian state officials.⁸ The "grand vizier" (*sukkallu dannu*) had two distinct functions: he was a high judicial authority, often working in cooperation with the "chief judge" (*sartinnu*), and he had a position in Babylonia, as he received letters from several Babylonian cities, most likely as a direct representative of the king. For example, he was involved in the preparations for Sargon's residence in Babylonia during the years 710–707.⁹ The "chief eunuch" (*rab ša rēši*) had a political influence at the court because he belonged to the close circle of the king. He was in command of the central army of Assyria, the royal corps. Several officials were eunuchs, their physical inability to father children ensuring their loyalty to the king; they seem to have been regarded almost like adopted children.¹⁰ In addition, the "majordomo" (*ša pân ekalli*) was in charge of supply and maintenance for the occupants of the royal palace, the Assyrian army, and the royal administration.

All of these high officials were counted among the magnates, the "great ones" (GAL.MEŠ), along with the most important "governors" (*bêl pahâti* or *šaknu*) of the provinces, appointed at the king's discretion, and with the king's personal delegates (*qēpu*, "trustworthy man"), who advised the rulers of allied states and reported directly back to Sargon. However, the high officials had a hierarchic position above that of the provincial governors, who referred to them as their lords. Equipped with the royal seal, the magnates governed in the king's stead and on the king's behalf. The relationship of this group of about one hundred to two hundred men with the king was foremost bureaucratic and impersonal, based on rules intended to ensure fair treatment. It was different for the high officials. Sargon is depicted in a relief of Khorsabad in conversation with one of them: without his bodyguard and attendants, the king faces the high officer wearing his sword, eye to eye, which meant an almost equal footing, great favor and trust.¹¹ However, in this relief, the high official is probably Sargon's

---

7. SAAS 11:162–63 (with bibliography).
8. SAAS 11:163.
9. SAAS 11:97–98, 164–65.
10. Omar N'Shea, "Royal Eunuchs and Elite Masculinity in the Neo-Assyrian Empire," *NEA* 79 (2016): 214–21.
11. Radner, "Running the Empire" (Louvre, AO 19873-4).

son, the crown prince Sennacherib. Sargon tried to keep an equilibrium of power between the magnates, whose influence neutralized each other and stabilized the empire. They were no longer chosen from the ancient noble families that had previously held hereditary positions of power; posts were awarded on merit rather than through family ties. Those who benefited from royal favor enabled their family and people within their circle to enjoy advantages, but they knew that they were revocable at any time. All the magnates had regular meetings with the king. It is debated whether this meant that they represented a kind of royal council, an Assyrian cabinet. Most of them were dispatched either to a province or to a foreign court, and assembling them all for a state council would have represented a logistical challenge, although each of them had a deputy (šaniu, "second one") who could handle local affairs in his absence. It seems that the king's magnates convened to settle judicial disputes, especially cases where petitions against administrative officials had been raised.[12] However, during the reign of Sargon, this system was somewhat modified (see below).

The power of the Neo-Assyrian Empire was based on a strong army of conquest. The army of conscripts who provided military service (ilku) only during the summer, when the agricultural calendar permitted the absence of farm workers, was transformed into an army of professionals by the mid-eighth century at the latest. Tiglath-pileser III and all his successors had armed forces of specialized soldiers.[13] For example, the army of Sargon during his campaign in Babylonia was composed of contingents raised in Assyria: a corps of Arameans, commanded by the chief of the "royal eunuchs" (ša rêš šarri); units of cavalrymen and charioteers from Babylonia, Chaldea, and Samaria; a unit of deportees from Carchemish and Hamath, incorporated into the Assyrian army; and troops of the royal

---

12. Simo Parpola, "The Assyrian Tree of Life: Tracing the Origins of Jewish Monotheism and Greek Philosophy," *JNES* 52 (1993): 189 n. 106; SAAS 11:166–67.

13. Andreas Fuchs, "War das Neuassyrische Reich ein Militärstaat?," in *Krieg-Gesellschaft-Institutionen: Beiträge zu einer vergleichenden Kriegsgeschichte*, ed. Burkhard Meissner, Oliver Schmitt, and Michael Sommer (Berlin: Akademie, 2005), 35–60; Dezsö, "Reconstruction of the Army of Sargon," 93–140; Postgate, "Invisible Hierarchy," 331–60; Robin Archer, "Chariotry To Cavalry: Developments In The Early First Millennium," in *New Perspectives on Ancient Warfare*, ed. Garrett G. Fagan and Matthew Trundle, HW 59 (Leiden: Brill, 2010), 57–80; Karen Radner, "The Assyrian Army," http://tinyurl.com/SBL1722b; John Marriott and Karen Radner, "Sustaining the Assyrian Army among Friends and Enemies in 714 BCE," *JCS* 67 (2015): 127–43.

guard.¹⁴ The marching order of the Assyrian army came under the aegis of gods: it began with the regiments of Nergal and Adad; they were followed by that of Ishtar, formed by the royal guard around Sargon, with the troops of Sîn and Shamash on his right- and left-hand sides, respectively. The supreme commander of the army was the Assyrian king, even if he did not participate in all the campaigns. He was primarily assisted by the commander-in-chief. The Assyrian army was formed by several corps adapted to the different terrains; for example, in difficult mountains, there were sappers for opening roads; in plains, charioteers were used; for besieging fortified cities, there were poliorcetic specialists; couriers were used for reconnaissance operations; there were also specialists in naval operations.

The "land of Assur" (*māt Aššur*) was the contemporary designation for Assyria. Altaweel defined the Assyrian heartland as the area between the Lesser Zab in the south, Mosul in the north, Wadi Tharthar and Jebel Sheikh Ibrahim in the west, and Jebel Qara Chauq and the Khazir river in the east.¹⁵ However, the core region of Assyria can be better described as the Assur-Nineveh-Arbela triangle (fig. 1): Assur (modern Qalaat Sherqat) in the south, Nineveh (modern Mosul with the mounds of Kuyunjik and Nebi Yunus) in the north, and Arbela (modern Erbil) in the east.¹⁶ It means the roughly triangular area east of the Tigris, north of the Lesser Zab and southwest of the mountain range where Taurus and Zagros meet. As a matter of fact, this area was under the continuous rule of the Assyrian kings from the fourteenth to the seventh centuries.¹⁷ It was not affected by the loss of territory due to the creation of new Aramean states in the eleventh century, in particular in the Jezireh. When Adad-narari III and his successors undertook to restore Assyria's old borders, they did not need to reestablish control in the Assur-Nineveh-Arbela triangle, because they had not lost it. The main historical Assyrian cities were located in the Tigris valley, on promontories that protected them from the violent floods of the river, such as Nineveh, Nimrud, and Assur. The other cities settled on the eastern plateaus, such as Khorsabad, Imgur-Enlil (Balawat), and Arbela.¹⁸

---

14. Joannès, *The Age of Empires*, 55.
15. Mark Altaweel, *The Imperial Landscape of Ashur: Settlement and Land Use in the Assyrian Heartland*, HSAO 11 (Heidelberg: Heidelberger Orientverlag, 2008), 6.
16. Radner, "Ashur-Nineveh-Arbela Triangle," 321–29.
17. Karen Radner, "Provinz: Assyrien," *RlA* 11:45–48.
18. Joannès, *Dictionnaire de la civilisation mésopotamienne*, 90.

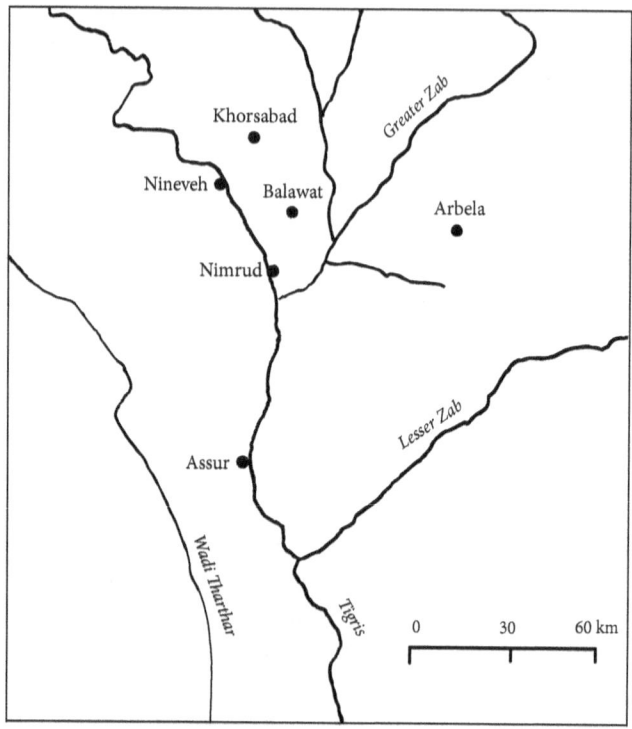

Fig. 1. The Assur-Nineveh-Arbela Triangle. NOTE: The localization of some toponyms is not precisely known and is presented in the maps throughout this volume as approximate

Assur lay on the western riverbank of the Tigris, in contrast with most of the regions of the triangle, which were situated east of the river. The particular location of Assur provided its control over the important road leading to the Euphrates and Khabur valleys. It was situated at the fringes of the desert, north of the artificially irrigated lands of Babylonia. It was also the point of contact with the pastoralists who made use of this arid area. Assur was the first capital of Assyria and occupied this site until the ninth century, except for the isolated attempt of Tukultî-Ninurta I, who, in the thirteenth century, built a new city next to Assur (Kâr Tukultî-Ninurta). Assur lost its chief political role in 879 under the reign of Ashurnasirpal II, who made Nimrud the new capital of Assyria. Nimrud became the seat of royal power and state administration, and the court moved to the new location. It remained the capital of Assyria until the reign of Sargon who lived there until 710–707, when he was in Babylon, and 706, year of the inauguration of his new capital, Khorsabad. Nimrud was not a new foundation but had roughly a millennium of recorded history and was well integrated in the regional road network.[19] Nimrud occupied a central position between Assur (ca. 70 km as the crow flies), Nineveh (ca. 35 km), and Arbela (ca. 60 km). It was situated just north of the Tigris's confluence with the Greater Zab. A canal dug to the Zab gave it a direct river connection with Arbela, which was located alongside one of the Zab's affluents. Nimrud became one of the largest Neo-Assyrian capitals, with a surrounding wall 7.5 km long and a surface area of 380 ha. Choosing Nimrud as capital meant that the influence of the three cities of the triangle, Assur, Nineveh, and Arbela, was substantially weakened. However, these three cities remained famous because of their old, prestigious sanctuaries: that of Ashur at Assur, those of Ishtar at Nineveh and Arbela.[20] No Assyrian king could ignore these gods, their shrines, and their festivals. Assur was the main god invoked by Sargon; Ishtar, more rarely mentioned, was named "the queen of the battle," for instance, in the Cyprus stela.[21]

Nineveh, situated on the eastern riverbank of the Tigris in front of modern-day Mosul, was mentioned several times in the Bible, for example, in the account of the prophet Jonah who had received from Yahweh the mission to preach to the city and its inhabitants because of their iniquitous behavior, as characterized in Nah 1:9–11, 14; 2:4; 3:19. Nineveh was used as a summer residence by the Assyrian kings until the reign of Sargon. At that time, it played a major role as the crown prince Sennacherib dwelled there to exercise the regency when his father was absent. The archives of Nimrud were partly moved to Nineveh, possibly before being transferred to Khorsabad, which was only 16 kilometers away. When Sennacherib ascended the throne, he chose Nineveh as the new capital of his empire and refitted its architecture.

Arbela, located on the western fringes of the Zagros, controlled the roads eastward, in particular through the neighboring mountain pass of Kikuri. It was starting from Arbela that Sargon undertook his campaigns

---

19. Max E. L. Mallowan, *Nimrud and Its Remains* (London: Collins, 1966); Radner, "Ashur-Nineveh-Arbela Triangle," 323–25.

20. G. van Driel, *The Cult of Aššur*, SSN 13 (Assen: Van Gorcum, 1969); Robert P. Gordon and Hans M. Barstad, eds., *"Thus Speaks Ishtar of Arbela": Prophecy in Israel, Assyria, and Egypt in the Neo-Assyrian Period* (Winona Lake, IN: Eisenbrauns, 2015); Claus Wilcke, "Inanna/Ištar," *RlA* 5:74–87.

21. *ARAB* 2.180.

to the east. Arbela was also located on the important road leading alongside the Zagros down to the Diyala and Babylonia. The city, under the name Urbilum, was already known in the third millennium. However, the ancient site is buried under the modern city of Erbil and the possibility of unearthing it remains limited. Archaeological excavations have started only recently.[22] Arbela developed mainly in the reign of Ashurbanipal, who made it one of his main residences. A relief of the north palace of Ashurbanipal showed the city, identified by name, with its walls, its fortified acropolis, and the temple of Ishtar.[23]

After having resided in Nimrud, Sargon in turn decided in 717 to build his new capital, Khorsabad, only 18 kilometers from Nineveh. What were the reasons for the Assyrian kings to move to new capitals? First, such an initiative supposed that the Assyrian Empire had become sufficiently opulent, thanks to the spoils and tributes from the submitted populations. According to Radner, the building of a new capital was an intentional strategy to strengthen the position of the king at the expense of old urban elites.[24] This seems to be a good reason as far as Sargon is concerned because he had met violent opposition from the elites when he ascended the throne (see above). It can be assumed that the new capital was not only a new political center, but was also populated by selected loyal supporters of the king, easy to control, in contrast to the traditional elites. The construction of Khorsabad also redirected resources previously under the control of Nineveh, mainly agricultural lands, personnel, and water, with the consequence of lowering the economic potential of Nineveh. Another reason for building a new capital was ideological: the will of the Assyrian king to realize a prestigious achievement that surpassed those of his predecessors. The operations of building are recounted in detail in the royal inscriptions, on the same level as the military expeditions.

The great cities, centers of power, were becoming more and more populated by inhabitants coming from the entire Near East, mainly employed as civilian and military administrators and officials, craftsmen, and workers. The regional agricultural environment of these cities was not sufficient for feeding them all. Outside these great cities, the countryside had only

---

22. Karel Nováček, "Research of the Arbil Citadel, Iraq: First Season," *PA* 99 (2008): 265, 276–78; Radner, "Ashur-Nineveh-Arbela Triangle," 322–23.

23. Radner, "Ashur-Nineveh-Arbela Triangle," 321–22, 328, and fig. 2 (Louvre, AO 19914).

24. Ibid., 324–25.

small towns and villages, where the peasants had very limited estates of about 20 ha on average, except when they worked on royal and temples estates. Bêl-dîni, the governor of Damascus, for example, possessed 580 ha of cereal lands in the district of Guzana in upper Mesopotamia.[25] Those who had the favor of the king took advantage of their situation to convert their profits by buying land. The taxes and duties owed to the king were so heavy that the cities tried to obtain exemptions from taxes and forced labor (*kidinnûtu, zakûtu*).

The plain of upper Mesopotamia, an almost empty land except for small urban centers such as Kahat and Harran, was considered a natural westward extension of Assyria. From the mid-eighth century, the policy for the development of this region became more systematic. The Assyrians tried to valorize it by integrating the local Aramean populations, by implanting Assyrian colonies and a great number of deportees in the valleys of Khabur and Balih.[26] The region of Harran, with its famous sanctuary of Sîn, became the western pole of the heartland of Assyria. It was also a base for the campaigns to the west. A series of documents related to a census in the region of Harran was found in the royal palace of Nineveh; they are attributed by most scholars to the beginning of Sargon's reign. This census registered the families cultivating mainly vineyards and cereals, in lands belonging to members of the court or of the royal family.[27] Upper Mesopotamia illustrates the process of fusion between Assyrian and Aramean cultures, as is shown from the mixed documents in cuneiform and alphabetic Aramaic, discovered, for example, at Dûr-Katlimu (Sheikh Hamad) or Burmarina (Shioukh Fauqâni) on the Euphrates. Arrapha was another natural extension of Assyria. The ancient site is covered by the modern town of Kirkuk; therefore, it could not be excavated and is known only from the texts; it belonged to Assyria from the time of the Middle Empire.[28]

---

25. Joannès, *The Age of Empires*, 61–62.

26. Hartmut Kühne, "The Assyrians on the Middle Euphrates and the Ḫābūr," in *Neo-Assyrian Geography*, ed. Mario Liverani, QGS 5 (Rome: Universita di Roma "La Sapienza," 1995), 79–83.

27. Joannès, *The Age of Empires*, 67, 73–77.

28. Katarzyna Grosz, *The Archive of the Wullu Family*, CNIP 5 (Copenhagen: Carsten Niebuhr Institute of Ancient Near Eastern Studies, University of Copenhagen, 1988).

The Assyrian Empire was divided into several provinces of different sizes. From the reign of Tiglath-pileser III onward, the number of provinces substantially increased from around fifteen due to the conquest of new territories, the transformation of some vassal states into provinces, and the partition of large provinces.[29] Usually, a province was designated by the name of its capital or the name of its region.[30] For more centralization, some provinces which were in border areas were placed under the responsibility of a high official; for example, the province of the commander-in-chief (*turtānu*) was formed with the territories between the Euphrates and the Balih; the province of the chief cupbearer (*rab šāqê*) was located in the Tur Abdin range and the high Tigris valley; the province of the treasurer (*mašennu*) was situated in the mountains north of Assyria; the province of the palace herald (*nāgir ekalli*) was located in the area of Habruri, north of Arbela. The provinces of heartland Assyria were smaller in size compared with the other Assyrian provinces.[31] However, all the governors were expected to provide the same contributions to the central administration, regardless of the size of their provinces, as appears from the records on the building of Khorsabad.[32] This means that all the provinces were theoretically expected to have approximately the same economic potential. According to a likely hypothesis, the small provinces had to be more densely populated, which was achieved by the settling of more deported populations.[33] In addition, the productivity would have been substantially increased by the large-scale irrigation projects supporting Nimrud, Khorsabad, and Nineveh.[34]

The functions of a province governor (*šaknu*) were the following: he had first to receive and share the tribute, sending part of it to the capital, keeping a part for entertaining his local troops, and building reserves for the royal army, while retaining some for his own needs. The governor was also in charge of collecting and transmitting all the information concerning

---

29. SAA 11:1, 1.20.

30. Joannès, *Dictionnaire de la civilisation mésopotamienne*, 699–702.

31. Radner, "Ashur-Nineveh-Arbela Triangle," 322, fig. 1, 327–29.

32. Simo Parpola, "The Construction of Dur-Šarrukin in the Assyrian Royal Correspondence," in Caubet, *Khorsabad, le palais de Sargon II*, 47–77.

33. Radner, "Ashur-Nineveh-Arbela Triangle," 327–28; Bustenay Oded, *Mass Deportations and Deportees in the Neo-Assyrian Empire* (Wiesbaden: Reichert, 1979), 28, 116–35.

34. Jason A. Ur, "Sennacherib's Northern Assyrian Canals: New Insights from Satellite Imagery and Aerial Photography," *Iraq* 67 (2005): 343.

his province.³⁵ His reports were sent to the capital chancellery, controlled by the crown prince, before being presented to the king. Messages exchanged between the king and the governors could be delivered either by letter or by envoy, with an unprecedented speed, as shown, for example, in a letter from the crown prince Sennacherib to his father Sargon.³⁶ Some high officials who had several functions, among which was the responsibility of a province, sent local delegates, such as the "trustworthy man" (*qēpu*) for handling the provincial affairs in their stead. From the reign of Tiglath-pileser III on, the important posts were entrusted to a group of three persons: the titular, his assistant (*šaniu*), and a third man (*šalšu*). This chain of command was probably intended to optimize the governance and to limit personal ambitions.³⁷ The royal seal was given to the king's representatives as a manifestation of authority and a sign of trust. Hundreds of copies of the royal seal were in circulation, yet only seal impressions on clay tablets are preserved. It represented the Assyrian king, identifiable by his headdress, fighting with his sword against a standing roaring lion.³⁸ Every document bearing the impression of the royal seal had the same value as a direct command from the king and his subjects had to act accordingly.³⁹ However, royal orders could be refused if the seal was suspected not to be genuine, as was the case recorded in a letter to Sargon: "The signet ring which he delivered is not made like the signet rings of the king, my lord. I have a thousand signet ring(-sealed letters) of the king, my lord, with me and I have compared it with them—it is not made like the signet ring of the king, my lord!"⁴⁰

At the beginning of Sargon's reign, governorship of a central Assyrian province no longer necessarily meant a successful career in state

---

35. Peter Dubovský, *Hezekiah and the Assyrian Spies: Reconstruction of the Neo-Assyrian Intelligence Services and its Significance for 2 Kings 18–19*, BibOr 49 (Rome: Biblical Institute Press, 2006).

36. SAA 1:29, no. 31; Karlheinz Kessler, "'Royal Roads' and Other Questions of the Neo-Assyrian Communication System," in Parpola, *Assyria 1995*, 129–36; Karen Radner, "Royal Pen Pals: The King of Assyria in Correspondence with Officials, Clients and Total Strangers (8th and 7th Centuries BC)," *PapyVind* 8 (2015): 61–72.

37. SAAS 11:161–68; Postgate, "Invisible Hierarchy," 331–60.

38. Karen Radner, "The Delegation of Power: Neo-Assyrian Bureau Seals," in *L'archive des fortifications de Persépolis: État des questions et perspectives de recherches*, ed. Pierre Briant, Wouter F. M. Henkelman, and Matthew W. Stolper, Persika 12 (Paris: de Boccard, 2008), 481–515.

39. SAA 5:168, no. 234.

40. SAA 5:86, no. 125.

administration as had been the case previously. It now was more prestigious to govern one of the newly created provinces. Governorship of a central Assyrian province was considered for an official at a more junior stage in his career. For instance, Nabû-bêlu-kain was first governor of Arrapha, then of the Median new province of Harhar/Kâr-Sharrukîn, and finally he was named "vizier" (*sukkallu*), one of the main state offices.[41] The most experienced governors were appointed to rule over the newly created and distant provinces. This change was also reflected by the fact that the governors who were made eponyms after the king, were only the most important ones, those who had the governorship of new provinces, for example, in 712 the eponym was Sharru-êmuranni, governor of Zamua.[42]

---

41. Stefan Zawadzki, "The Question of the King's Eponymate in the Latter Half of the 8th Century and the 7th Century BC," in Parpola, *Assyria 1995*, 383–89; John Nicholas Postgate and Raija A. Mattila, "Il-Yada' and Sargon's Southern Frontier," in Frame, *From the Upper Sea*, 251–54, no. 50; *PNA* 2.2:815–17.

42. SAAS 2:60; *PNA* 3.21234–37.

4
THE CONQUEST OF THE WEST

The first campaign of Sargon, probably in 720, after he had solved his internal problems, was directed against Babylonia. He could not accept that Merodach-baladan, the chief of the tribal political unit of Bît-Yakin, had seized anew the throne of Babylon in 721. The first of Sargon's battles occurred near Dêr, a Babylonian city under Assyrian control. Contrary to what he claimed, he was not victorious and learned that he was not yet ready to expel Merodach-baladan from the throne of Babylon (see below). Therefore, he decided to campaign, immediately after, against the western coalition led by Iaûbidî of Hamath. Moreover, the conquest of the west was a constant purpose of the Assyrian kings who were attracted by the wealth of the western states, fascinated by the Mediterranean Sea, and also intended to make the Assyrian Empire a maritime empire. The control or conquest of Egypt, which had dominated the Levantine region in the second millennium, was another of their dreams. However, at the beginning of Sargon's campaigns, no plan or program is clearly discernible. Rather, he seemed to respond to various challenges in different areas, as and when they arose, such as the western coalition against Assyria. But, is that completely true?

Palestine

The kingdom of Israel, known to the Assyrians as *Bit-Humri*, "House of Omri," lost its northern territories and coastal regions after the conquest of Damascus by Tiglath-pileser III in 732 BCE (fig. 2). This Assyrian king had established the new provinces of Megiddo and Dor.[1] He had replaced

---

1. Ephraim Stern, "Hazor, Dor and Megiddo in the Time of Ahab and under Assyrian Rule," *IEJ* 40 (1990): 12–30; Nadav Na'aman, "Province System and Settle-

king Peqah with Hoshea, chosen to serve as a loyal executor of Assyrian interests. The south of the kingdom of Israel remained independent as long as Hoshea was a faithful Assyrian vassal. According to biblical evidence, the only one that exists, Hoshea stopped paying tribute and sought alliance with "So, king of Egypt" (2 Kgs 17:3–6; 18:9–10), possibly Osorkon IV of Tanis.[2] Shalmaneser V put king Hoshea in jail and attacked Israel, which possibly had no more king because, in the Nimrud Prisms, reference was then made to the "Samarians" rather than to the "king of the Samarians." The seizure of Samaria took place in the fourth year of Hezekiah of Judah and the seventh year of Hoshea of Israel, after a siege of three years. Assuming that the traditional dates of Hezekiah's reign (719–699) and Hoshea's reign (731–722) are correct, Shalmaneser V would have seized Samaria in 722 BCE.[3] The seizure of Samaria was also attributed to him by the Babylonian Chronicle: "He (Shalmaneser V) ruined Samaria (URU Šá-ma/ba-ra-ʾ-in iḫ-te-pi)."[4] The toponym with the determinative URU is very likely the city (not the region) of Samaria.[5] As a matter of fact, the verb ḫepû had several meanings: "to ruin," "to destroy," "to plunder," "to ravage": it is unclear whether Samaria was seized after the breaking of its walls or simply ravaged.[6] The archaeological record does not indicate

---

ment Pattern in Southern Syria and Palestine in the Neo-Assyrian Period," in Liverani, *Neo-Assyrian Geography*, 106–7; Karen Radner, "Israel, the 'House of Omri,'" in *Assyrian Empire Builders*, http://tinyurl.com/SBL1722c.

2. Or Piye/Piankhy: Na'aman, "Historical Background," 210–11; Alberto R. W. Green, "The Identity of King So of Egypt: An Alternative Interpretation," *JNES* 52 (1993): 106; Erik Hornung, Rolf Krauss, and David Warburton, eds., *Ancient Egyptian Chronology*, HdO 83 (Leiden: Brill, 2006), 494.

3. Gershon Galil, *The Chronology of the Kings of Israel and Judah*, SHANE 9 (Leiden: Brill, 1996), 83–97; Paul Garelli and André Lemaire, *Le Proche-Orient Asiatique: Tome 2; Les Empires mésopotamiens, Israël*, 3rd ed., Nouvelle Clio (Paris: Presses universitaires de France, 1997), 321. For a different chronology, see M. Christine Tetley, "The Date of Samaria's Fall as a Reason for Rejecting the Hypothesis of Two Conquests," *CBQ* 64 (2002): 59–77; Tetley, *The Reconstructed Chronology of the Divided Kingdom* (Winona Lake, IN: Eisenbrauns, 2005).

4. Grayson, *Assyrian and Babylonian Chronicles*, 73, I, 28.

5. The other hypotheses, such as Sabara or the region of Samaria, are not relevant: Hugo Winckler, "Nachtrag," *ZA* 2 (1887): 351–52; Winckler, *Die Keilinschriften und das Alte Testament*, 3rd ed. (Berlin: Reuther & Reichard, 1903), 62; Na'aman, "Historical Background," 215–16.

6. Na'aman, "Historical Background," 211, 215–16; Stig Forsberg, *Near Eastern Destruction Datings as Sources for Greek and Near Eastern Iron Age Chronology*,

4. THE CONQUEST OF THE WEST

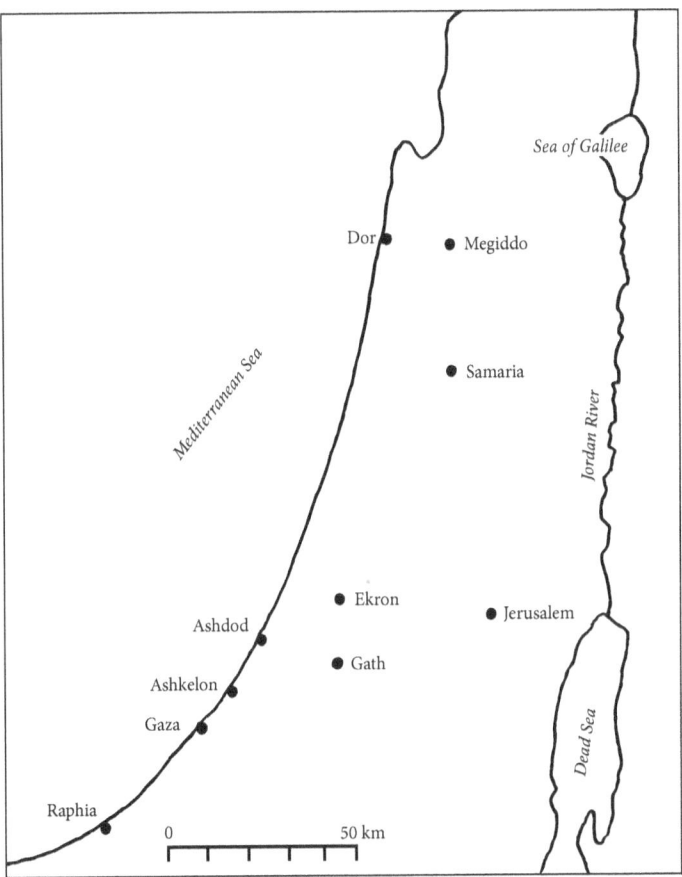

Fig. 2. Palestine

a complete destruction of the city, but the Assyrians' claim of having conquered a city did not mean its utter razing.[7]

As the Eponym Lists for Shalmaneser's reign mentioned three campaigns in 725, 724, and 723, with the name of the country or city broken away, it has been suggested that these three year campaigns referred to the three-year siege of Samaria mentioned in the Bible (2 Kgs 17:5).[8] This hypothesis is possible but needs to be confirmed by new evidence.

Archaeological and Historical Studies: The Cases of Samaria (722 B.C.) and Tarsus (696 B.C.), AUU.Boreas 19 (Stockholm: Almqvist & Wiksell, 1995): 48–49.

7. N. Avigad, "Samaria (City)," *NEAEHL* 4:1300–10.

8. SAAS 2:59. See J. W. Crowfoot, G. M. Crowfoot, and Kathleen M. Kenyon,

The conquest of Samaria was claimed by Sargon. His campaigns were represented in the reliefs of his palace of Khorsabad as a complement to his inscriptions. Room V seems to be devoted, at least partly, to his western campaigns, but it is difficult to identify the representation of Samaria because it is not mentioned in the accompanying captions; it is also uncertain whether the fragment of Assyrian inscription found in Samaria belonged to a Sargon stela.[9] However, Sargon's claim to the conquest of Samaria was clearly asserted in eight different inscriptions.[10] In the Great Summary Inscription, he affirmed: "I besieged and conquered Samarina (Samaria)." The Nimrud Prism (D and E) was the most detailed: "[The inhabitants of Sa]merina, who agreed [and plotted] with a king [hostile to] me, not to endure servitude and not to bring tribute to Assur and who did battle, I fought against them with the power of the great gods, my lords." The Assur Charter and the Annals mentioned the participation of Samaria in the Iaûbidî of Hamath's coalition in year 2, which is 720 BCE. However, the conquest of Samaria was attributed to the very beginning of Sargon's reign in the first damaged lines of the Annals. The conquest and plundering of Samaria were briefly mentioned in four other inscriptions.

The fall of the Northern Kingdom of Israel as a result of the conquest of Samaria has been studied in several articles and books. However, the question is still debated because not all the problems have been solved. The theories proposed can be divided into six main groups.[11] According

---

Samaria-Sebaste III: The Objects from Samaria (London: Palestine Exploration Fund, 1957), 35 and pl. IV; Frame, "Tell Acharneh Stela," 51 and n. 5.

9. Norma Franklin has proposed an identification on Slab 4. Upper register (4-4), Slab 5. Upper register (5-U), and Slabs 8 and 9. Upper register (8-U and 9-U): "A Room with a View: Images from Room V at Khorsabad, Samaria, Nubians, The Brook of Egypt and Ashdod," in *Studies in the Archaeology of the Iron Age in Israel and Jordan*, ed. Amihai Mazar, JSOTSup 331 (Sheffield: Sheffield Academic, 2001), 266–72; Franklin, "The Room V Reliefs at Dur-Sharrukin and Sargon II's Western Campaigns," *TA* 21 (1994): 255–75; Crowfoot, Crowfoot, and Kenyon, *Samaria-Sebaste III*, 35 and pl. IV; J. E. Reade, "Sargon's Campaigns of 720, 716, and 715 B.C.: Evidence from the Sculptures," *JNES* 35 (1976): 99–102; Frame, "Tell Acharneh Stela," 51 and n. 5.

10. ARAB 2.55; Fuchs, *Inschriften Sargons II*, 197 (Great Summary Inscription); Gadd, "Inscribed Prisms of Sargon II," 179–82 (Nimrud Prism, D and E). ARAB 2.133–35; Saggs, "Historical Texts and Fragments," 11–20 (Assur Charter). ARAB 2.4–5; Fuchs, *Inschriften Sargons II*, 87–89 (Annals); 34, ll. 19–20 (Cylinder Inscription); 76 (Small Summary Inscription); 261 (Palace Door); 63 (Bull Inscription).

11. Winckler, *Keilschrifttexte Sargons*, 1:62 (Theory 1). Na'aman, "Historical

to the first theory, the conquest of Samaria has to be ascribed to Sargon because the Babylonian Chronicle referred to another city, and the biblical evidence is either irrelevant or erroneous. This theory is unlikely since Samaria is clearly mentioned in the Babylonian Chronicle in relation to Shalmaneser V's reign. According to the second theory, Sargon brought an end to a siege initiated by Shalmaneser. However, the mention of the capture of Samaria by Shalmaneser appears to be the most natural way to understand the Babylonian Chronicle and the biblical testimony. A variant of this theory consists in dating the siege and fall of Samaria to 721–719/8; however, this reconstruction of the chronology, based on a radically reconstructed Hebrew chronology, is problematic because it cannot be exactly synchronized with Assyrian, Phoenician, and Egyptian chronologies.[12] The third theory proposes that the fall of Samaria took place at the very end of the reign of Shalmaneser, so that Sargon could legitimately claim its conquest. But this theory does not make a distinction between the two kings' actions: Shalmaneser's action was clearly directed against Hoshea's rebellion while Sargon's action was connected with the participation of Samaria in the revolt of Iaûbidî of Hamath. According to the fourth theory, Sargon usurped his predecessor's accomplishment, or possibly he simply put down a minor revolt of Samaria after it was already an Assyrian province. Since Sargon's claim was thoroughly integrated into his western campaigns of 720, he probably did not usurp the conquest of Samaria; moreover, he asserted that he himself installed his official over it as gov-

---

Background," 206–25 (Theory 2). Olmstead, *Western Asia in the Days of Sargon*, 45–47 (Theory 3). Reade, "Sargon's Campaigns," 100; see also Edwin R. Thiele, *The Mysterious Numbers of the Hebrew Kings*, rev. ed. (Grand Rapids: Zondervan, 1983), 163–72 (Theory 4). Jeremy Hughes, *Secrets of the Times: Myth and History in Biblical Chronology*, JSOTS 66 (Sheffield: JSOT Press, 1990), 208–9; John H. Hayes and Jeffrey K. Kuan, "The Final Years of Samaria (730–720 B.C.)," *Bib* 72 (1991): 153–81; Jeffrey K. Kuan, *Neo-Assyrian Historical Inscriptions and Syria-Palestine* (Hong Kong: Alliance Bible Seminary Press, 1995), 193–207 (Theory 5). Tadmor, "Campaigns of Sargon," 22–40; Becking, *Fall of Samaria*, 21–45 (Theory 6). For discussion of the theories, see, e.g., Becking, *Fall of Samaria*, 21–56; Galil, *Chronology of the Kings*, 83–97; Anton Schoors, *Die Königreiche Israel und Juda im 8. und 7. Jahrhundert v. Chr.: Die assyrische Krise*, BiE 5 (Stuttgart: Kohlhammer, 1998); Younger, "Fall of Samaria," 461–82; Tetley, "Date of Samaria's Fall," 59–66.

12. Tetley, "Date of Samaria's Fall," 59–77; Tetley, *Reconstructed Chronology*; see Steven L. McKenzie, review of *The Reconstructed Chronology of the Divided Kingdom*, by M. Christine Tetley, *JHebS* 5 (2004–2005), http://tinyurl.com/SBL1722d.

ernor. According to the fifth theory, there were four conquests of Samaria between 727 and 719 BCE, three of them attributable to Shalmaneser and one to Sargon. The sources concerning Shalmaneser's reign do not attest three conquests of Samaria.

The sixth theory supposes that Samaria was conquered first by Shalmaneser, and a few years later by Sargon. This reconstruction appears to be the best way of understanding the data. Shalmaneser decided to subdue the rebellion of king Hoshea by besieging Samaria, his capital city, possibly over a three-year period (725, 724, 723) according to the Eponym Lists. The city fell in 722, possibly in autumn (Elul/Tishri) because he was not able to deport the people of Samaria in the very short span of time between the conquest and his death.[13] Shalmaneser died shortly after the fall of Samaria in the month of Tebet 722. Sargon defeated the western coalition in 720, his second year of reign, and proceeded to recapture Samaria because this city had participated in Iaûbidî's coalition which "gathered together (the people of) Arpad and Samerina (Samaria) and brought them to his side."[14]

Sargon turned the kingdom of Israel, partly reduced by Tiglath-pileser III, then by Shalmaneser V, into an Assyrian province. He rebuilt Samaria, which had not been completely destroyed: "I made it greater than it was before."[15] According to the standard practice of the time to incorporate enemy troops into the conquering forces, Sargon selected two hundred (or fifty in later versions) chariot crews.[16] Administrative documents from Nimrud indicate that the Samarian chariot corps was stationed in that city and was allowed to retain its group identity, which was unusual.[17] The Israelite heavily fortified and tank-like chariots, drawn by large breeds of strong horses, were appreciated. Sargon deported a significant number of Samaria's population to several locations throughout his empire: "I counted

---

13. Tadmor, "Campaigns of Sargon," 37 and n. 132.

14. *ARAB* 2.134; Eckhart Frahm, "A Sculpted Slab with an Inscription of Sargon II Mentioning the Rebellion of Yau-bi'di of Hamath," *AoF* 40 (2013): 46, l. 13.

15. *ARAB* 2.4.

16. Gadd, "Inscribed Prisms of Sargon II," 179–82 (200); Fuchs, *Inschriften Sargons II*, 197 (50).

17. John Nicholas Postgate, *The Tablets from Fort Shalmaneser*, CTN 3 (London: British School of Archaeology in Iraq, 1984), 35–41; Stephanie Dalley, "Foreign Chariotry and Cavalry in the Armies of Tiglath-Pileser III and Sargon II," *Iraq* 47 (1985): 31–36; Archer, "Chariotry to Cavalry," 57–80.

as spoil 27,280 people.... I settled the rest of them in the midst of Assyria."[18] Two biblical passages specify the places where they were deported: "The king of Assyria deported Israel to Assyria and settled them in Halah, on the Khabur, the river of Gozan and in the towns of the Medes" (2 Kgs 17:6; 18:11).[19] This deportation did not take place before 716, the date of Sargon's campaign to Media. Indeed these texts were written at least three generations after the first deportations, and they telescoped over many years, perhaps covering the entire period from Shalmaneser V to Ashurbanipal.[20] References to deported Israelites among the West Semitic personal names are found in Assyrian documents.[21] Some of them appear to have received preferential treatment. For example, Sama, a Samarian deportee, was highly placed at Sargon's court, advising him about matters pertaining to his homeland.[22]

While Tiglath-pileser III seems to have utilized a unidirectional deportation policy for Israelites in Galilee, Sargon conducted a bidirectional deportation, deporting Israelites from Samaria and settling others there: "I repopulated Samaria more than before. I brought into it people from countries conquered by my hands."[23] The only deportees to Samaria that he specified are some Arabian tribes in 715, probably for the purpose of diverting to that area some of the Arabian trade in which the nomad

---

18. Fuchs, *Inschriften Sargons II*, 197 (27,290 people); Gadd, "Inscribed Prisms of Sargon II," 179–82, ll. 4–6; SAAS 3:52, 70, 86. See Nadav Na'aman, "The Number of Deportees from Samaria in the Nimrud Prisms of Sargon II," *NABU* 1 (2000): 1, no. 1, who proposed to read "47,280 people" instead of "27,280."

19. On these toponyms, see John MacGinnis, "The Toponym Hara in I Chronicles 5.26," *NABU* 4 (2014): 154–56, no. 99.

20. Oded, *Mass Deportations and Deportees*, 20, 50: he considers up to 38 the number of deportations by Sargon, and up to 217,635 the total of deportees known from sources; K. Lawson Younger, "The Deportations of the Israelites," *JBL* 117 (1998): 201–27; Younger, "The Repopulation of Samaria (2 Kings 17:24, 27–31) in Light of Recent Study," in *The Future of Biblical Archaeology: Reassessing Methodologies and Assumptions*, ed. James K. Hoffmeier and Alan Millard (Grand Rapids: Eerdmans, 2004), 254–80.

21. Israel Eph'al, "The Samarian(s) in the Assyrian Sources," in Cogan, *Ah, Assyria*, 41–42; Becking, *Fall of Samaria*, 66–93.

22. Dalley, "Foreign Chariotry," 41; Younger, "Deportations of the Israelites," 219–24.

23. Gadd, "Inscribed Prisms of Sargon II," 178–82, ll. 37–39. See Younger, "Deportations of the Israelites," 216–17, 227.

tribes played a significant role.²⁴ The major deportation to Samaria took place in 710/709, from the main Babylonian cities and from the peripheral Aramean and Chaldean areas. Some groups of deportees are attested by their names: the "Avvim" in the district of Bethel and the "Chaldeans village" in northern Samaria (2 Kgs 17:24; Josh 18:23).²⁵ The analysis of personal names also throws light on the ethnic composition of the population, but without any precise dating.²⁶ Cuneiform tablets that appeared in Palestine after the Assyrian annexations and deportations were the product of Assyrian officials or of some of the Mesopotamian deportees to the region, but it is difficult to relate them precisely to Sargon's reign.²⁷

The kingdom of Judah probably received refugees from conquered Samaria; indeed Jerusalem's enlargement reflected an important population growth not to be explained in terms of gradual demographic growth.²⁸ Between the conquest of Jerusalem by Tiglath-pileser in 733 BCE and that of Sennacherib in 701, what happened in Judah during Sargon's reign? According to the traditional dates, Ahaz reigned in Judah

---

24. Becking, *Fall of Samaria*, 102–4; Fuchs, *Inschriften Sargons II*, 110; see Younger, "Deportations of the Israelites," 226–27. For a different view, see Israel Eph'al, *The Ancient Arabs: Nomads on the Borders of the Fertile Crescent 9th–5th Centuries B.C.* (Jerusalem: Magnes, 1982), 105–6.

25. See Nadav Na'aman, "Population Changes in Palestine Following Assyrian Deportations," *TA* 20 (1993): 104–24; Na'aman, "Province System and Settlement Pattern," 110–11.

26. Nadav Na'aman and Ran Zadok, "Sargon II's Deportations to Israel and Philistia (716–708 B.C.)," *JCS* 40 (1988): 40–42; Ran Zadok, "Israelites and Judaeans in the Neo-Assyrian Documentation (732–602 B.C.E.): An Overview of the Sources and a Socio-historical Assessment," *BASOR* 374 (2015): 159–89.

27. Nadav Na'aman and Ran Zadok, "Assyrian Deportations to the Province of Samerina in the Light of Two Cuneiform Tablets from Tel Hadid," *TA* 27 (2000): 159–88; Younger, "Repopulation of Samaria," 254–58. Some typical Assyrian clay vessels were also uncovered in seventh-century strata: Ephraim Stern, *The Assyrian, Babylonian, and Persian Periods, 732–332 BCE*, vol. 2 of *Archaeology of the Land of the Bible*, AYBRL (New York: Doubleday, 2001), 51.

28. Israel Finkelstein, "The Settlement History of Jerusalem in the Eighth and Seventh Centuries BC," *RB* 115 (2008): 499–519; A. M. Bagg, "Hezekiah's Jerusalem: Nineveh in Judah?" in Gaspa, *From Source to History*, 36. For another view, see Nadav Na'aman, "When and How Did Jerusalem Become a Great City? The Rise of Jerusalem as Judah's Premier City in the Eighth-Seventh Centuries B.C.E.," *BASOR* 347 (2007): 21–56.

around 735–719 and was succeeded by Hezekiah (719–699).[29] Does the quasi-absence of a mention of Judah in Sargon's inscriptions and in the Bible mean that Judah was not attacked by Sargon and remained a loyal vassal throughout his reign? There is no attestation that king Ahaz of Judah participated in Iaûbidî's coalition in 720, nor that king Hezekiah, who was approached in 712 by Yamani of Ashdod, participated in his anti-Assyrian coalition.[30] Neither is there evidence that the so-called Azekah Inscription has to be dated to the time of Sargon; it more likely described Sennacherib's campaign against Judah in 701.[31] However, even if Sargon's inscriptions did not explicitly mention any military campaign against Judah, in the Nimrud Inscription, Sargon described himself as "the subduer of Judah which lies far away" (*mu-šak-niš* KUR *Ia-ú-du šá a-šar-šú ru-ú-qu*).[32] The word *mušakniš* is a causative participle form from the verb *kanāšu*, "to submit," "to subjugate," "to bow down," "to make subject." It frequently referred to a military campaign but possibly referred only to the imposition of tribute. Isaiah described the invasion route followed by an unnamed enemy army approaching Jerusalem from the north (Isa 10:24–32).[33] These two passages were interpreted alternately in the sense of a military campaign conducted by Sargon against Judah or of a simple mention of the vassal relationship of Judah to Assyria.[34] In the absence of conclusive evidence in his inscriptions, in the representation of campaigns in the reliefs of the palace of Khorsabad, and in the biblical

---

29. Garelli and Lemaire, *Proche-Orient Asiatique 2*, 321. For discussion on different dates, see, e.g., Nadav Na'aman, "Hezekiah and the Kings of Assyria," in *Ancient Israel and Its Neighbors, Interaction and Counteraction: Collected Essays*, vol. 1 (Winona Lake, IN: Eisenbrauns, 2005), 99–102.

30. *ARAB* 2.195.

31. Na'aman, "Hezekiah and the Kings of Assyria," 108–11 (with bibliography). For another, unlikely, hypothesis, see Gershon Galil, "Conflicts between Assyrian Vassals," *SAAB* 6 (1992): 61–63.

32. *ARAB* 2.137; Winckler, *Keilschrifttexte Sargons*, 168, l. 8.

33. Marvin A. Sweeney, "Sargon's Threat against Jerusalem in Isaiah 10, 27–32," *Bib* 75 (1994): 457–63 (with bibliography), argued that the passage pertains to the campaign of Sargon in 720 BCE.

34. Tadmor, "Campaigns of Sargon II," 38 and n. 146; Becking, *Fall of Samaria*, 54–55; Sweeney, "Sargon's Threat against Jerusalem," 457–63; K. Lawson Younger, "Sargon's Campaign against Jerusalem—A Further Note," *Bib* 77 (1996): 108–10.

text, it is reasonable to conclude that Judah was not confronted with a military campaign during Sargon's reign.[35]

The king of Judah (unnamed) was mentioned as a "payer of tribute [and] tax to Assur" in the Prism Inscriptions from Nineveh, and in a letter, probably written around 716 by the governor of Nimrud.[36] Another letter, dated around 715, mentioned that the Judean king had sent a contingent of troops to support the Assyrian army on campaign.[37] It is not improbable that in 706 Hezekiah visited the new impressive city built by Sargon.[38] There was possibly a special relationship or even some kind of alliance between Judah and Assyria in the time of Sargon and his predecessors. If the women's names Atalia and Iabâ were really Hebrew names, it would mean that, in the second half of the eighth century, the Assyrian kings concluded marriage alliances with princesses from Jerusalem, as it was a common Assyrian practice to secure an alliance with a foreign state by marriage.[39] In short, the scarcity of sources on the relationship between Judah and Sargon does not allow any further advance to be made

---

35. Na'aman, "Hezekiah and the Kings of Assyria," 104–5.

36. *ARAB* 2.195; H. W. F. Saggs, *The Nimrud Letters, 1952: Cuneiform Texts from Nimrud V* (London: British School of Archaeology in Iraq, 2001), ND 2765.

37. Saggs, *Nimrud Letters, 1952*, ND 2608.

38. William R. Gallagher, *Sennacherib's Campaign to Judah: New Studies*, SHANE 18 (Leiden: Brill, 1999), 268; K. Lawson Younger, "Recent Study on Sargon II, King of Assyria: Implications for Biblical Studies," in *Mesopotamia and the Bible: Comparative Explorations*, ed. Mark W. Chavalas and K. Lawson Younger, JSOTSup 341 (London: Sheffield Academic, 2002), 319.

39. Ran Zadok, *The Pre-Hellenistic Israelite Anthroponymy and Prosopography*, OLA 28 (Leuven: Peeters, 1988), 168; S. Dalley, "Yabâ, Atalyā and the Foreign Policy of the Late Assyrian Kings," *SAAB* 12 (1998): 83–98; Dalley, "Recent Evidence from Assyrian Sources for Judaean History from Uzziah to Manasseh," *JSOT* 28 (2004): 387–401; Reinhard Achenbach, "Jaba und Atalja: zwei jüdische Königstöchter am assyrischen Königshof?" *BN* 113 (2002): 29–38. Peter Machinist, "Assyria and Its Image in the First Isaiah," *JAOS* 103 (1983): 719–37, has drawn attention to Neo-Assyrian images and idioms in the writing of First Isaiah. On the crucially important stimuli coming from Assyria in the Neo-Assyrian Empire, see Simo Parpola, "Assyria's Expansion in the 8th and 7th Centuries and Its Long-Term Repercussions in the West," in *Symbiosis, Symbolism, and the Power of the Past: Canaan, Ancient Israel, and Their Neighbors from the Late Bronze Age through Roman Palaestina; Proceedings of the Centennial Symposium, W. F. Albright Institute of Archaeological Research and American Schools of Oriental Research, Jerusalem, May 29–31, 2000*, ed. William G. Dever and Seymour Gitin (Winona Lake, IN: Eisenbrauns, 2003), 103–5.

regarding its interpretation. As far as we know, Judah was a vassal kingdom that did not clash with Assyria and paid tribute until Sargon's death in 705 BCE.

Philistia was organized during the eighth century in independent kingdoms centered around four cities: Ekron, Ashdod, Ashkelon, and Gaza. This region acted as a buffer zone between the expanding might of Assyria and Egypt. Therefore, the Philistine cities were too important in the national politics of the ancient Near East for Sargon to loosen control over them. Moreover, he did not want to upset the precarious trade relations that Assyria had with Egypt through Philistia.

Gaza was the southernmost of the Philistine cities on the *Via Maris*, an important trade route running along the Mediterranean seashore to the Nile Delta, and the end destination of the incense route across the Arabian Peninsula. Due to its exceptional position, Gaza was one of the main trading centers in the eastern Mediterranean. It was also very close to the border brook of Egypt.[40] Consequently, it was one of the first concerns of Sargon at the beginning of his reign. Hanunu was king of Gaza from the reign of Tiglath-pileser III. Early in the reign of Sargon, he probably took advantage of the political instability that accompanied his accession to the throne of Assyria. There is no document attesting that he allied with the anti-Assyrian coalition headed by Iaûbidî, king of Hamath; however, his revolt occurred at about the same period.[41] After smashing the coalition forces at Qarqar and subduing Samaria, Sargon marched south against Hanunu and his allies, among them troops dispatched by Egypt. He met the allied forces at Rapihu (modern Raphia), just south of Gaza, and defeated them: "Hanunu, king of Gaza, with Rêû, commander-in-chief of Egypt, who had come out against me at Rapihu to offer battle and fight, I defeated … Hanunu, king of Gaza, I seized with my own hand."[42] "I counted as booty the king of the city of Gaza who had not submitted my yoke."[43] Then he brought him in bonds to Assur, possibly in order to take part in a ritual

---

40. Paul K. Hooker, "The Location of the Brook of Egypt," in *History and Interpretation: Essays in Honour of John H. Hayes*, ed. M. Patrick Graham, William P. Brown, and Jeffrey K. Kuan, JSOTSup 173 (Sheffield: JSOT Press, 1993), 201–14.

41. Hayim Tadmor, "Philistia under Assyrian Rule," *BA* 29 (1966): 91.

42. *ARAB* 2.55; Fuchs, *Inschriften Sargon II*, 197, 25, and 344; *PNA* 3.1:1049.

43. Grant Frame, "The Inscription of Sargon II at Tang-i Var," *Or* 68 (1999): 36, 40, l. 23; ND3411: see Hooker, "Location of the Brook of Egypt," 207. See also *ARAB* 2.80, 92, 99.

victory celebration or to publicly swear loyalty to Sargon.[44] No more is mentioned about his fate. Gaza was not annexed as an Assyrian province but remained an autonomous vassal state, probably because of its strategic importance, both military and commercial. Was there a second campaign against Gaza in 716? Sargon was then campaigning in the Zagros, and the deportation of eastern populations to the Gaza region has been interpreted as inferring a campaign there.[45] There is no good evidence yet provided to suggest an Assyrian military campaign, but only a deportation.[46] Two fragmentary inscriptions read: "and the cities] on the border of the brook of E[gypt, a province which is on the shore of] the Western [Sea], I settled them; [to the hands of my prefect,] the sheikh of the city of Laban, [I entrusted them]." Sargon claimed to have encouraged trade between Egypt and Assyria: "of the country of Musur I opened the sealed (treasury), I mingled together Egyptians and Assyrians to make trade."[47] After having deported the population of the Raphia region, he probably decided to build a new independent trading emporium, following on from the trading post (*bît kâri*) built by Tiglath-pileser III. Building it, which started in 720, could have extended until 716, when the deportation of a population from the Zagros to it took place. This new trading emporium, partly populated by deportees from the Zagros region, was supervised by the Arab sheikh of Laban, a client king. Sargon's purpose was probably to control this militarily and commercially strategic region, in particular the vassal kingdom of Gaza, and Egypt. It has been suggested that the site of this trading emporium was Tell er-Ruqeish, on the Mediterranean coast, about 20 kilometers south of Gaza, excavated by Oren.[48]

---

44. *ARAB* 2.5, 118.

45. Tadmor, "Campaigns of Sargon II," 77–78; Tadmor, "Philistia under Assyrian Rule," 91–92; Nadav Na'aman, "The Brook of Egypt and Assyrian Policy on the Border of Egypt," *TA* 6 (1979): 71; Kenneth A. Kitchen, *The Third Intermediate Period in Egypt (1100–650 B.C.)*, 2nd ed. (Warminster: Aris & Phillips, 1986), 376; Sweeney, "Sargon's Threat against Jerusalem," 460.

46. Blakely and Hardin, "Southwestern Judah," 49–52.

47. Tadmor, "Campaigns of Sargon II," 77–78 (Prism fragment VA 8424 from Assur, and Prism fragment 79-7-8, 14 from Nineveh); Gadd, "Inscribed Prisms of Sargon II," IV, ll. 46–49.

48. E. D. Oren et al., "A Phoenician Emporium on the Border of Egypt" [Hebrew] *Qad* 75/76 (1986): 83–91; Oren, "Ruqeish," *NEAEHL* 4:1293–94; Alon Shavit, "Settlement Patterns of Philistine City-States," in *Bene Israel, Studies in the Archaeology of Israel and the Levant during the Bronze and Iron Ages in Honour of Israel Finkelstein,*

4. THE CONQUEST OF THE WEST

A few years later, Sargon had to face another rebellion in Philistia that he could not ignore due to the importance of Philistia, this time by Ashdod. The importance it had for the Assyrian king is reflected in the numerous mentions of this event in his inscriptions and representations of the campaign against Ashdod in the reliefs of Room V of his new palace.[49] As a matter of fact, there were two successive Ashdod rebellions. Azuri, king of Ashdod, refused to pay tribute to Sargon and plotted against him: "Azuri, king of Ashdod, plotted in his heart to withhold (his) tribute and sent (messages) of hostility to the kings round about me. Because of the evil he had done, I put an end to his rule over the people of his land and set up Ahî-Mîti, his full brother, as king over them."[50] Sargon thus followed the usual Assyrian practice, which consisted of support for a pro-Assyrian claimant to the throne of a vassal kingdom. The dating of this first Ashdod revolt is not quite clear. In the Annals, the two revolts are related together in the account of year 11, that is, 711. However, in the prism fragment S2022, a campaign is mentioned against Ashdod in year 9: "In my ninth campaign, against the city of Ashdod on the shore of the Great Sea I went ... the city of Ashdod" (*i-na* 9 *palê-ia a-na* [URU As-du-di ša a- ḫi*] [*ti*]-*amti rabīti a-*[*lik*...] [URU] *As-du-di*[...).[51] It is formulated in the same way as Sargon's campaign against Manneans and Medes in year 8.[52] Year 9 corresponds to 713 BCE. According to the Eponym Lists, in 713 Sargon sent his commander-in-chief against Ellipi and Musasir; Ashdod was not mentioned. In 712 he stayed in Assyria (*i-na māti*); in

---

ed. Alexander Fantalkin and Assaf Yasur-Landau, CHANE 31 (Leiden: Brill, 2008), 153. For other propositions of identifications, see Ronny Reich, "The Identification of the 'Sealed *kāru* of Egypt,'" *IEJ* 34 (1984): 33 n. 7 (with bibliography); André Lemaire, "Populations et territoires de la Palestine à l'époque perse," *Trans* 3 (1990): 46; Anson F. Rainey, "Herodotus' Description of the East Mediterranean Coast," *BASOR* 321 (2001): 60.

49. Franklin, "Room with a View," 270–71, figs 10.6 and 10.7. According to Alexander Fantalkin, "Ashdod-Yam on the Israeli Mediterranean Coast: A First Season of Excavations," *Skyllis* 14 (2014): 53, it was the representation of Ashdod-Yam and not of Ashdod or Gaza as has been proposed.

50. *ARAB* 2.30, 62, 193; Fuchs, *Inschriften Sargons II*, 132 and 326, ll. 241–245; 219 and 348, ll. 90–94.

51. *ARAB* 2.214; SAAS 8:44, ll. 13–16; see Tadmor, "Campaigns of Sargon II," 79–80.

52. *ARAB* 2.19; Fuchs, *Inschriften Sargons II*, 110, l. 127.

711 he conducted a campaign against Gurgum (Marqasa).⁵³ As it is not specified that Sargon stayed in Assyria in 713, we may suppose that, while he sent his *turtānu* ("commander-in-chief") against Ellipi and Musasir, he went to Ashdod in order to suppress Azuri's rebellion and to replace him with Ahî-Mîti. For an uncertain length of time, Ahî-Mîti ruled Ashdod and paid tribute and tax to Assyria; then the Ashdodites did not accept his rule any longer. They chose another king, Yamani, and started a new revolt. Sargon needed time to gather his troops to prepare a second campaign against Ashdod. In 712, he stayed in Assyria while these events occurred in Ashdod; the second campaign probably took place in 711: "The Hittites, plotters of iniquity, hated his rule and elevated (to reign) over them Yamani without claim to the throne, who like themselves did not know fear of my sovereignty. In the fury of my heart, I (did) not (stop) to gather the masses of my troops or to prepare the camp, but with my warriors, who do not leave the place of danger (?) at my side, I marched against Ashdod."⁵⁴ The second time, Sargon did not show the same clemency as after the first rebellion, he wanted to hit hard in order to punish this insubordinate city and to set an example for the neighboring Philistine cities. However, according to Isaiah, the leader of the Assyrian army was not Sargon himself but his commander-in-chief (Isa 20:1).⁵⁵ Why did Sargon himself probably conduct the first campaign against Ashdod in 713 and not the second more important one in 711? Tadmor assumed that the king's presence was required in that year for the building of his new capital of Khorsabad, but that is not convincing because in 711 he conducted a campaign against Gurgum.⁵⁶

Who was this Yamani, a man with no claim to the throne but who had a leading role among the insurgents? He attempted to form an anti-Assyrian coalition, approaching other Philistine cities, Judah, Moab, Edom, and the Delta ruler, Bakenrenef of Saïs. But his appeals went unanswered. Most of the inscriptions called him *Ia-ma-ni* and two texts *Ia-ad-na*.⁵⁷ Yamani

---

53. SAAS 2:47.
54. *ARAB* 2.30, 62, 193–95.
55. See Tadmor, "Campaigns of Sargon II," 77–80; Blakely and Hardin, "Southwestern Judah," 51; May, "Administrative and Other Reforms," 84.
56. Tadmor, "Campaigns of Sargon II," 79 n. 208.
57. Winckler, *Keilschrifttexte Sargons*, 82, l. 11; 114, ll. 95 and 101; 186, l. 18; 188, l. 40; Lie, *Inscriptions of Sargon II*, 41, l. 254 and n. 5 (*Ia-ad-na* and *I[a-x-n]a*, restored);

does not mean "Ionian" as has been proposed.[58] It was a personal name, similar to biblical names such as *Iamîn*, *Imnā* or *Imnaʿ*, and containing the root *ymn* designating the south in Semitic languages. *Ia-ad-na* was interpreted as a Ionian from (*Ia-*)*ad-na-na*, Cyprus.[59] *Ia-ad-na*, which is a hapax in Akkadian, is more probably a misreading or a miswriting on the part of Botta, as the signs *ad* and *ma* are very close.[60] Whether that is the case or not, Ionians had no connection with the revolt of Ashdod. When the Assyrian army marched on Ashdod in retaliation against Yamani, he wasted no time, left his family and palace, and fled to a territory outside Assyria's reach: "That Yamani heard of the progress (coming) of my march, from afar, and fled to the side (boundary) of Egypt which is on the border of Meluhha (Ethiopia), to be seen no more."[61] Some time later, the fugitive was caught and sent back to Sargon by the king of Meluhha: "in fetters, shackles and bonds of iron, he cast him and they brought him before me into Assyria, (after) a most difficult journey."[62] The siege and capture of Ashdod by the Assyrian commander-in-chief were violent, as is shown by the on-site discovery of three thousand skeletons buried in a mass grave, some of them displaying signs of decapitation, corresponding approximately to this date.[63] This episode is well-described in the Annals, wrongly attributed by Sargon to himself: "Ashdod, Gath, Asdudimmu, I besieged, I captured; his gods (of Yamani), his wife, his sons, his daughters, the property, goods (and) treasures of his palace, together with the people of his land, I counted as spoil."[64] As the excavations have shown,

---

SAAS 8:45, VII.b, l. 15; Hawkins, "New Sargon Stele," 154–55, l. 22 (*Ia-ma-ni*); I, 36, l. 220; II, pl. 9.

58. Simo Parpola, *Neo-Assyrian Toponyms* (Neukirchen-Vluyn: Neukirchener Verlag, 1970), s.v. "Jawan"; P. J. Riis, *Sūkās I: The North-East Sanctuary and the First Settling of Greeks in Syria and Palestine* (Copenhagen: Munksgaard, 1970), 133–34. See Tadmor, "Campaigns of Sargon II," 80 and n. 217; Josette Elayi and Antoine Cavigneaux, "Sargon II et les Ioniens," *OrAnt* 18 (1979): 59–63; Karen Radner, "Aššur-dūr-pānīya, Statthalter von Til-Barsip unter Sargon II. von Assyrien," *BaM* 37 (2006): 185–95.

59. Winckler, *Keilschrifttexte Sargons*, 82, 114, 186, 188.

60. Elayi and Cavigneaux, "Sargon II et les Ioniens," 61–63.

61. *ARAB* 2.30, 62, 193–95.

62. *ARAB* 2.63; Frame, "Inscription of Sargon II," 40, l. 19, 21.

63. M. Dothan, "Ashdod," *NEAEHL* 1:100 (with bibliography); Younger, "Recent Study on Sargon II," 315.

64. *ARAB* 2.30, 62.

after the destruction of Ashdod, the region's center of gravity was shifted to Ashdod-Yam (Asdudimmu), 5 km northwest.[65] Impressive fortifications were erected at Ashdod-Yam, probably in order to protect a man-made harbor, either before the rebellion or slightly afterward. Ashdod-Yam became one of the most important Assyrian international emporia at the empire's southwestern maritime frontier. Three fragments of a basalt stela that Sargon had erected at Ashdod in celebration of his victory were discovered in the acropolis of the city.[66] They are too damaged to be able to establish whether the conquest of Ashdod was mentioned on the stela. It may have been smashed in the aftermath of the great revolt of Ashdod against Assyria under the leadership of Hezekiah in 705 BCE.

Sargon ended Ashdod's autonomy, turning it into an Assyrian province and the new southwestern boundary of the empire: "These cities (Ashdod, Gath, Asdudimmu) I restored; people of the lands my hand had conquered, from [the mountains] of the East, I settled therein, [and set my official over them as governor]; with the people of Assyria I counted them, and they bore my yoke."[67] After having deported their inhabitants, he brought people from the East into these towns. The southern coast of Philistia up to the brook of Egypt, identified by some scholars with Nahal Besor, seems to have experienced an unprecedented demographic increase from the end of the eighth to the seventh century, whereas the area near Wadi el-Arish was sparsely inhabited at that time.[68] The most remarkable site was the fortified emporium of Tell er-Ruqeish (see above).

Gibbethon and Ekron are not mentioned in the preserved inscriptions of Sargon, but they are explicitly represented in the reliefs of Room V in the palace of Khorsabad. Gibbethon is referred to in the Bible as a Philistine border settlement (1 Kgs 16:15) and was identified with Tell Melat, but this identification is still inconclusive; Ekron is identified with Tel Miqne/ Khirbet Muqqanna.[69] It was probably in 720 that Sargon captured Gibbe-

---

65. Jacob Kaplan, "The Stronghold of Yamani at Ashdod-Yam," *IEJ* 19 (1969): 137–49; Israel Finkelstein and Lily Singer-Avitz, "Ashdod Revisited," *TA* 28 (2001): 231–59; Fantalkin, "Ashdod-Yam," 45–57.

66. Hayim Tadmor, "Fragments of an Assyrian Stele of Sargon," *Atiqot* English Series 9–10 (1971), 192–97; Kapera, "Ashdod Stele of Sargon II," 87–99.

67. *ARAB* 2.30, 62.

68. Na'aman and Zadok, "Sargon II's Deportations," 42–46; Na'aman, "Province System and Settlement Pattern," 111–13.

69. Franklin, "Room with a View," 259, 261, 269; Albenda, *Palace of Sargon*, Room V, pls. 95–96, 98.

thon and Ekron, after having seized Samaria and before capturing Hanunu of Gaza.[70] Ekron was transformed into a vassal state, which did not revolt until the accession of Sennacherib.

Sargon's reign had an immense impact on Palestine. This impact was quite obviously felt in the political and military history of the region: the kingdom of Israel was suppressed and its inhabitants scattered through deportations, most of the Philistine cities were reduced to subjugation, and the kingdom of Judah was subdued as an Assyrian vassal state. There was also a literary Assyrian impact preserved in biblical literature. It is not surprising that after Sargon's death, revolts occurred almost immediately in Palestine.

Syria

In the conquest of the West, Syria occupied the prime position because it was located on the first direct route to the Mediterranean Sea (fig. 3). Tiglath-pileser III had inaugurated the following policy: subduing the Aramean states of Syria in order to have access to the sea, to control the trade routes westward and northwestward, and to have access to the metal and wood resources from Amanus to Taurus. Sargon continued the same policy and started his military campaigns by suppressing the revolts in Syria in 720 (year 2), that is, as soon as he had secured his position in Assyria proper.

The first grave difficulty Sargon came up against was in 720, in the anti-Assyrian coalition led by Iaûbidî, king of the land of Hamath: "Iaûbidî of Hamath, a camp-follower, with no claim to the throne, an evil Hittite, was plotting in his heart to become king of Hamath, and had caused the cities of Arpad, Simirra, Damascus and Samaria to revolt against me, had unified them and prepared for battle."[71] All these cities had been defeated during the reigns of Tiglath-pileser III and Shalmaneser V and were now eager to regain their independence. Moreover, three of them, Arpad, Simirra, and Damascus, were not just vassal cities but had been turned into Assyrian provinces ruled by Assyrian governors.[72] The Assur

---

70. Younger, "Recent Study on Sargon II," 292–94; Nadav Na'aman, "Ekron under the Assyrian and Egyptian Empires," *BASOR* 332 (2003): 83 (Padi, a local ruler, was installed on the throne).

71. *ARAB* 2.55.

72. Ariel Barag, *Die Assyrer und das Westland: Studien zur historischen Geogra-*

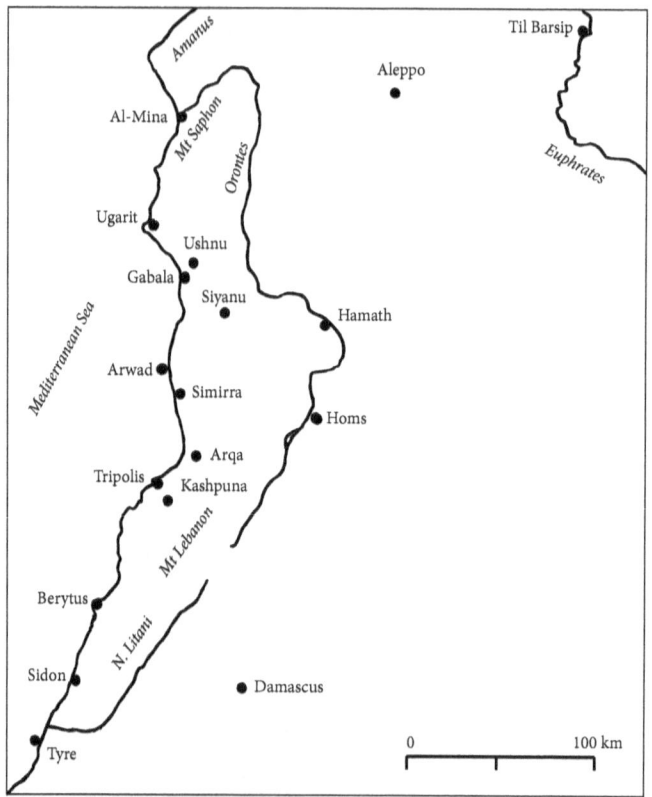

Fig. 3. Syria and Phoenicia

Charter provided complementary information: "Ilu-bidi the Hamathite, not the (rightful) throne-holder, unfitted for a palace, who in the shepherding of (his) people *did not consider their* destiny *but* for the god Assur, his land (and) his people sought evil, not good, and treated (them) with insolence ... he then killed, and did not leave a single person."[73] This damaged passage narrated two successive episodes: first the gathering of a broad coalition of allies, secondly Iaûbidî and his rebels apparently killing every Assyrian who happened to fall into their hands, possibly Assyrian administrators appointed by Tiglath-pileser III.

---

phie und Herrschaftspraxis in der Levante in 1.Jt.v.u.Z., OLA 216 (Leuven: Peeters, 2011), 233–36.
    73. Saggs, "Historical Texts and Fragments," 14, 15, ll. 17–21. See Frahm, "Sculpted Slab," 50.

4. THE CONQUEST OF THE WEST

Who was this Iaûbidî? In a few texts, he was named Ilu-bidi; it has been suggested that *Ilu-bi'di*, "El is behind me," was a throne name, which is doubtful.[74] *Iaū-bi'dî*, "Yahweh is behind me," was apparently a Yahwistic name, which raises various questions, all the more so because Samaria took part in his coalition. Among different hypotheses, some bands of Hebrews would have failed to enter Palestine and continued their migration northward, or Israelite adventurers would have seized power far from home, or the Assyrians would have thought of Yahweh as El.[75] The Yahwistic form of his name remains tantalizingly unclear, and how exactly Iaûbidî ascended the throne in the land of Hamath is unknown.

The description of Iaûbidî's rebellion was followed by Sargon's prayer invoking Sîn for giving him the victory: "[*I lifted my hands*] to Sîn, the king of the gods and lord of the lands [... who *vanquishes*] the foes and destroys the enemies, my lord, and implored him (to help me) [*conquer*] the land of Hamath, overthrow [... *and*...] the wide land of Amurru."[76] The battle between the Assyrian army and the coalition forces took place at the fortified city of Qarqar on the Orontes, probably corresponding to the modern city of Hamath: "I mustered the masses of Assur's troops and at Qarqar, his favorite city, I besieged and captured him, together with his warriors. Qarqar I burned with fire."[77] Sargon did not spare Iaûbidî; he flayed him, dying his skin red, "like wool." He destroyed and/or burned the city of Qarqar and devastated the whole land of Hamath: "The land of Hamath to its farthest border I destroyed like a flood. Iaûbidî, their king, together with his family, his warriors, as captives of his land, I carried away to Assyria, in bonds. 300 chariots, 600 cavalry troops, bearers of shield and lance, I selected from among them and added them to my royal host ... my

---

74. *ARAB* 2.5, 118, 134; Gadd, "Inscribed Prisms of Sargon II," 200, l. 22; Fuchs, *Inschriften Sargons II*, 35, Zyl. 25; 89, Ann. 23; *PNA* 2.1:526.

75. *PNA* 2.1:497. See Stephanie Dalley, "Yahweh in Hamath in the 8th Century BC: Cuneiform Material and Historical Deductions," *VT* 40 (1990): 21–32; Edward Lipiński, *The Aramaeans: Their Ancient History, Culture, Religion*, OLA 100 (Leuven: Peeters, 2000), 316; Frahm, "Sculpted Slab," 49–51.

76. Frahm, "Sculpted Slab," 46, 47, ll. 16–19.

77. *ARAB* 2.55. On the identification of Qarqar, see Josette Elayi and Alain G. Elayi, *Recherches sur les poids phéniciens*, TransSup 5 (Paris: Gabalda, 1997), 27–31; Elayi and Elayi, *Arwad, cité phénicienne du nord*, TransSup 19 (Pendé: Gabalda, 2015), 87–88.

official as governor I set over them."⁷⁸ If he flayed Iaûbidî, of course he carried him dead. He could not immediately take with him all the prisoners and booty because he first went southward to seize Samaria and Gaza. He may have brought them to Assyria with his army on his way back from the south. Sargon had several commemorative monuments set up in places that were symbolic of his conquests and where they could be seen by many people. On the Tell Acharneh stela, badly damaged, Sargon describes the campaign against Iaûbidî and mentions five places where he set up stelae, one of them in the land of Hamath, possibly at Tell Acharneh on the Orontes.⁷⁹ Another stela also seems to have been set up in the land of Hamath, maybe at Sheizar on the Orontes.⁸⁰ This partly broken stela, on side B, bears a historical report of the conquest of the land of Hamath in 720, while side A relates events up to the latter years of Sargon's reign (708–705 BCE). Therefore, this stela was not erected in celebration of the 720 victory but during a much later campaign. There is no mention of this possible campaign in the inscriptions, but the stela could have been set up on Sargon's way to another military expedition. Four fragments, currently in the Oriental Institute of the University of Chicago, have recently been related to a fragment of a basalt stela found at Tell Tayinat (ancient Kullania).⁸¹ This stela was one of the stelae erected by Sargon in the important centers of the kingdom of Hamath, and it reported, among other historical events, the destruction of Hamath.

After having deported many people of Hamath to Assyria, Sargon deported other people to the land of Hamath: people from the land of Karalla and Ittî, ruler of Allabria, in year 6 (716), and Daiukku, a Mannean governor and his family, in year 7 (715). In year 2 (720), he also had six thousand three hundred guilty Assyrians settled in Hamath: "their transgression I disregarded, I had mercy on them."⁸² He gave no details

---

78. *ARAB* 2.183; Fuchs, *Inschriften Sargons II*, 278, VIII, 25 (epigraph of this battle represented in the reliefs of the palace of Khorsabad).

79. Frame, "Tell Acharneh Stela," 52, Col. iii, l. 6'.

80. W. G. Lambert, in *Ladders to Heaven: Art Treasures from Lands of the Bible*, ed. Oscar W. Muscarella (Toronto: McClelland and Steward, 1981), 125 and no. 83; Hawkins, "New Sargon Stele," 151–64.

81. Jacob Lauinger and Stephen Batiuk, "A Stele of Sargon II at Tell Tayinat," *ZA* 105 (2015): 54–68.

82. *ARAB* 2.56; Fuchs, *Inschriften Sargons II*, 37, ll. 32–33; 98–100, ll 84–90; 208, l. 56; Hawkins, "New Sargon Stele," 169, ll. 5–8; Frame, "New Cylinder Inscription," 72; 74, l. 23; 78; K. Radner, "The Assyrian King and His Scholars: The Syro-Anatolian

4. THE CONQUEST OF THE WEST

of the fault they had committed, but no doubt he referred to the turbulent period of 722–721 when he had to fight against Assyrian opponents in the heartland of the empire in order to save his throne; probably they had not supported his claim to the throne. Sargon was conscious and proud of having crushed the anti-Assyrian coalition of Iaûbidî just as his ancestor Shalmaneser III had vanquished, at the same place of Qarqar, the coalition led by Irhulena, king of the land of Hamath, in 853: "Taxation, tribute, the bearing of the basket, the going on campaign like that which the kings my fathers on Irhulena the Hamathite had imposed I imposed on them (the inhabitants of the land of Hamath)."[83]

Damascus and Arpad were the other two Aramean states that in 720 participated in the anti-Assyrian coalition led by Iaûbidî. Damascus was a powerful Aramean state that was captured by Tiglath-pileser III in 732 BCE, after a siege of the capital city of Rezin that lasted forty-five days. Damascus was established as an Assyrian provincial capital, closing the list of its independent rulers. Iaûbidî the Hamathite had caused Damascus to revolt against Sargon, in spite of the presence of provincial Assyrian administration, and he had coordinated the Damascus revolt with the coalition.[84] After the defeat of Qarqar, Damascus became an Assyrian province as previously. Sargon deported Manneans to Damascus: "the people of the cities of Sukkia, Bâla, Abitikna, Pappa, Lalluknu, I tore away from their places and settled them in Damascus and the Hittite-land."[85] In the Annals, this deportation is dated from year 5 (717) but more likely followed on from Sargon's campaign against the Manneans in year 6 (716). Arpad, modern Tell Rifaat, is located northeast of Aleppo, between Hamath and Carchemish. This kingdom, founded by Gûsh around 890, better known as Bît-Agusi, was conquered by Tiglath-pileser III in 740 and turned into an Assyrian province.[86] After the defeat of Qarqar, Arpad became an Assyrian province again.

---

and the Egyptian Schools," in Luukko, *Of God(s), Trees, Kings, and Scholars*, 236; *PNA* 1.2:370, 2.1:587–88.

83. Hawkins, "New Sargon Stele," 160, ll. 9–12; *PNA* 2.1:564.

84. *ARAB* 2.5, 9, 55–56, 197. On Damascus, see, e.g., Lipiński, *Aramaeans*, 347–407 (with bibliography).

85. *ARAB* 2.9, 55–56; Fuchs, *Inschriften Sargons II*, Ann. 76; Prunk. 57; Zyl. 28.

86. *ARAB* 2.5, 55, 134; Fuchs, *Inschriften Sargons II*, Ann. 25; Prunk. 33. On Arpad, see, e.g., Lipiński, *Aramaeans*, 195–219.

Carchemish (modern Jerablous) on the Euphrates did not participate in Iaûbidî's coalition. However, its king, Pisîri, who reigned around 738–717, revolted against Sargon. The Assyrian king blamed the "wicked Hittites" such as him and the king of Hamath, "who did not fear the name of the gods, who plotted mischief."[87] Pisîri's revolt occurred in year 5 (717): "I lifted my hand to Assur, my lord, and brought him and his family out (of the city) in chains. Gold, silver, together with the property of his palace and the rebellious people of Carchemish, who were with him, with their goods, I carried off and brought (them) into Assyria. 50 chariots, 200 cavalry-men, 300 foot soldiers, I selected from among them to my royal host."[88] Carchemish was annexed to Assyria. The people of Carchemish deported to Assyria were replaced, as usual, by people of Assyria, without precision, who settled in this new Assyrian province. Sargon erected a stela in Carchemish; a small fragment of it has been discovered.[89] A fragment of brick inscribed "Palace of Sargon, king of the universe, king of Assyria," was unearthed at Tell Amarna, a small site 8 kilometers south of Carchemish, similar to another brick found in Carchemish.[90] As an Assyrian palace was more probably built in Carchemish than in the small Tell Amarna, the brick was probably brought from Carchemish in order to be reused in later buildings. Another fragment of a Sargon inscription was found at Til Barsip, modern Tell Ahmar, south of Carchemish on the upper Euphrates. Yet, this fragment was possibly part of a bull colossus, not of a stela, and it must date from after the conquest of Babylonia in 710 BCE. It is impossible to know during which campaign this inscription was engraved at Til Barsip; in any case not when Sargon passed by Mount Saphon (ṣapuna),

---

87. *ARAB* 2.92, 99; Hasan Peker, *Texts from Karkemish. I: Luwian Hieroglyphic Inscriptions from the 2011–2015 Excavations*, OrientLab.Series Maior 1 (Bologna: Ante Quem, 2016), 36–40, 49.

88. *ARAB* 2.8, 118; Gadd, "Inscribed Prisms of Sargon II," 180, col. iv, l. 13; Fuchs, *Inschriften Sargons II*, Ann. 72, 74, 76; Zyl. 26; XIV.9; 54.22; Stier 17; Frame, "Inscription of Sargon II," 36, 40, l. 18; Frame, "New Cylinder Inscription," 82; Hawkins, "New Sargon Stele," 154–55, ll. 25–26. On Carchemish, see, e.g., Nadav Na'aman, "The Historical Portion of Sargon II's Nimrud Inscription," *SAAB* 8 (1994): 17–20; Lipiński, *Aramaeans*, 175–77; *PNA* 3.1:997.

89. Frame, "Tell Acharneh Stela," 53 (with bibliography).

90. C. Leonard Woolley and Richard D. Barnett, *Carchemish 3: Report on the Excavations at Jerablus on Behalf of the British Museum; The Excavations in the Inner Town* (London: British Museum, 1952), 265; Onhan Tunca, "Un fragment de brique inscrite néo-assyrienne provenant de Tell Amarna (Syrie)," *BaM* 37 (2006): 179–84.

modern Djebel el-Aqra, located 40 kilometers north of Ugarit because that was in 712 (year 10).[91]

In short, most of the Aramean states revolted in a coalition against Sargon at the beginning of his reign. In 720, he had to severely suppress all the rebellions and to resubjugate these states just as they had already been during Tiglath-pileser III's reign. It was vital for his empire that Syria remained completely pacified. Later, in 717, he had the kingdom of Carchemish turned into an Assyrian province.

Phoenicia

Phoenicia was not impacted much by Sargon's conquest of the West, except for Simirra. From 738 BCE, the northern cities of Phoenicia, such as Gabala (Jeble), Ushnu (Tell Daruk), Siyanu, Simirra, Arqa, and Kashpuna, had been subjugated by Tiglath-pileser III. After a violent repression, he turned the Phoenician city of Simirra into the capital of an Assyrian province.[92] He relied on the strategic importance of this province for controlling the Phoenician cities, primarily Arwad, which had revolted against him, and for supervising Mediterranean trade. Apparently, Simirra did not easily accept its Assyrian province status because in 720 it participated in the anti-Assyrian coalition of Iaûbidî. After the defeat of Qarqar, Simirra again became an Assyrian province as previously. It does not seem to have recovered its autonomy after Sargon's reign, as is shown by the mention of its Assyrian governor Iddin-ahhe, eponym in year 688.[93]

Phoenician cities are not mentioned in Sargon's inscriptions, except for Tyre, as we shall see later. Apparently, they did not revolt and were loyal vassals. In fact, they were probably included in the tributary "kings of the seashore" (*šarrāni ša a-ḫi tam-tim*) who sent tribute to Sargon in year 7 (715), together with the kings of the desert.[94] It is possible to get

---

91. Walter Farber and K. Kessler, "Eine Inschrift Sargons II. aus Til Barsib," *RA* 67 (1973): 163–64; Frame, "Tell Acharneh Stela," 53; *ARAB* 2.28; Radner, "Aššur-dūr-pānīya," 185–95.

92. Josette Elayi, "The Phoenician Cities and the Assyrian Empire in the Time of Sargon II," *Sumer* 42 (1986): 129–32; Elayi, *Histoire de la Phénicie*, 168–74; Elayi and Elayi, *Arwad*, 94–97; Massimo Botto, *Studi Storici sulla Fenicia. L'VIII e il VII secolo a.C.*, Quaderni di orientalistica pisana 1 (Pisa: Università degli studi di Pisa, 1990), 19–62.

93. *ARAB* 2.5, 55; *SAAS* 2:61.

94. Lie, *Inscriptions of Sargon II*, 22–23, l. 124; Fuchs, *Inschriften Sargons II*, 110, l. 124.

an idea of the Tyrian tribute to Shalmaneser III from a representation on the Balawat bronze door bands: the king and queen of Tyre are standing on the shore of their island city, looking at the boats carrying their tribute and gifts.[95] Sargon's scribes did not usually differentiate between Phoenician kings and the other kings of the Mediterranean seashore. There were in fact three groups in the west from an Assyrian perspective: the rulers of the hinterland, those of the seashore, and those of the midst of the sea, a new category that appeared during Sargon's reign. It corresponds to the progressive extension of the Neo-Assyrian Empire westward.[96] The Phoenician cities were also regarded as "Hatti," a general term that at that time designated the populations of the Near East.

As long as the Phoenician cities accepted his rule, Sargon had no reason to trouble the trade of Phoenician products and handicraft. He also needed Phoenician wood, in particular for the building of his new capital Khorsabad. He accorded great importance to the acquisition of timber, as shown by its representation in the reliefs of his new palace, shown in the forefront because he considered it as one of his greatest successes.[97] He called upon Phoenician and Cypriots as specialists in exploiting and carrying wood. He had the transport of tree trunks represented, first by land from the Phoenician forests of Mount Lebanon or the Cyprian mountains, then their transport by sea to Assyria. Maritime transport passed first through a fortified city on a rocky island, probably Tyre. Then the wood was conveyed to a second fortified city on a flat island. This city can be identified as Arwad due to the symbol of the fish-tailed bearded deity, Baal Arwad, next to it.[98] Arwad was used as a transit city for wood transport. Then the wood reached a third city at the mouth of the Orontes, which

---

95. L. W. King, *Bronze Reliefs from the Gate of Shalmaneser King of Assyria B.C. 860–825* (London: British Museum, 1915), pl. XIII; Elayi, *Histoire de la Phénicie*, 147–48.

96. Josette Elayi, "Terminologie de la Mer Méditerranée dans les *Annales* assyriennes," *OrAnt* 23 (1984): 75–92.

97. Pauline Albenda, *A Mediterranean Seascape from Khorsabad*, Assur 3.3 (Malibu, CA: Undena, 1983): 1–34; Albenda, *Palace of Sargon*, pls. 21–23; Elisha Linder, "The Khorsabad Wall Relief: A Mediterranean Seascape or River Transport of Timbers?," *JAOS* 106 (1986): 273–81.

98. Josette Elayi and Alain G. Elayi, "Ba'al Arwad," in *ACFP 5*, ed. Antonella Spanò Giammellaro (Palermo: Università di Palermo, 2005), 129–33; Elayi and Elayi, *Arwad*, 101–2.

could have been Al-Mina. It was then conveyed on the lower Orontes, finally on the Euphrates, to its destination in Assyria.

Was Tyre mentioned in a badly damaged passage of the Annals, dated from year 7 (715), as has been proposed?[99] Sargon would have provided troops to Tyre in order to fend off Ionian pirates who were threatening its maritime network. This interpretation is groundless because there is no reason to restore ^{URU}ṣur-r]i in this text. It concerned a military expedition of Sargon or of his commander-in-chief conducted against an enemy in relation with Ionians and Que, as we shall see later.[100]

The seizure of Tyre was briefly mentioned in a text duplicated on four cylinders found in Khorsabad and dated from 706.[101] The Annals could not report this event because they did not deal with the latter years of Sargon's reign. Lulî, king of Tyre, identified with Elulaios of Josephus, seems to have reigned thirty-three years, from about 728 to 695.[102] He probably succeeded Mattan II who had paid a heavy tribute to Tiglath-Pileser III in 729. In spite of his title of "king of the Sidonians" (šar URU ṣi-du-un-ni) in Akkadian inscriptions, the enumeration of his towns in the Annals of Sennacherib clearly showed that he was king of Tyre and Sidon.[103] It is difficult to say when the double kingdom of Tyre and Sidon began and whether it continued to exist without interruption under this form until Sargon's reign.[104] Ittobaal I, who had reigned from about 888 to 856, was already named "king of Tyrians and Sidonians." He had established a kind of bicephalous kingdom, similar to that of David, king of Israel and Judah, and after him that of Solomon.[105] Qurdi-ashur-lâmur, an Assyrian official settled at Ushu, controlled the Assyrian tax-collectors of both Tyrians and Sidonians exploiting the forests of Mount Lebanon, which would mean that there was one kingdom at that time. The dating of his letters is

---

99. Fuchs, *Inschriften Sargons II*, Ann. 118; Karen Radner, "Tyre and the Other Phoenician City-States," in *Assyrian Empire Builders*, http://tinyurl.com/SBL1722e.

100. Elayi and Cavigneaux, "Sargon II et les Ioniens," 72–74.

101. Winckler, *Keilschrifttexte Sargons*, pl. 43; *ARAB* 2.118.

102. Elayi, *Histoire de la Phénicie*, 172–73.

103. Daniel David Luckenbill, *The Annals of Sennacherib*, OIP 2 (Chicago: Univeristy of Chicago Press, 1924), 29, ll. 41–43.

104. Josette Elayi, "Les relations entre les cités phéniciennes et l'Empire assyrien sous le règne de Sennacherib," *Sem* 35 (1985): 20–21 (with bibliography); Elayi, *Histoire de la Phénicie*, 143–45, 174.

105. Elayi, *Histoire de la Phénicie*, 143–44.

debated, but the end of Tiglath-pileser III's reign is more likely than the first half of Sargon's reign.[106]

When Sargon established control through his officer over Kition, Tyre's colony, whom Kition had revolted against, Lulî could not accept it and he probably acted immediately, possibly around 709 BCE, in order to reconquer Kition. Consequently, we may suppose that the corrupt text of Josephus dealt with Lulî's action: "Upon the revolt of the Kitieis, he put out to the sea and restored them by his side" (Josephus, *A.J.* 9.283–287). Josephus quoted Alexander Polyhistor, who in turn quoted the third century Greek author, Menander of Pergamon, who could indirectly go back to the Tyrian annals of the eighth century. Errors have crept into the story through these successive transmissions, which have led scholars to attribute the siege of Tyre told by Josephus to various kings of Assyria. This unsuccessful five-year siege cannot be ascribed to Shalmaneser V's rule because he reigned for only five years and he probably fought in Palestine for three years. Nor can it be ascribed to the beginning of Sargon's reign because it would have been mentioned in the first part of the Annals; besides, this energetic king would not have accepted beginning his reign by remaining on this failed siege. Because of Lulî's action in Cyprus, the Assyrian army, probably led by an officer of Sargon, as the king was in Babylon, invaded Phoenicia. He subjugated all the Phoenician cities and signed a peace treaty with them. Several cities, including Sidon, Ushu, and perhaps Akko, revolted against Tyre and made allegiance to Assyria. The Tyrians refused to do so, and the Assyrian officer returned to attack Tyre with sixty ships equipped with eight hundred rowers provided by the other Phoenicians. The Tyrians confronted them with only twelve ships, dispersed them, and captured five hundred prisoners. Tyre won the battle, but the Assyrian officer, before leaving, placed guards on the river and aqueducts to prevent the Tyrians from going to fetch drinking water. The siege, or rather the blockade of Tyre, lasted five years, during which time the Tyrians resisted. Indeed, this five-year siege was not a true blockade either because Tyrians had wells and cisterns and could probably go and fetch water with their boats, which visibly had not been blocked. The name of the king of Assyria involved in this expedition is written in several ways: Selampsas, Salmanasses, Elampsas. Although

---

106. H. W. F. Saggs, "The Nimrud Letters 1952: Part II," *Iraq* 17 (1955): 127–28, letter XII, ll. 11, 15, 21 (ND2715); *PNA* 3.1:1021–22.

this corrupt name approximates somewhat to Shalmaneser, it means nothing because the Akkadian name was first translated into Phoenician, then into Greek by several successive authors. Moreover, was it the name of the king or the name of the officer, which is unknown, who conducted this operation?

The fact that the seizure of Tyre was mentioned so briefly in Sargon's inscriptions, contrary to his habit, can be explained by the fact that he preferred not to mention his failure. The Assyrian forces probably hit the Tyrians, but he certainly did not vanquish them. Either Sargon expressed a desired, but not obtained, victory (there are other examples of this), or he anticipated the issue of the siege in progress. The failure of the Assyrian campaign against Tyre would explain the punitive expedition of Sennacherib against Lulî in 701 BCE, related in his inscriptions. After two campaigns intended to solve urgent problems, the first campaign of Sennacherib westward was directed against Lulî. He wanted to solve a problem left by his father Sargon, and he could not accept the existence of a rebellious Phoenician king at the beginning of his reign.

The first victim of Sargon's Cyprus campaign was Tyre because it needed its colony of Kition, which was the hub of its maritime business and its indispensable stopover en route to its colonies in the western Mediterranean. King Lulî had no choice but to recapture Kition, but Sargon could not accept that. The other cities integrated in the double kingdom of Tyre and Sidon took advantage of Lulî's difficulties by revolting against him, starting with Sidon, which wanted to regain its autonomy. If they made allegiance to the king of Assyria, it was also because they did not want to endure the same difficulties as the rebel city of Tyre.

After his expedition to Cyprus, Sargon had a fleet again. If the numbers given by Josephus are accurate, the ships provided by the other Phoenicians probably had to be supplemented by Cypriot or Cilician ships to reach the total of sixty, while Tyre had only twelve ships. The naval victory of Tyre is surprising given its numerical inferiority. If we ignore the reality of numbers, what is clear is only that Sargon was unable to overcome the fleet of Lulî or seize the island city of Tyre. He then organized its blockade to cut the water supply as had already been done before him, for example, in the fourteenth century, by Zimredda the king of Sidon. If the blockade of Tyre did actually last five years, as written by Josephus, it could have occurred between 709 and 705.

The Tyrians managed to survive by digging wells to reach groundwater and using cisterns. However, all the accumulated difficulties probably began to erode the power and prosperity of Tyre. For the duration of the blockade, the double kingdom of Tyre and Sidon no longer existed in its entirety. Luckily for Lulî, the sudden death of Sargon released the blockade and enabled him to recover at least some of his dissident cities such as Sidon. The Assyrian administration, however, had not disappeared from Ushu, and the timber trade continued to be controlled and taxed.

Cyprus

The Greek name of the island of Cyprus came from its rich copper deposits. In the Late Bronze Age, Cyprus had been part of the international trade and diplomatic network under the name Alashiya. In Sargon's inscriptions, Cyprus was named Iadnana or Adnana, and the land of Ia was mentioned as a "district" (*nagiu*) of the land of Iadnana. The interpretation of Iadnana as "island of Adnana" (*ia' Adnana*) is not relevant since some inscriptions clearly mentioned that Ia was a district of Iadnana. The name Iadnana could link the island to the Sea Peoples of the *dnn* from Egyptian sources of 1200 BCE, to the *dnnym*, inhabitants of the Cilician coast according to the local inscriptions from the eighth century, and to the *Danaoi* of Homer.[107] Although Cyprus presents an apparent unity because it is an island, its regions were characterized by a geographic and ethnic diversity. In the first millennium BCE, it was divided into twelve natural areas and around ten autonomous political units, small city-states ruled by local kings.[108] The Cypriot city of Kition, modern Larnaka, seems to be the oldest permanent Phoenician colonial settlement; the site was occupied

---

107. Claude Baurain, *Chypre et la Méditerranée orientale au Bronze Récent: Synthèse historique* (Paris: de Boccard, 1984); Vassos Karageorghis, *Cyprus from the Stone Age to the Romans* (London: Thames & Hudson, 1982); Robert S. Merrillees, *Alashia Revisited*, CahRB 22 (Paris: Gabalda, 1988); A. T. Reyes, "Notes on Iron Age Kingdoms of Cyprus," *BASOR* 308 (1997): 65–68; Karen Radner, "The Stele of Sargon II of Assyria at Kition: A Focus for an Emerging Cypriot Identity?," in *Interkulturalität in der Alten Welt: Vorderasien, Hellas, Ägypten und die vielfältigen Ebenen des Kontakts*, ed. R. Rollinger et al., Philippika 34 (Wiesbaden: Harrassowitz, 2010), 429–49; Radner, "The Many Kingdoms of Cyprus," in *Assyrian Empire Builders*, http://tinyurl.com/SBL1722f.

108. Anne-Marie Collombier, "Organisation du territoire et pouvoirs locaux dans l'île de Chypre à l'époque perse," *Trans* 4 (1991): 21–43; Maria Iacovou, "Historically Elusive and Internally Fragile Island Polities: The Intricacies of Cyprus's Political Geography in the Iron Age," *BASOR* 370 (2013): 15–47.

4. THE CONQUEST OF THE WEST

from the thirteenth century. According to Josephus (*Antiquitates judaicae* 9.283–287), Hiram I king of Tyre conducted an expedition against a city, probably Kition, that refused to pay tribute and again brought it under his domination. Thus the Tyrian colony of Kition could have been founded by Abibaal, Hiram I's father, who reigned before 970. It was meant to ensure Tyre's control over the copper exports.

The island of Cyprus was not under the domination of Sargon's predecessors and was never mentioned in Assyrian inscriptions previous to Sargon's reign: "the name of whose land, since the far-off days of the moon-god's time, not one of the kings, my fathers who (ruled) Assyria and Babylonia, had heard."[109] Most of Sargon's inscriptions related to Iadnana are either damaged, repetitive, or propagandistic.[110] The first problem was to identify Iadnana with Cyprus. A prism from Nimrud mentioned the stela of Sargon that was erected at Iadnana: "I caused to be inscribed upon a stone monument, and left it (to stand) unto the future in the land of Ia, a district of the land Iadnana."[111] Because this stela of Sargon was discovered in Cyprus, the identification of Iadnana with Cyprus is established.

The hypothesis according to which the Assyrian intervention to help Tyre against pirates in 715 contributed to restore Tyre's control over the Cypriot kingdoms is groundless because it is based, as we have seen, on an erroneous reading and interpretation of a damaged passage of the Annals. The Cyprus events started in 709 (year 13) according to the chronology of the Annals, and ended before 707. We have to place in this short period the events mentioned in the Assyrian inscriptions and by Josephus: the subjugation of Kition (and of other Cypriot cities?) by Sargon, the revolt of the Tyrian colony of Kition against Tyre, the reconquest of Kition by Lulî king of Tyre, the allegiance of seven kings of Ia and the erection of the Sargon stela in Cyprus.

All these events are much debated, in particular the following one: Did Sargon send a military expedition to Cyprus? In other words, did he really conquer Cyprus? The first question is to know how he was able to reach

---

109. *ARAB* 2.70, 186.

110. J. Renger, "Neuassyrische Königsinschriften als Genre der Keilschriftliteratur: Zum Stil und zur Kompositionstechnik der Inschriften Sargons II. von Assyrien," in *Keilschriftliche Literaturen: Ausgewählte Vorträge der XXXII; Rencontre assyriologique internationale, Münster, 8.-12.7.1985*, ed. Karl Hecker and Walter Sommerfeld, BBVO 6 (Berlin: Reimer, 1986), 109–28.

111. Gadd, "Inscribed Prisms of Sargon II," 192–93, ll. 42–44.

the island despite the lack of a fleet and maritime knowledge.[112] He could use any fleet belonging to his vassals in coastal locations, Phoenicians or Cilicians. Three other objections were opposed to the conquest: the seven kings of Ia made allegiance to Sargon spontaneously, not by force. If there was a military campaign in the island, it would have been recorded on Sargon's stela found in Cyprus.[113] Other than this stela, there is no evidence of any Assyrian presence in Cyprus and no clear statement in Sargon's inscriptions that the Assyrians conquered the island. The answer to these objections is that, even if the seven kings are mentioned as spontaneously making allegiance, there is evidence in other inscriptions of a military intervention by one of Sargon's officers, and Sargon claimed explicitly: "I subdued 7 kings of the land of Ia."[114] The back of Sargon's stela is no longer preserved, but it may have been inscribed and possibly contained an extensive account of some military action, such as an expedition to Cyprus. Moreover, the conquest of Cyprus by Sargon seems to be attested by some elements in the inscriptions of the subsequent kings. Prisoners from Cyprus were employed as sailors by Sennacherib; as Sennacherib did not mention any campaign to the island, these prisoners were probably those captured by Sargon a few years earlier.[115] It is also clear that Assyria maintained its hegemony over Cyprus after Sargon's conquest, based on the list of Cypriot vassals enumerated by Esarhaddon and Ashurbanipal who participated in the Assyrian building projects.[116]

There was a military expedition in 709 (year 13), sent to Cyprus by Sargon, conducted by one of his officers: "my officer, who is fearless in

---

112. Nadav Na'aman, "The Conquest of Yadnana according to the Inscriptions of Sargon II," in *Historiography in the Cuneiform World*, ed. Tvi Abush et al., RAI 45 (Bethesda: CDL, 2001), 360–61.

113. Florence Malbran-Labat, "Inscription assyrienne," in Marguerite Yon, *Kition dans les textes: Testimonia littéraires et épigraphiques et corpus des inscriptions*, Kition Bamboula 5 (Paris: Editions Recherche sur les civilisations, 2004), 352; Frame, "Tell Acharneh Stela," 54–55; Radner, "Stele of Sargon," 435–36; Anna Cannavo, "Histoire de Chypre à l'époque archaïque: analyse des sources textuelles" (PhD diss., Université Lumière Lyon, 2011), 332; Barbara N. Porter, "Audiences for the Cyprus Stela of Sargon II," in *Leggo! Studies Presented to Frederick Mario Fales on the Occasion of His 65th Birthday*, ed. Giovanni B. Lanfranchi et al., LAOS 2 (Wiesbaden: Harrassowitz, 2012), 670.

114. *ARAB* 2.54, 80, 92, 99.

115. Luckenbill, *Annals of Sennacherib*, 73, ll. 59–60.

116. *ARAB* 2.690, 876.

battle, with my royal guard, I dispatched to have vengeance on (?) him (or avenge him?)."[117] The following hypothesis was proposed for this badly damaged passage: the seven kings of Ia had been paying tribute for a long time to some local city or ruler to whom they were subject. They rebelled against this local authority and possibly asked Sargon for military aid.[118] Although this hypothesis is plausible, there is no information regarding such a hierarchy of powers in Cyprus at that time. The other hypothesis proposed, according to which Shilta, king of Tyre, was the authority controlling the seven kings of Ia, is groundless.[119] The name "Tyre" is restored; "Shilta" is partly restored and was possibly a Cypriot king, but certainly not the king of Tyre, who at that time was Lulî, in fact the king of the double kingdom of Tyre and Sidon.[120]

When did the revolt of the Tyrian colony of Kition, mentioned by Josephus (*A.J.* 9.283–287), occur? Possibly after the military expedition of Sargon's officer and its submission to the Assyrian tribute. Maybe the Kitians found that having to pay twice, both to the Assyrian king and to the Tyrian king, was too heavy a burden. There was probably a logical sequence of events, starting from 709: submission of Kition to the Assyrian tribute, revolt of Kition against Tyre, then reconquest of Kition by king Lulî. Afterward, Kition was probably submitted to a double tribute again. The strong link between Kition and Lulî is illustrated by the fact that he fled to Cyprus after the campaign of Sennacherib against Tyre in 701.[121]

Another difficulty is in dating the two other events: allegiance of the seven kings of Ia and erection of the stela in Cyprus. According to the inscriptions, these seven kings "had heard from afar, in the midst of the sea, of the deeds which I was performing in Chaldea and the Hittite-land, their hearts were rent, fear fell upon them, gold, silver, furniture of ebony and boxwood, of the workmanship of their land they brought before me in Babylon, and they kissed my feet."[122] However, in the damaged passage of

---

117. *ARAB* 2.44.

118. Elayi and Cavigneaux, "Sargon II et les Ioniens," 65–66; Fuchs, *Inschriften Sargons II*, 337 n. 387.

119. Nadav Na'aman, "Sargon II and the Rebellion of the Cypriote Kings against Shilṭa of Tyre," *Or* 67 (1998): 239–47; Na'aman, "Eloulaios/Ululaiu in Josephus, *Jewish Antiquities* IX, 284," *NABU* 1 (2006): 5–6, no. 1.

120. Fuchs, *Inschriften Sargons II*, 337 n. 387, and 414; Frame, "Tell Acharneh Stela," 54–55 n. 11; *PNA* 3.1:1112.

121. Elayi, "Relations entre les cités phéniciennes," 21–23.

122. *ARAB* 2.70, 186.

the Annals quoted above, the allegiance of the seven kings is mentioned as coming after the military expedition: "…] they heard (or saw) the might of Assur's troops and, at the mention of my name, they became afraid and their arms collapsed. They brought to Babylon, into my presence, gold, silver, utensils of ebony and boxwood, the manufacture of their land, and [as Assyrians?] I counted them."[123] It is difficult to know, from these two somewhat diverging versions, whether they surrendered when they saw the Assyrian army sent by Sargon to Cyprus or when they heard of the Assyrian conquests, in particular in Cilicia against the Ionians, their compatriots. Either way, the allegiance of the seven kings occurred when Sargon was in Babylon, that is, in 710, 709, 708, or 707 (years 12 to 15), according to the Babylonian Chronicle and the Eponym Lists. The exact date is uncertain, however 708 has been proposed by some authors.[124] The number of kings (seven) has been questioned, compared with the ten kings of Cyprus enumerated in the lists of vassals in Esarhaddon's and Ashurbanipal's inscriptions. Was there an attraction between the number of kings and that of days? The number of days, seven days to reach Cyprus from the Levantine coast, is wrong because it is far too excessive; therefore, it was probably attracted by the number of kings. This number did not necessarily change from seven to ten between the reigns of Sargon and Esarhaddon. The seven kings mentioned in Sargon's inscriptions only concerned the district of Ia, not the whole island.[125]

The Sargon stela (Berlin Museum, VA 968) was discovered in 1844 at the site of Bamboula, to the west of the old harbor of Kition. Sargon, identified by the inscription, is dressed in a long fringed robe with the royal headdress, holding a mace in his left hand and raising his right hand in prayer. Eight symbols representing Assyrian and Babylonian gods are engraved in front of the king's head: Assur, Sîn, Ishtar, Adad, Marduk, Nabû, Sebet, and Shamash. It was fashioned out of black basalt stone, available in the Troodos massif, by an Assyrian craftsman. The primary position of the stela was "on the top (or in front) of Baal-harri, a mountain

---

123. *ARAB* 2.44; Fuchs, *Inschriften Sargons II*, 397.

124. Fuchs, *Inschriften Sargons II*, 382; Hawkins, "New Sargon Stele," 163–64.

125. Elayi and Cavigneaux, "Sargon II et les Ioniens," 65. For another view, see Einar Gjerstad, *The Swedish Cyprus Expedition: Vol. IV, Part 2, The Cypro-geometric, Cypro-archaic and Cypro-classical periods* (Stockholm: Swedish Cyprus Expedition, 1948), 449.

4. THE CONQUEST OF THE WEST

[...] of the country of Iadnana," possibly Mount Stavrovouni.[126] The stela was dated from his third year on the throne of Babylon, that is, 708.[127]

Each stela carried its own specific message and addressed a particular audience in the place where it was erected; it was a medium by which Assyrian propaganda was communicated. What was the significance of Sargon's Cyprus stela? Mesopotamian cuneiform script was not in local use in Cyprus at that time. Only a few scribes employed by local merchants trading with Assyria would have been able to read the stela erected there. Some scholars believe that the inscription was read aloud to the uneducated public, but it had to be translated into the local dialect, Phoenician in the area of Kition. However it was done, the inscription and the image depicted on the stela complemented one another. The stela's significance as Sargon's dedication to the gods was apparent to any observer: the king's gesture of prayer and at least some of the divine symbols were immediately recognizable. In the Cypriot perception, the stela carried the prestige of Sargon and proclaimed his power. Thus, one of the purposes of the stela would have been to intimidate potential Cypriot rebels, both as a reminder and a warning. The erection of this royal stela, acting as a substitute for Sargon's presence, was also intended to mark the western perimeter of Assyrian influence, of the "officially existing world."[128] Sargon was proud to describe his empire as going from the island of Cyprus to the island of Dilmun. That is why the account of the delegation of Cypriot rulers was often juxtaposed with that of the submission of Upêri, king of Dilmun, "who like a fish set up his home in the midst of the Sea of the rising sun."[129] This was a new motif in Neo-Assyrian inscriptions as, previously, the extent of the empire was said to go from the Mediterranean to the Persian/Ara-

---

126. Malbran-Labat, "Inscription assyrienne," 348, ll. 51–53, and 351; Radner, "Stele of Sargon," 432–33, with different hypotheses.

127. Malbran-Labat, "Inscription assyrienne," 348, ll. 20–22, and 350; Hawkins, "New Sargon Stele," 163–64. For a date in 707, see Hayim Tadmor, "Notes on the Stele of Sargon II from Cyprus" [Hebrew], ErIs 25 (1996): 286–89; Radner, "Stele of Sargon," 434.

128. Mario Liverani, *Prestige and Interest: International Relations in the Near East, ca. 1600–1100 B.C.*, HANE/S 1 (Padova: Sargon, 1990), 59; Irene Winter, "Art in Empire: The Royal Image and the Visual Dimensions of Assyrian Ideology," in Parpola, *Assyria 1995*, 376; Radner, "Stele of Sargon," 440–45; Porter, "Audiences for the Cyprus Stela," 669–75.

129. *ARAB* 2.43, 70, 81, 92, 99, 185; Malbran-Labat, "Inscription assyrienne," 348, ll. 23–30, and 350; *PNA* 3.2:1390.

bian Gulf; it also expressed a better Assyrian knowledge of the Mediterranean.[130] Another important aim of this stela was a ritual act: Sargon sent a message to the gods, who alone could keep him alive and ensure his future military successes. He addressed Assyrian and Babylonian gods, but, for the first time, he also considered the Cypriot maritime gods, whom he did not know by name: "the gods who dwell in the midst of the Great Sea."[131] As suggested on the stela, some ceremony, including sacrifices, may have taken place at the time it was erected or later in commemorative rituals. Finally, Sargon explicitly intended this stela for his successors: "I leave (it) for ever to my royal descendants. In future days, a succeeding king shall see the stele and read it, the name of the great gods may he honor, my stele let him anoint and perform sacrifices; he must not change its location."[132] He uttered curses against anyone who might destroy his stela or erase his name. These curses give an insight into Sargon's worst fears: the extinction of his name and his dynasty, the absence of mercy for him, or the decline in the number of his people through want, famine, hunger, and plague, living as hostages at the usurper's court.

On the whole, Sargon was, on the one hand, very interested in subjugating the island of Cyprus in order to provide a new unprecedented western frontier to his empire. On the other hand, he was too busy from 710 to 707 in Babylonia to conduct the military expedition to Cyprus himself; therefore, he sent his officer to solve some kind of problem that occurred there and to submit the island to Assyrian tribute. The Tyrian colony of Kition revolted against Lulî who reconquered it around 709. Around 708, seven kings from the district of Ia went to Babylon and submitted to Sargon who had a stela erected in the area of Kition. The Cyprian cities lost their independence and became vassals of the Assyrian Empire until Ashurbanipal's reign. However, because of their insularity, they were probably not closely controlled nor submitted to paying tribute with regularity.

Egypt

After Egypt's failed attempt to once more gain a foothold in western Asia in 853 BCE at the battle of Qarqar, the Assyrians continued to domi-

---

130. Elayi, "Terminologie de la Mer Méditerranée," 75–92.
131. *ARAB* 2.189.
132. *ARAB* 2.188–89; Radner, "Stele of Sargon," 442.

4. THE CONQUEST OF THE WEST

nate the region. Tiglath-pileser III seized Gaza in 734; its king Hanunu first escaped to Egypt, then gave allegiance to Assyria and was allowed to reascend his throne. The Assyrian king reached the border of Egypt, which was unable to fight against him during one of its most chaotic and politically fragmented periods.[133] Osorkon IV, a pharaoh more probably of the Twenty-third Dynasty rather than of the Twenty-second, was little more than ruler in Tanis and Bubastis, in Lower Egypt.[134] The Nubians of the kingdom of Kush threatened Egypt from the lands of the south. The Kushite king Piye or Piankhy left his Nubian capital of Napata and invaded Egypt around 727 BCE. The Twenty-Fifth Dynasty, known as the Ethiopian or Kushite Dynasty, was a line of rulers originating in Kush, who succeeded in reunifying Lower and Upper Egypt.[135] From the reign of Tiglath-pileser III onward, the policy of Assyria consisted in maintaining diplomatic contacts with some rulers of the Delta and, from the reign of Sargon onward, also with the kings of Kush. Assyria wanted to control the terminal ports of the lucrative international trade routes leading from Arabia and Egypt northward through the *Via Maris*.

Historically and economically, Gaza enjoyed a close relationship with the Nile Delta, and when Hanunu revolted against Sargon in 720, it was natural for him to seek protection in Egypt against the Assyrian king. He made an alliance with an Egyptian ruler whose name is lost, who sent him "Rêû, commander-in-chief of Egypt."[136] Who was this Rêû? It has been suggested that he was either a commander of Osorkon IV of Tanis, Tefnakht of Sais, or Piankhy. However, another hypothesis seems more

---

133. Nicolas-Christophe Grimal, *A History of Ancient Egypt* (Oxford: Blackwell, 1992), 412–13; Kitchen, *Third Intermediate Period in Egypt*; Erik Hornung, Rolf Krauss, and David Warburton, *Ancient Egyptian Chronology*, HdO 83 (Leiden: Brill, 2006), 234–64, 494.

134. Karl-Heinz Priese, "Der Beginn der Kuschitischen Herrschaft in Ägypten," ZÄS 98 (1970): 20; Robert M. Porter, "Osorkon III of Tanis: the Contemporary of Piye?," *GM* 230 (2011): 111–12; Aidan Dodson, "The Coming of the Kushites and the Identity of Osorkon IV," in *Thebes in the First Millennium BC*, ed. Elena Pischikova (Newcastle upon Tyne: Cambridge Scholars, 2014), 6–12.

135. Barbara Brannon, *The Kingdom of Kush* (Pelham: Benchmark Education, 2005); Christian Dereser, "Die 25. Dynastie: Ägypten unter Nubischer Herrschaft," *Kemet* 20 (2011): 20–23.

136. *ARAB* 2.5, 55; Fuchs, *Inschriften Sargons II*, Ann. 53, 55; Prunk. 25, 26; *PNA* 3.1:1049.

likely.¹³⁷ Piankhy died in 722/721 after a reign of about thirty-three years. Shabaka, his younger brother, succeeded him on the throne of Kush and conquered Egypt in February 720. Osorkon IV and the other rulers of the Delta surrendered, but they were allowed to keep their former domains and authority. In the battle near Raphiu, Shabaka himself did not fight, but sent his commander-in-chief Rêû. According to the Assyrian accounts, Hanunu and his ally Rêû were defeated: "I defeated them and Rêû ran off alone like a shepherd (*rē'û* in Akkadian), whose sheep have been carried off, and he went up (disappeared or died?)."¹³⁸ One relief of Room V in the palace of Khorsabad recorded this campaign, along the brook of Egypt; one of the foes has been identified with an upper Nile Nubian.¹³⁹ Even though he was weakened as a result of his defeat in 720, Shabaka maintained a hostile policy toward Assyria until his death around 707/706 (year 15).¹⁴⁰

Neither Egypt nor even a part of it was conquered by Sargon. In his inscriptions, the so-called river of Egypt was usually considered as the southern border of his empire: "I cut down all my foes ... as far as the border of Egypt," "(I am) the king who brought under his sway ... all the desert as far as the river of Egypt."¹⁴¹ However, a passage of the Cyprus stela is more pretentious because in it he claimed to have subjugated all peoples, including those of Egypt: "the peoples from the Upper Bitter Sea to the Lower Bitter Sea I brought under one rule, and from Egypt to [Mushki] I brought them in submission to my feet."¹⁴² In fact, according to the Assyrian inscriptions, tribute was sent to Sargon by two Egyptian rulers. It is reported that Piru king of Egypt, together with Samsi queen of the Arabs, and Itamar the Sabean sent their tribute (*madattū*) to Sargon in 715.¹⁴³ Another inscription states that Shilkani, king of Musri (Egypt),

---

137. Dan'el Kahn, "The Inscription of Sargon II at Tang-i Var and the Chronology of Dynasty 25," *Or* 70 (2001): 11–13 (with bibliography).

138. *ARAB* 2.5 (*ip-par-šid*).

139. Pauline Albenda, "Observations on Egyptians in Assyrian Art," *BES* 4 (1982): 8; Franklin, "Room V Reliefs," 265–66 and fig. 4; Franklin, "Room with a View," 267–69, and fig. 10.4.

140. Kahn, "Inscription of Sargon II," 7, 12–13, 18. For other dates, see, e.g., Frédéric Payraudeau, "Retour sur la succession Shabaqo-Shabataqo," *NeHeT* 1 (2014): 115–27 (with bibliography).

141. *ARAB* 2.54, 82, 96–97, 118.

142. *ARAB* 2.183.

143. *ARAB* 2.18, 55.

sent to Sargon in 716 a gift (*tāmartu*) of "12 great horses whose like did not exist in Assyria."[144] Tadmor noted the discrepancy of one year between the tribute and this gift and suggested that the scribe of the Annals erred by one year in his dating and that Piru and Shilkani were the same person.[145] It is more likely that they were two different persons, Shilkani sending a gift in 716, and Piru sending his tribute in 715.[146] Who were they? Shilkani was probably Osorkon IV (So from the biblical book of 2 Kings) who wanted to seek help from Sargon. Piru was another ruler, probably Shabaka, the recognized king of Egypt, who submitted to tribute by the Assyrian power. Osorkon IV perhaps was punished immediately and deposed from kingship because he deviated from the anti-Assyrian policy of his overlord. As was stated above, it was also in 716 that Sargon settled eastern populations on the border brook of Egypt and developed international trade in this area.

Egypt was then mentioned in Sargon's inscriptions in relation with the revolt of Ashdod, in fact only with the second revolt raised by Yamani in 711. Before starting his revolt, in 712, Yamani tried to obtain the participation of Bakenrenef of Sais, named Bocchoris by Manethon, in an anti-Assyrian coalition. This Delta ruler was a son of Tefnakht who had inaugurated the Twenty-fourth Dynasty around 720/719 and reigned eight years. Bakenrenef did not answer Yamani's appeal, possibly because he was himself swamped by difficulties. It is reported in another inscription that Piru, king of Musri, that is to say Shabaka, could not or did not wish to help Yamani.[147] However, when his revolt against Assyria failed, Yamani fled in 711 to Piru (Shabaka) who was an opponent of Sargon. He received asylum from Shabaka until the end of his reign: "Yamani of Ashdod feared my weapons, left his wife, his sons and his daughters, fled to the border of Egypt which is on the frontier of Meluhha and lived there like a thief (outlaw)."[148] Even if his life during this long exile from around 711 to 707 was hard, Shabaka did not extradite Yamani. But after Shabaka's death, which occurred shortly after the twenty-fourth of November 707, his successor Shabatka changed his policy toward Assyria. As a gesture of

---

144. Gadd, "Inscribed Prisms of Sargon II," 180; Younger, "Recent Study on Sargon II," 312.
145. Tadmor, "Campaigns of Sargon," 78.
146. SAAS 8:131; Kahn, "Inscription of Sargon II," 9, 13, 18.
147. SAAS 8:46, 74, and 131, VII.b, ll. 30–33.
148. *ARAB* 2.79.

goodwill or because of his "fear of the splendor of Assur," he extradited Yamani to Sargon, bringing him himself into Assyria, "after a most difficult journey."[149] The dates of the reigns of Shabaka and Shabatka are still debated. There are three main hypotheses: a coregency between the two pharaohs, a division of the kingdoms of Kush and Egypt ruled by Shabaka and Shabatka respectively, or an inversion of their reigns, Shabatka preceding Shabaka.[150] However, the Tang-i Var inscription, dated from 706, clearly indicates that Shabatka, who extradited Yamani, was on the throne in 706.[151] Problematic data such as the fake Turin stela were used to prove the coregency, but in fact there is no trace of double dating in the texts, and the reliefs on the monuments never represent both rulers performing religious rites jointly. It is inconceivable too that, in a divided kingdom, the two kings ruled in Thebes in the same year, using different dating methods. The interpretation of Kahn seems to be the most plausible: Shabaka acceded to the throne around 720 for a reign that lasted at least fifteen years (year 15 being attested); he was succeeded by Shabatka around 707/706.[152]

Even if relations between Assyria and Egypt were difficult during a chaotic and politically fragmented period, Sargon succeeded in suppressing the revolts of Gaza and Ashdod in spite of Egyptian support for the rebels. He positioned Assyria as the strongest power in the Levant, controlling the border of Egypt, and he moved skillfully with the different powers of the moment. He protected Assyrian international trade interests in the southern Levant. He entrusted a local ruler, the sheikh of Laban as gate-

---

149. *ARAB* 2.63, 80.

150. See, e.g., Anthony Spalinger, "The Year 712 BC and its Implications for Egyptian History," *JARCE* 10 (1973): 95–101; Frank Yurco, "Sennacherib's Third Campaign and the Coregency of Shabaka and Shebitku," *Serapis* 6 (1980): 221–40 (first hypothesis). Donald B. Redford, "A Note on the Chronology of Dynasty 25 and the Inscription of Sargon II at Tang-i Var," *Or* 68 (1999): 58–60 (second hypothesis). Michael Bányai, "Ein Vorschlag zur Chronologie der 25. Dynastie in Ägypten," *JEgH* 6 (2013): 46–129; Payraudeau, "Retour sur la succession Shabaqo-Shabataqo," 115–27 (third hypothesis).

151. Frame, "Inscription of Sargon II," 36, ll. 20–21, 52–54. Nadav Na'aman has proposed to restore Shabatka in the broken inscription of Sargon at Malatya: "Šapataku' of Meluḫḫa in a Second Inscription of Sargon II," *NABU* 3 (1999): 64, no. 65.

152. Dan'el Kahn, "Was There a Co-regency in the 25th Dynasty?" *AeL* 16 (2006): 275–91; Kahn, "Inscription of Sargon II," 1–18.

keeper facing Egypt, in the same way as Tiglath-pileser III had appointed Idibi-ilu, the sheikh of an Arabian tribe.

Finally, what was the goal of Sargon's policy in the west throughout his reign? Did he change it along the way? Did he succeed in applying it? It was not, as some scholars have suggested, a policy of "Assyrianization," a kind of colonialism, meaning that the Assyrians were convinced of their own superiority, and that they brought in civilization and Assur, the king of the gods.[153] Just like his predecessors, Sargon was a pragmatist; he considered the conquest of the west as a success if he obtained maximum profit with the minimum investment.[154] Using the prestige-oriented propaganda in his royal inscriptions, he pointed to his invincibility and superiority with the help of the gods. His message to the conquered people was simple: never resist, be loyal and obedient, pay the tribute and the taxes, and provide military assistance such as a war fleet and various services. The same conditions did not apply to all peoples: autonomous vassals such as Phoenician cities and Gaza, and Assyrian provinces such as Samaria and Ashdod could coexist. Sargon handled the different regions with care and made local differences. Northern Syria was special due to its proximity to Assyrian heartland. Conversely, Cyprus was so distant, lost in the middle of the sea, that it was not necessary and not possible to exercise tight control over it. If a social entity, such as the Phoenicians or the inhabitants of Gaza, was irreplaceable and useful for profit (maritime or desert trade) and strategy, he experimented with different types of domination. In line with usual Assyrian practice, parts of the territories of rebellious vassal states were cut off and given to the neighboring pro-Assyrian vassals. The objective of deportations was to intimidate, to undermine local resistance, and to acquire human resources for Assyrian projects. The deportees had to become productive as rapidly as possible by working at their old professions in their new homes. Houses were built for them and their families.[155] Sargon succeeded, at the very beginning of his reign in 720, in solving most of the problems in the west, stabilizing it in order to achieve maximum profit and then turning to focus on other problematic regions of

---

153. See, e.g., Liverani, "Ideology of the Assyrian Empire," 297–317; Parpola, "Assyria's Expansion," 99–111.

154. Angelika Berlejung, "The Assyrians in the West: Assyrianization, Colonialism, Indifference, or Development Policy?," in *Congress Volume: Helsinki, 2010*, ed. Martti Nissinen, VTSup 148 (Leiden: Brill, 2010), 21–61.

155. SAA 15:28–29, nos. 40–41.

his empire. However, the western front was not definitively stabilized, as new problems occurred in Carchemish in 717, in Ashdod in 713 and 711, in Cyprus in 709, and in Tyre between 709 and 705. Either he intervened personally or, more frequently, he sent his officer. The most serious issue that he failed to solve at the end of his reign was the rebellion of Tyre. In fact, the western front was one of the most, if not the most, important part of the Assyrian Empire, but also one of the most difficult to control.

5
The Northwest of the Empire

The geographical and political scene in the northwest of the Assyrian Empire, that is to say, Anatolia, was quite confusing for two reasons: (1) there were no fixed borders defining the limits of states and (2) territorial control was constantly changing (fig. 4). The chief states in the second half of the eighth century were: Mushki, and the ancient Neo-Hittite states, Que, Hilakku, Samal, Tabal, Bit-Purutash, Gurgum, Kummuhu, and Kammanu. These states roughly formed a line along the Taurus Mountains from the Mediterranean to the upper Euphrates. Anatolian states were not a core concern in Sargon's foreign policy—on the condition that they provided Assyria with the product of their mines and forests and remained not too warlike. They represented a peripheral goal for him, only taken into consideration when he had solved the other main problems. In fact, the riches of the Levantine coastal trade provided by the Phoenicians and the fabulous wealth of Egypt were far more substantial than the riches of Anatolia. The powers of the Urartians and Elamites were more difficult to confront than the weakened and divided powers of the northwestern states.[1] In addition, the Assyrian chariotry had difficulty in this mainly mountainous country.

---

1. Albert Kirk Grayson, "Assyrian Expansion into Anatolia in the Sargonid Age (ca. 744–650 BC)," in *The Relations between Anatolia and Mesopotamia*, ed. H. Erkanal, V. Donbaz, and A. Uğuroğlu, RAI 34 (Ankara: Türk Tarih Kurumu Basımevi, 1998), 131–35; Simo Parpola, "Assyria's Expansion in the Eighth and Seventh Centuries and Its Long-Term Repercussions in the West," in Dever and Gitin, *Symbiosis, Symbolism, and the Power of the Past*, 99: Lydia in western Anatolia was not reached before Ashurbanipal's reign. See also Ezek 27:12 (Tabal and Mushki).

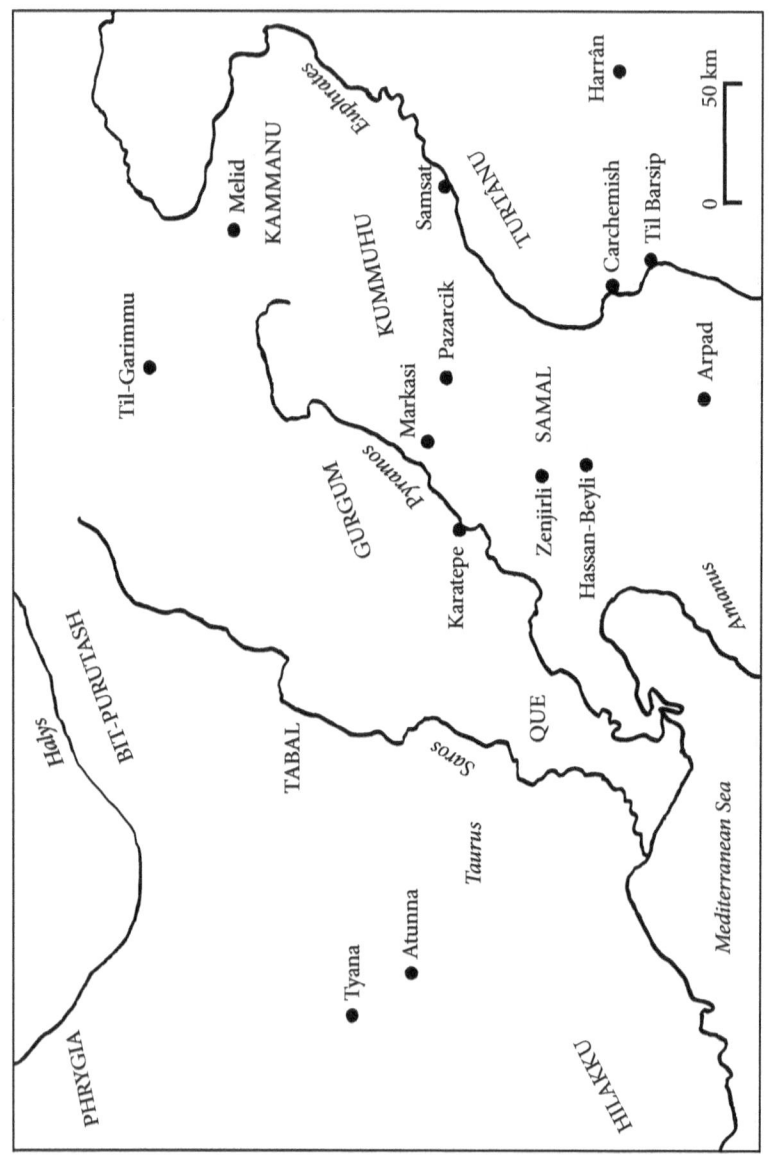

Fig. 4. The Northwest of the Empire

Mushki/Phrygia

It has always been in dispute as to whether Phrygia corresponds to the land of Mushki.[2] The term used in Assyrian inscriptions was "Mushki," while "Phrygia" was used in Greek sources. A related question is the following: was Mitâ of Assyrian sources the same king as Midas in Greek sources? Even if Mitâ was a current name from the Hittite period onward, Mitâ the king of Mushki appears to be the same as the Phrygian king Midas.[3] However, this does not mean that the Mushki people should be equated with the Phrygians. The oldest attestation of the Mushki in the sources is the victory won by Tiglath-pileser I over twenty thousand soldiers of Mushki, conducted by their five kings who had seized Kutmuhi (Kummuhu).[4] They were infiltrating and attempting to settle in the upper Tigris and the Khabur regions. The wide geography of the ethnic name Mushki from eastern to western Anatolia could mean the existence of two different ethnic units or migratory movements from west to east, or the reverse.[5] The prevailing hypothesis is that the Mushki were a patchwork of some twenty tribes, assembled in the last quarter of the eighth century by a unique king: Mitâ/Midas.[6] The organization of his kingdom seems completely different from that of other kingdoms of the ancient Near East. The exact location and extent of his kingdom is not precisely known: Gordion in central Anatolia was supposed to be its capital.[7]

---

2. See, e.g., Anne-Marie Wittke, *Mushki und Phryger: Ein Beitrag zur Geschichte Anatoliens vom 12. bis 7. Jh. v. Chr.*, TAVO 99 (Stuttgart: Reichert, 2004); Wittke, "Remarks on the Early History of Phrygia (Twelfth to Eighth Century BC)," in *Anatolian Iron Age 6: The Proceedings of the Sixth Anatolian Iron Age Colloquium Held at Eskişehir, 16–20 August 2004*, ed. Alton Çilingiroğlu and Antonio Sagona, ANESSup 20 (Leuven: Peeters, 2007), 335–46; Gocha R. Tsetskhladze, "Thracians versus Phrygians: About the Origin of the Phrygians Once Again," in Çilingiroğlu, *Anatolian Iron Age 6*, 283–310; G. Fielder, "Les Phrygiens en Tyanide et le problème des Mushki," *ResAnt* 2 (2005): 394–98.

3. See, e.g., Oguz Soysal, "A New Join to the Mita-Text (BO 8742) and a Duplicate of the Zannanza-Affair (Bo 8757)," *NABU* 4 (2014): 145–48, no. 93; *PNA* 2.2:755–56; Fielder, "Phrygiens en Tyanide," 396–97.

4. *ARAB* 1.221.

5. On the different hypotheses, see Aram V. Kossian, "The Mushki Problem Reconsidered," *SMEA* 39 (1997): 253–66.

6. Fielder, "Phrygiens en Tyanide," 396–97.

7. Wittke, "Remarks on the Early History of Phrygia," 335, 340, and map 1.

When Tiglath-pileser III came to the throne in 744, his main concern throughout his reign was to defeat the powerful kingdom of Urartu, which had extended its control as far as part of western Anatolia. He won the first battle in 743 and incorporated Kummuhu and Gurgum into the Assyrian Empire. Except for an unsuccessful insurrection of Tabal, a number of states in the region, such as Kammanu, Kummuhu, Gurgum, and Que, paid tribute to the Assyrian king; however, Phrygia is not mentioned in Tiglath-pileser III's inscriptions.[8] Thus it seems to have remained fairly docile until Sargon's reign.

The policy of Midas was original: to avoid open conflict with Assyria, he preferred to make alliances with the various small states east of Phrygia and to encourage them to rebel against Assyria. These allies hence constituted a buffer zone between Phrygia and Assyria. As a result, Sargon was obliged to fight, not directly against Midas, but against Midas's allies. For example, in 717, when Pisîri king of Carchemish revolted against Assyria, he "sent (messages of) hostility against Assyria to Mitâ of the land of Mushki."[9] Sargon severely repressed his revolt, bringing Pisîri and his family in chains and turning Carchemish into an Assyrian province (see above). However, he made no offensive against Midas. Why? Maybe he was too far away or too powerful; either way, he preferred not to attack him for the time being. Early in Sargon's reign, Phrygia and Urartu formed an alliance against Assyria and were joined by Kammanu and Gurgum. According to the Annals, the first direct attack of Sargon against Phrygia occurred in 715. Midas, after hearing about the conquest by Sargon's governor over his own territory and the submission of several neighboring rulers to the Assyrian king, submitted to him in 709 (year 13).[10] A letter found at Nimrud was written by Sargon to Ashur-sharru-usur, the Assyrian governor of Que.[11] In this letter, unfinished and apparently never sent, perhaps due to a change in the political situation, Sargon was answering his governor who had reported that king Midas, who until that time had been hostile toward Assyria, had now taken the first steps toward a rapprochement: "As to what you wrote to me: 'A messenger [of] Mitâ the Mushki has come to me, bringing me 14 men of Que whom Urik had sent

---

8. *ARAB* 1.769, 772, 797, 801.
9. *ARAB* 2.8.
10. *ARAB* 2.43.
11. *PNA* 1.1:218–19.

to Urartu as an embassy'—this is extremely good!"[12] According to the new satisfactory situation, Sargon gave him his instructions. The chronological problem surrounding this important text has been much debated. At first, a low dating had been proposed: 709 (year 13), on the basis of the account of the Annals for that year. The letter was naturally linked with the submission of Midas.[13] However, the new edition published by Parpola offers improvements for some of the damaged areas of the tablet, in particular in lines 8–9: "without a battle [or any]thing, the Mushki has given us his word and became our ally!"[14] It is explicitly stated that no battle on the part of Sargon was needed to result in Midas's friendly attitude. On the contrary, in the Annals, Midas is said to have turned to peaceful relations after he had seen "the destruction of his country and the deportation of his people."[15] The letter cannot be ascribed to an Assyrian king previous to Sargon because he said in the Annals: Midas "had not made his submission to (any of) the kings who lived before me."[16] The most plausible date for this letter is 715 (year 7), before the beginning of Assyria's hostilities against Phrygia and after the nomination of Ashur-sharru-usur as governor of Que.[17]

Assyria's hostilities against Phrygia indirectly started through campaigns against Midas's allies (see below).[18] In 718 (year 4), Kiakki of Shinuhtu, a king of Tabal who had broken a treaty with Assyria, was defeated. In 717 (year 5), Carchemish was annexed after the discovery of Pisîri's intrigues with Midas. In 715 (year 7), the Assyrian campaign was directed against the land of Phrygia by recapturing cities of Que that had been taken by Midas.[19] This campaign resulted in an Assyrian foray into Midas's territory but did not stop him from making continuous incursions into Que and Tabal. In 713 (year 9), Sargon continued to fight against Midas's allies, defeating Ambaris king of Tabal, who had

---

12. SAA 1:4, no. 1, ll. 3–7 (ND 2759).
13. H. W. F. Saggs, "The Nimrud Letters, 1952: Part IV," *Iraq* 20 (1958): 202–8; John Nicholas Postgate, "Assyrian Texts and Fragments," *Iraq* 35 (1973): 13–36; followed by *PNA* 1.1:218–19.
14. SAA 1:4, no. 1, ll. 8–9.
15. Lie, *Inscriptions of Sargon II*, 68–69, l. 454.
16. *ARAB* 2.22, 71.
17. As proposed by Giovanni B. Lanfranchi, "Sargon's Letter to Aššur-šarru-uṣur: An Interpretation," *SAAB* 2 (1988): 59–64.
18. *ARAB* 2.55, 137.
19. *ARAB* 2.16, 18, 118.

"sent a messenger to Rusâ of Urartu and Mitâ of Mushki, (proposing) to seize (his) territory."[20] Even after the defeat of Rusâ in 714, his weakened position was less apparent in Anatolia. In 711 (year 11), Sargon took four cities on the border of Phrygia and Urartu, and "so as to make no exit … blocked their gates."[21] In 709, the Assyrian governor of Que made raids, three times, in the land of Phrygia, with some success (see below).[22] Midas's submission was reported immediately after these campaigns: "(he) sent his messenger to me, to the Sea of the rising sun (where I was), (offering) to do (feudal) service and to pay tribute and gifts."[23]

Therefore, 715 appears to have been a crucial year for Sargon's northwestern policy. Pressed both by Phrygia and Urartu, he initiated campaigns in those two directions. This would explain why he appeared, in the Nimrud letter ND 2759 mentioned above, so happy with Midas's initiative, and so well disposed toward him. After 709, no further mention of Midas was made in Sargon's inscriptions. The Assyrian king claimed that he had submitted Phrygia: "Sargon … the mighty king … who placed his yoke on the land of Mushki."[24] In fact, he had not conquered Mushki but several lands that he enumerated "up to the land of Mushki."[25] The evidence, other than the Assyrian inscriptions concerning the Midas-Sargon relationship, is very meager, but it does exist, as is shown by art and artifact finds in Phrygian and Assyrian sites, such as animal-headed situlae and vessels without handles.[26] Phrygia was not mentioned in Assyrian inscriptions again until Esarhaddon's reign: a king of Phrygia, whose name is lost, addressed a query to Shamash, asking whether he might attack a fortress of Melid.[27]

Que, Hilakku, Samal

The Assyrian Que of Sargon's inscriptions probably corresponds to the plain of Cilicia Pedias. It is a well-defined geographical entity, bounded

---

20. *ARAB* 2.24, 55; *PNA* 1.1:99–100.
21. Lie, *Inscriptions of Sargon II*, 34–37, ll. 209–219.
22. Ibid., 66–67, ll. 445–446.
23. *ARAB* 2.43, 71; Fuchs, *Inschriften Sargons II*, Prunk. 150–52.
24. *ARAB* 2.137; Gadd, "Inscribed Prisms of Sargon II," 199–200, l. 14.
25. *ARAB* 2.118.
26. Oscar W. Muscarella, "Relations between Phrygia and Assyria in the Eighth century B.C.," in Erkanal, *Relations between Anatolia and Mesopotamia*, 149–57.
27. SAA 4:6–7, no. 4.

by the Mediterranean to the south, the Taurus Mountains to the north, the Amanus range to the east and the mountains of Cilicia Traccheia to the west.[28] Cilicia Traccheia could correspond to Assyrian Hilakku. However, if that is so, then it needs to be explained why this land was given to Tabal (see below), which would have supposed a contiguous territory, inasmuch as Sargon set over them one official as governor; but the extent of Tabal at this time is unknown.[29] The main passes by which entry could be gained into Que were few from the western coastal strip: the so-called Cilician Gates and Amanus Gates. The Assyrian kings entered Que when they were en route for Tabal. In Sargon's inscriptions, Que and Hilakku are always presented as different territories. Hilakku is not mentioned in the inscriptions of his predecessors, but Que was conquered by Shalmaneser III; both states are conventionally known as "Neo-Hittite."[30] King Urik (Urikki, Awarikku) of Que was one of the tributaries of Tiglath-pileser III, who paid tribute to him from 743, his third year.[31]

Sargon's inscriptions presented him as "the conqueror of Hilakku," the one "who uprooted Hilakku" and "who deported (the people) of the land of Hilakku," without any dating.[32] In 713 (year 9), according to the Annals, he gave Hilakku to Ambaris of Tabal. However, the scribes had no precise idea of what Hilakku was because, in one inscription, they used the determinative for "land" (KUR) and in another inscription the determinative for "city" (URU).

Sargon's campaigns in Que were directed against two different adversaries: Midas of Phrygia (indirectly) and the Ionians, as if the region was divided into two parts and shared between two different owners. It is interesting to note that, in both cases, the date of the conquest is presented in

---

28. See, e.g., A. Erzen, "Kilikien bis zum ender der Perserherrschaft" (PhD diss., Universität Leipzig, 1940); John Bing, "A History of Cilicia during the Assyrian Period" (PhD diss., Indiana University, 1969); Paolo Desideri and Anna M. Jasink, *Cilicia: Dall'età di Kizzuwatna alla conquista macedone* (Turin: Le lettere, 1990); Olivier Casabonne, *La Cilicie à l'époque achéménide*, Persika 3 (Paris: de Boccard, 2004), 21–49; Elizabeth French, "Cilicia," in *The Philistines and Other "Sea Peoples" in Text and Archaeology*, ed. Ann E. Killebrew and Gunthar Lehmann, ABS 15 (Atlanta: Society of Biblical Literature, 2013), 479–84.

29. *ARAB* 2.25, 55.

30. *ARAB* 2.600, 674, 682. See Trevor Bryce, *The World of the Neo-Hittite Kingdoms: A Political and Military History* (Oxford: Oxford University Press, 2012).

31. *ARAB* 1.769, 772, 801; *PNA* 3.2:1414.

32. *ARAB* 2.80, 92, 99.

the same imprecise way: "since distant days" (*ul-tu ūmī* (UD.MEŠ) *ru-qu-ú-ti*).³³ The date of the Phrygian conquest of some cities in Que probably did not occur during Tiglath-pileser III's reign because his inscriptions did not mention any problem in this vassal kingdom. A date between 718 and 715 has been proposed.³⁴ However, the expression "since distant days" seems to mean more than only three years. Either the Phrygian conquest of Que dated from the very beginning of Sargon's reign or from Shalmaneser V's reign, but no conclusion can be reached due to the lack of documentary evidence. The delivery, by Midas to Ashur-sharru-usur, of "14 men of Que whom Urik had sent to Urartu as an embassy," in the context of an exchange of prisoners of war, was probably related to the Phrygian conquest, but no date is indicated.³⁵ Concerning the date of the establishment of Ionians in Que, documentation is also lacking. The letter sent by Qurdi-ashur-lâmur to Tiglath-pileser III around 730 related an attack of Ionians who arrived by sea and their defeat at the cities of "⸢Samsim⸣[uruna?], ... Harisu, and...."³⁶ Samsimuruna was a Phoenician city (Baalbek?), but the names of these cities are too damaged to be interpreted. However, this event did not take place in Cilicia but on the Levantine coast; Qurdi-ashur-lâmur was an Assyrian official in charge of the coastal strip from Kashpuna to Tyre, and possibly settled at Ushu opposite Tyre.³⁷

According to the Nimrud letter ND 2759, dated to 715, Urik, king of Que and vassal of Assyria, was forced to move over to the Phrygian side. His sending of envoys to the king of Urartu was a consequence of good relations established between Phrygia and Urartu.³⁸ Urik was already king of Que under Tiglath-pileser III's reign. He is known from the Phoenico-Luwian bilingual inscriptions of Karatepe, a site about 100 kilometers

---

33. *ARAB* 2.16 (concerning Ionians), 18 (concerning Midas); Fuchs, *Inschriften Sargons II*, Ann. 118, 126.

34. Lanfranchi, "Sargon's Letter," 63.

35. SAA 1:4–5, no. 1, ll. 4–6, 16–25.

36. ND 2370. H. W. F. Saggs, "The Nimrud Letters, 1952: Part VI," *Iraq* 25 (1963): 77; Frederick Mario Fales, *Lettere dalla corte assira* (Venice: Marsilio, 1992), 52–54, no. 3; Robert Rollinger, "The Ancient Greeks and the Impact of the Ancient Near East: Textual Evidence and Historical Perspective (ca. 750–650 BC)," in *Mythology and Mythologies*, ed. Robert M. Whiting, MSym 2 Helsinki: Neo-Assyrian Text Corpus Project, 2001), 237 and n. 20 (updated transliteration by Simo Parpola from the SAA database).

37. Elayi, *Histoire de la Phénicie*, 163–65.

38. Lanfranchi, "Sargon's Letter," 63.

northeast of Adana, written by Azitawada, vassal of Urik and king of the Danunians (*Dnnym*), from the Phoenician damaged inscription of Hassan-Beyli in north Amanus, and from the Phoenician and Luwian bilingual inscription of Cineköy, which throws new light on the importance of the "House of Mopsos," an important dynasty of southern Anatolia.[39] When Sargon discovered the treason of Urik, his vassal, he punished him; Que was no longer a kingdom, but became an Assyrian province, with an Assyrian governor, Ashur-sharru-usur. The date of the transformation of Que into an Assyrian province has been debated, but it was most likely in 715, which is now also confirmed by the new reading of Sargon's letter: it occurred before Sargon's military actions in Que. Ashur-sharru-usur had been made governor of Que in reaction to Urik's attempt to develop an independent policy.[40] The hypothesis of a mixed government, a kind of coregency or superintendence between the Assyrian governor and the local king, is not convincing.[41]

The reconquest of the cities captured by Midas is related in the Annals in two passages dated from 715 (year 7): "⌈I defeated⌉ Mitâ, king of Mushki, in his province. The cities of Harrua and Ushnanis, fortresses of the land of Que, which he had held by force since distant days I restored in their (former) status."[42] The second passage is slightly different: it mentions one additional city, its name being partly lost (*Ab-*), and after their capture, Sargon "carried off their spoil." A third passage in a Nimrud prism, not so propagandistic, mentions two battles: "twice I made defeat of him," probably when he captured the cities of Harrua and Ushnanis. These cities were fortresses (*ḫalṣu*) on the northwestern border of Que, in the direction of Phrygia, but they are not yet identified.

---

39. François Bron, *Recherches sur les inscriptions phéniciennes de Karatepe*, HEO 11 (Geneva: Droz, 1979), 167–68; Jean Deshayes, Maurice Sznycer, and Paul Garelli, "Remarques sur les monuments de Karatepe," *RA* 75 (1981): 54–60; André Lemaire, "L'inscription phénicienne de Hassan-Beyli reconsidérée," *RSF* 11 (1983): 9–19; Edward Lipiński, "Phoenicians in Anatolia and Assyria," *OLP* 16 (1985): 82–83 (this inscription is possibly mentioned in a treaty of peace between Urik and Sargon); Halet Çambel ed., *Corpus of Hieroglyphic Luwian Inscriptions: Vol. 2, Karatepe-Aslantaş; The Inscriptions; Facsimile Edition*, UISK 8.2 (Berlin: de Gruyter, 1999).

40. Elayi and Cavigneaux, "Sargon II et les Ioniens," 67–68; Lanfranchi, "Sargon's Letter," 63.

41. Saggs, "The Nimrud Letters: Part IV," 206; Postgate, "Assyrian Texts and Fragments," 28.

42. *ARAB* 2.16, 18; Gadd, "Inscribed Prisms of Sargon II," 183–84, col. v, ll. 34–40.

The Annals reported, for 709 (year 13), some fights in Que. While Sargon was waging war against Merodach-baladan, the Assyrian governor of Que "made raids into his (Midas's) province, three times."[43] This unnamed governor was still probably Ashur-sharru-usur, who maybe remained in office until Sargon's death in 705.[44] He fought along the western border of Que, a region belonging to Midas. When the terrain was favorable, he used chariotry, but where it was steep, his one thousand warriors went on foot: "Two of the fortresses which defended his province, which were situated on a steep mountain, at the side of staggering [cliffs], ... he captured and smote the picked troops who fought his battle(s).... His strong cities, together with the towns of their environs, he destroyed, he devastated, he burned with fire."[45] These fortresses are unnamed, but this mountainous region west of Que could refer to Hilakku. Apparently, this defeat deeply affected Midas because he decided to submit by sending his ambassador to Sargon on the Elamite border, "bringing a message of peace (and) 1000 trophies (?) of warriors."[46] From 709 to the end of Sargon's reign in 705, Midas apparently behaved as a docile vassal.

The second problem to solve in Que was the Ionian issue. The question of the presence of Greeks in the Near East is much debated, with an abundant bibliography, mainly by scholars specializing in Greek studies. Their approach has long been dominated by a Hellenocentric ideology, and still today is sometimes biased.[47] Leaving aside the ideology, let us focus on the capture of the Ionians by Sargon: they were designated in

---

43. *ARAB* 2.42.

44. André Lemaire, "Aššur-šarru-uṣur, gouverneur de Qué," *NABU* 1 (1987): 5–6, no. 10; *PNA* 1.1:218–19.

45. *ARAB* 2.42.

46. Lie, *Inscriptions of Sargon II*, 69, 451. The meaning of *zīm panī* is uncertain: a part of the equipment or of the body of soldiers collected by the victor as evidence of his triumph; *CAD*, s.v. *zīmu*.

47. Josette Elayi, "La présence grecque dans les cités phéniciennes sous l'Empire perse achéménide," *REG* 105 (1992): 305–27 (with bibliography); Elayi, *Pièges pour historiens et recherche en péril* (Paris: Idéaphane, 2004), 72–78; Alexander Fantalkin, "Identity in the Making: Greeks in the Eastern Mediterranean during the Iron Age," in *Naukratis: Greek Diversity in Egypt; Studies on East Greek Pottery and Exchange in the Eastern Mediterranean*, ed. A. Villing and U. Schlotzhauer, BMRP 162 (London: British Museum, 2006), 199–208; Fantalkin, "Did Ionian or Carian Mercenaries Serve in the Neo-Assyrian Army?" (paper presented at Ionians in the East and West, International Conference, Empuries/L'Escala, Spain, 26–29 October 2015).

the Sargon's inscriptions and more generally in Assyrian inscriptions by the word *Iam(a)naiia* or *Iam(a)naīa*. The Greek Ἰωνες was borrowed from the Akkadian: *Yâw(a)nya* (inhabitants of the country *Yâwan*) > *Iawones > Iaones > Iônes.[48] The capture of Ionians by Sargon was apparently a fairly important event for him since it was mentioned eight times in the inscriptions of the palace of Khorsabad: Display Inscription of Salon XIV, Bull Inscription, Pavement Inscription, Cylinder Inscription, and in four duplicated prisms from Nimrud.[49] These Ionians are designated as "those who (lived) in the midst of the sea" (*ša ina qabal tamtim*). This expression was used for the first time in Sargon's inscriptions for designating the people of Cyprus (see above). Therefore, the origin of these Ionians, or of some of them, was most probably Cyprus.[50]

The next question is: where did their capture occur? The hypothesis of Cyprus in relation with the Assyrian expedition to this island in 709 is not convincing (see above).[51] The two events are never connected in Sargon's inscriptions. The localization of the capture of Ionians on the seashore of Que is more likely. The first argument is that the difficulties encountered by Sargon in this region were similar to those encountered by his son Sennacherib, a few years later, in 696 BCE. People from Ingirrâ and Tarzi (Tarsus) contributed their help to Kirua for the revolt of Hilakku and seized the Que road, blocking the traffic.[52] The late testimony of Berossos, which seems reliable, reported who these people were: in a naval battle

---

48. John A. Brinkman, "The Akkadian Words for 'Ionia' and 'Ionian,'" in *Daidalikon: Studies in Memory of Raymond V. Schoder, S.J.*, ed. Robert F. Sutton (Wauconda, IL: Bolchazy-Carducci, 1987), 53–71. See, e.g., P. R. Helm, "'Greeks' in the Neo-Assyrian Levant and 'Assyria' in Early Greek Writers" (PhD diss., University of Pennsylvania, 1980); Giovanni B. Lanfranchi, "The Ideological and Political Impact of the Assyrian Imperial Expansion on the Greek World in the Eighth and Seventh Centuries BC," in *The Heirs of Assyria: Proceedings of the Opening Symposium of the Assyrian and Babylonian Intellectual Heritage Project Held in Tvärminne, Finland, October 8–11, 1998*, ed. Sanna Aro and Robert M. Whiting, MSym 1 (Helsinki: Neo-Assyrian Text Corpus Project, 2000), 7–34; Rollinger, "Ancient Greeks," 233–64.

49. *ARAB* 2.80, 92, 99, 118. Prism ND 3411: Gadd, "Inscribed Prisms of Sargon II," 199, l. 19.

50. Elayi and Cavigneaux, "Sargon II et les Ioniens," 64–65, followed by Rollinger, "Ancient Greeks," 248.

51. Winckler, *Keilschrifttexte Sargons II*, 1:xl n. 6; Elayi and Cavigneaux, "Sargon II et les Ioniens," 65–67.

52. *ARAB* 2.286–89.

near the shore of Cilicia, Sennacherib defeated Greek invaders (*Graeci* in the Latin text, *Join* in the Armenian text).⁵³ The second argument is based on the context where the capture of Ionians took place. It was always in the same geographical context: south of Asia Minor, more precisely Cilicia Pedias, that is, Que. In the first and third inscriptions where Ionians are mentioned, this event is placed between the capture of Shinuhtu, city of Tabal, and the deportation of people of Kasku, Hilakku, and Tabal. The grammatical link *ma* between the capture and the deportation means either a simple geographical link or that Ionians established on the shore of Hilakku were deported.⁵⁴ In the second inscription, the event is placed between the restoration of the captured fortresses of Que and the capture of Kammanu and Gurgum.⁵⁵ In the fourth inscription, it is placed after a lacuna and before the conquest of Shinuhtu and Bit-Purutash.⁵⁶ The last inscription, duplicated on four cylinders, is the most explicit: "(I am the king), mighty in the battle, who caught the Ionians out of the midst of the sea as a fisherman, like fish, and subdued Que and Tyre."⁵⁷ The event preceded the capture of Shinuhtu. A logical link (*ma*) is established between the capture of Ionians, and the capture of Que and Tyre. The relation with Que is normal since the capture of Ionians occurred in Que. The relation with Tyre is less clear: according to my hypothesis on the siege of Tyre (see above), Sargon boasted by anticipating the issue of a siege in progress.

When did the capture of Ionians occur? The use of the metaphor of fishing indicates that this event took place on the seashore or even at sea. The prisms of Nimrud specify that Sargon caught the Ionians "in the midst of the sea": a naval battle is not excluded as Sargon could dispatch, for example, some Phoenician fleets; the conquest of an island is also possible because there are several small islands along the Que-Hilakku coastline. The capture of Ionians did not happen during the campaigns conducted by the governor of Que in 709 because these campaigns were explicitly directed against Midas of Phrygia.

---

53. L. W. King, "Sennacherib and the Ionians," *JHS* 30 (1910): 331; W. Röllig, "Griechen," *RlA* 3:643–47; Elayi and Cavigneaux, "Sargon II et les Ioniens," 68–69 (with bibliography).
54. *ARAB* 2.80, 99.
55. *ARAB* 2.92.
56. Gadd, "Inscribed Prisms of Sargon II," 199–200, ll. 18–20.
57. *ARAB* 2.118; Fuchs, *Inschriften Sargons II*, 34, 290, l. 21.

Sargon's first campaign against Que in 715 (year 7) seems to be the best period in which to place the capture of Ionians. The campaign against Phrygia and the confrontation with Ionians were probably two stages of a single Assyrian strategy: to relieve both Phrygian and Ionian pressure on Que. A text, unfortunately damaged and which has been misunderstood, in all likelihood referred to this event: "… country (?) which on the shore (in the midst?)] of the sea, is settled, which from days long (past), had defeated Que and which [had blocked?] the road (?), to the sea I went down against them, and slew them, great and small, with the sword."[58] Instead of "country," it could be "city" (ālu) or "fortress" (ḫalṣu). In fact, the Assyrian scribes had no clear idea of who these Ionians were because they used alternatively the determinative for "man" (LÚ), "city" (URU), or "country" (KUR). Sargon was obliged to go down to be able to reach this enemy: this means that they were on the seashore, not on an island. They could have blocked the road to the Cilician Gates, as happened later during Sennacherib's reign in 696. The phrase "great and small" could mean that these people were accompanied by their families, women and children. In the inscription, the battle with these people is followed by the capture of the cities of Midas, which could follow a chronological order. Who were these people who had established their domination, since a long time, on a coastal part of Que, the other part being occupied by the Phrygians? They could have been Ionians coming from Cyprus, who had conquered the southeastern part of Que and controlled the Cilician Gates. When had they become established in Que? They were not initially a problem in Que, which was mentioned in the Tiglath-pileser III's inscriptions: Urik king of Que was an obedient vassal. Therefore, the arrival of the Ionians possibly happened during Shalmaneser V's reign. They were neither simple traders nor pirates because they settled in Que by occupying a part of the territory. It is well-established that Sargon encouraged trade, as is shown in south Philistia and Egypt, and he would not have fought against merchants—he never disturbed the Greek merchants settled at Al-Mina, at the mouth of the Orontes, because they merely founded a commercial establishment without trying to conquer or control the region. According to Lanfranchi, the pressure on Que by both Phrygians and Ionians implied a political and economic alliance between them.[59] It is true that Midas had good relations

---

58. *ARAB* 2.16; Fuchs, *Inschriften Sargons II*, 109, 319, ll. 117–119; Elayi and Cavigneaux, "Sargon II et les Ioniens," 72–73.

59. Lanfranchi, "Ideological and Political Impact," 19–20.

with Greeks; he was the first foreign king to send gifts to Delphi, and he dedicated his throne to the Pythian Apollo.[60] However, this is not sufficient to give substance to the hypothesis of a connection between Phrygians and Ionians in Que. As a matter of fact, the settlement of Ionians in Que looks like a kind of colonization. We lack reliable and sufficient information to go further into the controversial question of the presence of Greeks in the Near East, but it is worth reiterating that the mere discovery of Greek ceramics in a site does not validate Greek presence; the ceramics could have been imported and used by local people.[61]

Bar-rakib, king of Samal (Zenjirli, modern Höyük in Gaziantep province), had understood what material advantages were to be gained from military cooperation with Assyria.[62] He stressed how he had been raised to a superior rank of kingship as a consequence of his alliance with Tiglath-pileser III and he probably continued his cooperation with Sargon.

In short, Sargon could not leave the problems of Que unsolved because the Cilician and Amanus Gates had to remain open for communication with northern states such as Tabal. The problem of the Ionians was solved in 715 by expelling them and the problem of Phrygia in 709, with the submission of Midas. Samal was probably a vassal state loyal to Assyria.

Tabal, Bit-Purutash

After the fall of the Hittite Empire, several allied states, known in Assyrian sources as Tabal, developed at the southern end of the Anatolian plateau. The term Tabal was also used in Sargon's inscriptions for designating a specific state in the Kayseri region and its capital, also named Bit-Purutash/Bit-Purutish.[63] The Assyrian and Luwian hieroglyphic inscrip-

---

60. Herodotus, *Hist.* 1.14.2.

61. See, e.g., Rollinger, "Ancient Greeks," 252 n. 124: "From the archaeological point of view there is only one very scanty hint which might refer to a Greek presence in the Assyrian heartland: a small sherd from Nineveh."

62. *KAI*, 215, ll. 10–12; 216, ll. 8–11; Giovanni B. Lanfranchi, "Consensus to Empire: Some Aspects of Sargon II's Foreign Policy," in *Assyrien im Wandel der Zeiten*, ed. Harmut Waetzoldt and Harald Hauptmann, RAI 39; HSAO 6 (Heidelberg: Heidelberger Orient-Verlag, 1997), 84–85; Lipiński, *Aramaeans*, 238–47; K. Lawson Younger, *A Political History of the Arameans: From Their Origins to the End of Their Polities*, ABS 13 (Atlanta: SBL Press, 2015).

63. SAA 1:250, rev. l. 8′ (URU.*tab*.URU); *ARAB* 2.25: Ambaris king of Bit-Purutash; 2.55: king of Tabal. For the location of Bit-Purutash, see J. D. Hawkins, "A

tions revealed that, in the eighth century, Tabal experienced a period of significant change in the degree of political cohesion, as is shown by the appearance of local inscriptions and rock reliefs found in the western Taurus. Tabal belonged to a contested periphery, subject to the competing foreign powers of Assyria, Phrygia, and Urartu.[64] The term Tabal was used for Assyrian administrative convenience, without any political meaning, because it encompassed several small states, having porous and shifting borders. Thus the exact location and extent of Tabal remain elusive. However, at the most, it was bound in the south by Que and Hilakku, in the west by Phrygia, in the north by the Halys river, and in the east by Gurgum, Kummuhu, Kammanu, and Urartu. This part of Anatolia was isolated, rugged, easy to defend, therefore making both internal political cohesion and external conquest difficult. Tabal was coveted because of its natural resources such as silver, alabaster, and wood, as well as its strategic position on the northern side of the Cilician Gates, controlling the eastern routes to the Anatolian plateau.

Tabal was the object of Assyrian aggression for the first time in the ninth century. In 836, Shalmaneser III made a campaign in Tabal, encountered a Tabalian king, Tuatti, with his son Kikki, and received submission from twenty kings of Tabal.[65] Tiglath-pileser III's inscriptions listed, in 738 and 732, several Tabalian tributary states, such as Tabal, Atunna, Tuhana, Istunda, and Hubishna.[66] The Tabalian states were inclined to fight among themselves, which was more desirable than their unity from Assyria's point of view because this facilitated its own objectives in the region. Assyria could exploit the desire for power of local elites such as Hulli/Hullû (Luwian Hulis), who could remain independent but used Assyrian backing to maintain his position.[67]

Hieroglyphic Hittite Inscription from Porsuk," *AnSt* 19 (1969): 107–8. On Neo-Hittite states, see Bryce, *World of the Neo-Hittite Kingdoms*.

64. Sarah C. Melville, "Kings of Tabal: Politics, Competition, and Conflict in a Contested Periphery," in *Rebellions and Peripheries in the Cuneiform World*, ed. Seth Richardson, AOS 91 (New Haven: American Oriental Society, 2010), 87–109.

65. Shigeo Yamada, *The Construction of the Assyrian Empire: A Historical Study of the Campaigns of Shalmaneser III (859–824 B.C.) Relating to His Campaigns to the West*, CHANE 3 (Leiden: Brill, 2000); *PNA* 3.2:1327.

66. *ARAB* 2.772, 801; J. D. Hawkins and J. N. Postgate, "Tribute from Tabal," *SAAB* 2 (1988): 36–37; Melville, "Kings of Tabal," 93–98.

67. Melville, "Kings of Tabal," 97 and n. 46.

Urartu and Phrygia, seeming intent on expanding into the Taurus region, represented a serious threat to Assyria's northwestern borders. It became a priority for Sargon to prevent a Phrygian-Urartian alliance. From Phrygia and Urartu's points of view, an Assyrian presence in Anatolia would represent a danger for both of them; therefore they plotted against Assyrian interests there. Sargon's strategy consisted of maintaining control over Tabal and Que in order to prevent easy communication between Phrygia and Urartu. During his whole reign, Tabal was subjected to pressure from these three powers, though it remained under Assyrian control. The existence of several foreign powers attempting to control Tabal increased the competition within and between the Tabalian states. Sargon was obliged to get more and more involved in Tabal. His inscriptions testify to the continuous progress in the international struggle to control Tabal.

He followed a deliberate "divide and conquer" strategy toward the Tabalian states. His first campaign in Tabal took place in 718 against Kiakki of Shinuhtu who had forgotten his oath, decided not to pay tribute anymore, and intrigued with Midas: "I overthrew Shinuhtu, his royal city, like a storm. Himself, together with his warriors, 7,350 people, his wife, his sons, his daughters, the people of his palace, together with much property, I reckoned as its booty," "I burned Kiakki, their king with the torch," then "Shinuhtu, his royal city, I gave to Mattî (Kurtî) of Atunna and imposed upon him (the payment of) more horses, mules, gold and silver than he had paid before."[68] Sargon deported the people of Shinuhtu to Assur. The ruler Kiyakiya, mentioned on a stela from Aksaray, seems to be the same as Kiakki and therefore, Shinuhtu can be identified with modern Aksaray.[69] Atunna has been identified with the site of Kululu because it is mentioned on many occasions in economic documents on lead strips found at this site.[70]

---

68. *ARAB* 2.7, 55, 80, 92, 99, 118, 137; *PNA* 1.2:431–32.

69. Mustafa Kalaç, "Niğde'de Bulunan Bir Havatanrısı Steli," in *VIII Türk Tarih Kongresi: Ankara, 11–15 Ekim 1976; Kongreye sunulan bildiriler* (Ankara: Turk Tarih Kurumu Basımevi, 1979), 239–43; J. D. Hawkins, "The Political Geography of North Syria and South-East Anatolia in the Neo-Assyrian Period," in Liverani, *Neo-Assyrian Geography*, 99; Melville, "Kings of Tabal," 95–96.

70. J. D. Hawkins, "The Kululu Lead Strips Economic Documents in Hieroglyphic Luwian," *AnSt* 37 (1987): 136–43; Hawkins, "Political Geography of North Syria," 99.

5. THE NORTHWEST OF THE EMPIRE

The letter of Sargon to Assur-sharru-usur ND 2759, dated from 715 (see above), described a military conflict between three vassals of Sargon: the kings of Atunna and Istunda on the one hand, and Urpalâ king of Tuhana on the other: "As to what you wrote: 'Urpalâ [*may slip away*] from the king my lord, on account of the fact that the Atunneans and Istuandeans came and took the cities of Bit-Paruta away from him'—now that the Phrygians have made peace with us and..., what can all the kings of Tabal do henceforth?... Move about as you please, do whatever you have to do ... until I come."[71] Urpalâ is known as Warpalawas from the epichoric hieroplyphic Luwian inscriptions of Tabal.[72] He is entitled "king of the city Tuwana (Tuhana, Tyana)," ruled from 738, and the distribution of his inscriptions indicates that he ruled the area of the Tyanites and controlled the upper end of the Cilician Gates. The situation described in Sargon's letter was complicated, but he was worried by the capture of villages belonging to Bit-Purutash by men from Atunna and Istunda. Once Midas had made peace with him, he knew that the Assyrians and the Phrygians together would be able to subdue these Tabalian states. For the time being, he let them fight between themselves and allowed his governor full scope for managing this affair until he came in person if necessary.[73]

Sargon had decided to encourage Tabal proper/Bit-Purutash in its claim of sovereignty over the other Tabalian states because he sought to control this area of fundamental strategic importance. Tiglath-pileser III had already replaced the royal clan with Hullî, "the son of nobody," after Uassurme had failed to pay tribute.[74] In 713 (year 9), Sargon restored Hullî to the throne of Tabal proper/Bit-Purutash, from which he had been removed by Shalmaneser V: "Hullî on his royal throne [I placed]. [The people of Bit-]Purutash I gathered together and put under his hand."[75] Then he replaced Hullî by his son Ambaris, without giving any reason: "Ambaris of Tabal, whom I had placed upon the throne of Hullî, his father,

---

71. SAA 1:6, no. 1, ll. 43–56; *PNA* 3.2:1417–18.

72. G. Galil, "Conflicts between Assyrian Vassals," 38–39; Hawkins, "Political Geography of North Syria," 99–100 (with bibliography).

73. Galil, "Conflicts between Assyrian Vassals," 56–58; Melville, "Kings of Tabal," 101–2; however, their analyses are based on a wrong date of the letter (709 instead of 715).

74. *ARAB* 1.802.

75. *ARAB* 2.24. See Fuchs, *Inschriften Sargons II*, Ann. 68–69, 194–95; Melville, "Kings of Tabal," 99–100 n. 51.

to whom I had given my daughter, together with the land of Hilakku, which did not belong to the territory of his father, and had extended his land."[76] By giving Ambaris his daughter Ahat-Abisha, Sargon raised him above the other vassal states in this area; it was possibly at that time that a diplomatic mission from Tabal received particularly rich gifts.[77] The fact that the dowry-land of Hilakku was not adjacent to the land of Bit-Purutash could suggest that he wanted to check any territorial ambitions Ambaris might have.[78] In distributing territories and powers among the Tabalian kings, he aimed at preventing any state from becoming too strong.

However, Ambaris plotted with Rusâ of Urartu, Midas of Phrygia, and other kings of Tabal to drive the Assyrians from the region. Sargon responded vigorously to the treason of Ambaris, "a foolish man, not keeping faith," in as much as he had forgotten the favors received: "Ambaris, together with his family, relatives, the seed of his father's house, the nobility of his land, I carried away to Assyria, together with 100 of his chariots. There I settled Assyrians, who feared my rulership, I set my officers and governors over them and imposed upon them tribute and tax."[79] He had resettled people of Tabal in the province of Parsua; although he said that he installed other conquered people in place of the Tabalian deported population, the archaeological evidence is lacking for the moment.[80] As far as we know, neither Phrygia nor Urartu sent any troops to aid their alleged ally. Several hypotheses have been proposed for identifying the officer put in charge of the new Assyrian province of Tabal, but none is convincing.[81]

Other Tabalian kings plotted against Assyria. In 718, Kurtî of Atunna had received the city of Shinuhtu, previously belonging to Kiakki (see above). Instead of feeling grateful to Sargon, he "⌜put his trust⌝ in [Mitâ] of Mushki."[82] The damaged prism fragment relating this event does not

---

76. *ARAB* 2.25, 55.

77. SAA 7:73–77, no. 58; *PNA* 3.2:1240.

78. Melville, "Kings of Tabal," 100.

79. *ARAB* 2.25, 55, 118, 214; Frame, "Inscription of Sargon II," 39–40, l. 22; Gadd, "Inscribed Prisms of Sargon II," 183, ll. 20–33.

80. SAA 15:36–37, no. 54; Sanna Aro, "Art and Architecture," in *The Luwians*, ed. H. Craig Melchert, HdO 68 (Leiden: Brill, 2003), 288–91.

81. Postgate, "Assyrian Texts and Fragments," 31; J. D. Hawkins, *Corpus of Hieroglyphic Luwian Inscriptions: Inscriptions of the Iron Age; Vol. 1, Part 2; Text, Amuq, Aleppo, Hama, Tabal, Assur Letters, Miscellaneous, Seals, Indices*, UISK 8.1 (Berlin: de Gruyter, 2000), 428 n. 46; Melville, "Kings of Tabal," 101.

82. *ARAB* 2.214; *PNA* 2.1:642.

enable historians to know at what moment between 718 and 713 he betrayed Sargon. However, Kurtî was a pragmatist and he returned posthaste to the Assyrian fold. He "saw the defeat of Am(ba)ris and the plundering of ... and his courage failed; [to (offer) payment of tribute and] tax, (to submit) to the yoke of Assur, they sent their messenger bearing a [friendly?] message to Sikris of the land of the Medes, into my presence and [kissed my feet]."[83]

However the removal of Ambaris and the annexation of Tabal as an Assyrian province did not solve Assyria's problems in Tabal. In 705, Sargon personally led an army to Tabal. This campaign is mentioned in the Babylonian Chronicle.[84] However, the Eponym Lists for 705 (year 17) mention a campaign against Gurdî the Kulummean.[85] The place of the battle is disputed: among others, it could have been at Til-Garimmu or in another place against the Cimmerians (see below).[86] Instead of reestablishing Assyrian supremacy over Tabal, the battle of 705 was lost by the Assyrians and resulted in Sargon's death. The withdrawal of Assyria, the increasing Cimmerian threat, and the decline of Urartu and Phrygia, freed the Tabalian states from the three imperial powers. Tabal became isolated again, and it also resulted in the disappearance of monuments and Luwian inscriptions from this area.

Gurgum

The Neo-Hittite kingdom of Gurgum had Markasi/Markasa (modern Marash) as its capital and is located west of Tabal and about 120 km northwest of Carchemish. Indications of the geography of Gurgum are given by some inscriptions. The stela of Pazarcik, on the Marash-Malatya road, bears an inscription of Adad-narari III and a secondary inscription of Shalmaneser IV; it records the establishment of the boundary (*tahūmu*) between Gurgum and Kummuhu by Adad-narari III after a battle dated to 805 BCE.[87] The Iran stela of Tiglath-pileser III also provides information on

---

83. *ARAB* 2.214.
84. Grayson, *Assyrian and Babylonian Chronicles*, 76, chr. I, ll. 6'-7'.
85. SAAS 2:60.
86. Melville, "Kings of Tabal," 103.
87. V. Donbaz, "Two Neo-Assyrian Stelae in the Antakya and Kahramanmaras Museums," *ARRIM* 8 (1990): 5–24; Manfred Weippert, "Die Feldzüge Adadnararis III.

this boundary.[88] The hieroglyphic inscriptions of Marash and its environs mention either the city of Gurgum or Markasi.[89] Gurgum was the western neighbor of Kummuhu, and its territory included principally the plain of Marash on an upper stretch of the Ceyhan where this river is joined by the Aksu coming down from Pazarcik. To the north, it is separated from the plain of Elbistan by high mountains. There is a rift valley running southward down the east side of the Amanus to the ʿAmuq plain. The small state of Samal, possibly turned into an Assyrian province by Shalmaneser V and not mentioned in Sargon's inscriptions, marked the end of Gurgum territory (see above).[90]

Gurgum was an Assyrian vassal kingdom, with new boundaries confirmed by Adad-narari III, then by Shalmaneser IV on the stela of Pazarcik. In his year 3 (742), Tiglath-pileser III repressed the Neo-Hittite alliance including Tarhu-lara, king of Gurgum.[91] Tarhu-lara was allowed to remain on the throne and he paid tribute to Assyria regularly.[92] However, the boundary of Gurgum was moved again in favor of Samal, as mentioned in the Panamuwa inscription: "and his lord Tiglath-pileser, king of Assyria, [added to] his territory towns from the territory of Gurgum."[93]

Sargon's activity in the region of Gurgum was essentially that of consolidation and fortification against two major powers: Phrygia and Urartu. King Tarhu-lara of Gurgum had a long reign, at least thirty-one years from 742, year 3 of Tiglath-pileser III, to 711, the date of Sargon's campaign against Gurgum. In Sargon's inscriptions, Gurgum is mentioned as a large country: "the whole territory of the wide land (*māt*) of Gurgum."[94] Bîtpaalla is also mentioned as a tribe or a land.[95] It could be the name of the

---

nach Syrien: Voraussetzungen, Verlauf, Folgen," *ZDPV* 108 (1992): 55–60; Hawkins, "Political Geography of North Syria," 93–94.

88. Levine, *Two Neo-Assyrian Stelae from Iran*, 11–24; RINAP 1:84–85, 35.i.25′–26′.

89. W. Röllig, "Maraş," *RlA* 3:703–4; J. D. Hawkins, "Marqas" *RlA* 7:352–53; Hawkins, "Political Geography of North Syria," 93–94 (with bibliography).

90. Hawkins, "Political Geography of North Syria," 101, fig. 1.

91. *ARAB* 1.769.

92. *ARAB* 1.769, 772, 797, 801.

93. *KAI*, 40, no. 215; J. C. L. Gibson, *Textbook of Syrian Semitic Inscriptions: 2, Aramaic Inscriptions; Including Inscriptions in the Dialect of Zenjirli* (Oxford: Oxford University Press, 1975), 80–81; see Galil, "Conflicts between Assyrian Vassals," 58.

94. *ARAB* 2.79, 92, 99.

95. *ARAB* 2.29, 61.

dynasty on the throne of Gurgum if Palalam (Laramas I) was regarded as the dynastic founder.[96] There are two different accounts of Sargon's campaign to Gurgum, either against Tarhu-lara or against his son Mutallu. Mutallu (in Assyrian) was the same as Muwatalis (in hieroglyphic Luwian), the name of several kings of Gurgum, in connection with the famous ruler of the Hittite imperial period, Muwattalli.[97] Mutallu of Gurgum must not been confused with the contemporary Mutallu of Kummuhu.[98] In a prism from Nimrud, Tarhu-lara, together with Tarhun-azi of Melid, did not favorably receive the favors given by Sargon and instead sent messages of hostility against Assyria to Midas. Sargon defeated the two kings: "with their wives, sons and daughters, gold, silver, property and possessions, the treasures of their palaces, together with the heavy spoils of their countries, I carried away to Assyria."[99] He settled anew Gurgum and Melid with Suteans and appointed his officer as governor, either for both or one of the two states, but the rest of the inscription is missing. The same campaign against Tarhu-lara is reported in the Display Inscription of Salon XIV, the Bull, and the Pavement inscriptions.[100]

However, in a damaged passage of the Annals dated from 711 (year 11) and in the Display Inscription, the account concerned the son, not the father: Mutallu slew Tarhu-lara "with the sword, and without my permission seated himself on the throne, and ruled his land."[101] Then the account is almost the same: Sargon defeated Mutallu and deported him with his family and his treasures into Assyria. He placed his officer as governor over Gurgum. This contradiction could be solved if there were two campaigns: the first one against Tarhu-lara before 711 and the second against Mutallu in 711. In fact, this previous first campaign is alluded to twice in the inscriptions, first in this sentence: "Tarhu-lara, of the city of Markasi, (in) whose kingdom I had brought order (out of) confusion," and second in the following sentence: "the people of Gurgum... I pardoned once more."[102]

---

96. Fuchs, *Inschriften Sargons II*, Ann. 238; Prunk. 86; 428; Robert M. Porter, "Dating the Neo-Hittite Kinglets of Gurgum/Maraş," *Anatolica* 29 (2003): 8.

97. Porter, "Dating the Neo-Hittite Kinglets," 8; *PNA* 3.2:1315, 2.2:785.

98. *ARAB* 2.27, 45, 64.

99. Gadd, "Inscribed Prisms of Sargon II," 183–84, ll. 49–66; *SAAS* 2:47; Frame, "New Cylinder Inscription," 67.

100. *ARAB* 2.79, 92, 99; Fuchs, *Inschriften Sargons II*, Ann. 237; Prunk. 83; XIV.10; S4.28; Stier 26.

101. *ARAB* 2.29, 61.

102. *ARAB* 2.29, 61; Gadd, "Inscribed Prisms of Sargon II," 183, ll. 43–44.

It is possible that Sargon first campaigned against Tarhu-lara reestablished order in Gurgum and submitted him without driving him out of the throne. But afterward, his son Mutallu slew his father and took the throne without Sargon's permission, behaving as a "foolish, wicked man." The Assyrian king was so angry that, in 711, he made a second important campaign: he captured Mutallu and bound his hands, suppressed the local dynasty and turned Gurgum into an Assyrian province. The scribes who summarized Sargon's campaigns in the last years of his reign could have confused the father and the son, and the two campaigns, the first one having passed off somewhat unnoticed. The hypothesis of Gadd, according to which Tarhu-lara was deposed in 712 and was then killed by his son in 711, is less likely because there was no interruption of the local dynasty.[103]

Kummuhu

Kummuhu (Kummuhi, Kummuh) was another Neo-Hittite kingdom, located in the region between Carchemish and Melid and known in classical times as Commagene.[104] It was both a land and a city in Sargon's inscriptions. For Sargon, Kummuhu was "in the Hittite-land" and its king, like those of Carchemish, Hamath, and Ashdod, were "wicked Hittites."[105] The natural boundaries of Kummuhu were fairly well defined. It was situated just north of the present border between Syria and Turkey. It is encircled to the east by the curve of the Euphrates and separated from the northern kingdom of Melid by a mountain range. The capital city of Kummuhu is identified with the modern city of Samsat (classical Samosata). The excavations of this important site have not been published, only reported in preliminary notices.[106] Unfortunately the site is now lost, having been flooded in 1989 by the waters of the Atatürk dam. The remains dating to the later kingdom of Commagene (163 BCE–72

---

103. Gadd, "Inscribed Prisms of Sargon II," 185.

104. J. D. Hawkins, "Kummuḫ," *RlA* 6:338–40; see *Qumaha* in the Urartian source, and *Kummaha* in Hittite Empire texts: Hawkins, "Political Geography of North Syria," 92.

105. *ARAB* 2.41, 69; Fuchs, *Inschriften Sargons II*, Stier 18; Rukiye Akdoğan and Andreas Fuchs, "Ein Inschriftenfragment Sargons II. im Museum zu Ankara," *ZA* 99 (2009): 82–86.

106. Machteld Mellink, "Archaeology in Asia Minor," *AJA* 84–95 (1980–1991); Jörg Wagner, ed., *Gottkönige am Euphrat: Neue Ausgrabungen und Forschungen in Kommagene* (Mainz: von Zabern, 2000), 74, fig. 99.

CE) are much better known than those of the kingdom of Kummuhu, in particular from the ruins of the mountaintop sanctuary of Nemrud Dag. The Malpinar rock inscription, in Luwian hieroglyphics, mentions the "city Kumaha."[107] The main local Luwian hieroglyphic inscriptions are those of Boybeypinari and Ancoz.[108]

The political boundary of Kummuhu to the south is not known. The districts of Kishtan and Halpi are mentioned in Tiglath-pileser III's inscriptions as belonging to the state of Kummuhu.[109] It is unclear how far along the Euphrates its territory extended. King Qatazili (Hattushili) of Kummuhu allied with the Assyrian kings Ashurnasirpal II and Shalmaneser III, and close relations continued with Adad-narari III who helped Ushpilulume (Shuppiluliuma) to protect his borders. The Assyrians established new boundaries, commemorated by boundary stones. The stela of Pazarcik, inscribed by Adad-narari III after 805, established the boundary between Kummuhu and Gurgum to the benefit of Kummuhu (see above). This boundary was confirmed on the stela by Shalmaneser IV in 773. However, Kushtashpi of Kummuhu was forced to accept the hegemony of Sarduri II of Urartu, according to a Urartian inscription of Turushpa.[110] When Tiglath-pileser III fought against the Neo-Hittite alliance, Kushtashpi proved himself a loyal ally of Assyria. As a consequence, after the defeat of Urartian forces and during the long conquest of Syria, Tiglath-pileser III used Kummuhean troops fighting as part of the Assyrian army. When Damascus became an Assyrian province in 732, two thousand warriors of the king of Kummuhu are mentioned as part of the Assyrian forces in this province.[111]

The close relations between Assyria and the kings of Kummuhu continued into the reign of Sargon. After the annexing of Carchemish in 717, of Kammanu in 712 and of Gurgum in 711, Kummuhu was the last remaining buffer state between Assyria and Urartu on the northwestern

---

107. Mustafa Kalaç and J. D. Hawkins, "The Hieroglyphic Luwian Rock-Inscription of Malpinar," *AnSt* 39 (1989): 107–12.

108. Hawkins, "Political Geography of North Syria," 93 (with bibliography).

109. *ARAB* 1.813; for their location, see Michael C. Astour, *The Arena of Tiglath-pileser III's Campaigns against Sarduri II (743 B.C.)*, Assur 2.3 (Malibu, CA: Undena, 1979), 9–14.

110. Karen Radner, "Hatti's Heirs: Kummuhi and the Other Neo-Hittite Kingdoms," in *Assyrian Empire Builders*, http://tinyurl.com/SBL1722g.

111. SAA 1:135, no. 172, ll. 27–28.

front. Sargon put so much trust in Mutallu, his ally of Kummuhu, that in 712 (year 10), he gave him the city of Melid and its surrounding area.[112] Suddenly, Mutallu withheld tribute and tax from Assyria and allied with Argishti II, king of Urartu; according to the Annals, it occurred in year 13 (709), while according to the Eponym Lists, it was in 708.[113] It is quite unclear why Mutallu of Kummuhu decided to break with the long-term alliance between Assyria and Kummuhu; according to Radner, it may have seemed the only way to preserve his kingdom's independence.[114] However, during the long period of good relations from the beginning of Sargon's reign and earlier, it is uncertain whether Mutallu was on the throne. The first year of attestation of his reign is 712. He was possibly a new king who, for some unknown reason, had decided to change his political stance toward Assyria. Sargon was very angry with this "wicked Hittite, who did not fear the name of the gods, a planner of evil, plotter of iniquity, (who) put his trust in Argishti, king of Urartu."[115] He sent Assyrian forces, including battle chariots and cavalry, against Mutallu. When the king of Kummuhu saw the approach of the expedition, he escaped from his city and was not seen anymore; it seems likely that he sought refuge in Urartu. As he was still alive, he represented, in Sargon's eyes, a risk for the loyalty of the Kummuheans toward Assyria. For example, he kept under close watch a group of augurs from Kummuhu, travelling with the Assyrian army.[116]

Sargon besieged and captured the capital city of Mutallu and sixty-two strong cities of his land. He took all Mutallu's family, his wife, sons, and daughters, as hostages to Nimrud, and deported the people of Kummuhu to the border of Elam.[117] He plundered the property, goods, and all kinds of valuables in Mutallu's palace. Kummuhu was annexed to Assyria and reorganized. He resettled it with Chaldeans from Bît-Yakin and put it under the control of his officer as governor (*turtānu šumēlu*, "commander-in-chief of the left"). He was thus resurrecting an ancient practice used by

---

112. *ARAB* 2.27; Fuchs, *Inschriften Sargons II*, Ann. 220–21; Lanfranchi, "Consensus to Empire," 81; Frame, "New Cylinder Inscription of Sargon," 67–68.

113. *ARAB* 2.64; SAAS 2:48.

114. Karen Radner, "Assyrians and Urartians," in *The Oxford Book of Ancient Anatolia, 10,000–323 B.C.E.*, ed. Sharon R. Steddman and Gregory McMahon (Oxford: Oxford University Press, 2011), 740.

115. *ARAB* 2.64; Fuchs, *Inschriften Sargons II*, Ann. 403–4.

116. SAA 5:122, no. 163.

117. *ARAB* 2.41; R. Campbell Thompson, "A Selection of the Cuneiform, Historical Texts from Nineveh (1927–32)," *Iraq* 7 (1940): 87–88, ll. 22–26.

Shalmaneser III, which consisted of appointing the highest military officers in areas where major conflicts were to be expected. He selected 150 chariots, 1,500 cavalry, 20,000 bowmen, and 1,000 shield (and) lance bearers and put them under the Assyrian governor's control. Even if Urartu had suffered a severe defeat in 714, its influence in the northwest had not disappeared. Therefore, losing the protection of the king of Kummuhu against Urartu was a damaging situation for Sargon. The transformation of the buffer kingdom of Kummuhu into an Assyrian province was clearly a far more cost-effective strategy. However, this new annexation represented an extension of the Assyrian Empire, which was another objective of Sargon. The region remained under the direct control of Assyria until the end of the Assyrian Empire and the conquest of the city of Kummuhu by Nebuchadnezzar II, who stationed a garrison there.

During the long period of good relations between Kummuhu and Assyria, there was an exchange of specialists between the two allied powers. This is attested by the presence of ritual experts in the ancient Anatolian art of augury from Kummuhu at the royal court of Nimrud where they conducted rituals on behalf of the Assyrian king.[118] Kummuhean troops fought as part of Assyrian army, as well. Cultural transfer is also attested from Assyria to Kummuhu, in the shape of rock reliefs, sculptured blocks and fragments, which is evidence for Assyrian sculptors, or at least for their influence.[119]

Kammanu/Melid

The "wide land" of Kammanu was another Neo-Hittite kingdom, located north of Kummuhu, comprising several cities, such as Til-Garimmu, usually identified with modern Gürün, and its royal city Melid/Melid-du.[120] This city on the Euphrates corresponds to the classical Melitene and

---

118. Radner, "Assyrian King and His Scholars," 232–33, 236.
119. Ibid.
120. *ARAB* 2.26; Fuchs, *Inschriften Sargons II*, 441; Marcella Frangipane, "Melid," *RlA* 8:42–52; Andreas Fuchs, "Sargon II," *RlA* 12:51–61. John Garstang and O. R. Gurney, *The Geography of the Hittite Empire* (London: British Institute of Archaeology at Ankara, 1959), 47; Fuchs, *Inschriften Sargons II*, 465; Simo Parpola and Michael Porter, *The Helsinki Atlas of the Near East in the Neo-Assyrian Period* (Helsinki: Neo-Assyrian Text Corpus Project, 2001), 17; Hawkins, "Political Geography of North Syria," 90, finds it best placed in the plain of Elbistan.

is identified with Arslantepe, 7 kilometers northeast of modern Malatya. The extent of the territory of Kammanu is defined by the Luwian hieroglyphic inscriptions, centered in the plain of Malatya on the west bank of the upper Euphrates, below the junction of the Kara-Su and Murad-Su branches. Westward, it extended along the routes to Anatolia and into the plain of Elbistan.[121]

Kuzi-Teshub, king of Carchemish, is mentioned in some inscriptions of Malatya as the grandfather in the genealogies of local rulers, where he is entitled "Great king, hero of Carchemish."[122] In the ninth century, the site of Melid attained high levels of monumental structures, and from Urartian and Assyrian inscriptions is known to have been a strategic kingdom and a flourishing cultural center.[123] Assyrian pressure was strong during the three campaigns of Shalmaneser III in 844, 836, and 835. However, during the first half of the eighth century, Assyrian pressure was replaced by Urartian pressure. Argishti I and Sarduri II defeated the ruler of Melid Khilaruata and forced him to pay tribute.[124] The political situation of Melid changed in 743, after the Kishtan battle won by Tiglath-pileser III over Sarduri II of Urartu and his allies, such as Melid. Thereafter, Melid was subject to Assyrian tribute. The ceremonial hall excavated in Melid, dated to ca. 750–710, corresponds to the period of Assyrian dominance after 743.[125]

Three inscriptions of Sargon have been found at Arslantepe/Melid, two under the pavement of an Assyrian palace, and a badly damaged cylinder fragment north of the mount, probably dated to or after 707, possibly mentioning the annexation of Melid.[126] Only one letter from Sargon's

---

121. Hawkins, "Political Geography of North Syria," 88–90.

122. J. D. Hawkins, "Kuzi-Tešub and the 'Great Kings' of Karkamiš," *AnSt* 38 (1988): 99–108; Hawkins, "Political Geography of North Syria," 88.

123. Marcella Frangipane and Mario Liverani, "Neo-Hittite Melid: Continuity or Discontinuity?," in *Across the Border: Late Bronze-Iron Age Relations between Syria and Anatolia*, ed. K. Alishan Yener, ANESSup 42 (Leuven: Peeters, 2013), 359–60.

124. Mario Liverani, "Melid in the Early and Middle Iron Age, Archaeology and History," in *The Ancient Near East in the Twelfth–Tenth Centuries BCE, Culture and History: Proceedings of the International Conference held at the University of Haifa, 2–5 May, 2010*, ed. Gershon Galil et al., AOAT 392 (Münster: Ugarit-Verlag, 2012), 340–41 (with bibliography); *PNA* 1.1:129–30.

125. Frangipane and Liverani, "Neo-Hittite Melid," 360.

126. As suggested by Andreas Fuchs; Frame, "New Cylinder Inscription of Sargon," 68–80.

reign mentions Melid, but regrettably, in a damaged context.[127] At the beginning of his reign, the kingdom of Kammanu, ruled by king Gunzinânu (Kunzinânu), was a loyal tributary state. At some point prior to 712, Sargon removed Gunzinânu from his royal city of Melid and put a new king, Tarhun-azi, on the throne.[128] He is designated as "Meliddean" and sometimes as "Kammanean."[129] His removal is briefly mentioned in the inscriptions, without giving the reason. However, it is stated that, under Tarhun-azi's reign, the people had to perform the same *ilku-* and *ṭupšikku-* duty as during the preceding reign.[130] This means that Gunzinânu had for a time acknowledged Assyrian overlordship, but had then done something regarded as treasonous to Assyria, possibly by ceasing to pay tribute. No doubt Sargon had chosen a king favorable to Assyria to replace him.

However, in 712 (year 10), after an undefined period of time, the new king Tarhun-azi also rebelled against Assyria. He broke his oath of loyalty to Sargon, stopped paying tribute, and sent to Midas, king of Phrygia, "hostile messages against Assyria."[131] The campaign against Melid in 712 is not mentioned in the Eponym Lists; Sargon is said to have stayed in Assyria and probably sent his commander-in-chief to march against Tarhun-azi. However, in the Annals, he could not relate one year without a campaign: "in the anger of my heart, I smashed Meliddu, his royal city, together with the cities of its environment, like pots."[132] As usual, his reaction was much more violent because the rebel had been chosen and installed on the throne by himself. Tarhun-azi fled to the city of Til-Garimmu, some 110 km northwest of Melid, if it has been correctly identified with modern Gürün. However, the people of Til-Garimmu, fearing Assyrian might, threw Tarhun-azi into fetters, opened the city gates, and surrendered to the Assyrian army. Sargon possibly destroyed Til-Garimmu because it is mentioned that, afterward, he "rebuilt" or "restored" this city. Together with Tarhun-azi, Sargon took his wife, his sons, his daughters, and five thousand fighters as captives to Assur. The kingdom of Kammanu was turned into an Assyrian province and put under the control of one of

---

127. SAA 1:149, no. 189, l. 13.
128. *ARAB* 2.26, 60; Fuchs, *Inschriften Sargons II*, Ann. 204–6; Stier 26–27; XIV 9–10; S4, 23–24; Frame, "New Cylinder Inscription of Sargon," 67.
129. Gadd, "Inscribed Prisms of Sargon II," 183, l. 59, 185.
130. *ARAB* 2.60.
131. *ARAB* 2.26.
132. *ARAB* 2.26, 60; SAAS 2:47, 60.

Sargon's eunuchs. It was resettled by "Suteans, archers (and) fighting men," people from the east who had been conquered by Sargon. He gave the city of Melid and its surrounding area to Mutallu, king of the neighboring state of Kummuhu (see above). Contrary to the Annals and the prisms from Nimrud, in other inscriptions of Sargon Gunzinânu is presented as the last king of Kammanu before the transformation of his kingdom into an Assyrian province: "Gunzinânu of Kammanu I tore out of Melid, his royal city, and over these lands (Neo-Hittite states), I sent governors."[133] It could be an error on the part of scribes who had confused the two kings of Kammanu: Gunzinânu and Tarhun-azi.[134] One building (A 1139+), dated ca. 710–680, could correspond to the short phase of Assyrian provincial presence in Melid after its conquest.[135] Sargon made substantial investments to protect the new Assyrian border, including the fortification of Til-Garimmu, and the construction of the so-called "Cappadocian wall." This wall is attested over a distance of more than 100 kilometers along the watershed between the Euphrates and the Halys.[136]

When, in 708, the kingdom of Kummuhu was turned into an Assyrian province after the rebellion of Mutallu, it is likely that the city of Melid, which Sargon had given to him, was retaken by Sargon, along with the land of Kummuhu. In 705, at Sargon's death, Melid may have fallen out of Assyrian control. The site began to decline afterward. Sennacherib campaigned against an independent Til-Garimmu in 695, but it is not certain whether it controlled Melid.[137] During the reign of Esarhaddon, it may have formed part of the kingdom of Tabal, under Mugallu, a king hostile to the Assyrians. The destruction of the site of Arslantepe in the late seventh century could possibly be attributed to the Cimmerians.

Even if the northwest of Sargon's empire did not represent a primordial goal for him, he was obliged to take interest in it for economic and strategic reasons. He wanted to exploit the forests of Amanus, the min-

---

133. *ARAB* 2.79, 92, 99.

134. For the identification of these two kings in the Luwian hieroglyphic inscriptions, see J. D. Hawkins, "Hittites and Assyrians at Melid (Malatya)," in Erkanal, *Relations between Anatolia and Mesopotamia*, 75.

135. Frangipane and Liverani, "Neo-Hittite Melid," 360; Liverani, "Melid in the Early and Middle Iron Age," 342–44.

136. Andreas Müller-Karpe, "Auf dem Rücken der Berge: Die kappadokische Mauer in Anatolien," *AW* 40.4 (2009): 21; Karen Radner, "Tabal and Phrygia: Problem Neighbours in the West," in *Assyrian Empire Builders*, http://tinyurl.com/SBL1722h.

137. Frangipane, "Melid," 42–52.

eral resources of the Taurus range and of Anatolia, and to use the Cilician fleets for his maritime battles. He was obliged to control the accesses to the inland riches, particularly via the Cilician and Amanus Gates. He had to prevent an alliance, by preventing contact, between two powers that were dangerous for Assyria: Phrygia and Urartu. The Neo-Hittite states were uncontrolled and turbulent states, difficult to reach in the mountains, at times allied, at times fiercely competitive. Sargon did not intend to conquer Phrygia, but only some areas taken by Midas that he considered important to conquer, such as Que because of its strategic position. His strategy consisted in relieving both Phrygian and Ionian pressure on Que. As for Phrygia, he was satisfied with the submission of Midas in 709. Sargon's behavior toward the northwestern states, which were so different from each other, depended on the attitude of the local kings, but he tried essentially to adapt himself to the various situations. Tabal was a group of several small dissimilar states. Sargon followed a "divide and conquer" strategy toward them, encouraging Bit-Purutash in its claim for sovereignty over all the Tabalian states. It was a failure, and he was obliged to annex the whole of Tabal as an Assyrian province, which did not solve the problems of this region. He was confronted with the rebellions of the kings of Gurgum and Kammanu, and was obliged to turn these kingdoms into Assyrian provinces, too. Even the kingdom of Kummuhu which, for a long time, had close relations with Assyria, finally rebelled against Sargon in 712; it also had to be annexed. These conquests meant that there were no more buffer states between Assyria and Urartu, but after the defeat of Urartu in 714, Sargon extended his empire in the northwest in order to prevent the remaining Urartian ambitions from controlling this area.

6

THE WARS IN THE NORTH OF THE EMPIRE

The political scene in the north of the Assyrian Empire was dominated by the powerful and concurrent kingdom of Urartu (fig. 5). The Assyrian capital Nineveh and the Urartian capital Turushpa were only about 240 km apart as the crow flies. But they were separated by the Oriental Taurus ridge culminating at more than 3,000 m and by a strip of buffer states, kingdoms, or provinces. Some of them were independent, others were under Assyrian or Urartian domination. From west to east, there were the following states: Shubria, Amidi, Tushhan, Ukku, Kumme, the Mashennu and Rab-Shaqe provinces, Mannea, Hubushkia, Musasir, and Mannea. It is difficult to study them otherwise than from an Assyrian or Urartian perspective because of the lack of autochthonous sources, both archival and monumental. These states, partly corresponding to the ancient Mittani, are described linguistically and culturally as Hurrian states.[1] The struggle between Sargon and the king of Urartu passed necessarily through them and brought them into total upheaval.

Shubria, Amidi, Tushhan

East of Kammanu/Melid was located the kingdom of Shubria (Shubarû, Shubru) and the birthplace of the Tigris.[2] Shubria was the Assyrian name,

---

1. Karen Radner, "Between a Rock and a Hard Place: Muṣaṣir, Kumme, Ukku and Šubria; the Buffer States between Assyria and Urarṭu," in *Biainili-Urartu: The Proceedings of The Symposium Held in Munich 12–14 October 2007*, ed. Stephan Kroll et al., Acta Iranica 51 (Leuven: Peeters, 2012), 243–64; Andreas Fuchs, "Urartu in der Zeit," in Kroll, *Biainili-Urartu*, 135–61.

2. Karlheinz Kessler, "Šubria, Urartu and Aššur: Topographical Questions around the Tigris Sources," in Liverani, *Neo-Assyrian Geography*, 55–62; Parker, *Mechanics of Empire*, 227–30; Radner, "Between a Rock and a Hard Place," 261–64.

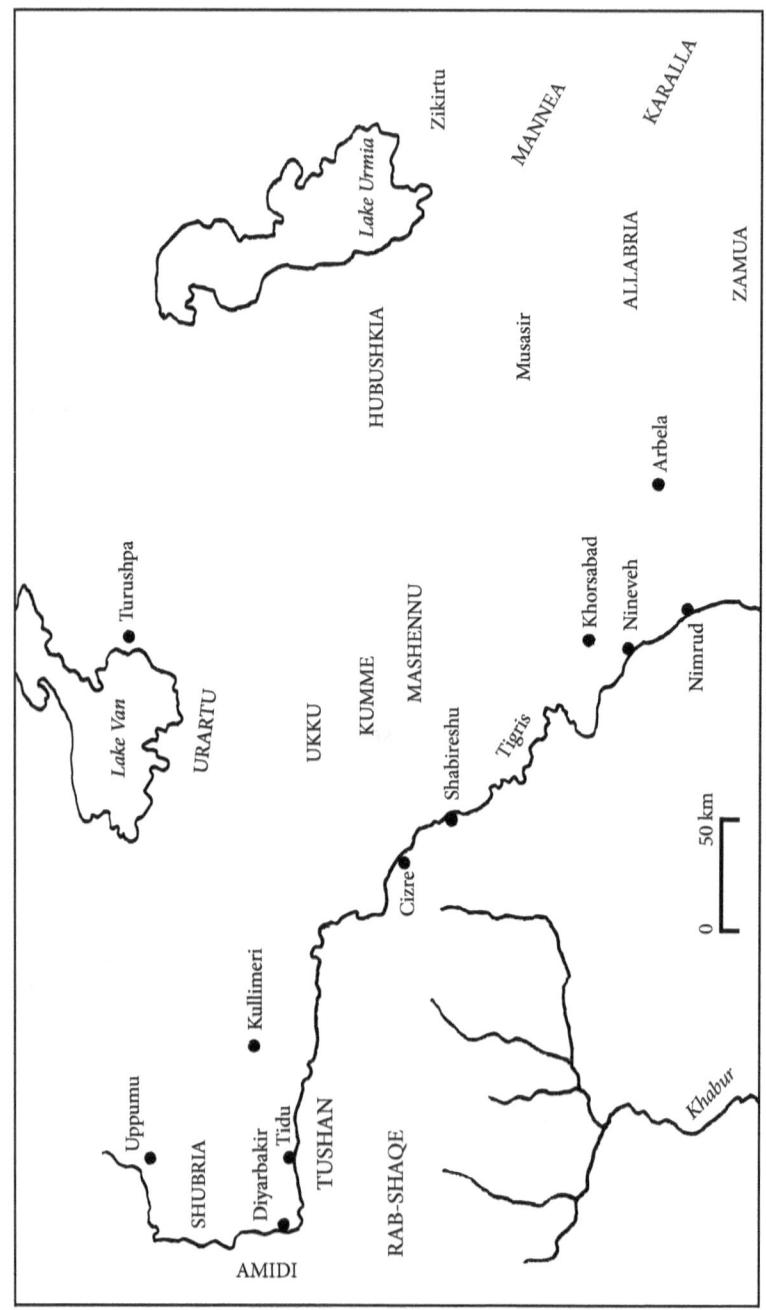

Fig. 5. The North of the Empire

designating a "northern country." The Urartians called it Qulmeri after its capital city (Kullimeri in Akkadian).[3] It could correspond to the corrupted form *klmd*, one of the trading partners of the Tyrians in the Bible (Ezek 17:23). Because of the lack of local sources, the name by which the inhabitants designated their country is unknown. Indeed, the Shubrian language was not understood by Assyrians, who required the assistance of interpreters.[4]

The kingdom of Shubria was situated in the mountainous area on the upper Tigris, stretching from the Tigris in the west to the mountain ranges in the north and the east that bordered on Urartu.[5] The western and southern boundaries of Shubria were the Tigris. The long frontier, common with Urartu, suggests that Shubria was under Urartian control. However, the fact that this frontier was mountainous with only a few connecting roads, often blocked in winter, probably limited this control.[6] The real danger for political control came from the south, that is, from Assyria. The rulers of Shubria succeeded in keeping their state independent until the reign of Esarhaddon, who annexed it. Their two prominent residences were, in Sargon's reign, Kullimeri and Uppumu/Pumu. Only the identification of Uppumu is fixed: modern Fum, near Lice, which controlled the important road used for crossing the difficult mountain range northward. There was possibly a refuge sanctuary at Uppumu, at the nearby Tigris Grotto, the riverine cave system at Birkleyn, represented on the Balawat Gates of Shalmaneser III.[7]

The proposals for identifying Kullimeri are uncertain; for example, the site of Grê Migro, or modern Arzen, or Silvan have been proposed.[8] In 673 Shubria was divided into western and eastern Assyrian provinces: Uppumu being located in the west, Kullimeri must be sought in the eastern part of Shubria. Kullimeri seems to have been the target of an Urartian campaign under the reign of king Minua, but this city was not mentioned in Assyrian inscriptions before Sargon's reign. Shubria was regarded by Sargon as a

---

3. I. M. Diakonoff and S. M. Kashkai, "Qulmēre," *RGTC* 9:69.
4. SAA 5:85–86, 147, 152, nos. 108, 203, 212.
5. Radner, "Between a Rock and a Hard Place," 260.
6. Kessler, "Šubria, Urartu and Aššur," 55.
7. Tamás Dezsó, "Šubria and the Assyrian Empire," *ActAnt* 46 (2006): 37; Radner, "Assyrians and Urartians," 744; Radner, "Between a Rock and a Hard Place," 264.
8. Kessler, "Šubria, Urartu and Aššur," 57–58; Radner, "Between a Rock and a Hard Place," 260–61.

fully independent state. It is difficult to say how relations with such entities were managed, as the relations depended on the rank between the different independent kingdoms. The prerogatives of the individual rulers enable their degree of independence and importance to be gauged. For example, King Hu-Teshub of Shubria was able to refuse the extradition of deserters to the Assyrian government, or to deny the consignment of timber cut in his territory to Assyrian officers.[9] This points to his total independence from Assyrian provincial government. However, the Assyrians were interested in the resources of Shubria, especially timber, and probably also metals.[10] Just like his predecessors, Sargon had an insatiable need for wood, which was needed to build his new capital Khorsabad. His relations with Shubria were probably comparable to his relations with other small more or less independent states: a treaty (*adū*) between the Assyrian king and the king of Shubria would have been the basis for Assyrian rights of access. Under this treaty, Shubria was seen by the Assyrian administration as belonging to the Assyrian zone of influence. The fact that the Assyrians were depleting the woodlands along the upper Tigris was a source of conflict between Sargon and his northern neighbors. Even if the Shubrians did not allow logging in their territory, and were sometimes at odds with the Assyrians, they were not asked for permission to cut timber; for example, Sha-Ashur-dubbu, governor of Tushhan, sent a cavalry-escorted logging team.[11] A report on the Shubrians of Kullimeri was sent to Sargon by Ashîpâ, possibly governor of Tushhan (see below).[12] During the reign of Sargon, the king of Shubria was Hu-Teshub, who had a Hurrian name. However, two other Shubrians named in the correspondence of Sargon had Aramean names. Shubria appears to have been a multiethnic state at that time made up of, among others, Hurrians, Arameans, and probably Urartians and Assyrians.[13] According to a fragmentary letter, "The Shubrian (king) is compiling a detailed report in Kullimeri"; the question is for whom he compiled that report: for Sargon or for the king of Urartu?[14] Tension between Assyria, Shubria, and Urartu, especially over logging,

---

9. SAA 5:xxi, 26–29, 46–47, nos. 33, 35, 52; *PNA* 2.1:483.
10. Parker, *Mechanics of Empire*, 230.
11. SAA 5:25–26, no. 32; *PNA* 3.2:1179–80.
12. SAA 5:21, no. 25; Parker, *Mechanics of Empire*, 222–23; *PNA* 1.1:142.
13. Parker, *Mechanics of Empire*, 230.
14. SAA 5:21, no. 25.

was so intense that it is difficult to answer the question. Shubria seems to have maintained a political balance between the two major powers.

Conversely, the two states of Amidi and Tushhan, south of Shubria, were Assyrian provinces. Amidi/Amadînu (ancient Bit-Zamani, classical Amida) was located some 50 kilometers west of Tushhan and is to be identified with modern Diyarbakir. This state was mentioned among the conquests of Tiglath-pileser III.[15] Several letters from Amidi, in the correspondence of Sargon, illustrate how important the Assyrian exploitation of timber was in this area. Assyrian cuneiform scribes were put at the local rulers' disposal to facilitate the required correspondence with Assyria. However, Assyrian language was not the only language used for the exchange of messages, even when communicating with Assyrian officials, as we know from a letter in Hurrian from the king of Shubria to an Assyrian magnate.[16] For example, one letter reported that one thousand two hundred door beams and one thousand two hundred roof beams had been floated down the Tigris; another letter referred to two thousand door beams and five hundred roof beams.[17] Even if much of the old forest growth in the provinces of Amidi and Tushhan had been greatly depleted before the Neo-Assyrian period, the extraction of timber could still continue in the mountains of the north during the reign of Sargon. The mountainous area just on the northern edge of Shubria, along the Murad-Su river and the border of Urartu, seems to have been one of the favorite areas for woodcutting at that time. Access to the forests and forwarding logs involved having to cross the territory of Amidi. The Assyrians encountered many difficulties because of the hilly ground, the conflicts between the small states, and the proximity of the Urartians. A road along the Murad-Su valley is possible in theory, but would have been dangerous because of the continuous clashes with the Urartians, who probably controlled huge sectors of the southern river valley. Although this region was undoubtedly claimed by the Urartians as being their own, the Assyrians still staked their claim to its economic exploitation. As it has not been

---

15. Parker, *Mechanics of Empire*, 59 and nn. 21–22, 228 and n. 1007.

16. SAA 5:29–30, no. 35.

17. SAA 5:6–8, nos. 5, 7. It is possible to have an idea of the number of trees necessary for Khorsabad by comparison with the Urartian fortress Ayanis in which forty thousand trees were used; see Altan A. Çilingiroğlu, "How Was an Urartian Fortress Built?," in *A View from the Highlands: Archaeological Studies in Honour of Charles Burney*, ed. Antonio Sagona, ANESSup 12 (Leuven: Peeters, 2004), 214.

extensively surveyed, it is impossible for the moment to identify the roads used for transport through Amidi, Tushhan, and Shubria.

Assyrian operations to obtain the precious wood for the building of Khorsabad are described in detail in a group of letters. The Assyrian governors of Amidi and Tushhan were the main actors. It appears that part of the area where the Assyrians cut their wood was claimed directly by the Urartians. This resulted in military clashes, as reported in some letters.[18]

A group of letters sent to Sargon by Liphur-Bêl, the governor of Amidi, dealt with wooden beams cut in the vicinity of Eziad, a settlement possibly taken from the Urartians by Tiglath-pileser III and added to the Amidi province. Eziad served as an Assyrian fortress with a garrison and watchtower under the jurisdiction of the governor of Amidi. This place was located near a river used as a route for transporting the logs but has not yet been identified. The Urartians were assembled in the fortified places on the other side of the Murad-Su River. Stone extraction was also conducted in this area under Sargon's reign. The cutting and transport of bull colossi or stone thresholds is attested by several letters, such as one sent by Liphur-Bêl, from Amidi; the long distance involved does not appear to have posed a major problem.[19]

The Assyrian province of Tushhan was located south of the kingdom of Shubria and east of the Assyrian province of Amidi. Its capital had the same name and corresponds to modern Ziyaret Tepe. A large number of letters from the correspondence of Sargon pertained directly to the administration and management of the province of Tushhan. Thirteen letters were written by Sha-Ashur-dubbu, governor of Tushhan and eponym in 707.[20] The other ten letters were written by Ashipâ, an official holding a high administrative position in the upper Tigris, probably also governor of Tushhan, at the beginning of Sargon's reign.[21] A new tablet found in the 2009 season of excavations at Ziyaret Tepe, in the governor's palace of the capital of Tushhan, gives evidence of a peripheral language in the late eighth century, with a variety of linguistic backgrounds (Assyrian, Hurrian, Luwian, and possibly Indo-Iranian).[22] Ashîpâ informed Sargon

---

18. SAA 5:6, nos. 5–6; Kessler, "Šubria, Urartu and Aššur," 62–64.
19. SAA 5:14, 91–94, nos. 17, 115, 117–18.
20. SAA 5:23-35, nos. 31–43; SAAS 2, nos. 48, 60; Parker, *Mechanics of Empire*, 222–23.
21. SAA 5:18-23, nos. 21–30.
22. John MacGinnis, "Evidence for a Peripheral Language in a Neo-Assyrian

mainly about the activities of the enemy state of Urartu and of the independent state of Shubria, beginning with the usual formula: "the forts and the land of the king my lord are well." One of the main preoccupations of Assyrian officials on the northern frontier was to gather military intelligence about Urartu. The possibility of a large-scale conflict between Assyria and Urartu was evoked by Ashîpâ; he was keeping watch because six Urartian governors had assembled their troops along the borders and he described Urartian troop movements. A fragmentary letter reported: "I have sent out (spies) to go and inquire; (when) they return with a detailed report, I shall write to the king, my lord." Ashîpâ denounced to Sargon the ambiguous policy of the king of Shubria, who seized and protected Urartian deserters on their way toward Assyria, while he held back Assyrian deserters and delayed their extradition with the excuse of illness.[23] In one letter, dated before the Assyrian campaign of 714, he mentioned that a messenger sent by Sargon had warned him of an impending attack from Urartu. For the Assyrian king's attention, he listed the preparations he had made for defense in supplies, the stationing of soldiers, and the protection of the local inhabitants and domesticated animals.[24] Several towns mentioned in the letters sent by the two governors of Tushhan to Sargon, such as Tasi (Tasa?), Penza, and Eziad, have not yet been located, as this region has not been extensively surveyed. Their localization partly depends upon the understanding of the network of routes used for military strategy and for the transport of timber and other goods toward Assyria.[25] Depending on whether Tasi and Penza belonged to the sphere of influence of different Assyrian provinces (formerly to the province of Amidi, later to the province of Tushhan), whether both once belonged to Urartu, and if there had been direct access to them via the kingdom of Shubria, it meant that control of the main route to the north via Uppumu was essential to the Assyrians.

Several letters in the correspondence of Ashîpâ and Sha-Ashur-dubbu to Sargon are related to the economy of the province of Tushhan. Some

---

Tablet from the Governor's Palace in Tušhan," *JNES* 71 (2012): 13–20; John MacGinnis and Timothy Matney, "Archaeology at the Frontiers: Excavating a Provincial Capital of the Assyrian Empire," *JAAS* 23 (2009): 1–21; MacGinnis and Matney, "Ziyaret Tepe: Digging the Frontier of the Assyrian Empire," *CWA* 37 (2009): 30–40.

23. SAA 5:18, 27–30, nos. 21, 34–35.
24. SAA 5:18, no. 21; Parker, *Mechanics of Empire*, 223–24.
25. Kessler, "Šubria, Urartu and Aššur," 63–67.

of them dealt with the problems of transport of wood beams, of fruit tree saplings for the royal parks, and of shipments of red wool and hewn stone objects to the Assyrian king.[26] Ashîpâ indicated the amount of straw available for the horses and pack animals of the Assyrian army; he also explained that since there had been little rain, he was obliged to sell his surplus straw to the deputy and all the village managers who had come down from the mountains to purchase it.[27]

Ukku, Kumme

When Tiglath-pileser III began to annex the strip of former vassal states and initiated their transformation into Assyrian provinces, he was reacting against the emergence of the rival power of Urartu that had led to the defection of his allies. However, the distinction between vassal states and Assyrian provinces continued to exist under Sargon's reign. Vassal states were allowed to keep their nominal independence, especially when they were situated in mountainous regions that impeded effecting and maintaining direct Assyrian control.[28] Ukku and Kumme were vassal states controlled by Sargon.

Ukku had a unique geographical and therefore political position. According to Sennacherib, it was located "behind Mount Nippur," north of the Cudi Dagi, in the region where the Turkish provinces of Siirt and Hakkari intersect.[29] Ukku could correspond to Hakkari and was situated exactly between Assyria and Urartu, opposite a Urartian province of unknown name, in one of the most rugged mountains areas in southeastern Turkey.[30] This geographic position gave Ukku its special political status. Permanent Assyrian control in Ukku was impracticable. Several letters in the correspondence of Sargon's reign indicated that snow and ice often blocked the mountain trails for a good part of the year. The high mountain passes were completely snowbound in winter, making the Assyrian army inefficient. Moreover, the transportation of siege machines, chariots, and other equipment across this arduous mountain would have

---

26. SAA 5:22–23, 26–29, nos. 27–29, 33–34.
27. SAA 5:18, no. 21; Parker, *Mechanics of Empire*, 224–27.
28. Karen Radner, "Representing Assyrian Interests in the Vassal States," in *Assyrian Empire Builders*, http://tinyurl.com/SBL1722i.
29. Parker, *The Mechanics of Empire*, 94–97.
30. Radner, "Between a Rock and a Hard Place," 257–60.

been very difficult and time consuming for the Assyrians. Another reason why Sargon did not want to annex Ukku was probably the proximity of this state to Urartu. Any Assyrian occupation of Ukku would have provoked direct confrontation between Assyria and Urartu. Sargon most certainly wanted to avoid such a situation in this logistically difficult zone. He considered it much more valuable to keep Ukku as a buffer state between Kumme, his loyal vassal, and the frontier of Urartu.

In 697, Sennacherib conducted a campaign against Maniye, king of Ukku, who fled: he "pursued the people dwelling therein who had like birds flown to the summit of the inaccessible mountains and defeated them at the summit."[31] A relief of Sennacherib's palace in Nineveh represented the city of Ukku, without fortifications but with buildings depicted as tower-like structures.[32] This small independent and peripheral state was an important component of the Assyrian geopolitical attitude toward the northern frontier. Beyond annexation and vassalage, Sargon's other method of control was the manipulation of independent states as buffers between Assyria and his enemies.

Although Ukku is mentioned in sixteen letters dated from Sargon's reign, the name of the king is not written; he is only referred to as "the Ukkean."[33] However, the crown prince was named Bazia, and king Maniye who was defeated by Sennacherib was possibly on the throne already, at least at the end of Sargon's reign. The letters of Ashur-rêsûwa, the royal delegate of Kumme, provide some information about the precarious situation of Ukku. This small state was beyond direct Assyrian control, so Assyria was forced to send spies to gather information. In a series of espionage letters, the Assyrians expressed great concern about communications between Ukku and Urartu. However, at the same time, Ukku probably had certain vassal obligations toward Urartu. For example, the Ukkeans had informed the Urartians about a fort that the Assyrians were constructing in Kumme. According to another letter, the king of Ukku had been sent by the Urartians to meet with the king of Kumme in order to persuade him to throw off the Assyrian yoke.[34] The two kings met in Elizki, a town located in a mountain pass between Ukku and Kumme, identified with

---

31. Luckenbill, *Annals of Sennacherib*, 37–38, 72; RINAP 3:117–18, 135, 152; *PNA* 2.2:677.
32. Radner, "Between a Rock and a Hard Place," 258–59 and fig. 17.07.
33. SAA 5:136, no. 190; Parker, *Mechanics of Empire*, 95 and n. 437.
34. SAA 1:44, no. 41.

the Süvrihalil pass, which shows that a neutral territory could exist even between small states.

After Sargon's campaign of 714 and the weakening of Urartu, it appears from the correspondence of his reign that the Ukkeans became more open to friendly relations with the Assyrians. It even appears that at this time Sargon tried to impose on the Ukkeans some vassal obligations such as tribute. There were also some Ukkean laborers serving the Assyrians; for example, one hundred Ukkeans, together with sixty Kummeans, are reported to be transporting logs for them.[35]

Kumme was a small realm, also located in the Taurus mountain range, in the upper reaches of the Lesser Khabur on the modern border between Turkey and Iraq, perhaps near the Turkish town of Beytüshshebap. It could be reached either by following the Lesser Khabur or by following the Hezil Cay and then crossing the Tanintanin pass to meet the Khabur at the village of Basharan.[36] The proximity of Zümrüt Kaplicalari ("emerald hot springs"), a thermal spring with water at a temperature of forty-four degrees Celsius, could fit with the location of the temple of the storm god Teshub of Kumme, one of the most important in the Near East and known from the time of Zimri-Lim of Mari.[37] The geographical proximity between Kumme and Ukku is clear from several letters of the correspondence of Sargon's reign.

Kumme was one of the small states to the north of Assyria that enjoyed the leadership of a local ruler. It had been allied with Assyria since the reign of Adad-narari II. However, at some point in Sargon's reign, Kumme was no longer a trusted ally but had become a full-fledged Assyrian vassal, possibly because it failed to check Urartu's expansion into the Cudi Dagi. It was ruled by Ariye and Ariazâ; it is not clear whether the latter was his son and crown prince or whether the two men were corulers.[38] They appear to have had separate jurisdictions because their subordinates were listed independently and they provided laborers separately to the Assyrians. However, Ariye was the superior, he was in charge of the city of Kumme where he maintained a palace, and he was named the "city lord" (*bēl āli*)

---

35. SAA 5:87, no. 111.

36. Radner, "Between a Rock and a Hard Place," 254–55 (with other proposals of localization).

37. Ibid., 256 (with bibliography).

38. SAA 5:175, no. 243; Parker, *Mechanics of Empire*, 90; PNA 1.1:130–31.

of Kumme.³⁹ This title was normally used to refer to recently subjugated vassal rulers, which is contradicted by the fact that Argishti II, the new king of Urartu, complained about not having received any greetings from Kumme since his accession, meaning a partial autonomy of this state, at least in Urartian eyes.

Ariye of Kumme had certain obligations to Sargon, guaranteed by a treaty: to supply manpower, horses, and timber, and mainly to provide intelligence reports on the other states of the region. His state was in an excellent strategic position; it was located on the direct mountain route leading from Assyria's heartland to the center of Urartu. At the same time, he entertained close relations with the king of Urartu and also provided him with men and information.⁴⁰ Ariye was in fact a "double spy"; he was encouraged by Sargon to be a spy working for Urartu because this was seen as a good way of gaining access to Urartu and gathering intelligence about it—the Assyrian system of espionage was highly efficient.

Unknown historical developments led to a change in relations between Kumme and Assyria and in the status of this state. Kumme was permanently controlled by the presence of an Assyrian ambassador (*qēpu*, "trustworthy man") at Ariye's court. This ambassador was Ashur-rêsûwa, whose seventeen letters have been preserved.⁴¹ He reported, for example, about the organization of timber transportation to Assyria; he provided information on Assyrian-Urartian espionage and counterespionage and unveiled a Urartian plan to kidnap Assyrian governors present in Kumme's territory. But some of his activities were perceived by many Kummeans as oppressive and invasive, for example, when he overinfluenced Ariye's decisions and considered Kumme's trade with Urartu as illegal. The financial burden that resulted from regular tribute payments to the Assyrians possibly also led to resentment by the local population. The letters reported a general uprising in Kumme, a murderous conflict with some local dignitaries. How this ended for Ashur-rêsûwa personally is unknown, but it resulted in a significant increase in Assyrian control. Kumme's autonomy was probably no longer respected. It is likely that this state was incorporated into the provincial system of the Assyrian Empire; Kumme was possibly too small to become a separate province, but was integrated in a larger administrative structure such as the neighboring

---

39. SAA 1:95, no. 117.
40. SAA 5:76–77, nos. 95, 105.
41. SAA 5:70–80, nos. 84–100.

Assyrian province of Birtu. Moreover, the fact that the Kummeans found themselves under the control of a mere cavalry officer was considered an insult. When Argishti II of Urartu questioned the conspicuous absence of messengers from Kumme at his court, he received the following answer from Kumme: "Since we are the slaves of Assyria, a foreman of the cavalry is our superior; only the houses of Kumme are left to us.... We cannot put our feet anywhere."[42] The fact that Kumme had an ancient and famous temple had not stopped Sargon. There is evidence that Kummeans were deported to Guzana.[43]

Forests still dominated much of the landscape in the mountains of Kumme, as in Ukku, and the Assyrians exploited these resources. It is known from the correspondence that Kummean laborers were helping the Assyrians fell trees, and that the Kummean king was sending saplings to be planted in Khorsabad. Letters also reveal some subtle means of resistance to Assyrian demands—openly rejecting Assyrian control would have been a dangerous course. For example, the Kummeans responsible for transporting the logs could dither and hesitate before complying with Assyrian demands.[44] Kumme was no longer mentioned in Assyrian sources after Sargon's reign, possibly because it was absorbed by the Assyrian province of Birtu, but it is uncertain whether Kummean independence was put to an end once and for all.[45]

The Mashennu and Rab-Shaqe Provinces

The Assyrian Mashennu province was located to the east of Kumme, including the Cizre plain that was annexed by Tiglath-pileser III. It should be remembered that Mashennu was the title of one of the Assyrian king's inner circle of high officials. These high officials had several duties, and in particular they were in charge of certain, sometimes volatile, provinces.[46] Therefore, some Assyrian provinces had no official geographical name but were instead referred to as *māt Mašennu*, "the province of the *Mashennu* (treasurer)," or *māt Rab šāqê*, "the province of the *Rab-Shaqe* (chief cupbearer)." The Assyrian governor of the Mashennu province during almost

---

42. SAA 5:76–77, no. 95, ll. 12–18.
43. SAA 1:95, no. 233.
44. Parker, *Mechanics of Empire*, 94.
45. Radner, "Between a Rock and a Hard Place," 257, doubts it.
46. Parker, *Mechanics of Empire*, 84.

6. THE WARS IN THE NORTH OF THE EMPIRE

the whole reign of Sargon was Tab-shar-Ashur. He held the office of the eponym in 717 BCE.[47] Thirty-four letters (probably even forty) can be attributed to him in the Sargonic corpus. Royal inscriptions (annals, stelae, and display inscriptions) and chronographic texts are lacking for the reconstruction of the history of the Mashennu province and other small northern states. Fortunately, a large group of letters dated to the reign of Sargon conveys information on the internal workings of the Assyrian empire, making for a more colorful and complicated record of this historical period. Tab-shar-Ashur was one of Sargon's highest and most trusted officials. He was not only governor of the Mashennu province, but also the chief coordinator and supervisor of the construction of Khorsabad.[48]

The Mashennu province was close to the state of Kumme, because its governor was closely involved in relations with Kumme and Ukku. Its capital was probably Shabireshu, an important city and road station; it is likely that this city should be equated with the site of Basorin Höyük in the Cizre plain.[49] However, Tab-shar-Ashur reported in a letter on the availability of timber along the upper stretches of the Greater Zab river; this would imply that the jurisdiction of the governor of this province had reached as far east as the headwaters of the Greater Zab river, in modern Iran.[50] The acquisition of timber was a major reason for incursions into these highland regions.

The correspondence of Tab-shar-Ashur provides precious information on the economy of his province and on his functions as governor of this province. The acquisition of timber was an Assyrian priority, especially during the construction of Khorsabad. The governor also ensured the cultivation of the fields in his province, the most productive being in the Cizre plain. He sent grain shipments to Assyria but was also responsible for providing the inhabitants of his province with food. He not only paid rations to regular soldiers, but also to villagers whose main occupation was farming and who served in the Assyrian army only in fulfillment of their corvée duty.[51] The correspondence of Tab-shar-Ashur informs us

---

47. SAAS 2, nos. 46, 60, 174.
48. According to Parpola, "Construction of Dur-Šarrukin, 51; *PNA* 3.2:1344–46.
49. Karlheinz Kessler, *Untersuchungen zur historischen Topographie Nordmesopotamien: Nach Keilschriftlichen Quellen Des 1. Jahrtausends V. Chr.*, TAVO 26 (Wiesbaden: Reichert, 1980), 122–49; Parker, *Mechanics of Empire*, 88.
50. SAA 1:58–59, no. 62.
51. Parker, *Mechanics of Empire*, 87 (with bibliography).

that governors and magnates were obliged to provide equipment, chariots (one hundred from the Mashennu province) and horses to the Assyrian army.⁵² It is difficult to know whether this equipment was intended for the troops stationed in the province or for an upcoming campaign in preparation. The Assyrian governor was also obliged to prepare for imminent campaigns by providing infrastructure, for example, by building a bridge to aid Sargon's Assyrian army in crossing a river.⁵³ He gathered military intelligence and controlled the activities of neighboring states, receiving reports from their rulers, for example, a Kummean report concerning a shipment of carnelian.⁵⁴ He was also responsible for the building and maintenance of outposts along the frontier. Thus, Sargon's campaigns relied heavily on the mobilization of resources from the provinces. Although the royal inscriptions give the impression that Sargon himself led nearly all the military expeditions, it was impossible to maintain a vast empire only by ideologically charged offensives conducted by the Assyrian king. The correspondence shows that governors, who had an array of military men and equipment at their disposal, conducted their own military expeditions in their provinces and even in distant areas. A fragmentary letter, probably written by Tab-shar-Ashur, mentioned a campaign in Mannea that he apparently directed.⁵⁵

It would appear that Tab-shar-Ashur probably did not remain governor of the Mashennu province until the end of Sargon's reign.⁵⁶ He was in all likelihood replaced late in Sargon's reign by Ashur-dûr-pânîya as the treasurer and governor of the Mashennu province, as is suggested in nine letters attributed to him.⁵⁷ Like his predecessor, he was in charge of the cutting and transportation of stones; he was involved in the allocation of work assignments and several letters were concerned with the problem of fugitives, which seems to have been particularly acute during his tenure. The Mashennu province probably still existed during Ashurbanipal's reign, as

---

52. SAA 1:47–48, nos. 48–49.
53. SAA 1:46–47, no. 47.
54. SAA 5:200, no. 284.
55. SAA 5:199, no. 282.
56. *PNA* 3.2:1344–46.
57. Parker, *Mechanics of Empire*, 88; *PNA* 1.1:180. For another interpretation, see SAA 5:38–48, nos. 45–53 (Letters from the Rab-Shaqe province).

it is mentioned in a lexical list of Neo-Assyrian provinces, generally dated from this time.[58]

Just like the Mashennu province, the Rab-Shaqe province was an Assyrian province under the control of a high official, the "chief cupbearer." Twelve letters written by Nadi-ilu, chief cupbearer of Sargon, are said to come from the Rab-Shaqe province.[59] Ten letters, written by Ashur-dûr-pânîya, are attributed to the same province.[60] In fact, as we have seen, this official was more probably the successor of Tab-shar-Ashur as governor of the Mashennu province at the end of Sargon's reign. However, the most difficult problem is the localization of the Rab-Shaqe province. According to some scholars, it was located in the Tur Abdin, a calcareous mountain in north Mesopotamia, flanked by two volcanoes: the Elim Dag at its eastern extremity and the Karaca Dag at its western extremity.[61] For other scholars, it was located much further to the east, somewhere in the Iranian Zagros; Bususu is said to be a town in the Rab-Shaqe province, but it has not yet been identified.[62] It is difficult to choose between these two hypotheses. The Rab-Shaqe province is mentioned in a lexical list of Neo-Assyrian provinces, which means that it still existed at the time of Ashurbanipal.[63]

Mannea

Before analyzing the Assyrian campaigns against the kingdom of Urartu, it is necessary to consider the kingdom of Mannea, which the Urartian king unceasingly tried to remove from Assyrian influence. Urartu and Mannea are often quoted together in Sargon's inscriptions.[64] One of the official reasons given by Sargon for justifying his campaign in the north was to help the loyal Manneans: "I restored quiet in the disrupted Mannean land"; "the

---

58. SAA 11:1, no. 1, l. 17, and xiii–xiv.
59. SAA 5:54–59, nos. 62–73.
60. SAA 5:46–53, nos. 52–61.
61. SAA 1:186, no. 238; SAA 5:40–48, nos. 46–53; Bradley J. Parker, "Garrisoning the Empire: Aspects of the Construction and Maintenance of Forts on the Assyrian Frontier," *Iraq* 59 (1997): 77–87.
62. Kessler, *Untersuchungen zur historischen Topographie*, 159–82; Parker, *Mechanics of Empire*, 88–89.
63. SAA 11:4, no. 1, I, l. 20.
64. E.g., *ARAB* 2.92, 99, 118.

harassed Manneans I caused to inhabit abodes of peace."[65] Mannea was in fact caught between the two major powers, Assyria and Urartu, and had more or less the following principle: my enemy's enemy is my friend.[66]

The kingdom of Mannea bordered the Assyrian provinces of Parsua and Bît-Hamban on the eastern flank of the Zagros, and of Zamua in the region of Sulaymaniyah in Iraqi Kurdistan. It occupied Iranian Kurdistan, western Azerbaijan, and a part of eastern Azerbaijan. Assyrian sources described Mannea as a country having many cities and fortresses, fine horsemanship, and prosperous agriculture. However, archaeological searches in Mannea are only now starting in Iran, Azerbaijan, and Kurdistan provinces at the sites of Qalaichi Tepe, Qale Bardine, Rabat Tepe, and Kul Tarike.[67] The first known discovery is the so-called stela of Bukân, which was found in Qalaichi Tepe.[68] The upper part of the stela is broken; the end of an Aramaic inscription is preserved. It is dated, on paleographic grounds, to the end of the eighth century. Its interpretation is still debated.[69] Among hypotheses, it could be a treaty or an alliance between a Mannean king and a possibly Syrian partner. One aspect of this riddle is the use of Aramaic script and language in this place at that time. What can be

---

65. *ARAB* 2.12, 79.

66. Karen Radner, "Mannea, a Forgotten Kingdom of Iran," in *Assyrian Empire Builders*, http://tinyurl.com/SBL1722j.

67. H. Rezvani and K. Roustaei, "A Preliminary Report on Two Seasons of Excavations at Kul Tarike Cemetery, Kurdistan, Iran," *IrAnt* 42 (2007): 139–84; Bahman Kargar and Ali Binandeh, "A Preliminary Report of Excavations at Rabat Tepe, Northwestern Iran," *IrAnt* 44 (2009): 113–29; Yousef Hassanzadeh, "Qalʻe Bardine, a Mannean Local Chiefdom in the Bukân Area, North-Western Iran," *AMIT* 41 (2009): 269–82; Y. Hassanzadeh and H. Mollasalehi, "New Evidence for Mannean Art: An Assessment of Three Glazed Tiles from Qalaichi (Izirtu)," in *Elam and Persia*, ed. Javier Alvarez-Mon and Mark B. Garrison (Winona Lake, IN: Eisenbrauns, 2011), 407–17.

68. Rasoul Bashash Kanzaq, "Lecture complète de l'inscription de Bukân," in *Recueil d'articles du 1er colloque: Langues, inscriptions et textes anciens, Shiraz 12–14 Esfand 1370 (2–4 mars 1991)* (Tehran, 1375/1996), 25–39; André Lemaire, "Une inscription araméenne du VIIIe siècle av. J.-C. trouvée à Bukân," *SIr* 27 (1998): 15–30; Lemaire, "L'inscription araméenne de Bukân et son intérêt historique," *CRAI* (1998): 293–300; Israel Ephʻal, "The Bukān Aramaic Inscription: Historical Considerations," *IEJ* 49 (1999): 116–21.

69. F. M. Fales, "Evidence for West-East Contacts in the Eighth Century BC: The Bukān Stele," in Lanfranchi, *Continuity of Empires (?) Assyria, Media, Persia*, ed. Giovanni B. Lanfranchi, Michael Roaf, and Robert Rollinger, HANE/M 5 (Padova: S.A.R.G.O.N., 2003), 131–47 (with bibliography).

said is that Aramaic was not routinely spoken in Mannea, as is attested by a letter mentioning the need for a Mannean interpreter at the Assyrian royal court, where Aramaic was understood.[70]

In the southern Urmia basin, Mannea encountered Urartian influence. Once Tiglath-pileser III had created Assyrian provinces in Iran in 744, the kingdom of Mannea found itself caught in a stranglehold between Urartu in the north and Assyria in the west and south. Iranzû, king of Mannea, became an Assyrian vassal from 744, paying an annual tribute of horses, cattle, and sheep. He needed Assyrian military aid against Urartian expansionism. Tiglath-pileser III proved to be a reliable protector when the Assyrian army defeated the Urartian forces in 743. In return, the alliance with Mannea, the most powerful state in the region, guaranteed protection to the new Assyrian provinces. Twice, in 744 and 737, Iranzû met the king of Assyria, as is specifically mentioned on a stela erected in Iran during his second campaign in this region.[71]

After the beginning of Sargon's reign, the close relationship between Assyria and Mannea continued. Iranzû was still king of Mannea until at least 719, during a long reign of more than twenty-five years. He remained a loyal vassal of Assyria and succeeded in preserving the unity of the kingdom of Mannea. Sargon appreciated the horses from Mannea, in particular the famous steeds from the eastern region of Mesu, which were crucially important for the Assyrian army. This importance emerged from a letter written by the crown prince Sennacherib: "A messenger of the Mannean (king) has come to me bringing a horse as the audience gift and giving me the regards of the Mannean. I dressed him (in purple) and put a silver bracelet on his arm."[72]

The political situation in Mannea changed in 719 due to the pressure of the two powerful neighbors' conflicts, which caused the kingdom's political fragmentation. Assyria no longer appeared to all Manneans as their protector against the incursions of their Urartian enemy. The Manneans became divided into two groups: one loyal to Assyria and the other openly favoring an alliance with Urartu. The anti-Assyrian faction was headed by Mitatti. A number of Mannean cities rebelled against King Iranzû and joined Mitatti. The status of Mitatti is not quite clear; he was not merely

---

70. SAA 11:29, no. 31.
71. RINAP 1:84.35i.15′–2′; 87.iii.24–30; *PNA* 2.1:563.
72. SAA 1:28–29, no. 29, ll. 22–26.

a subject of the Mannean king Iranzû, but his most dangerous rival.[73] Officially, Assyrian sources considered Zikirtu a Mannean province and Mitatti as the governor of Zikirtu, subject of Iranzû. Even if Mitatti was never called "king" of Zikirtu, the fact that his capital Parda was considered to be a royal city seems to point to him as a king. Most probably, in 719, there were two independent Mannean kingdoms, one pro-Assyrian and one pro-Urartian, each fighting for supremacy. King Iranzû may well have been old and could no longer maintain the unity of Mannea. Either he called on Sargon for help, or Sargon decided to come to his aid when he was informed of his critical situation. However, he did not hold a high opinion of Iranzû: "an obedient slave who bore my yoke."[74] The spread of the revolt was suppressed thanks to heavy Assyrian military aid. Sargon's campaign in year 3 (719) is described in detail in the Annals. Some Mannean cities rebelled, helped by Mitatti: "Shuandahul and Durdukka, strong cities, planned to fight against Iranzû, the Mannean, their king and lord, who was subject to me, and they put their trust in Mitatti of Zikirtu. Mitatti of Zikirtu gave them his warriors with their cavalry, and (this) aid was provided for them."[75] Sargon captured and burned these cities and smashed their fortified walls with battering rams, hence flattening them completely. Then he carried off the people and their possessions. Other Mannean cities committed a worse sin in his eyes: in their revolt against Iranzû, "they conceived a wicked plan of tearing up the roots of (their) land," and they came to terms with Rusâ I, king of Urartu. Sargon deported these populations "in Hatti of Amurru." An attack of the town of Pasashi, possibly Panzish, in 719 or 715, was represented in a relief of Sargon's palace.[76] A letter of Tab-shar-Ashur referred to this decorative program: "[The king, my lord], knows that our [previous] campaign which we directed against Mannea [is depicted] o[n the walls of] the ol[d] palace."[77] However, Zikirtu seceded from Mannea and became an independent state. Now the earlier Mannea kingdom was actually divided into two Mannean kingdoms: the Assyrian vassal state of Mannea having Izirti as its capital and the independent state of Zikirtu, allied with Urartu, with its capital city Parda.

---

73. *PNA* 2.1:563, 2.2:757.
74. *ARAB* 2.56.
75. *ARAB* 2.6.
76. Reade, "Sargon's Campaigns," 99.
77. SAA 5:199, no. 282, ll. 6–10.

The disintegration of the political unity of Mannea was amplified by the death of king Iranzû and the following war of succession. Iranzû had two sons: Azâ and Ullusunu. Sargon installed Azâ on the throne of Mannea, who reigned from 719 to 716, with the Assyrian approval.[78] But his brother Ullusunu contested his claim. A strong coalition of governors of the Manneans was formed against Azâ, supported by the Urartian king. In the ensuing battle between the two factions, Azâ was killed: "Rusâ, the Urartian, encouraged the men of Uishdish, Zikirtu, and Misiandu, the great chiefs of the Manneans, to revolt and hostility, and they cast the corpse of Azâ, their lord, out on Mount Uaush, a precipitous mountain."[79] The opposition set up Ullusunu, Azâ's brother, as king. Ullusunu placed his trust in King Rusâ of Urartu, and gave him twenty-two of his fortresses as a bribe. He also gained Ashur-lêi of Karalla and Ittî of Allabria as his allies against Sargon.

In 716 (year 6), Sargon conducted another campaign in Mannea, captured and burned several cities of Izirtu, the royal city of the Manneans. He captured Bag-dâti of Uishdish, flayed him, "and showed him to the Manneans." However, Ullusunu displayed political pragmatism and submitted to Sargon. The Assyrian king understood that it was in his best interest to forget Ullusunu's rebellion: "Ullusunu, the Mannean, and all of his land gathered together as one man and seized my feet. I had mercy upon them. I forgave his transgression, on the royal throne [I placed him]."[80] Sargon had proclaimed him king of Mannea. But Rusâ of Urartu quickly managed to turn the situation to his advantage. He confiscated twenty-two of Ullusunu's fortresses as booty. He pronounced words of suspicion against him and established another Mannean governor, Daiukku, as a new leader. He supported him and ensured his compliance by taking his son as hostage.[81] Sargon was obliged to conduct another campaign in Mannea in 715 (year 7) to restore the situation. He besieged and recaptured the twenty-two fortresses taken by the Urartians and returned them within the border of Assyria. He defeated Telusina of Andia and seized the province of Uishdish (Ugishti in the Urartian Annals). Daiukku and his family were captured

---

78. *PNA* 1.1:238.
79. *ARAB* 2.56.
80. *ARAB* 2.10 (Bag-dâti flayed in 716); *PNA* 1.2:251 (flayed in 714), 2.1:587–88, 3.2:1374–75.
81. *ARAB* 2.12–13; *PNA* 2.2:370.

and deported to Assyria. Sargon set up a stela proclaiming "the might of Assur in Izirti, the royal city of the Manneans."

In spite of Assyrian interventions, the problems were not solved and Urartu became more aggressive. Southern Urmia, on the Urartian border, was constantly troubled by military attacks, sometimes by Mannean troops on Urartian cities, sometimes by Urartian troops on Mannean cities. Mitatti ruled again over Zikirtu, in open contempt of Assyria, and made incursions into pro-Assyrian Mannean territory with Urartian military aid.[82] In 714 (year 8), Sargon conducted a new campaign, first to solve the problems of Urartian incursions into Mannea, then to fight directly against Urartu. The eighth campaign of Sargon is well-known from the Annals and other inscriptions, but mainly from his famous letter to "Assur, father of the gods," probably written by Nabû-shallimshunu, the royal scribe, in which he recounted the events of this campaign in detail. This letter is full of geographic details and written in an unusually rich prose. Between the opening epistolary formula and the colophon, the body of the report, 420 lines long, is made up of fifteen sections of unequal length, with ruled lines demarcating the sections. The different scholars writing about it do not agree on the purpose of this letter: an initial report on a military campaign to be abridged for the year-by-year edition of the Annals, an experimental text never meant for wide circulation, a letter intended to be actually read, a complex compositional history reflecting separate authors or differing historical circumstances.[83] The first phase of the campaign (episodes one to five) is concerned with Mannea and recounts Sargon's progress through the Zagros, collecting tribute from submissive vassal kings and rulers. In the campaign of 714, Sargon's army was not a fighting machine of war-hungry warriors, but a heterogeneous group of specialists who were rela-

---

82. SAA 1, no. 29; SAA 5:70, 101, nos. 84, 131.

83. François Thureau-Dangin, *Une relation de la huitième campagne de Sargon (714 av. J.-C.)*, TCL 3 (Paris: Geuthner, 1912); *ARAB* 2.139–78; A. Leo Oppenheim, "The City of Assur in 714 B.C.," *JNES* 19 (1960): 133–47; F. M. Fales, "Narrative and Ideological Variations in the Account of Sargon's Eighth Campaign," in Cogan, *Ah, Assyria*, 129–47; Louis D. Levine, "Observations on Sargon's Letter to the Gods," *ErIs* 27 (2003): 111*–19*; Kathryn F. Kravitz, "A Last-Minute Revision to Sargon's Letter to the Gods," *JNES* 62 (2003): 81–95; Victor A. Hurowitz, "'Shutting Up' the Enemy-Literary Gleanings from Sargon's Eighth Campaign," in *Treasures on Camels' Humps: Historical and Literary Studies from the Ancient Near East Presented to Israel Eph'al*, ed. Mordechai Cogan and Dan'el Kahn (Jerusalem: Magnes, 2008), 104–20; May, "Administrative and Other Reforms," 100.

tively rarely engaged in combat because they preferred to use intimidation, not brute force, to seize enemy settlements, and relied on speed, safety, and access to resources.[84]

Sargon intervened at the request of his vassal Ullusunu, king of Mannea, to drive back king Rusâ of Urartu, who had encroached on Ullusunu's territory. Among the kings that he met, some were submissive, friendly, groveling, or terrified, some were hostile and consequently defeated. Ullusunu received Sargon in his fortress of Sirdakku. He supplied flour and wine to feed the Assyrian army. He prostrated before Sargon and offered him large draft horses, cattle, and sheep as tribute. He delivered his eldest son to him, together with a peace offering, and inscribed his son's succession to the throne on a stela. Sargon promised Ullusunu and his nobles that he would overthrow Urartu, restore their boundaries, and pacify the distressed people of the Mannean land. This convivial meeting ended with a banquet: "Before Ullusunu, their king and lord, I spread a groaning banquet table, and exalted his throne high above that of Iranzû, the father who begot him. (The people of this land) I seated with the people of Assyria at a joyous banquet; before Assur and the gods of their land they did homage to my majesty."[85]

Sargon had a quite different attitude toward the other Mannean king of Zikirtu, the renegade Mitatti. The Assyrian army invaded Zikirtu, defeated the troops of Mitatti, some of them stationed in the mountain passes; he captured and destroyed many of his cities, battering them into heaps of ruins. Rusâ of Urartu came promptly to his ally Mitatti's aid, but in vain.[86] Their joint forces suffered a terrible defeat at the battle of Mount Uaush: "I filled the gullies and gorges with their horses while they, like ants in distress, made their way over most difficult trails."[87] What was the fate of Mitatti of Zikirtu after this defeat? "Parda, his royal city, I burned with fire, and he, together with the people of his land, ran away to be seen no more."[88] However, a diplomatic relationship was established with the probable new king of Zikirtu, controlled by an Assyrian representative, Issar-shumu-iqisha, who was installed there.[89]

---

84. Marriott and Radner, "Sustaining the Assyrian Army," 127–37.
85. *ARAB* 2.149.
86. SAA 5:123, no. 164; *PNA* 3.1:1054–57.
87. *ARAB* 2.155.
88. *ARAB* 2.19, 56.
89. SAA 5:125, no. 169; SAA 11:29, no. 31. There is no reason to think that the

In 713 (year 9), Sargon conducted an expedition against the rebels in the Persian mountains, in particular in Karalla. On his way, he received the tribute of Ullusunu, the Mannean king.[90] After Sargon's reign, Mannea had several conflicts with Assyria during the reigns of Esarhaddon and Ashurbanipal. But afterward, its fate much improved and, according to the Babylonian Chronicle, Mannea came to Assyria's aid in 616, in its confrontation on the Middle Euphrates with the Babylonian king Nabopolassar. However, it was not a success.[91]

Urartu

The name Urartu (Uruatri/Uratri) was the conventional name that Assyrians gave to this state, alternately with Nairi until the ninth century. But its self-designation was Biainili, a name preserved to the present day as "Van." The name Urartu lives on in the form of "Ararat," the highest mountain in the region (5,167 m), a dormant volcano, supposed to be the landing place of Noah's ark.[92] Relevant texts on Urartu are numerous but very unevenly distributed: Assyrian material is much more substantial and far more diverse in nature than the Urartian material.

The kingdom of Urartu was located to the north of Assyria; its capital Turushpa (or Tushpa), modern Van Kalesi, was situated on an impregnable rock high above saltwater Lake Van. Urartu occupied the mountainous area between and around the three lakes of Van in eastern Turkey, Urmia in northwestern Iran, and Sevan in Armenia, and the valley of the Murad-Su up to its confluence with the main branch of the Euphrates. Because of the high mountains, there was very limited access to this area. Coming from the south, that is from Assyria, there existed only a limited number of opportunities to cross the mountain barrier northward. The main road was the road from modern Lice to the valley of the Murad-Su and further to Bingöl. There remain some doubts as to whether the dif-

---

unnamed king of Zikirtu was Mitatti, with Radner, "Mannea, a Forgotten Kingdom of Iran."

90. *ARAB* 2.23–24.

91. Grayson, *Assyrian and Babylonian Chronicles*, 91, chron. 3, ll. 1–5.

92. Mirjo Salvini, *Nairi e Ur(u)atri: Contributo alla storia della formazione del regno di Urartu*, Incunabula Graeca 15 (Rome: Edizioni dell'Ateneo, 1967), 18–31; Joannès, *Dictionnaire de la civilisation mésopotamienne*, 882–85; Radner, "Assyrians and Urartians," 735.

ficult track from Hani via Karabegan (Mirvan) to Palu was much used in antiquity.[93] The difficulty of access to Urartu, protected by the mountains of oriental Taurus and Zagros, explains why it could not really be placed under Assyrian control. For the same reason, Urartu hesitated to penetrate into the Syrian plain and upper Mesopotamia.

Urartu had developed a prosperous agricultural economy thanks to the irrigation of the large fluvial valleys and by the breeding of horses in the high steppe areas. Its mining resources allowed the development of bronze and iron metallurgy. The Urartians had a military and political model similar to that of Assyria. They developed a policy of aggressive expansion founded on a powerful army. They conducted annual military campaigns, plundering, destroying, and deporting populations just like the Assyrians, sometimes with the same ferocity. Urartu was a centralized state with a net of vassal states paying tribute. The great expansion of Urartu started under the reigns of kings Ishpuini and Minua, who took advantage of the weakness of Assyria and subjugated Musasir, Parsua, Alzi, and Melid. Argishti I extended Urartian influence northward into Erebuni, modern Erevan, Assyria on the upper Euphrates, and in Arrapha. His son Sarduri II defeated the forces of Assur-narari V at Arpad in 754, striking a hard blow against Assyria's political standing in a region where the Assyrian king was formerly overlord and arbiter in all border conflicts. Tiglath-pileser III reversed the situation by the victory of 743 at the same place. The local rulers, considered untrustworthy, were replaced by loyal officers appointed directly by the Assyrian king as the head of the Assyrian provinces of Arpad, Hamath, and Ukku. The threat of Urartu on its northern border could have been one reason why Assyria replaced the system of vassals and allies by the creation of provinces under direct Assyrian control. The capture of Turushpa has been questioned: "In Turushpa, Sarduri's city, I shut him up and slew many of his warriors before his (city's) gates. My royal image I set up in front of Turushpa."[94] Sometime after 743, one of Tiglath-pileser's officers urged him to try again to seize Turushpa for

---

93. Kessler, "Šubria, Urartu and Aššur," 56; Joannès, *Dictionnaire de la civilisation mésopotamienne*, 883–84.

94. *ARAB* 1.785; M. Salvini, "Assyrie-Urartu: Guerres sans conquêtes," in *Guerre et conquête dans le Proche-Orient ancien: Actes de la table ronde du 14 novembre 1998 organisée par l'URA 1062 "Études sémitiques,"* ed. Laïla Nehmé, AntSem 4 (Paris: Maisonneuve, 1999), 55–58; RINAP 1:129, 156, 181.

glory, but the king of Assyria preferred to avoid any direct confrontation with Urartu for the remainder of his rule.[95]

In the light of the ongoing Assyrian expansion in the northwest in Sargon's reign, some northwestern states are known to have sought Urartu's protection against Assyria (see above). However, in most cases, these attempts seem to have been either unsuccessful or the diplomatic delegations never even reached their destination. This does not mean that Urartu had given up its expansionist policy. It was keeping quiet on the western front in order to concentrate its military presence in northeastern Iran where it attempted to replace Assyria as the overlord of its regional vassal kingdoms, such as Mannea and Zikirtu. This resulted in a period of sustained war from 719 to 714, which was fought neither in Assyria nor in Urartu; war was fought by proxy in Mannea and Zikirtu. The Urartian border was closely watched by Assyrian spies and Assyrian intelligence reports informed Sargon when Urartu encountered internal difficulties such as a revolt in Turushpa and an incursion of Cimmerians.[96] These events could explain why Sargon chose this moment for a definitive strike against his traditional enemy.

Cimmerians (Κιμμέριοι in Greek) were mentioned for the first time in Sargon's inscriptions. The provenance of these Cimmerian rider nomads is indicated in a letter of Sargon's correspondence: "The Cimmerian (king) has departed from Mannea [...] and entered Urartu."[97] This contradicts the assertion of Herodotus, saying that Cimmerians entered Anatolia coming from Caucasus (*Hist.* 4.11-12). According to the letter, they came from Mannea, that is, Iranian Kurdistan. The origin of Cimmerians was in central Transcaucasia.[98] The battle between the Urartians and Cimmerians is reported in four letters written by the crown prince Sennacherib and Ashur-rêsûwa.[99] Rusâ, king of Urartu, was defeated: "The troops of the Urartian king have been defeated on his expedition against the Cimmerians. The governor of Waisi has been killed; we do not have detailed information yet, but as soon as we have it, we will send you a full report." Eleven Urartian

---

95. Radner, "Assyrians and Urartians."
96. SAA 5:109, no. 144; Mirjo Salvini, "Sargon et l'Urartu," in Caubet, *Khorsabad, le palais de Sargon II*, 143–44.
97. SAA 5:109–10, no. 145; Salvini, "Sargon et l'Urartu," 143.
98. Askold I. Ivantchik, *Les Cimmériens au Proche-Orient*, OBO 127 (Fribourg: Presses Universitaires; Göttingen: Vandenhoeck & Ruprecht, 1993), 28.
99. SAA 1:29–33, nos. 30–32; SAA 5:75, no. 92; Ivantchik, *Cimmériens*, 30.

6. THE WARS IN THE NORTH OF THE EMPIRE

governors had been killed; two other governors had been taken prisoner by the Cimmerians. After their defeat, the Urartians feared an invasion by Sargon: "they are very much afraid of the king, my lord. They tremble and keep silent like women." What was the date of the Urartian defeat by the Cimmerians? It possibly occurred in 715 or spring 714, before the eighth campaign of Sargon in June 714.[100] Two other lacunary letters mentioned a conflict between Urartians and Cimmerians during Sargon's reign.[101] Both occurred earlier than 714; either this conflict is related to the fighting between Urartians and Cimmerians, or it concerned an earlier conflict.

Sargon, after the account of his outstanding victory of Mount Uaush against Rusâ and Mitatti, decided not to have dealings with Mannea anymore but to attack Urartu directly: "I stopped my march on Andia and Zikirtu which lay before me, and set my face toward Urartu."[102] Sargon's itinerary during this campaign cannot be reconstructed completely, in spite of the numerous geographical details given in the description of the campaign, because several toponyms are unknown and because some stipulations such as a march from "head" to "foot" of Urartu were mere figures of speech. Any reconstruction of the itinerary on the basis of the available facts involves choices between conflicting pieces of evidence.[103] Hypotheses on Sargon's itinerary fall into three categories: (1) he went north of both Lake Urmia and Lake Van, (2) he made a circuit of Lake Urmia only, (3) he approached the southern and western shores of Lake Urmia without circling either lake.[104] The third hypothesis is the most accepted one, for example by Levine.[105] The victory on the slopes of Mount Uaush was followed by a march through Urartian territory. The last stages of the eighth campaign, except for the unplanned diversion to Musasir, correspond to the second part of Shalmaneser III's expedition of 856.[106] Mount Uaush

---

100. Ivantchik, *Cimmériens*, 47; Salvini, "Sargon et l'Urartu," 143.

101. SAA 5:109–10, nos. 144–45; Ivantchik, *Cimmériens*, 47–51.

102. *ARAB* 2.157; Kravitz, "Last-Minute Revision to Sargon's Letter," 82–83.

103. Paul Zimansky, "Urartian Geography and Sargon's Eighth Campaign," *JNES* 49 (1990), 21.

104. Ibid., 4 (with bibliography).

105. Louis D. Levine, "Sargon's Eighth Campaign," in *Mountains and Lowlands: Essays in the Archaeology of Greater Mesopotamia*, ed. Louis D. Levine and T. Cuyler Young, BMes 7 (Malibu, CA: Undenaa, 1977), 135–51; Levine, "Observations on Sargon's Letter," 111*–19*; accepted by Salvini, "Sargon et l'Urartu," 133–57.

106. Mirjo Salvini, "Some Historic-Geographical Problems concerning Assyria and Urartu," in Liverani, *Neo-Assyrian Geography*, 46.

was located in the area of Uishdish, to the south of Lake Urmia, but its identification with Sahend to the east of Lake Urmia is no longer accepted. After Uishdish, the course of the campaign becomes difficult to determine. The next step was Subi, a border district considered as Urartian or Mannean, possibly the area bordering the southeast shore of Lake Urmia near Miyanduab. The city Ulhu, described as a model of Urartian architecture and organization, could be the enormous fortress of Sardurihurda, modern Qalatyah in the Godar Cay valley.[107] Then Sangibutu, which corresponded to one of the two following localities: Bit Sangibutu, a northeastern area near the Urartian border, or Bit Sangi, a more southeastern area along the route to Media or maybe the plain of Khoi. Then Armarili, which was the plain of Salmas, along the southern or eastern border of Urartu. Afterward, Sargon invaded the country of Ayadi, "on the shore of the sea, at the foot of great mountains (probably Lake Urmia)."[108] Then he crossed three rivers: Alluria, Qallania, and Innâ, probably in the plain of Urmia, which could have been Qasemlu Cay, Baranduz Cay, and Berdesur Cay.[109] The province of Uaiais, on the lower border of Urartu, near Nairi, could correspond to the plain of Urmia, controlled by the fortress of Qaleh Ismail Aqa, and other sites in the districts of Salmas and Khoi. It appears that Sargon did not want to penetrate further inside enemy territory. Therefore, he did not advance as far as the shore of the lake, probably because it becomes marshy north of the mouth of Nazlu Cay and the narrow passage between mountains and marshes is controlled by the fortresses of Qiz Qalek and Kuh-e Zambil. Sargon was facing two options: either to attack the heart of Urartu by capturing the capital Turushpa, or to go back to Assyria, considering mainly the economic benefit of the campaign. He considered the first option too risky for him and his army, and wisely chose the second.[110] On his return route, he attacked the fortress of Qaleh Ismail Aqa, the largest Urartian fortress located east of Zagros, and seized only the rear part (*kutallu*), as he killed the prisoners outside the fortress, before the main entrance, not inside.

---

107. Oscar W. Muscarella, "The Location of Ulhu and Uiše in Sargon II's Eighth Campaign, 714 B.C.," *JFA* 13 (1986): 465–75; Salvini, "Sargon et l'Urartu," 139; see Zimansky's objections, "Urartian Geography," 18.
108. *ARAB* 2.166.
109. *ARAB* 2.167; Salvini, "Sargon et l'Urartu," 139.
110. Salvini, "Sargon et l'Urartu," 140.

Rusâ, king of Urartu, the great enemy of Sargon, appeared only in some episodes. The first phase of the campaign culminated in the confrontation on Mount Uaush (episode five, lines 91–166). The account of the letter stressed Sargon's piety and heroism, in contrast to Rusâ's cowardice and ignominy. The parallelism between the two kings is lengthily and meticulously expressed by chosen words.[111] Rusâ did not observe the commands of the gods of Assur and Marduk while Sargon observed the oath of the gods Enlil and Marduk. Rusâ was a "mountain man, the seed of a murderous line"; Sargon was "the seed of Assur, the city of wisdom and broad understanding." Rusâ did not respect the oath of Enlil and every year did not fail to overstep his boundaries; Sargon respectfully adhered closely to the words of the great gods and never overstepped the boundaries the gods had set. Rusâ's lips babbled foolishness and vicious talk, he did not observe the solemn command of Shamash, the great judge of the gods, and had no common sense. In contrast, Sargon spoke well and honestly; he abhorred lies and did not pronounce wicked and treacherous words; he heeded the judgment of Shamash and was "the wise one among all kings." Sargon's masculinity as a great warrior contrasted with Rusâ who behaved "like a woman in labor." Rusâ was so afraid of the army of Assur who filled the ascents and descents of the mountains with the corpses of Urartian warriors, that he left Turushpa, his royal city, and fell ill: "he laid stretched on his bed, his mouth refusing food and drink; a fatal injury he inflicted upon himself."[112] At that moment of the letter, Rusâ seemingly dead, Sargon celebrated his victory with singers and musicians, and offered splendid sacrifices to his gods.

In the second phase of the campaign (episodes six through twelve, lines 167–305), Sargon advanced into Urartian territory, with no more confrontations with enemies. The whole country had been abandoned by the Urartian inhabitants, who had fled into the mountains. Quite uncharacteristic of Assyrian royal inscriptions, Sargon gave positive descriptions of the foreign civilization that he discovered there. In a respectful and even admiring manner, he described the enemy's palaces, fortresses, and irri-

---

111. *ARAB* 2.152–56; Marc Van de Mieroop, "A Study in Contrast: Sargon of Assyria and Rusa of Urartu," in *Opening the Tablet Box: Near Eastern Studies in Honor of Benjamin R. Foster*, ed. Sarah C. Melville and Alice L. Slotsky, CHANE 42 (Leiden: Brill, 2010), 417–34; van de Mieroop, "The Madness of King Rusa: The Psychology of Despair in Eighth Century Assyria," *JAH* 4 (2016): 16–39.

112. *ARAB* 2.155.

gation works: "A palace, a royal dwelling, he (Rusâ) built by the side of the river, for his enjoyment. With cypress beams he roofed it, and (thus) made the odor thereof pleasant."[113] There was another opposition between order and chaos, which made this letter unusual. The Assyrian troops devoured the abundant stores of food and destroyed all the magnificent palaces, mighty fortresses, irrigation works, and the rest, for example: "Into Ulhu, the store city of Rusâ, I entered triumphantly.... The mighty wall ... I smashed like a pot and leveled it to the ground." Sargon destroyed and burned the trees, the crops, the fields, the meadows, "and made their smoke cover the face of heaven like a cyclone." There is a narrative pattern that exhibits a distinct before-and-after: the condition of the enemy's cities before Sargon's arrival is contrasted with their condition after the Assyrian destruction. Several interpretations were proposed for explaining the opposition presented between order and chaos.[114] Whatever the explanation, one thing is clear: Sargon wanted to mask his failure not to have captured Rusâ.

Rusâ was not mentioned in the letter from line 152 to line 402. Then a passage at the end of the sack of Musasir is interpreted as a kind of decoronation of King Rusâ: "one statue of Rusâ, with two of his horsemen, (and) his charioteer, with their shrine, cast in bronze, on which was engraved his own haughty (inscription), 'With my two horses and one charioteer, my hand attained to the kingdom of Urartu'; (these things) together with his great wealth, which was without calculation, I carried off."[115] Rusâ heard of the sack of Musasir and committed suicide: "When Rusâ heard this, he threw himself on the ground, tore his clothes, and his arms hung limp. He ripped off his headband, pulled out his hair, pounded his chest with both hands, and threw himself flat on his face. His heart stopped and his liver burned. Screams of pain kept rising from his lips."[116] This description, using rare words and expressions, has no parallels in Assyrian royal inscriptions. However, the letter stopped just short of declaring Rusâ absolutely dead. In fact, the letter's account of the eighth campaign was driven by ideology and has to be corrected by other inscriptions. Thus, Sargon's Annals for the following year (year 9, 713) mention Rusâ as a potential

---

113. *ARAB* 2.161.
114. Kravitz, "Last-Minute Revision to Sargon's Letter," 92 (with bibliography).
115. *ARAB* 2.173; Van de Mieroop, "A Study in Contrast," 429.
116. *ARAB* 2.175; Van de Mieroop, "A Study in Contrast," 427.

participant in an anti-Assyrian conspiracy.[117] Other evidence supports Rusâ's continued presence on the scene after 714, at least for a time; he possibly retook Musasir after its sack by Sargon.[118] Exactly how soon Rusâ died after the eighth campaign is unknown but before 708, when his successor is mentioned. Other Sargon texts, dated to later in his reign, mentioned Rusâ's death, a suicide with his own dagger, when he probably actually died.[119]

Hubushkia, Musasir

On his return march from his eighth campaign, Sargon first went to the area of Hubushkia where he received the tribute of King Ianzû: "From Uaiais I departed, to the district of Ianzû, king of the Nairi-land, I drew near. Ianzû, king of Nairi, came to meet me from Hubushkia, his royal city, a distance of 4 *bêru*, and kissed my feet. His tribute, horses broken to the yoke, cattle, and sheep, I received from him in Hubushkia, his city."[120] According to the Annals, Sargon had received the tribute from King Ianzû on another occasion, in year 7 (715).[121] It was probably during his campaign of 715 to Mannea where he captured twenty-two fortresses taken by the Urartians (see above). However, the details of this campaign remain somewhat obscure because the Annals are fragmentary at this point. King Ianzû was the ruler of an independent kingdom. According to the royal inscriptions, he appeared as a loyal vassal of Assyria during the reign of Sargon. However, several letters in the Sargon correspondence indicate that the king of Hubushkia was apparently forced to change sides at least twice, depending on the pressure exerted on him in turn by each of the two powers, Urartu and Assyria. He marched together with Rusâ in his

---

117. *ARAB* 2.25.
118. SAA 5:xvii, xx; Kravitz, "Last-Minute Revision to Sargon's Letter," 94 (with bibliography).
119. Kravitz, "Last-Minute Revision to Sargon's Letter," 94 and n. 59; for a different view, see Michael Roaf, "Did Rusa Commit Suicide?," in *Organization, Representation, and Symbols of Power in the Ancient Near East: Proceedings of the Fifty-Fourth Rencontre assyriologique internationale at Würzburg, 20–25 July 2008*, ed. Gernot Wilhelm, RAI 54 (Winona Lake, IN: Eisenbrauns, 2012), 771–80; Roaf, "Could Rusa Son of Erimena Have Been King of Urartu during Sargon's Eighth Campaign?," in Kroll, *Biainili-Urartu*, 187–216.
120. *ARAB* 2.21, 56, 168.
121. *ARAB* 2.13; *PNA* 2.1:492.

military preparations. Then, in 715, he paid tribute to Sargon who visited his city or passed in its vicinity. He then cooperated with Rusâ before the battle on Mount Uaush. Finally, he went to pay tribute to Sargon at the end of the eighth campaign.[122]

There is a problem of location for both Nairi and Hubushkia. In Sargon's inscriptions, Nairi is presented as a country (KUR) and Hubushkia as a city (URU).[123] Earlier, the term "Nairi" was an equivalent of "Urartu" in Assyrian inscriptions and had a wide geographical spread in the late eighth century, but on his eighth campaign, Sargon was only concerned with a small part of Nairi, the area of Hubushkia, a city in Nairi-land. The location of this independent kingdom is still debated and various hypotheses have been proposed; among others, the basin of Bohtan-Su, the headwaters of the upper Zab, or the Khaneh plain.[124] Based on several sources, Hubushkia must be located not very far from the north of Assyria, toward the eastern rather than the western end of the northern boundary. Hubushkia was often associated with Musasir. On his return march in 714, Sargon proceeded from Uaiais to Hubushkia and then to Musasir, probably by following the route of Rawanduz. After departing from Uaiais, the Assyrian king received a deputation of his vassal Ianzû, who had marched from Hubushkia, his royal city, for four double hours (*bêru*), which means more than 40 kilometers (see below).[125] In contrast with this statement, it is then stated that Sargon received tribute in the city of Hubushkia: this could be a simple *topos*. The location of Hubushkia, royal city of the small kingdom of Nairi, was possibly in the region of the Dohan plain on the western fringes of the Zagros mountains.[126]

Three groups of sources concerning the sack of the sanctuary of Musasir have been preserved: Sargon's royal inscriptions describing his campaigns in the north, mainly his eighth campaign, Urartian royal

---

122. SAA 5:xviii and 97, no. 123.

123. Fuchs, *Inschriften Sargons II*, Ann. 104, 148; Prunk. 54; Frame, "New Cylinder Inscription," 72, l. 30; 74, 78 (Hubushkia: URU); Fuchs, *Inschriften Sargons II*, ibid. (Nairi: KUR). Walter Mayer, *Assyrien und Urartu I. Der Achte Feldzug Sargons II. im Jahr 714 v. Chr.*, AOAT 395/1 (Münster: Ugarit-Verlag, 2013), 152, 156.

124. Levine, "Sargon's Eighth Campaign," 143–44; Zimansky, "Urartian Geography," 19; Salvini, "Sargon et l'Urartu," 142, 147 n. 41; Giovanni B. Lanfranchi, "Assyrian Geography and Neo-Assyrian Letters: The Location of Hubuškia Again," in Liverani, *Neo-Assyrian Geography*, 127–37 (with bibliography).

125. *CAD* B, 208.

126. Karen Radner, *Assyrian Empire Builders*, http://tinyurl.com/SBL1722k.

inscriptions describing Rusâ I's invasion of Musasir, and letters of Sargon's correspondence related to military and cultic activities in Musasir.[127] The name of the sanctuary in Urartian sources was "Ardini," derived from Hurrian *arte-ni, "the city." The Assyrian name was "Musasir," derived from the region's designation as "Musru" in the inscriptions of Shalmaneser I and Tiglath-pileser I (thirteenth to eleventh century BCE). It was described as a "holy city founded in bedrock," having a sanctuary within its limits. However, the city was perhaps known locally under another name, as in the so-called Bukân stela, Musasir's deity Haldi is invoked in Aramaic as "Haldi of BS/Z'TR."[128] On an Assyrian cylinder seal belonging to Urzana, Musasir's king during Sargon's reign, Musasir is designated as "the city of the raven, of which, like a snake in difficult mountains, the mouth is open."[129] Musasir was already attested as a transregional center of considerable cultural influence centuries before the dynasty founded by Ishpuini in the late ninth century took control of Urartu.

Even if the general location of Musasir's territory is known, the identification of the site remains uncertain. From the itinerary of Sargon's campaign of 714, described in his Letter to Assur, Musasir should be situated somewhere in the impressive mountain range that had to be crossed when approaching from the region west of Lake Urmia in order to reach Assyria, on Sargon's return march from Urartu. Two bilingual stelae were erected by the Urartian kings Ishpuini, Minua, and by Rusâ I, one at the pass of Kelishin and the second at Topzawa; two other fragmentary stelae, possibly duplicates, were found at Mergeh Karvan and at Movana. These stelae

---

127. G. W. Vera Chamaza, "Der VIII Feldzug Sargons II. Eine Untersuchung zu Politik und Historischer Geographie des späten 8. Jhs. v. Chr. (I)," *AMI* 27 (1994): 91–92 (Assyrian royal inscriptions); Mirjo Salvini, "La bilingue urarteo-assiria di Rusa I," in *Tra lo Zagros e l'Urmia: Ricerche storiche ed archeologiche nell' Azerbaigian iraniano*, ed. Maria Rosaria Belgiorno, Paolo Emilio Pecorella, and Mirjo Salvini, Incunabula Graeca 78 (Rome: Edizioni dell'Ateneo, 1984), 79–96; N. V. Arutunjan, *Korpus Urartskich klinopisnych nadpisej* (Jerevan: Gitutjun, 2000) (Urartian royal inscriptions); Beatrice André-Salvini and Mirjo Salvini, "The Bilingual Stele of Rusa I from Movana (West-Azerbaijan, Iran)," *SMEA* 44 (2002): 5–66; SAA 5, xvii–xviii (Sargon's correspondence).

128. Radner, "Between a Rock and a Hard Place," 245–46 (with bibliography).

129. Thureau-Dangin, *Une relation de la huitième campagne de Sargon*, xii; Ralf-Bernhard Wartke, *Urartu: Das Reich am Ararat*, KAW 59 (Mainz: von Zabern, 1993); *PNA* 3.2:1420–21.

were possibly erected in the vicinity of Musasir.[130] The pass explicitly mentioned in Sargon's Letter to Assur should be identified between the Seko massif and the Baradost massif (Mount Andaruttu) connecting the valley of Mergazur with that of the Greater Zab. Musasir was separated from Assyria by the Baradost mountain range, and from Urartu by the main Zagros range (Mount Uaiais reaching over 3,600 m). The Baradost pass through the mountains was well suited for carrying the rich spoils taken by Sargon from Musasir to Assyria, including 6,110 people and hundreds of mules, cattle, and sheep. Any archaeologist working in the northern Zagros area would of course wish to discover Musasir. Excavations have been conducted since 2005 at Rabat Tepe, a settlement site some 15 kilometers northeast of Sardasht in the Iranian province of western Azerbaijan; the Iron Age remains discovered at this site have given rise to the hypothesis that they were the ruins of Musasir. Because of the apparent similarity of the two toponyms, some scholars suggested that Musasir should, instead, be identified with the fortified Iron Age site of Mudjesir, near Rawanduz and Topzawa, in the Soran district of the province of Erbil, and a survey was conducted there in 2015.[131]

Due to the location of Musasir between Assyria and Urartu, Urzana, king of Musasir, found himself caught between two empires. He first opted to ally with Assyria for a long time and was, at the beginning of Sargon's reign, a vassal of Assyria. However, Rusâ I, king of Urartu, could not tolerate such behavior any longer and promptly sent his army to intervene. In spite of Urzana's resistance, Rusâ captured Musasir and imposed a heavy tribute on its citizens; Urzana tried to flee to Assyria but was recaptured and reappointed to the throne in spite of his previous pro-Assyrian orientation. The Urartian military expedition against Musasir, described in the bilingual inscriptions of Rusâ of Topzawa and Mergeh Kervan, is to be dated sometime before Sargon's eighth campaign in 714. As a lunar eclipse was suggested by Sargon's remarks preceding the attack on Musasir, the date of that attack would have been 24 October 714 BCE, which left about one month for campaigning before the beginning of bad

---

130. Radner, "Between a Rock and a Hard Place," 247–50 (with bibliography).

131. Ibid., 251–54 (with bibliography); Dlshad A. Marf, "The Temple and the City of Muṣaṣir/Ardini: New Aspects in the Light of New Archaeological Evidence," *Subartu* 8 (2014): 18–29; Karen Radner, F. Janosch Kreppner, and Andrea Squitieri, *Exploring the Neo-Assyrian Frontier with Western Iran: The 2015 Season at Gird-i Bazar and Qalat-i Dinka*, PPP 1 (Gladbeck: PeWe-Verlag, 2016).

climatic conditions.[132] The elimination of Assyrian influence on Musasir was not well received in Assyria and is reflected in Sargon's Letter to Assur where he vilified Urzana: "a worker of sin and iniquity, who broke the oath by the gods and recognized no rule, a wicked mountaineer, who sinned against the oath taken by Assur, Shamash, Nabû, and Marduk, and revolted against me."[133] Sargon explained that Urzana's behavior had hastened the return march of his expedition because the king of Musasir failed to come bringing his gifts and kissing his feet, withheld his tribute, tax, and gifts, and not once did he send his messenger to greet him. The reason given in the letter for justifying the raid on Musasir seems to be a plausible explanation; yet the profit-earning perspective of plundering a very rich sanctuary could be another motivation. Sargon was furious and suddenly changed the course of his eighth campaign in order to invade Musasir. From Hubushkia, he dispatched the majority of the army home via the direct route. He, however, took with him a small picked force, did not follow the usual road to Musasir, but went across the mountains, in order to catch the city unaware.

This episode was therefore an appendage to the eighth campaign and also brought the campaign to its close. In fact, equal weight was accorded to the defeat of Rusâ of Urartu and to the despoliation of Urzana of Musasir: both were separate, but equal, highlights of the campaign. The Musasir narrative (lines 309–414) constituted the third and last phase of the campaign, with three scenes: the coronation scene, the god Haldi at the gate, and Rusâ's decoronation.[134] After Urzana's abandonment of his city, before the account of Sargon's entry into it and its plundering, the Letter to Assur described the coronation of the Urartian king, in Musasir, in the presence of god Haldi: "In the presence of Haldi, his god, (the people of Urartu) would set the crown of lordship on him, and the scepter of the kingship of Urartu they would give him to carry and his people would call out his name."[135] Musasir was not presented as Urzana's capital but as the abode of the Urartian kingship, the dwelling-place of Haldi, identified as the indispensable divine legitimator of Urartu's kingship. Is there any historical basis for the assertion that the Urartian coronation took place in Musasir, a small state outside the boundaries of Urartu proper? The Urartian capital

---

132. Oppenheim, "City of Assur," 137; Zimansky, "Urartian Geography," 21.
133. *ARAB* 2.169.
134. Kravitz, "Last-Minute Revision to Sargon's Letter," 81–88.
135. *ARAB* 2.171; Kravitz, "Last-Minute Revision to Sargon's Letter," 86.

Turushpa would seem a more likely site for the Urartian coronation, but documentation on this subject is lacking. External evidence supports Haldi's status as the principal god of the Urartian kings and the importance of Haldi's shrine in Musasir to the Urartian dynasty. Therefore, the assertion that the Urartian king was crowned in Musasir, whether true or not, would have seemed reasonable to a contemporary Assyrian audience.

The second scene of the account was related to Haldi at the gate. It interrupted Sargon's judgment concerning the fate of the citizens of Musasir: "regarding Haldi, the trust of Urartu, I ordered that he be brought out. Before the (city) gate, I victoriously sat him down."[136] The narrative created an image of Haldi as Sargon's captive. This god, who was sometimes referred to as "Urzana's god" and who had formerly presided over the Urartian coronation, was dragged from his temple and exhibited, as a simple captive, to the public. After having plundered the temple, Sargon then carried off Haldi and Bagbartu, his consort, to Assyria.[137] The narrative then seemed to be drawing to a close with the long and detailed booty list and the announcement that Musasir had been made an Assyrian province. However, it was interrupted by the third and final scene, with the sudden reappearance of Rusâ, king of Urartu: a scene of Rusâ's decoronation, in contrast to the first scene of the Urartian coronation. In reality, Rusâ was out of Assyrian reach when he heard of the sack of Musasir, and the description of his reaction more likely reflected wishful thinking than an eye-witness account by someone in Assyrian service.

Each of the three parts of the narrative—coronation, humiliation of Haldi, and Rusâ's de-coronation—conjured up a visual image linking Rusâ to Haldi and Musasir. It disrupted an otherwise coherent account of Urzana's flight and the sack of Musasir. It was impossible that the Letter to Assur ended by focusing on the list of riches carried off from Musasir. The author of the letter preferred to refocus at the end on Rusâ, Sargon's defeated Urartian rival. The conclusion had to adhere to the Assyrian ideology's heroic principle of royal omnipotence.[138] It had to make clear to the audience that Sargon had prevailed over Rusâ, Sargon's most significant adversary during his eighth campaign. In ideological terms, Sargon's sack of Musasir and his capture of Haldi had stripped the kingship of Urartu

---

136. *ARAB* 2.172.
137. *ARAB* 2.59, 173, 176, 183, 213.
138. Hayim Tadmor, "Propaganda, Literature, Historiography: Cracking the Code of the Assyrian Royal Inscriptions," in Parpola, *Assyria 1995*, 326–27.

of its divine legitimacy. Although Rusâ had escaped, due to an error committed by Sargon, his kingship had been deprived of its effective existence. The link between Rusâ's elimination and Haldi's capture was even more explicit in Sargon's Display Inscription, composed some seven years later.[139]

In fact, the Musasir booty itself testified to a long relationship between the Urartian dynasty and the shrine of Haldi, in particular the statues of the Urartian kings Sarduri, Argishti and Rusâ (lines 400–403), their votive gifts (line 401), and cultic equipment belonging to the kings of Urartu, used for offering sacrifices to Haldi, for example "11 cups of silver belonging to Rusâ" (lines 358, 398). Sargon spoiled not only the sanctuary of Musasir, but also the royal palace of Urzana, with their "treasure-houses," including all kinds of objects "which the enemies had carried off from city, palace and temple of Assur and Marduk, in countless quantities."[140] The vast quantity of spoils and the difficulty in bringing them back to Assyria were underlined by Sargon: "The property of the palace of Urzana and Haldi, together with their enormous wealth, which I carried off from the city of Musasir, I laid on (the backs) of my wide-spreading armies, in their immensity, and had them carry it into Assyria."[141] As he only had a small elite troop with him in Musasir, he probably called in the rest of his army to help carry the spoils. Even if the length of the list of spoils was exaggerated, Sargon was very proud of the plundering of Musasir, as is shown from its celebration, both in his official statements (mainly his Letter to Assur) and in the decoration of the most prominent Assyrian buildings: the facade of the Assur temple and the stone reliefs displayed on the walls of Room XIII in his palace of Khorsabad. The upper register in this room represented part of a siege in a mountainous country, and the lower register, damaged, showed the arrival of Sargon and his warriors in a city inhabited by men wearing animal skins, the sack of the city, and the Assyrians departing with their loot. The Haldi shrine is represented, with its unique roof construction and its facade decorated with shields, spears and statues. The figure caption reads: "I besieged and captured Musasir."[142]

---

139. Fuchs, *Inschriften Sargons II*, 215, ll. 76–77.
140. *ARAB* 2.174.
141. *ARAB* 2.175.
142. Reade, "Sargon's Campaigns," 98; Nicholas Gillmann, "Le temple de Musasir, une nouvelle tentative de restitution," *SAAB* 18 (2010): 245–63; Radner, "Between a Rock and a Hard Place," 252–53.

What status did Sargon give to Musasir after its capture? Urzana's family was deported, and the city was annexed to Assyria. However, once again, Urzana managed to be forgiven as Sargon reinstalled him on the throne of Musasir, apparently thinking Urzana's loyalty would be guaranteed by holding his family hostage. In reality, King Urzana was tightly controlled because the region was administered by Gabbu-ana-Ashur, the palace herald (*nāgir ekalli*) and his deputy Shulmu-bêli, who, together with Ashur-rêsûwa, the Assyrian delegate in Kumme, were responsible for monitoring Musasir. In a letter, Gabbu-ana-Ashur declared that "nobody may take part in the (religious) service (in Musasir) without the king's (Sargon's) permission."[143] The Assyrians prohibited a cultic gathering of local governors to prevent the fomenting of Urartian religious and nationalistic feelings and imposed a preemptive measure whose transgression would constitute a warning sign of increasing Urartian resistance. They also closely observed whether Urzana complied with the imposed yoke, involving such obligations as tribute delivery, summoning people, and making regular visits to Assyria. Nonfulfillment of any of these obligations needed to be adequately explained, in order not to be interpreted as a sign of disloyalty. For example, when Urzana delayed paying the tribute and giving regular homage to Sargon, he tried to justify himself by blaming the climate.[144]

Assyrian dominion over Musasir did not last very long however, as is shown from a group of undated letters, but which can be attributed to the period following the eighth campaign of 714. The clue for dating these letters is a letter of Urzana mentioning a previous visit of Sargon to his city, with a veiled reference to the sack of Musasir: "Could I hold him back? He did what he did."[145] The Urartians, initially led by Rusâ I, then by Argishti II, progressively recovered their control over Musasir, as can be seen from Sargon's correspondence. Thus, in one letter, Urzana described his desperation at seeing two Urartian governors disrespecting Sargon's order forbidding religious activities in Musasir: the governor of Waisi and the governor "next to the Ukkean" came and performed service in the temple of Haldi, and at the same time other governors were on their way to Musasir.[146] Therefore, Sargon gradually lost Assyria's control over Musasir once

---

143. SAA 5:111–12, no. 147, r., ll. 3–7; *PNA* 1.2:413–14, 3.2:1275.
144. SAA 5:105–7, 110–11, nos. 136, 139, 146.
145. SAA 5:xvii and 112, no. 147, ll. 10–11.
146. SAA 5:110–11, no. 147; Peter Dubovský, "Conquest and Reconquest of Muṣaṣir in the Eighth century BCE," *SAAB* 15 (2006): 143–44.

again. Connecting the events described in the letter of Urzana and those described in the Topzawa stela, Lanfranchi argued that Rusâ, shortly after the withdrawal of Sargon's troops, restored cultic activities in Musasir. The statue of Haldi was possibly returned to his temple in 713.[147] The reconquest of Musasir may have ended with some kind of purge.[148] A damaged passage in the Eponym Lists mentioned, for year 713, an uncertain event related with Musasir: "[the] nobles in Ellippa; ... entered his new house; [t]o Musasir."[149] However, there is no indication that Sargon intervened again in this region; he seems to have observed the progressive loss of Musasir through the eyes of his officials, sending alarmist reports to him on the evolution of the situation. One result of the capture of Haldi for the Urartian king was that, from that time onward, a series of Haldi temples were built in Urartu. Musasir was not the only ancient cult center and independent kingdom situated on the border region between Assyria and Urartu: the other one was the cultural center of Kumme, home of the storm god.

In the light of these different events, the original objectives of Sargon in his eighth campaign become clear. The account of this campaign in the Letter to Assur was driven by ideology and can be deciphered in the light of these events. Urartu was a major power facing Assyria, however a frontal attack would have been costly if not impossible.[150] After having neutralized the influence of Urartu on the northwestern front, the destruction of Urartu's power base north and northeast of Mannea, like Andia and Zikirtu, was sufficient to ensure the political objective of stability in the central Zagros, as was possibly the main objective of the campaign. In reality, this campaign was a monument to Sargon's military genius: he could deviate from his original design when the situation demanded, and turn the campaign so as to achieve a far greater impact than had originally been thought possible. It is significant that Urartu was not devastated, for no such effect can be seen.[151] Urartu continued to be a major power under kings Argishti II and Rusâ II, and the major building projects of

---

147. Oppenheim, "City of Assur," 145 and n. 22.
148. SAA 5:87, no. 112; Dubovský, "Conquest and Reconquest of Muṣaṣir," 145 and n. 10.
149. SAAS 2, nos. 47, 60.
150. Levine, "Sargon's Eighth Campaign," 149.
151. Boris B. Piotrovskij, *Urartu: The Kingdom of Van and its Art*, ed. Peter S. Gelling (London: Adams & Mackay, 1967).

enormous fortresses at Karmir Blur and Bastam can be ascribed to their reigns. However, it had to fight against the Cimmerian riders who devastated part of its territory. After 714, Urartu ceased to challenge Assyria in the Zagros. The importance of Sargon's eighth campaign was the end of the Assyrian-Urartian confrontation in the northeast, which was the Assyria's major military objective in this area. Even if, in 709, Urartu sent some troops south of its border with Kummuhu, the conflict between Assyria and Urartu had ended, without, to our knowledge, any formal peace treaty being concluded. As a matter of fact, to the Assyrian mind, Urartu was on the one hand the archenemy and eternal temptation for its northern vassals, but on the other hand it was a mirror image in the mountains, similar to Assyria with its administrative structure, referring to provinces and governors and using various specifically Assyrian titles for Urartian officers. Despite periods of tension between Assyria and Urartu, there were also opportunities for the exchange of goods, people, and ideas, in this region of intersecting cultures.[152]

---

152. Levine, "Sargon's Eighth Campaign," 149; Paul E. Zimansky, *Ecology and Empire: The Structure of the Urartian State*, SAOC 41 (Chicago: Oriental Institute of the University of Chicago, 1985), 89–94; Radner, "Assyrians and Urartians," 740–48.

7
Neutralization of the Eastern States

Continuing eastward and southeastward beyond Mannea, we reach the states and provinces of western Iran (fig. 6). From antiquity onward, conflicts occurred between the states of the Iranian plateau and those of the plain of Mesopotamia. Among the proposed etymologies, the country name "Iraq," in middle-Persian, meant the "low lands," compared with Iran, which is dominating the plain. The Iranian plateau is separated from the Mesopotamian plain by the large, long Zagros range extending from the mountains of Armenia in the north to the Gulf of Oman in the south. It culminates at more than 4,000 m and represents a barrier difficult to cross, in other words, a natural border between the modern countries of Iran and Iraq.[1] The central Zagros was inhabited by mountain dwellers, often considered as plunderers and unsubmissive people, designated by the general terms "Lullubi" and "Gutti." Assyria was always threatened by raids coming from Zagros populations; however, the political parceling of the different polities prevented them from becoming a serious danger. Among the polities of central Zagros, there were some vassals of Assyria and five Assyrian provinces, two of them created by Sargon. The precise status of Media—a powerful state or various small polities—is still in debate. Ellipi was a kingdom southward in Zagros, and still further south, Elam was an important power, dangerous for Assyria, mainly because of its alliance with Babylonia.

---

1. Louis D. Levine, "Geographical Studies in the Neo-Assyrian Zagros I," *Iran* 11 (1973): 14–27; Levine, "Geographical Studies in the Neo-Assyrian Zagros II," *Iran* 12 (1974): 99–105.

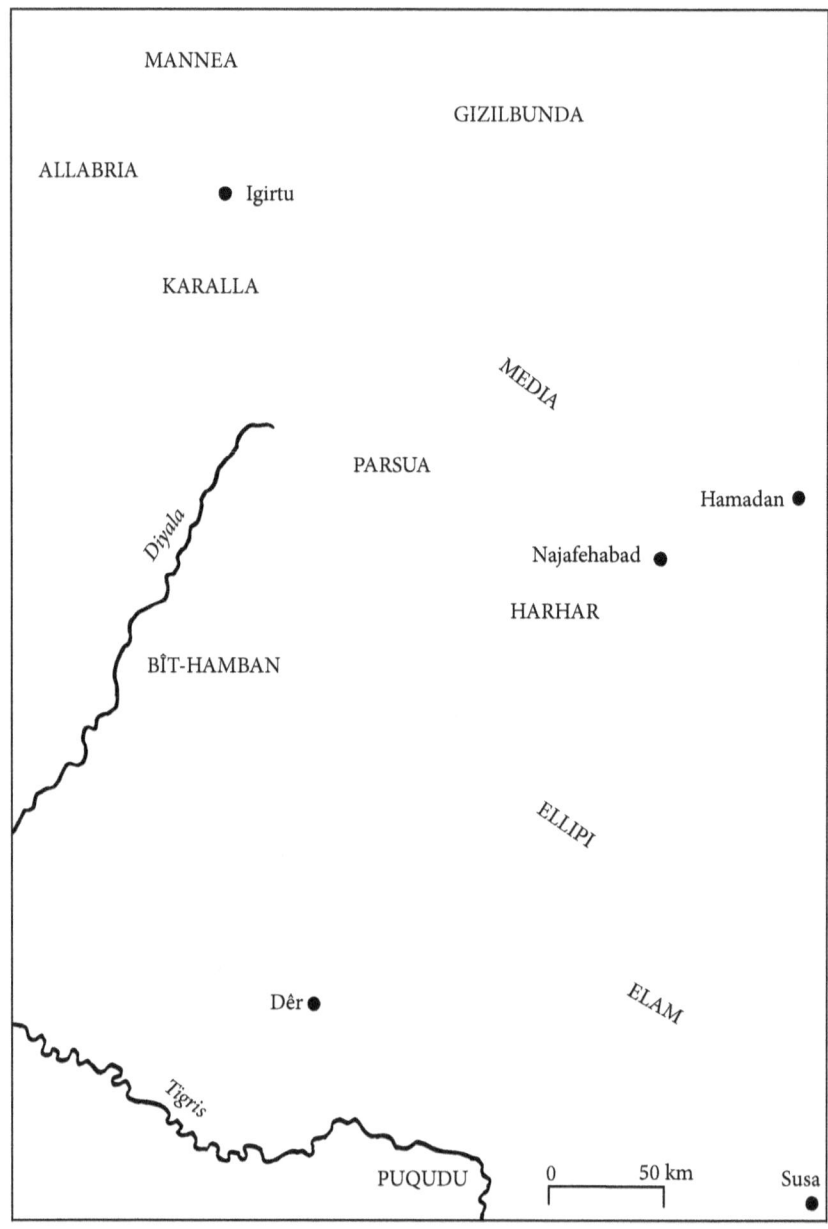

Fig. 6. The Eastern States

Central Zagros

The majority of the toponyms belonging to the Zagros and western Iran cannot be localized with certainty; their historical geography in the Neo-Assyrian period is still controversial.[2] The results of the proposals of localization are contradictory on many points and simply confirm the state of uncertainty.[3] Even when the localization of a toponym seems to be correct, neither the extension nor the borders of its territory are known; therefore, the maps can only indicate approximate political regions.[4]

It is necessary to take into account the cultural attitudes of the Assyrians toward the Zagros world in order to better understand their military and political actions. These attitudes probably also guided the choice of the institutional solutions which Sargon adopted in the regions annexed to his empire. It is important to establish to what extent they influenced the deviations from the standard annexation policy and the effects provoked in short- and long-term perspectives.[5] The inhabitants of the Zagros are presented in the Assyrian inscriptions as "bad" enemies who behave in various detestable and evil ways toward the "good" Assyrian king, but that was a general image for all the enemies of Assur. However, in the royal inscriptions of both Tiglath-pileser III and Sargon, there was a specific concept of ideologically oriented judgments about the nature, culture, lifestyle, and political institutions of the Zagros peoples. It consisted of a mixture of standard prejudices and factual observations. Assyrian elites considered the Zagros peoples as barbarians and the epithet "mountain dwellers" carried a strongly negative connotation: they had a subhuman nature and lacked any civilized character, as opposed to the inhabitants of the urbanized plain. The concept of mountain life was considered culturally inferior, as had already been proclaimed in the ancient Sumerian texts. For example, the inhabitants of the eastern mountains were stereotypically represented as wearing animal skins in the Assyrian palace iconography such as in the relief of the siege of Musasir (see above). The Assyrian

---

2. J. E. Reade, "Kassites and Iranians in Iran," *Iran* 16 (1978): 137–43; Reade, "Iran in the Neo-Assyrian Period Geography," in Liverani, *Neo-Assyrian Geography*, 31 (with bibliography).

3. SAA 15:xxiv.

4. See, e.g., Reade, "Iran in the Neo-Assyrian Period Geography," 37, fig. 5.

5. Giovanni B. Lanfranchi, "The Assyrian Expansion in the Zagros and the Local Ruling Elites," in Lanfranchi, *Continuity of Empire*, 81.

chancery also stressed that some Zagros polities, having a tribal or familial organization, were at a lower institutional level of development than Assyria. Since the lifestyle of Zagros populations was prevailingly determined by transhumant pastoralism, this mobility implied, from the Assyrian point of view, a lower level of civilization, and a primitive social status which was not regulated through a structured organization. This mobility suggested a certain degree of unlawfulness and, consequently, in a difficult geographical context, the impossibility to impose strict control and hence in practice, a regime of almost total impunity.

In the inscriptions of Sargon, the rulers of the Zagros polities were not designated by the title of *šarru* ("king"), but of *bēl āli*, conventionally translated as "city lord."[6] Lexically, it was not possible to equate the rulers of the Zagros with any other official structure in a rooted bureaucracy. It was necessary for the Assyrians to have an institutional definition and classification of the local ruling elites, which derived from the management of the annexed provinces. They were designated "city lords" because it was obviously impossible to call them "kings." In the other parts of the empire, in most of the annexed countries, the Assyrian governor replaced the local king and entered into an institutional relationship with the local bureaucracy. In large areas of the Zagros, it was different because the new Assyrian governor was faced with the preexisting village structure of his provincial territory and the local rulers connected with this structure. The local rulers were retained together with the Assyrian governor. There were relatively few deportations of populations in the Zagros as was customary in the other parts of the empire, where it was the main instrument for permanently and definitely securing annexations. Sargon did not consider deportations a necessary corollary of annexations in the Zagros. In fact, the mountains offered so many possibilities both for flight and for local resistance that it would have been very expensive or even impossible to catch a substantial part of the population in order to make an efficacious deportation. The emphasis in the inscriptions celebrating the successful capture of fugitives in the mountains shows the enduring difficulty in controlling the mountain territories effectively. The low capacity of resistance of the village-structured political system suggested to Sargon that it was not worth making an effort of radical stabilization; the costs of such an attempt would have been much greater than the expected results. That is

---

6. Fuchs, *Inschriften Sargons II*, Zyl. 33.

why he chose to have a tolerant approach to the local polities, which would have minimal negative effects on the establishment of Assyrian political supremacy. Therefore, the annexations in the Zagros were not carried out with the goal of establishing a strict territorial control of the type established, for example, in the west; that would have required profound social restructuring after their conquest.

If Sargon was aware that the polities of the Zagros, with their primitively structured society, could not seriously threaten Assyria and that the Zagros ruling elites were conscious of the Assyrian military superiority, why did he undertake to expand his empire in this area? The Assyrian expansion in the Zagros could clearly not be an answer to aggressions or dangers coming from the mountain peoples, as has been assumed by some scholars.[7] The main reason invoked is the Assyrian economic demands, which is not true since the Zagros regions had no specific products that could be considered worth the heavy costs of annexation. There were neither precious mineral resources nor stones, as in the Taurus and Amanus ranges. In his inscriptions, Sargon celebrated the mineral wealth of the western mountains, meaning indirectly that the eastern mountains were not considered productive in the same way.[8] Precious stones such as lapis, imported from Afghanistan, could be obtained through trade, gifts, or tribute. No precious wood like the renowned Amanus or Lebanon cedar is mentioned for Zagros. Besides, the costs of transporting wood from Zagros would have been very expensive. Cattle, sheep, and goats could be obtained through tribute and were available from other parts of the empire. The need for horses is often given as the main reason for Assyrian involvement in the Zagros, because they were useful for cavalry and chariotry, which were the main offensive elements in Sargon's army. However, horses could be bred elsewhere, in the provincial foothill regions, and horses from Zagros could be obtained through direct trade, as is attested since the reign of Tiglath-pileser III.

The reasons for the annexation of the difficult mountain territories of the Zagros can probably be explained by political needs.[9] It depended on specific emergencies in the international situation in which the potential role of the Zagros polities was considered to be crucial. Even if territorial

---

7. For the reasons given by different scholars, see Lanfranchi, "Assyrian Expansion in the Zagros," 96–104.

8. *ARAB* 2.28.

9. Lanfranchi, "The Assyrian Expansion in the Zagros," 98–104.

expansion was expensive by the requirement of garrison military forces, the most urgent need was the suppression of military support to the rival power, the recruitment of new allies, and the military aid. The prime aim of Sargon was to prevent the Zagros ruling elites from providing troops and horses to Urartu. The annexation occurred in the year that immediately preceded a direct confrontation of Sargon in the battlefield with Urartu. If he had not made an expansion in the polities of Zagros, those already allied with Urartu would have confirmed their alliance with it, those who were still independent would have entered into the Urartian sphere of influence, and those who had been loyal to Assyria would have changed their allegiance for Urartu. Therefore, Sargon tried to neutralize the polities of Zagros by giving them relatively mild conditions: almost no deportations while preserving the local rulers and institutional structures, even in the Assyrian provinces.

Among the small polities, some were vassals of Urartu, others were vassals of Assyria. Allabria was a small polity along the southern Mannean border. Ullusunu, the king of Mannea, had caused Ittî, the city lord of Allabria, to revolt against Sargon and called on him to become a vassal of Rusâ of Urartu. Sargon, in his campaign of 716 (year 6) in Mannea on his way to Media, defeated him: "Ittî, together with his family, I tore away, and settled them in Hamath."[10] However, in Prism B from Nineveh, this action is ascribed to 717 (year 5).[11] The new ruler of Allabria, Bêl-aplu-iddina, provided intelligence reports on Urartu to Sargon and brought him his tribute of horses, cattle, and sheep in 713 (year 9), during his campaign against the rebels in the Persian mountains.[12] Another small polity, Karalla/Karallu, was the neighbor of Allabria along the southern Mannean border. Ashur-lêi, its city lord, who was also influenced by Ullusunu of Mannea (see above), revolted against Sargon and made allegiance to Rusâ of Urartu. During the campaign of 716, more likely than 717, Sargon destroyed Karalla, flayed Ashur-lêi, and deported his people to Hamath.[13] He added Karalla and its district to the Assyrian province of Lullumî

---

10. *ARAB* 2.10, 56, 118; *PNA* 2.1:587–88, 3.2:1374–75.

11. *ARAB* 2.202; cf. Na'aman, "Historical Portion of Sargon," 19.

12. *ARAB* 2.24, 145, 210; *SAA* 5:164; *PNA* 1.2:286–87.

13. *ARAB* 2.56, 79, 92, 99, 118 (translation doubtful), 137, 183, 209; Frame, "Inscription of Sargon II," 37, 39, l. 16; Abraham and Klein, "New Sargon II Cylinder Fragment," 256; *PNA* 1.1:193.

(Zamua).¹⁴ The capture of Ashur-lêi of Karalla was considered by Sargon as an important exploit, representing it on a relief in his palace of Khorsabad, with the following inscription: "Ashur-lêi of Karalla, I bound hand and foot with iron fetters."¹⁵ The mention of the destruction of Karalla is followed, in the inscriptions, by that of Shurda and the submission of Adâ, its city lord.¹⁶ Sargon also captured Shêp-sharri, city lord of Shurgadia and added this city to the Assyrian province of Parsua.¹⁷ During the campaign of 713 (year 9), more likely than 714 (year 8), Sargon had to face a new revolt in Karalla: "The people of Karalla had driven out my officer and had made Amitashshi, brother of Ashur-lêi, ruler over them."¹⁸ Sargon defeated Amitashshi in Mount Ana and probably returned Karalla to the Assyrian province of Zamua (the inscription is damaged at this juncture). A list of toponyms and the inscription of Tang-i Var give the information that in 706 (year 16), Sargon stayed in Assyria, but that "his eunuch, the governor," possibly of Zamua, campaigned against Karalla; the inscription of Tang-i Var probably commemorated these Assyrian military actions in the land of Karalla.¹⁹

Gizilbunda was another small state in central Zagros, situated between Mannea and Media, as is mentioned in the Letter to Assur of Sargon: "a district, which is situated in remote mountains in a distant place, barring the way like a barricade in the region of the country of the Manneans and of the country of the Medes."²⁰ None of the previous kings had ever seen the dwelling place of their inhabitants, heard their name, or received their tribute. Two city lords of Gizilbunda, Zîzî of Appatar and Zalâ of Kitpatai, heard about the approach of Sargon during his eighth campaign in 714: "terror overcame them in their land, and they sent me their tribute, draft horses without number, cattle and sheep from their cities."²¹ The city lords of other small polities, such as Namri, Sangibuti, and Bît-Abadani,

---

14. Tadmor, "Campaigns of Sargon," 23–24; Levine, *Two Neo-Assyrian Stelae from Iran*, 38–39, ll. 31–32; SAA 15:xxiv.
15. *ARAB* 2.125; Reade, "Sargon's Campaigns," 98.
16. *ARAB* 2.23.
17. *ARAB* 2.10, 56; *PNA* 3.2:1261.
18. *ARAB* 2.79, 99, 118, 183; *PNA* 1.1:102.
19. SAAS 2:47, 60; Frame, "The Inscription of Sargon II," 37–38, 56.
20. *ARAB* 2.149.
21. *ARAB* 2.19, 149; Abraham and Klein, "New Sargon II Cylinder Fragment," 256; *PNA* 3.2:1433, 1447.

brought their tribute and submitted to Sargon when he was in the Assyrian province of Parsua.[22]

In fact, in central Zagros there were three Assyrian provinces that had been created before Sargon's reign. In the first half of the ninth century, Ashurnasirpal II had annexed various mountain valleys surrounding the Shehrizor basin, protesting that it was a reaction to the construction of a wall by a local ruler, blocking the pass leading to the mountains. He created the province of Zamua/Mazamua/Lullumî. He possibly wanted to deny Babylonia of important allies who, in the event of a conflict, might have represented a decisive element in the balance of power. In 744, during his second campaign, Tiglath-pileser III created two more provinces in central Zagros: Bît-Hamban and Parsua/Parsuash (future Parsu/amash, the modern Fars), west of Media and north of Ellipi, although their exact location is still debated.[23] Bît-Hamban was possibly situated where the Diyala River leaves the Zagros range and Parsua in the region of Sanandaj in Iran. During his eighth campaign in 714, Sargon crossed the Assyrian province of Zamua: "Into the passes of Mount Kullar, a high mountain range of the land of the Lullumî, which they (also) call the land of Zamua, I entered."[24] When necessary, he added to this province neighboring rebellious polities such as Karalla (see above).[25] One governor of Zamua was Sharru-êmuranni who was eponym in 712.[26] The administration of the Assyrian province of Zamua is well documented by twenty-eight letters from two governors in the correspondence of Sargon. Eleven letters were sent by the governor Sharru-êmuranni, and eleven other letters by the governor Adad-issêa. Three letters were sent by Nabû-hamâtûa, deputy governor, one by Nabû-ahu-usur, royal bodyguard, and two letters were sent by Kushkâiu to Nabû-hamâtûa.[27] One letter is particularly noteworthy, that of Adad-issêa, governor of Zamua; he described very precisely the Assyrian army present in this province, chariotry, cavalry, infantry, Assyrians and auxiliaries.[28] Sargon encountered some problems in the

---

22. *ARAB* 2.118, 146, 209.
23. See various hypotheses in Lanfranchi, "The Assyrian Expansion in the Zagros," 81–82 and n. 16.
24. *ARAB* 2.142.
25. *ARAB* 2.142, 208–9.
26. SAAS 2:47, 60; *PNA* 3.2:1234–37.
27. SAA 5:107–20, nos. 141–61; *PNA* 1.1:27, 2.1:644, 2.2:801, 833–34.
28. J. N. Postgate, "The Assyrian Army in Zamua," *Iraq* 62 (2000): 89–108.

province of Bît-Hamban because Kimirra, a city of this province, revolted against Assyria; he captured Kimirra in 715 (year 7) and inflicted severe punishment on this city by deporting its population.[29] Therefore, he presented himself as having conquered Bît-Hamban. He may have encountered some problems with Parsua too, because he presented himself as the conqueror of Parsua, and in 714, he did not simply cross Parsua, but "went down against Parsua."[30]

Sargon created two more provinces in central Zagros: Kishesim and Harhar. In 716, during his sixth campaign to Mannea, he had to face a revolt from Bêl-sharru-usur, the city lord of Kishesim: he "spoke untruths to the city chiefs surr[ounding him]," an accusation difficult to interpret.[31] Sargon severely repressed his revolt: "Bêl-sharru-usur, of the city of Kishesim, my hand captured and himself, together with the property of his palace, I carried off to Assyria."[32] He turned Kishesim into an Assyrian province. This military action was so important to him that he represented it on a relief of his palace of Khorsabad, with a short inscription: "The city of Kishesim."[33] He imposed the Assyrian gods on the city and renamed it Kâr-Nergal, making it a *kāru*, "harbor," "trading station," one of the places at the borders of the empire focusing on commercial connections with the outside world in order to control, supervise, and tax trading activities. He mentioned in the Annals that he set up a stela. As the precise location of Kishesim is unknown, a question is raised: was the Najafehabad stela set up in this place or elsewhere? Before the sentence "At that time I made a stela," two toponyms are mentioned in the inscription of the stela: Uratas and Urattus, unless it was the same one with two different spellings.[34] This toponym has not been identified and in any case the inscription is too lacunary to know whether it was related to the location of the stela. According to Frame, the place of the erection of the stela possibly reads *Kisasi*, which could be equated with Kishesim.[35] Renamed Kâr-Nergal, Kishesim became the center of a province that also included, among

---

29. *ARAB* 2.15, 118.
30. *ARAB* 2.10, 56, 118, 146, 148-49; Olmstead, *Western Asia in the Days of Sargon*, 123–26.
31. Levine, *Two Neo-Assyrian Stelae from Iran*, 38–39, l. 36; *PNA* 1.2:328–30.
32. *ARAB* 2.10, 56, 79, 92, 99, 183, 203.
33. *ARAB* 2.125; Albenda, *Palace of Sargon*, Room II, pl. 126.
34. Levine, *Two Neo-Assyrian Stelae from Iran*, 44–45, 50.
35. Frame, "Tell Acharneh Stela," 56–57.

others, the regions of Bît-Sagbat, Bît-Hirmani, and Bît-Umargi. Six letters in the correspondence of Sargon were written by Ashur-bêlu-usur, who was either the governor of Kishesim or the successor or predecessor of Nabû-rêmanni, governor of Parsua.[36]

The most important Assyrian stronghold in western Iran was the city of Harhar. In 719, the inhabitants of Harhar had dethroned their city lord Kibaba and had withheld their tribute, mainly horses, ever since. They had "sent word to Taltâ of Ellipi to be his vassals" (see below).[37] The rebellion of Harhar was probably caused by the disapproval of many city lords against the pro-Assyrian politics of some of them. According to the Annals, Sargon repressed the revolt of the inhabitants of Harhar: "That city I captured and I carried off its spoil. People of the lands my hand had conquered I settled therein. I set my official as governor."[38] However, in the Display Inscription, Kibaba, the city lord of Harhar, was no longer dethroned by the inhabitants but was the leader of the revolt and consequently punished by Sargon in 716: "Kibaba, governor of Harhar, I besieged, I captured."[39] Whatever the real account, all the inscriptions mentioned that he changed the name Harhar to Kâr-Sharrukîn. The king of Assyria was proud of the conquest of Harhar; he gave it his name and he represented its capture in a relief in his palace of Khorsabad, accompanied by a short inscription: "The city of Harhar."[40] It is possible that Harhar, located near modern Kermanshah, corresponds to modern Malayer.[41] However, the stela that he erected in Harhar after his victory has not been found. In 716 and also the following year, in 715, Sargon had conquered and renamed more cities, annexed to the new province of Harhar/Kâr-Sharrukîn. He renamed them in the same manner, with compound names beginning with "Kâr-": Kâr-Nabû, Kâr-Sîn, Kâr-Adad, and Kâr-Ishtar. A slightly different term was Bît-Kari, which could be explained by the fact that it was a border-region with all its warehouses

---

36. SAA 15:xxiv; *PNA* 1.1:174–75, 2.2:862–64.
37. *ARAB* 2.11; Karen Radner, "An Assyrian View on the Medes," in Lanfranchi, *Continuity of Empire*, 50; *PNA* 2.1:614, 2.2:815–17.
38. *ARAB* 2.11.
39. *ARAB* 2.57.
40. *ARAB* 2.125; Albenda, *Palace of Sargon*, Room II, pl. 112.
41. Karen Radner, "Harhar (Place)," in *Assyrian Empire Builders*, http://tinyurl.com/SBL17221.

(*kāru*), a kind of "trading colony."⁴² Twenty-eight letters in Sargon's correspondence were written, most of them, by two governors of Harhar: Nabû-belu-kain (seven letters) and Mannu-kî-Nînua (sixteen letters).⁴³ These letters provide interesting details on several subjects relating to how this Assyrian province functioned, such as the procedures of succession for a governor and his introduction to the native rulers of his province. To renew their oaths of loyalty (*adê*) to Assyria, the city lords did not go to the provincial capital, but the Assyrian governor himself went to meet them individually in their respective cities. The new governor formulated the reciprocal obligations and their relationship: the city lords had to obey and communicate all kinds of information; the governor had to protect them against local enemies and to represent them before the king of Assyria. Sargon wished his new governor to be an impartial judge: "Your friend and your [enemy] should not be treated differently."⁴⁴ The Assyrian local governors suffered from the bad weather conditions in the mountains, with cold and snow, which slowed down the construction of the defensive infrastructure and often cut off communication with central Assyria.⁴⁵

Thus, Sargon solved the difficult problems that occurred in central Zagros quite effectively, mainly in 716 and 715. This region was organized into five Assyrian provinces and a few vassal polities. Sargon succeeded in setting up important military bases ready to intervene in case of conflicts with any of the powerful neighbors. He gained allies either by force or by persuasion. In short, he succeeded in neutralizing the whole of this complex area by specific actions. The local Assyrian governors were entrusted to maintain order among the local city lords left in power as independent vassals; for example, in 706, a revolt in Karalla had to be repressed, probably by the governor of Zamua.

Media

In contrast with Assyria, Urartu, or Babylonia, no Median inscription has been discovered. In fact, the existence of a Median language is still in debate. Before the discovery of cuneiform archives and archaeological

---

42. *ARAB* 2.14; SAA 15:xxvi and 40–41, no. 60, r. 9; cf. *CAD*, s.v. *kāru* A.
43. SAA 15:xv, xxvi–xxviii, and 37–50, nos. 55–74; *PNA* 2.2:695–96.
44. SAA 15: xxvii and 62, no. 91.
45. SAA 15:40–42, 56, nos. 60–61, 83.

excavations in Media, the current reconstructions of its history were based on classical sources: the works of Herodotus (principally) and of later historians. According to Herodotus, Deioces united the six Median tribes and founded the Median Empire, with Ecbatana (modern Hamadan) as its capital, reaching as far west as the river Halys in central Anatolia; he was elected to be their king (*Hist.* 1.95–106).[46] The victory of Cyrus over the Median king Astyages would have meant that the new Persian dynasty inherited the Median imperial structure; the Median state would have been the model of the Achaemenid Empire. The Greek information has no reliability because it was not based on direct knowledge of Media, but was collected in the learned circles of the Achaemenid Empire as foundation legends of the Median state; it can be used now in order to reconstruct Greek historiography.[47] Since the Medes were known to have destroyed the Assyrian Empire and to have been defeated by Cyrus II, the founder of the Persian Empire, a Median Empire, if any, could only have been located between 612 and 550.[48]

The royal Assyrian inscriptions, from Shalmaneser III to Esarhaddon, contain by far the most abundant information about Media. They present the advantage of being contemporary records and relating the growth of Median polities during almost two centuries, from ca. 850 to 670. Archaeological excavations in ancient Media, between Kermanshah and Hamadan, were particularly intensive and fruitful in the 1960s and 1970s: in Godin Tepe, Nush-i Jan, and Baba Jan.[49] One of the main results of these excavations was that they contradicted Herodotus's account; the Median sites underwent a notable development during the late eighth century, under Sargon's reign, and the seventh century but were diminished during the first half of the sixth century, when the assumed Median Empire was

---

46. S. Brown, "The *Medikos Logos* of Herodotus and the Evolution of Median State," in *Method and Theory: Proceedings of the London 1985 Achaemenid History Workshop*, ed. Amelie Kuhrt and Heleen Sancisi-Weerdenburg, AchHist 3 (Leiden: Nederlands Instituut voor het Nabije Oosten, 1988), 71–86; Jo Ann Scurlock, "Herodotos' Median Chronology Again!," *IrAnt* 25 (1990): 149–63.

47. Mario Liverani, "The Rise and Fall of Media," in Lanfranchi, *Continuity of Empire*, 1–2. The Achaemenid Empire was more influenced by Elam than by Media; see Pierre Briant, *Histoire de l'Empire perse* (Paris: Fayard, 1996), 35–38, 908–9.

48. Heleen Sancisi-Weerdenburg, "Was There Ever a Median Empire?," in Kuhrt, *Method and Theory*, 199; P. R. Helm, "Herodotus' *Mèdikos Logos* and Median History," *Iran* 19 (1981): 85.

49. Liverani, "Rise and Fall of Media," 2–4 (with bibliography).

said to have reached the peak of its development. The main archaeological features seem to have been similar to those of Mannea, for example, the development of public buildings at the end of the eighth century, before diminishing in the first half of the sixth century.

From an Assyrian perspective, the various population groups living in the Zagros, south of Mannea, were not very different as far as their economic, social, and political characteristics are concerned. They bred cattle and horses, and they appeared as a people of raiders. In a relief of the palace of Khorsabad, the Medes were always represented on horseback, never in chariots.[50] Sargon's inscriptions show that there were a very large number of Median settlements, several being fortified, but many of them were probably small villages, as the distinction between *ālu*, "city," and *kapru*, "village" is not clear. Medes are described as a settled, not nomadic people, living in cities or villages. Just like the other peoples of central Zagros, they were ruled by hereditary city lords, a political system deeply rooted in their societies. Even when Sargon integrated these polities into Assyrian provinces, he kept their city lords in place. In short, according to the Assyrian view, at that time there was not one Median kingdom, but many small independent polities, with no discernible element of unity among them.

Even though the Medes were well attested in Assyrian sources from the late ninth century onward, the geographical location of their settlements is not easy to decipher. While the Assyrians distinguished the Medes from other peoples living in central Zagros, it is unclear what exactly constituted their identity: Was it ethnic, linguistic, religious, economic, or political? As far as we know, they do not seem to be differentiated by economy, politics, or language. Sargon's inscriptions always mention the "country of the Medes," without referring to a clearly defined geographic region. The only indications we have are the following: "the distant Medes who live on the border of the Bikni mountains," "the border of distant Media of the rising of the sun," "the people who live in these cities trusted in their own strength, they recognized no government."[51] The distance between Mannea and Media was of 30 *bêru* (double hours), that is, approximately 324 km (see below).[52] He was boasting when he said: "none of the kings who went before me had ever seen their dwelling-places, heard their name

---

50. Albenda, *Palace of Sargon*, pls. 109–30 (Room 2).
51. *ARAB* 2.54, 79, 82, 96–99; Hawkins, "New Sargon Stele," 155, l. 9.
52. *ARAB* 2.150.

or received their tribute," because, for example, in 835, Shalmaneser III had already received the tribute from Median rulers.[53] The country of the Medes could be reached from Assyria via the Namri/Bît-Hamban–Parsua route, which was the Great Khurasan road, a part of the Silk Road, following the valley of the Diyala into the Zagros mountains, to the Iranian plateau.[54] There was a second route, difficult for large armies, however: along the Zab, crossing Mount Kullar, then Hubushkia, reaching Mannea and Gizilbunda. Several localities, cities or villages, at least forty-five, were mentioned in Sargon's inscriptions and correspondence, for example, Nartu, Bît-Kapsi, Zakruti (Zakruta), Shaparda, Sikris, and Uriakka (Urikaia).[55] The names of various Median cities and of their city lords were listed in the Najafehabad stela.[56] However, it is uncertain whether a great number of other localities, cities, or villages, some of them quoted with their city lords, were Median or not.

In both Tiglath-pileser III's and Sargon's inscriptions, the Medes were qualified as "mighty" (*dannu*): it is an unusual term here; the other foreign peoples were usually described with depreciatory appellations such as "wicked" or "treacherous," for example. The reasons for Sargon's campaign to Media seem to have been the same as for his campaigns to central Zagros: in the event of conflicts with the powerful neighbors, he gained new allies, or at least neutral polities. He was possibly interested in horses too, which could be obtained through tribute, or trade, which became increasingly important. The Median cities situated in the mountains along the Great Khurasan road had no doubt greatly profited from the trade between Mesopotamia and Iran and beyond. The heavily fortified strongholds, depicted in the reliefs of Sargon's palace, offered opportunities for the city lords to enrich themselves by imposing heavy tolls on the passing caravans. When the camel came into regular use by caravans, the possibility of trade across the Arabian desert competed with the two routes across central Zagros and Media; it completely changed the relationship between Assyria, Elam, and Babylonia: Elam and Babylonia became allies

---

53. *ARAB* 2.149; Radner, "Assyrian View on the Medes," 38–40.

54. Michael Roaf, "Media and Mesopotamia: History and Architecture," in *Later Mesopotamia and Iran: Tribes and Empires 1600–539 B.C.; Proceedings of a Seminar in Memory of Vladimir G. Lukonin*, ed. John Curtis (London: British Museum, 1995), 56–57, fig. 22.

55. *ARAB* 2.24; SAA 15:xvii, table 3.

56. Levine, *Two Neo-Assyrian Stelae from Iran*, ii, ll. 46–70.

in trade, blocking Assyrian interests. Such a change could be one of the reasons why Assyrian military involvement in the Zagros area decreased in the seventh century.[57]

Sargon did not enter Median territory in 719, when he campaigned in Mannea; he entered for the first time in 716, when he created the two new Assyrian provinces of Kishesim/Kâr-Nergal, and Harhar/Kâr-Sharrukîn (see above). According to Sargon's correspondence, the governor of Harhar/Kâr-Sharrukîn was responsible for Media as long as it was under Assyrian control. However, when the city lords, settlements, or groups of people integrated in this Assyrian province are not explicitly called "Median," one cannot be sure about their identity.[58] Sargon captured and integrated six independent cities into Harhar, four of which were identified as Median: Nartu, Sikris, Shaparda, and Uriakku.[59] After that he continued further into Median territory and received tribute from "28 city lords of the mighty Medes"; this part of his campaign is described in detail in the Najafehabad stela, unfortunately very damaged.[60] In 715, Sargon returned to Mannea and Media because the inhabitants of the new province of Harhar were revolting against Assyria. He crushed the revolt in a bloody battle: 4,000 heads of enemies were cut off; 4,820 persons were deported and several cities were renamed.[61] The conquered Median strongholds were turned into Assyrian fortresses. The province of Harhar was then perceived, at least partly, as Median territory: its governor reported on "the Medes around us," and Sargon said: "For the subjugation of the land of the Medes, I strengthened Kâr-Sharrukîn."[62] Therefore it is impossible to know what part of Media was, at that time, inside or outside the Assyrian province of Harhar. Nevertheless, the Median city lords continued to wield power, even over regions included in Assyrian provinces. In the same year, Sargon received tribute from "22 city lords of the mighty Medes," whether they were still independent or not.[63]

---

57. McGuire Gibson, "Duplicate Systems of Trade: A Key Element in Mesopotamian History," in *Asian Trade Routes: Continental and Maritime*, ed. Karl Reinhold Haellquist, Studies on Asian Topics 13 (London: Routledge, 1991), 36; Radner, "Assyrian View on the Medes," 52.
58. SAA 15:xxvii.
59. *ARAB* 2.11; Fuchs, *Inschriften Sargons II*, 103–5, 318.
60. Levine, *Two Neo-Assyrian Stelae from Iran*, ii, ll. 46–70.
61. *ARAB* 2.14; Fuchs, *Inschriften Sargons II*, 107–9, 319.
62. *ARAB* 2.15; SAA 15:11–12, 58, 66–68, nos. 15, 85, 98, 100.
63. *ARAB* 2.15.

Yet the conflict did not end and more Assyrian campaigns were necessary the following year and again the year after. In 714 (year 8), Sargon conducted his famous campaign against Urartu (see above). On his way, he collected the tribute of the Medes, before entering Mannean territory: "The tribute of ... 45 city lords of the mighty Medes, 4,609 horses (and) mules, cattle (and) sheep, in countless numbers, I received."[64] In 713 (year 9), Sargon returned to the country of the mighty Medes, after crushing a rebellion in Karalla. But it was a new Median region: "distant provinces ... (of) the mighty Medes, who had cast off the yoke of Assur, and were scattered over mountain and desert, like thieves, into all of their cities I cast gloom and turned all their provinces into deserted mounds."[65] The reference to the Medes of the desert is singular, and has fuelled the image of the Medes as nomads.[66] There was some unrest in the Median city of Uriakku which was somewhat "far out," on the border of Ellipi; the governor of Harhar ordered the replacement of Karakku, city lord of Uriakku, arrested his son Uppite and replaced him by Rametî who remained a loyal subject, at least until 708.[67]

After 713, the dual system installed by Sargon, with the Assyrian administration on the one hand and the local city lords on the other, seems to have found an equilibrium, as the troubles in Media and Assyria's Median provinces subsided. Probably the Assyrian governor had to control the long-distance trade and the collection of tribute, while the local city lords remained in power for local affairs.[68] From the military point of view, the presence of Sargon himself was apparently not considered necessary anymore. The royal correspondence shows that the collecting of tribute and the meeting with the local city lords were from now on in the hands of the Assyrian governor and magnates. The reliefs of the palace of Khorsabad also represented the Assyrian governors of Harhar, Parsua, Zamua, Arrapha, and Nisibina campaigning against the Medes; these campaigns were not recorded in Sargon's royal inscriptions.[69] Further, there was an

---

64. *ARAB* 2.23–24; Radner, "Assyrian View on the Medes," 54, table 5.
65. *ARAB* 2.23.
66. Radner, "Assyrian View on the Medes," 55.
67. SAA 15:xxviii and table III; *PNA* 2.1:606, 3.2:1391.
68. Liverani, "Rise and Fall of Media," 6.
69. Radner, "Assyrian View on the Medes," 56–57 and table 7.

increase of Median presence at the royal court of Assyria from at least the reign of Sargon.[70]

Ellipi

Ellipi was located between the eastern Assyrian provinces of Media and Elam, in central Zagros.[71] It was an independent kingdom whose ruler had the title of "king" (*šarru*) and not of "city lord."[72] In 716 (year 6), the anti-Assyrian people of Harhar contacted Taltâ/Daltâ, king of Ellipi, in order to become his vassals (see above).[73] The Annals do not report whether Taltâ answered; in any case, Harhar was conquered by Sargon. As Taltâ was always presented in Sargon's inscriptions as a loyal vassal, "a payer of tribute and tax to the kings, my fathers, who went before," he probably did not accept welcoming enemies of Assyria as vassals.[74] In 714 (year 8), during the campaign against Urartu, Sargon received the tribute of Ellipi.[75] In 713 (year 9), the Annals mentioned that the Assyrian king marched against the land of Ellipi, at the same time as he crushed the revolt of Amitashshi (see above), but the paragraph is badly damaged in the lines where Taltâ is mentioned.[76] However, during this campaign Sargon received the tribute of Taltâ of Ellipi, among the tributaries.[77]

At some moment of Sargon's reign, probably in 713 at the latest, Taltâ was confronted with a revolt in his kingdom, conducted by the whole of his land or at least part of it, and Sargon assisted him in crushing it: "Taltâ of the land of Ellipi, a subservient slave who bore the yoke of Assur, 5 districts of his borderland revolted against him and would not submit to his rule; I went to his aid, those districts I besieged, I captured; the people, together with their possessions and with countless horses, I carried off into Assyria, a rich plunder."[78] As can be seen, Taltâ was saved

---

70. Karen Radner, "The Medes, Purveyors of Fine Horses," in *Assyrian Empire Builders*, http://tinyurl.com/SBL1722m.
71. *ARAB* 2.23, 82, 96–99, 102; Frame, "The Inscription of Sargon II," 39–40, l. 30.
72. Fuchs, *Inschriften Sargons II*, Ann. 96; Prunk. 117.
73. *ARAB* 2.11; *PNA* 1.2:373.
74. *ARAB* 2.212.
75. *ARAB* 2.19.
76. *ARAB* 2.23.
77. *ARAB* 2.24, 147.
78. *ARAB* 2.58, 212.

and kept his throne, but Sargon paid for the rescue operation himself. This operation was described in detail in a damaged passage of Prism A from Nineveh, which ended thus: "[From] Taltâ, their king, [I received] an ⌜offering⌝. The land of Ellipi to its farther border, ⌜I caused to inhabit⌝ peaceful habitations."[79] However, Taltâ was probably aged, as he was already on the throne under Tiglath-pileser III and Shalmaneser V's reigns. A letter written very close to the time of his death by the governor of Harhar mentioned: "Concerning news of Taltâ: he does not leave the house and no one enters into his presence."[80] Either he was ill or he had perhaps just died (in 708 or 707) and his death was kept secret to prepare the succession. The death of Sargon's royal vassal was reported in the Display Inscription, in 707 (year 15), in a poetic way: he "reached the appointed limit (of life) and trod the path of death."[81] A war of succession for the throne of Ellipi occurred between Nibê and Ashpa-bara, sons of Taltâ's sisters. As they did not come to an agreement, a fight of revenge broke out. Nibê called for help from his neighbor, Shutruk-nahhunte II, king of Elam, who came to his rescue. Ashpa-bara begged aid of Sargon. The king of Assyria decided to rescue him but did not intervene himself. He sent seven of his officers, possibly governors of the eastern Assyrian provinces, with their armies: "The defeat of Nibê and the Elamite army, (which had come) to his aid, they brought about in the city of Marubishti. Ashpa-bara I placed on the royal throne, I repaired the damage Ellipi (had suffered) and put it under his control."[82] However, Ashpa-bara was not a loyal vassal like his father Taltâ; he was an intrigant and, five years later, he revolted against Sennacherib, who crushed his revolt during his second campaign. During his reign, Sargon succeeded in keeping good relations with Ellipi, mainly thanks to Taltâ; it was a large eastern kingdom and an important power. It served as a buffer state between the Assyrian provinces of Kishesim/Kâr-Nergal and Harhar/Kâr-Sharrukîn, and the hostile kingdom of Elam.[83]

---

79. *ARAB* 2.191.
80. SAA 15:xxix–xxxi.
81. *ARAB* 2.47, 65.
82. *ARAB* 2.47, 65; Abraham and Klein, "New Sargon II Cylinder Fragment," 255–56, l. 8'. On Ashpa-bara's intrigues, see SAA 15:45–47, 67–69, nos. 69, 100–101.
83. Reade, "Iran in the Neo-Assyrian Period," 41.

Elam

The kingdom of Elam is known from the proto-Elamite texts, the first Elamite dynasties beginning in the third millennium BCE. The borders of its territory changed substantially during its history. At the time of Sargon, during the Neo-Elamite Period II (743–646), it was located south of Ellipi, mainly in Susiana, extending southward down to the Persian/Arabian Gulf (Bashime) and westward as far as the eastern Zagros (Huhmur).[84] It bordered on south Mesopotamia, which explains its political choices. The sources for Elamite history corresponding to Sargon's reign are threefold: Neo-Elamite texts, the Babylonian Chronicle, and Assyrian texts (royal inscriptions and letters). Elam was a powerful state at that time. However, it was not in itself dangerous for Assyria, but through its alliance with Babylonia, the traditional enemy of Assyria. War, already difficult with Babylonia in the southern marshes, would have been more exhausting if it were necessary to fight against Elam in the eastern Zagros. The risk was also that other eastern states could be involved in the conflict and that the routes of communication with the Iranian plateau would be blocked. That is why, from the beginning of his reign, Sargon was very attentive to the policy followed by the Elamite kings.[85]

He was so conscious of the danger that his first military expedition was targeted at solving the problem of the Elam-Babylonia connection. Humban-nikash I, king of Elam (743–717), was supporting Merodach-baladan II, who had ascended the throne of Babylon in the month of Nisan 721.[86] Sargon decided to intervene immediately against them, and he met Humban-nikash near Dêr on the pretext that he was defending this city against an Elamite attack. Although the battle is dated in the Assyrian inscriptions, either from Sargon's accession year or from his first year, it seems more plausible that the date was 720 (year 2).[87] The city of Dêr is identified with the site of Tell Aqar, a major mound lying about a kilometer northwest of the modern town of Badra.[88] Dêr owed its importance to

---

84. Joannès, *Dictionnaire de la civilisation mésopotamienne*, 272–76; François Vallat et al., *Les Noms géographiques des sources suso-élamites*, RGTC 11 (Wiesbaden: Reichert, 1993).
85. Garelli and Lemaire, *Proche-Orient asiatique 2*, 120–21.
86. Grayson, *Assyrian and Babylonian Chronicles*, 73, chr. I, l. 32.
87. Tadmor, "Campaigns of Sargon," 25.
88. Barthel Hrouda, "Ergebnisse einer Ruinenbesichtigung im südöstlichen Iraq," *BaghM* 6 (1973): 7–18.

its location on the route connecting Susa with Babylonia. It was an important religious center for the city's god *Anu rabû* ("Anu-the-Great"). Dêr was perceived as Babylonian, but ethnically it was a patchwork, and it had been conquered by Adad-narari II; it then provided several eponyms and probably came under permanent Assyrian domination under Tiglath-pileser III. In 724, under Shalmaneser V, Il-Iada, possibly an Aramean sheikh, is described in a formal legal document as the governor of the land of Dêr. Therefore, Dêr was an Assyrian provincial capital at this date and this province probably remained in existence until 710.[89] Its boundaries can be guessed with some plausibility: the eastern limit seems to have been the first part of the Zagros range and the Diyala northward; the western and southern limits are uncertain. The province probably acted as a buffer state between Assyria and Elam, with its heavily fortified city.[90] Strategically, Dêr fulfilled several roles: it provided a bulwark against any Elamite incursion from the southeast; for Sargon it represented a foothold in the south from which the northern sector of Babylonia could be observed and contained; and it gave him control over the route into Babylonia in case of conflict.[91]

According to the Babylonian Chronicle, Merodach-baladan had gone with his army to the aid of Humban-nikash but did not reach the place of the battle in time and so withdrew. Assyrian and Babylonian inscriptions carried two opposite accounts of the battle of Dêr. Sargon said to be "the exalted prince, who came face to face with Humban-nikash, king of Elam, in the outskirts of Dêr and defeated him."[92] In contrast, the Babylonian Chronicle reads: "The second year of Merodach-baladan (II): Humban-Nikash (I), king of Elam, did battle against Sargon (II), king of Assyria, in the district of Dêr, effected an Assyrian retreat, (and) inflicted a major defeat upon them."[93] Both enemies, Sargon and Humban-nikash, claimed their victory. The result of the battle was probably indecisive, but it gave some respite to Sargon who took advantage of it to campaign in the west. The Assyrian position at Dêr was held and the situation along the border remained more or less unchanged, but Sargon waited ten years

---

89. Postgate and Mattila, "Il-Yada' and Sargon's Southeast Frontier," 235–54.

90. Levine, "Geographical Studies in the Neo-Assyrian Zagros II," 104.

91. Postgate and Mattila, "Il-Yada' and Sargon's Southeast Frontier," 251.

92. *ARAB* 2.55, 118, 137; Saggs, "Historical Texts and Fragments," 14–15, ll. 16–17; Castellino, "Frammento degli Annali," 72, ll. 7–8.

93. Grayson, *Assyrian and Babylonian Chronicles*, 73, chr. 1, ll. 33–34.

7. NEUTRALIZATION OF THE EASTERN STATES

before attacking his enemies in Babylonia and on the borders of Elam.[94] In fact, there is no clear mention of Elam in royal inscriptions and letters before 710.

In 710 (year 12), the king of Elam came to the aid of the king of Babylonia, Merodach-baladan. There is a problem concerning his name in the Annals: he is named Humban-nikash on one occasion and Shutur-nahhunte on several others.[95] There are some contradictions between the Assyrian and Neo-Elamite inscriptions concerning this period, in particular the confusion between Shutur-nahhunte and Shutruk-nahhunte.[96] The chronology concerning the Sargon period is now well-established: Humban-nikash I (743–717) and his successor Shutruk-nahhunte II (717–699), wrongly named Shutur-nahhunte in the Assyrian texts; Shutur-nahhunte reigned ca. 645–620. According to the Babylonian Chronicle, "Shutruk-nahhunte (II), his sister's son (of Humban-nikash) ascended the throne in Elam."[97] Consequently, the name of Humban-nikash in the Annals for 710 (year 12) was a scribal error because this king had died in 717.

The sources for the reign of Shutruk-nahhunte II are the Neo-Elamite inscriptions and the Assyrian and Babylonian records, all of which differ on some points. In his own inscriptions, the Elamite king reported that he led successful campaigns to enlarge his territory, endowed temples, and set up stelae for the gods. According to the Assyrian sources, the allies of Merodach-baladan and Shutruk-nahhunte were first defeated. Then the Assyrian king captured the Elamite fortresses of Samuna and Bâb-dûri: "Saninu (?) (and) Singamshibu (?), the commanders of the fortress(es), together with 7,500 Elamites, who were with them, and 12,062 people…, wagons, horses, mules, asses, camels, as well as their many possessions, I carried off. Samuna I rebuilt. I changed its name, calling it Bêl-ikîsha."[98] Shutruk-nahhunte was described in a very pejorative manner. First, he was a coward, afraid of Sargon's army and who, to save his own life, "took

---

94. SAA 15:xxxii–xxxv.
95. *ARAB* 2.31–35.
96. Gwendolyn Leick, *Who's Who in the Ancient Near East* (New York: Routledge, 2002), s.v. Shutruk-Nahhunte II (= Shutur-Nahhunte); François Vallat, "Šutruk-Nahunte, Šutur-Nahunte et l'imbroglio néo-élamite," *NABU* (1995): 37–38, no. 44; Jan Tavernier, "Some Thoughts on Neo-Elamite Chronology," *ARTA* 3 (2004): 1–44.
97. Grayson, *Assyrian and Babylonian Chronicles*, 75, chr. 1, l. 40.
98. *ARAB* 2.32–33.

refuge in the midst of the distant mountains."[99] Merodach-baladan, in turn afraid, sent rich presents to the Elamite king, asking for asylum: "His ⌜paraphernalia (?)⌝, his bed, his chair, his footstool (?), his royal ewer, his necklace, he gave to Shutruk-nahhunte, the Elamite, as bribes that he might avenge him. The wicked Elamite received his bribes, but feared my weapons, blocked his path and told him to go no (farther)."[100] In fact, the Elamite king, mocked and presented as a fool, refused to waste his forces in a hopeless battle. His purely defensive strategy met with success: at least neither Susa nor any other of Elam's royal cities were attacked by the Assyrians. Even if he is presented as having cheated his Babylonian ally, later on when Merodach-baladan had to retreat after the siege of Dûr-Yakin, he sought and found refuge in Elam.

Even after the conquest of Babylonia, Sargon had not finished the war against Elam: "I waged bitter warfare against the people of Elam," and was obliged to reinforce the defense on the Elamite border in 709 (year 13): "On the Elamite border, at Sagbat, I had Nabû-damqi-ilâni build a fortress to hinder any advance of the Elamite. That land I divided totally and turned it over to my official, the governor of Babylon, and my official, the governor of Gambulu."[101] The Sargon correspondence shows that the Elamite king recruited new troops and assembled them, maybe in order to march on Ellipi as was announced.[102] Three different Elamite attacks of varying size can be distinguished, but only the first campaign is dated as 707. In Sargon's Annals, there is a mention of an Elamite royal army intervening in the Ellipean war of succession, for helping Nibê on his demand (see above), but no other intervention later in that Ellipean war.[103] However, step-by-step, the Elamite king recovered his territorial losses and before Sargon's death there were even modest territorial gains at Assyrian expense. As for Dêr, in addition to the lasting Elamite menace, its surroundings were raided by the mountains dwellers of Qirbit: these enemies were not defeated before the reign of Ashurbanipal.[104] In 703, after Sennacherib had succeeded Sargon, Shutruk-nahhunte and Merodach-baladan set out together with a force of Elamite troops. After initial

---

99. *ARAB* 2.34.
100. *ARAB* 2.35.
101. *ARAB* 2.41–42; *PNA* 2.2:820.
102. SAA 15:xxxiii–xxxv.
103. *ARAB* 2.47.
104. SAA 15:xxxv (with bibliography).

successes, they were defeated: the Elamite king went back to Elam, where he was taken prisoner by his young brother Hallushu-inshushinak who usurped the Elamite throne in 699. Sargon never succeeded either in putting an end to the threat represented by the Elamite kingdom, or in definitively preventing any alliance between Elam and Babylonia.

In short, the eastern states formed a heterogeneous conglomerate, very difficult to handle and to control. Sargon understood that he had to adapt his attitude toward each of them. He spared the polities of central Zagros and Media by allowing the city lords to continue to rule, even after their integration into Assyrian provinces. His aim was to neutralize them in case of conflicts with Urartu or Elam and to establish important military bases ready to intervene. He protected Taltâ, king of Ellipi, who was his most loyal vassal in this eastern part of the Assyrian Empire. During his whole reign, Sargon tried to prevent any alliance between Elam and Babylonia, which would have proved extremely dangerous for Assyria. In fact, he never took the risk of attacking Elam elsewhere than on the borders of the Iranian plateau, and he did not succeed in defeating this powerful state.

8
Recurring Problems in the South

The political scene in the south of the Assyrian Empire was dominated by the powerful and concurrent kingdom of Babylonia, the main traditional enemy of Assyria (fig. 7). Recurring problems in the south accompanied the whole history of Assyria. In fact, the situation was more complicated than if there had been merely one enemy state, even though very powerful. In addition to the great city of Babylon and all the ancient Sumerian cities, the tribes, proceeding from nomadism through the various stages of sedentary life, played a major role during the time of Sargon. Moreover, these tribes were heterogeneous: Aramean tribes and Chaldean tribes. Arab tribes were apart, being either inside or outside the kingdom of Arabia (Qedar). Further, one must not forget Dilmun, which Sargon claimed as the southeastern border of his empire.

Aramean and Chaldean Tribes

The Aramean and Chaldean tribes were tightly associated with the history of Babylonia. Before considering their history, let us take a glimpse at their origin, their dwelling place, and the organization of these tribes, still uncertain and much debated. All around the well-established urban centers of southern Mesopotamia, there was a massive and, often, hovering presence of Aramean and Chaldean tribally based groups.[1] These tribes were partly settled in specific niches of the alluvial plain between the lower reaches of the Tigris and Euphrates (Uqnû and Surappi rivers) and were

---

1. Joannès, *The Age of Empires*, 112–14; F. M. Fales, "Moving around Babylon: On the Aramean and Chaldean Presence in Southern Mesopotamia," in *Babylon: Wissenskultur in Orient und Okzident*, ed. Eva Cancik-Kirschbaum, Margarete Ess, and Joachim Marzahn, Topoi 1 (Berlin: de Gruyter, 2008), 91–111 (with bibliography).

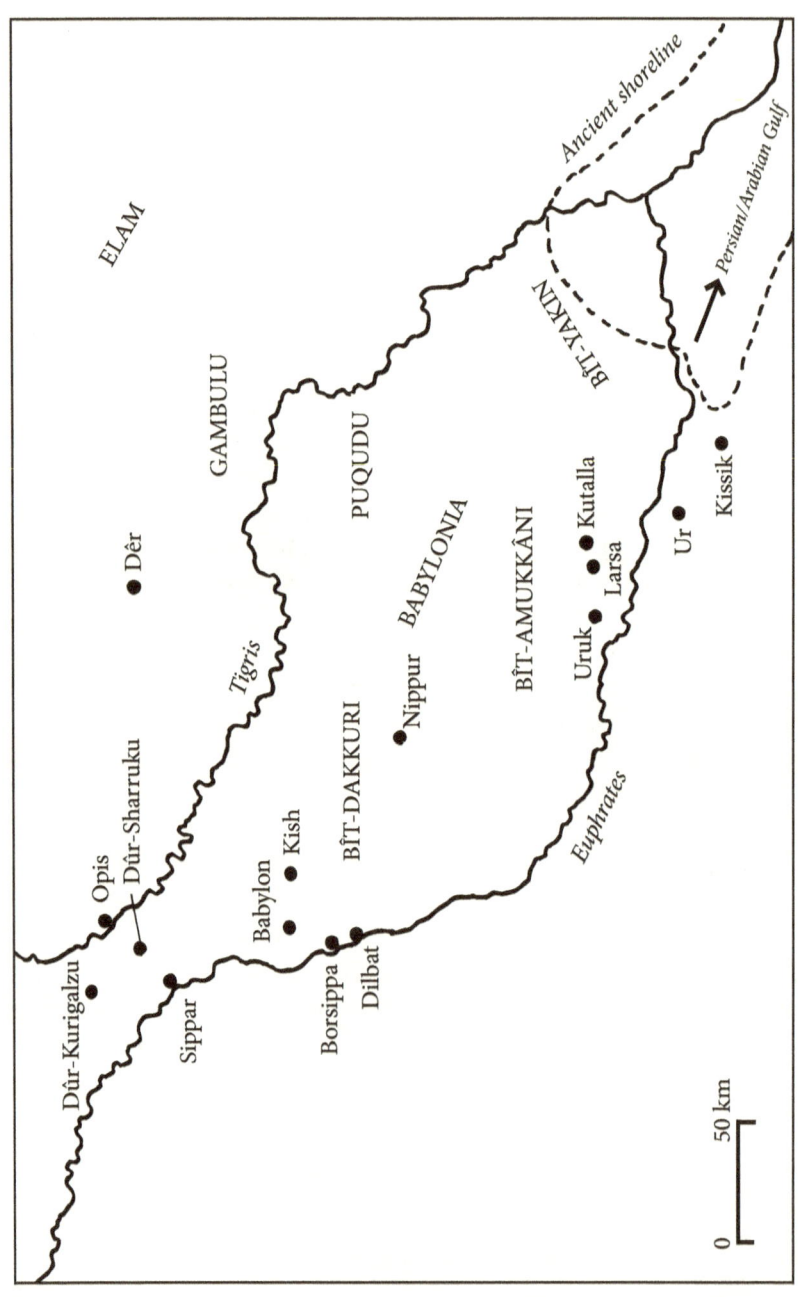

Fig. 7. The South of the Empire

partly circulating or settling in the countryside of the urban centers, most of all Babylon.

The origin of the Aramean tribal groups in this area still remains unclear, in spite of the several hypotheses proposed.[2] Aramean tribal groups are attested at least from the eleventh century as new occupants of strategic areas in the Jezirah, northern Mesopotamia, and the Syrian steppe. From this base, until 850 they opposed the Assyrian forces toward the Euphrates and westward into the area beyond the river and into the Levant. The first mention of the Arameans, associated with the Ahlamu, is in the military expedition organized against them by Tiglath-pileser I in 1111.[3] According to Babylonian sources, in the eleventh and tenth centuries, tribal groups called "Arameans" or "Suteans," a traditional designation for West Semitic nomads, looted Sippar and neighboring cities. The strong Assyrian military reaction during the late-tenth to early-ninth century could have forced these tribal groups to migrate downward and to occupy the vast southeastern plain between the Tigris and Elam. When the lower Tigris catchment area became the object of intense Assyrian military pressure, Tiglath-pileser III listed nearly forty names of tribal entities of unsubmissive Arameans.[4] The vast group of the Puqudu was active in the area surrounding Nippur (Nuffar).[5] Other places are indicated, such as Lahiru, to the east of the Tigris, "on the banks of the Tigris," between the Diyala and Dêr, or the marshy areas further south, along the Babylonian-Elamite border. Later, the Puqudu tribe, associated with anti-Assyrian activities, was operating from the southernmost sector of the alluvium. In general, the Aramean groups had great mobility, migrating between one enclave and another and giving rise to interregional movements, between the middle Euphrates and southern Mesopotamia. The scribes of Sargon described those who were in northwestern Babylonia:

---

2. Brinkman, *Political History*, 265–85; Brinkman, *Prelude to Empire: Babylonian Society and Politics, 747–626 B.C.*, OPSNKF 7 (Philadelphia: Babylonian Section of the University Museum, 1984); Lipiński, *Arameans*, 409–89; F. M. Fales, "Arameans and Chaldeans: Environment and Society," in *The Babylonian World*, ed. Gwendolyn Leick (New York: Routledge, 2007), 288–98.

3. *ARAB* 1.239; Françoise Briquel-Chatonnet, *Les Araméens et les premiers Arabes: Des royaumes araméens du IXe siècle à la chute du royaume nabatéen*, Encyclopédie de la Méditerranée 29 (Aix-en-Provence: Édisud, 2004), 9–17.

4. *ARAB* 1.771, 788, 804–5, 809.

5. Steven W. Cole, *Nippur in Late Assyrian Times ca. 755–612 BC*, SAAS 4 (Helsinki: Neo-Assyrian Text Corpus Project, 1996), 9–13.

"In that desert terrain, Arameans and Suteans—tent-dwellers, fugitives, thieves, and robbers—had come to dwell."[6]

The Aramean tribes rejected an ideology of unified leadership: each tribe having a specific "sheikh" (*nasiku*), as indicated in Sargon's inscriptions. These sheikhs were linked with several institutional or simply geographical entities, such as lands, cities, and even rivers. It resulted in a great degree of segmentation in their territories and distinctive ethnicity. For example, after their subjugation by Tiglath-pileser III, the Utua/Itua tribe was integrated into the Assyrian administration as a trustworthy corps of "military police."[7] Vaster tribal complexes, such as the Puqudu and the Gambulu, had retained their distinctive self-identification but had developed a number of inner clan subdivisions with reference to their specific sheikhs, who took individual courses of action, depending on the circumstances. The organization of some common tribal policies is possible but is not attested in the textual records.

In contrast to the long-attested Arameans, the Chaldeans (*Kaldu*) are not documented in written sources before 878 BCE. Their place names were characterized by the noun *Bīt*, "household," followed by the West Semitic personal name of an eponymic ancestor figure, which led to a connection being postulated with the northern and western Arameans in the general perspective of a shared heritage of ethnicity. However, their social, economic, and political structure was very different from that of the Arameans: it was rigidly centered upon the tribal unit of which all subjects were "sons" (*mār*). Such units in fact represented tribal confederations. The leader of each tribal confederation was called "chieftain" (*ra'su*). Although the structures of the Chaldean tribes were based on kinship ties, their way of life was basically sedentary in their southern Euphrates enclaves. They were occupied in stock raising and intraregional trade; in their well-watered territorial niches they practiced agriculture, including date-palm cultivation, and horse and cattle breeding. They seem to have alternated intensive agricultural exploitation along the rivers with periods of transhumance in steppe sectors.

The main Chaldean tribes occupied three territories from the Borsippa to the Ur regions and the marshlands. The first territory, going from north to south was Bît-Dakkûri, extending from Borsippa (modern Birs

---

6. John A. Brinkman, "Reflections on the Geography of Babylonia (1000–600 B.C.)," in Liverani, *Neo-Assyrian Geography*, 26–27.

7. *ARAB* 1.54, 99.

Nimrud) to Marad (modern Diwaniyah). Their second territory was Bît-Amukkâni, more or less between Nippur and Uruk. Bît-Yakin was their third territory, which occupied the south of the alluvial plain, including marsh areas. Other Chaldean territories were, for example, Bît-Shilâni and Bît-Saalli.[8] These Chaldean tribal territories comprised not only villages and small towns, but also several walled cities. For example, in Bît-Yakin Sargon captured "15 strongholds together with the towns," and he quoted each by name.[9] In his first campaign of Babylonia in 703, Sennacherib boasted about having conquered an unbelievable number of towns in these Chaldean territories: 33 walled cities and 250 hamlets in Bît-Dakkûri, 8 walled cities and 120 hamlets in Bît-Saalli, 39 walled cities and 350 hamlets in Bît-Amukkâni, 8 walled cities and 100 hamlets in Bît-Yakin, "a total of 88 strong, walled cities of Chaldea, with 820 hamlets."[10]

Moreover, the strategic position of the Chaldean territories along the westernmost and southern axes of the Mesopotamian plain had crucial implications for trade. The precious goods offered as tribute by the Chaldean chiefs to Tiglath-pileser III proved that they had full control of the trade routes crossing the Babylonian region, a vast commercial network that reached Mesopotamia from the Levant, northern Arabia, and Egypt by land.[11] A new southern Mesopotamian trade axis, using the recently introduced large-scale exploitation of the camel as a pack animal, was competing with the northern Mesopotamian axis, dominated by the Assyrian Empire, and would eventually replace it. Behind this new trade axis, the power of Chaldean tribes was increased by substantial commercial benefits, the support of Aramean and Arabian tribes, and the military cooperation offered by the Elamite state on the basis of economic advantages.[12] In the Chaldean social and political organization, the leader of each tribe recognized the status of one chief within a territorial-political complex that united the different Chaldean tribes. For example, in a Nimrud letter dated from the time of Tiglath-pileser III, the young Merodach-baladan was described as "one of the chieftains of the land of Chaldea."[13] All these

---

8. Frame, "Inscription of Sargon II," 37, 41, l. 35.
9. Gadd, "Inscribed Prisms of Sargon II," 186–87, ll. 50–58.
10. Luckenbill, *Annals of Sennacherib*, 52–54, ll. 39–50.
11. Fales, "Moving around Babylon," 96–97.
12. John A. Brinkman, "Elamite Aid to Merodach-Baladan," *JNES* 24 (1965): 161–66.
13. Saggs, *Nimrud Letters, 1952*, 25–26, ll. 5'-6'.

characteristics made the Chaldean tribes very different from the Aramean tribes: they represented a true danger to the Assyrian Empire.

Babylonia

Relations between Assyria and Babylonia (Kâr-Duniash) had always been contradictory and fluctuating: for example, in the ninth century, Marduk-zâkir-shumi I called for help from Shalmaneser III, then in turn helped the Assyrian king Shamshi-Adad V, then Shamshi-Adad V captured the new Babylonian king Marduk-balâssu-iqbi.[14] The consequence of this last Assyrian attack against Babylonia was a period of political confusion in this state from 811 to 769, and the reinforcement of the Chaldean confederations, with the seizure of power by several Chaldean chiefs of Bît-Yakin, Bît-Dakkûri, and Bît-Amukkâni. When the Babylonian king Nabû-nâsir called on Tiglath-pileser III for help in order to restore public order by neutralizing the Chaldean tribes, Babylonia completely lost its autonomy. From that moment on, it passed into Assyrian control, with only a few short periods of independence when some chiefs of the Chaldean tribes seized power.

Nabû-mukîn-zêri was the chief of the tribal political unit of Bît-Amukkâni and a personality of great prestige for several neighboring cities such as Nippur. In a period of strong dynastic instability in Babylon, this Chaldean chief had removed another rebellious candidate from the throne, Nabû-shuma-ukîn II, and assumed kingship in 732. The people of Babylon, deeply distrustful of the Assyrians and terrified of the Chaldeans, practiced forms of passive resistance, which seemed to lead nowhere, becoming prey to raids and other acts of violence. Tiglath-pileser III understood the danger and decided to intervene in Babylonian affairs: he marched against Nabû-mukîn-zêri and captured Shapiya, his capital in Bît-Amukkâni. In 728, he integrated Babylonia into the Assyrian Empire, becoming king of Babylonia, under the name of Pulû in order to spare the sensitivities of the Babylonians. By the expedient of the double throne of Assyria and Babylonia, he created the impression of an autonomous Babylonian region in the face of the Assyrian Empire.

---

14. Brinkman, *Political History*, 265–85; Peter Machinist, "The Assyrians and their Babylonian Problem: Some Reflections," *WBJb* (1984–1985): 353–64; Joannès, *The Age of Empires*, 112–18.

However, Tiglath-pileser III died in 727, a short time after taking over the Babylonian throne. His successor Shalmaneser V continued to occupy the throne of Babylon under the name Ulûlâyu, but little is known of his short reign (726–722). Merodach-baladan, the chief of the tribal political unit of Bît-Yakin, had by that time prepared the political and military scenario so as to be able to seize anew the throne of Babylon and to rule on much more effective terms than his Chaldean predecessor Nabû-mukîn-zêri. He had rallied all the Chaldean tribes and taken advantage of the troubles of the royal succession in Assyria to recapture all the Babylonian territories occupied by Tiglath-pileser III and to proclaim himself king of Babylon. According to the Babylonian Chronicle, "On the twelfth day of the month Tebet Sargon ascended the throne of Assyria. In the month Nisan Merodach-baladan ascended the throne of Babylon."[15]

Apart from the Assyrian heartland, Babylonia was for many reasons seen as the most precious and prestigious possession of the empire, and hence its loss represented a major blow for Sargon. Merodach-baladan II was, in Sargon's inscriptions, the one who surpassed all his enemies in terms of the burning hatred apparent at every mention of his name or deeds: "seed of a murderer, prop of a wicked devil, who did not fear the name of the lord of the lords, … violated the oath of the great gods and withheld his gifts, … the treacherous enemy."[16] Who exactly was Merodach-baladan? We know him by his biblical name (2 Kgs 20), his true name being Marduk-apla-iddina. In the royal inscriptions, he was also named "king of the land of Chaldea, who dwelled on the shore of the sea."[17] He claimed to be the grandson of Erîba-Marduk, a Chaldean chief who became king of Babylon from 769 to 761.[18] In the correspondence of Sargon, he was referred to not only by his proper name, but also as the "son of Yakin," that is, as a member or the head of the Chaldean tribe of Bît-Yakin. In some letters, he is named "son of Zerî," which could have meant a member or the head of a tribe called Bît-Zerî. What was this enigmatic Bît-Zerî? For the year

---

15. Grayson, *Assyrian and Babylonian Chronicles*, chr. 1, ll. 31–32.
16. *ARAB* 2.66; Fuchs, *Inschriften Sargons II*, 334 n. 365.
17. Frame, "Inscription of Sargon II," 37, 40, l. 25.
18. John A. Brinkman, "Merodach-baladan," in *Studies Presented to A. Oppenheim: June 17, 1964*, ed. Robert D. Biggs and John A. Brinkman (Chicago: Oriental Institute of the University of Chicago, 1964), 6–53; Joannès, *Dictionnaire de la civilisation mésopotamienne*, 523–25; SAA 19:xlvii–xlviii; *PNA* 2.2:705–11.

710, the Eponym Lists mentioned "To Bît-Zerî."[19] According to Fuchs and Parpola, the conglomerate of tribes and cities headed by Bît-Yakin was called Bît-Zerî: the "son of Yakin" and the "son of Zerî" would have been identical.[20] The senders of letters had a preference for one or the other of these names of Merodach-baladan.

As soon as possible after having solved his internal problems, probably in 720, Sargon decided to react strongly against the seizure of power by Merodach-baladan in Babylonia. The battle occurred near Dêr, a symbolic place, a Babylonian city under Assyrian control, between the territories of the two allied enemies: Merodach-baladan and Humban-nikash, king of Elam (see above). Even if Sargon confronted only the Elamites because of the delay of Merodach-baladan's troops, the meaning of the battle was clear: Sargon wanted to defeat the Babylonian king, a usurper "who exercised the kingship over Babylon against the will of the gods."[21] The outcome of the battle also seems to be clear: contrary to what he claimed, Sargon was not victorious against the king of Elam alone. However, it is possible that, on this occasion, he subjugated the Tuumuna and Têsa Aramean tribes.[22] Because he was unable to defeat Humban-nikash alone, he understood that he was not ready to expel Merodach-baladan from the throne of Babylon. Thus, it is clear why Sargon let Merodach-baladan carry on being king of Babylonia for ten more years: he probably first wanted to consolidate the Assyrian Empire, for example, by defeating the Elamite king separately, and to reinforce the Assyrian army. He waited patiently for the moment when he would be ready to solve the Babylonian problem definitively. In the meantime, he accumulated as much information as possible about the movements of his bitterest enemy, as can be seen from the correspondence preceding his attack against the Babylonian king in 710.[23]

The reported movements and whereabouts of Merodach-baladan can easily be matched with the evidence given in the Annals. Sargon's military expedition in Babylonia can be divided into four phases.[24] The first phase is known from the letters, but not reported in the royal inscriptions

---

19. SAAS 2:47, 60.
20. SAA 15:xv.
21. *ARAB* 2.4, 80.
22. *ARAB* 2.4, 118.
23. SAA 15:xv–xvi, 75–170; SAA 17:xv–xix and 22–47, nos. 20–51.
24. SAA 15:xvi–xxii.

in order to minimize its importance. For a short time, when Sargon was occupied by his campaign east of the Tigris, Merodach-baladan tried to impede Assyrian activities by counterattacking the Assyrian province of Dûr-Sharruku, probably relying on the news about the city's insufficient water supply, which would have made its capture easier. He advanced with his forces, together with Aramean troops from the Itua, Rubuu, and Litau tribes. Dûr-Sharruku was located in northeastern Babylonia; its capital of the same name was close to Opis and Ctesiphon and is probably to be identified with Mujailiat. It seems that the Chaldean campaign never even reached the vicinity of Dûr-Sharruku because it had no chance of success as, in this city, the Assyrian official Il-Iada was awaiting Merodach-baladan's forces with his troops. However, Sargon was very cautious and gave him the following order: "For these two months, be attentive and keep your guard strong until I come!"[25] During the first or the second phase, Merodach-baladan sent an embassy to Hezekiah, king of Judah, with letters and a present "for he had heard that Hezekiah had been sick" (2 Kgs 20), but probably more in search of an ally against Sargon; however, following Isaiah's advice, Hezekiah declined to revolt against Sargon.

The second phase was characterized by alarming news reaching Babylonia on the advance of Assyrian troops and by the diplomacy and secret negotiations conducted by Assyrian officers to win over tribes and cities in northern Babylonia. Il-Iada was the most important officer who organized these subversive activities in order to undermine Merodach-baladan's position in northern Babylonia.[26] The departure of Sargon's expedition is described with grandiloquence in his inscriptions: "Marduk, the great lord, saw the evil works of the (people of) Kaldu, which he hated, and decreed that his royal scepter and throne should be taken away. Me, Sargon, the humble king, he singled out from among all princes and exalted me…. At the command of the great lord Marduk, I set my chariots in order; I prepared the camp and gave the command to advance against the hostile and wicked people of Kaldu."[27] The secret negotiations can only be gleaned from the correspondence. For example, to establish an initial contact with the Aramean tribe of Ruaûa, a eunuch originating from this tribe was brought from as far away as Damascus.[28] Bît-Dakkûri

---

25. SAA 15:106–7, no. 156, ll. 8–10; *PNA* 2.1:515.
26. Postgate and Mattila, "Il-Yada' and Sargon's Southeast Frontier," 235–54.
27. *ARAB* 2.31.
28. *ARAB* 2.31–32, 54, 67, 99; SAA 15:4–5, no. 1, ll. 4–10.

was considered a friendly Chaldean territory by the Assyrians, who established an observation post in the city of Dûr-Ladini. The city of Sippar (Abu Habba) signaled to Il-Iada its readiness to cooperate. Conversely, Marduk-sharrani, an Assyrian official, was said to have instigated Merodach-baladan's attack on Dûr-Sharruku.[29] The reactions to the Assyrian offers depended on the degree of organization on the part of the different political entities in Babylonia. The well-organized Chaldean tribes such as Bît-Dakkûri and Bît-Amukkâni changed side and submitted en bloc. Less well-organized tribes and cities were divided into factions either siding with Merodach-baladan or ready to take up with Sargon. The Chaldean tribes generally viewed this war as an affair concerning Bît-Yakin only and remained passive, even allowing the Assyrians to make use of their territory. From the outset, the Aramean tribes were among the closest supporters of Merodach-baladan, in particular Puqudu and Gambulu. However, their support depended on the possession of a strong garrison. Merodach-baladan was aware of the success of the Assyrian diplomatic activities; he threatened the tribes who were likely to defect: "I will kill you!"[30] During the critical months of 710, efforts were made to avoid harm from either side during the transition of power.

On his march southward, Sargon did not go immediately toward Babylon but went along the eastern bank of the Tigris, first to Dûr-Athara, next to the Surappu river, which had been fortified by Merodach-baladan and surrounded by a ditch filled with water. Sargon besieged and captured the city: "my official I set over them as governor; 1 talent, 30 minas of silver, 200 *gur* of barley, one from every 20 cattle and one from every 20 sheep, as yearly tribute, I laid upon them."[31] A new province, Gambulu, was organized with Dûr-Athara, renamed Dûr-Nabû, as its capital. Sargon remained there for some time, sending his troops southward, as far as the Uknu territory, against Arameans and Elamites, possibly in order to prevent Elamite military aid from being sent to Merodach-baladan. Four chiefs of the Aramean tribe Hindara came and submitted to the Assyrian king. When the time was ripe to go to Babylon, Sargon crossed the Tigris and a branch of the Euphrates up to Dûr-Ladini in Bît-Dakkûri.

---

29. SAA 15:125–26, nos. 187–89; *PNA* 2.2:727.

30. SAA 15:135, no. 208.

31. *ARAB* 2.31; Robartus J. van der Spek, "The Struggle of King Sargon II of Assyria against the Chaldean Merodach-baladan (701–708 B.C.)," *JEOL* 25 (1978): 56–57; Frame, "New Cylinder Inscription," 72–74.

The third phase, with Merodach-baladan's retreat from Babylon and his fruitless attempt to obtain help from Elam, was shortly mentioned in the Babylonian Chronicle: "The twelfth year of Merodach-baladan: Sargon went down [to Akkad] and did battle against [Merodach-bala]dan. Merodach-baladan [retreated] before [him] (and) fled to Elam. For twelve years [Merodach-bala]dan ruled Babylon."[32] It was better described in the Annals: "Merodach-baladan heard of the approach of my expedition, he was seized with anxiety for his own (safety) and fled from Babylon to the city of Ikbi-Bêl, like a bat (?), at night. The inhabitants of his cities and the gods who dwelt therein he gathered together into one (body) and brought them to Dûr-Yakin, whose defenses he strengthened."[33] Merodach-baladan fled first to Jadbur in Elam and tried without success to buy help from Shutruk-nahhunte, king of Elam; unfortunately, the reports of his contacts with Elam are unclear or poorly preserved.[34] Apparently, he did not dare to fight the Assyrians, possibly because he had lost most of his forces in defending Dûr-Athara and maybe also because he had little support from the Babylonian population. The Assyrians had support in Babylon, as stated by Sargon: "The citizens of Babylon and Borsippa, the temple wardens, the *ummānī*-officials, skilled in workmanship, who go before and direct (the people) of the land, (all these) who had been subject to him, brought the 'remnant' (*ri-ḫat*) of Bêl and Sarpanit, (of) Nabû and Tashmetu, to Dûr-Ladini, into my presence, invited me to enter Babylon and (thus) made glad my soul."[35] A number of letters add important details to the royal inscriptions. The reports of Il-Iada were replaced by those of Sharru-êmuranni, Sargon's governor of Babylon. This means that Sargon's triumphal entry into Babylon must have taken place around the time when the retreating Merodach-baladan was about to cross the Tigris. The priests recognized Sargon as king of Babylon. He became king of Babylon by seizing the hands of Marduk, he sacrificed to the gods and set up in Merodach-baladan's palace. He stayed in Babylon for ceremonial purposes only. The Eponym Lists suggest that Sargon spent most of the remaining year 710 in Kish with his army.[36]

---

32. Grayson, *Assyrian and Babylonian Chronicles*, chr. 1, ii, ll. 1–4.
33. *ARAB* 2.31–32, 66–71, 80, 92, 99.
34. SAA 15:xxi; *PNA* 3.2:1296–97.
35. *ARAB* 2.35.
36. SAAS 2:47.

The fourth phase is concerned with the events following the seizure of Babylon. There is much speculation about Sargon's participation in the New Year festival in Babylon and over the fact that Merodach-baladan could have been forgiven and reinstalled as governor of Bît-Yakin.[37] The divergences of interpretation are mainly due to the gaps in the badly preserved texts.[38] Merodach-baladan turned to Iqbi-Bêl, but he could not stay there because, in the month of Iyyar (May) 709 (year 13), Sargon departed from Babylon to pursue him. Iqbi-Bêl and other cities surrendered to Sargon. Then Merodach-baladan took hostages and the gods from Ur (Tell Maqayyar), Uruk (Warka), Eridu, Larsa (Sinkara), Kisik (Tell Lahm), and Nimid-Laguda, and brought them to his ancestral city Dûr-Yakin.[39] He fortified his city, making an extra circumvallation at a distance of 60 meters further out around the city wall and dug a ditch 100 meters wide and 9 meters deep. Then he dug a canal from the Euphrates and inundated the surrounding territory, preparing his capital for the siege to come. There are no letters that referred directly to the war in the territory of Bît-Yakin because Sargon was in command of the operations and written reports were unnecessary.

First Sargon gained a victory over Merodach-baladan outside Dûr-Yakin and his troops carried off considerable spoils. Then he besieged the city of Dûr-Yakin, where Merodach-baladan had taken refuge, but he was unable to capture it; he cut down the orchards in order to persuade the inhabitants to surrender and he threw up a ramp: "But he, Merodach-b[aladan...] became afraid. His scepter (and) his throne he threw down before my messenger, he kissed the earth, his [great] walls [and his circumvallation to pull down] I ordered him and when he obeyed my command, I took pity on him."[40] Evidently Sargon did not take Dûr-Yakin in 709 because Merodach-baladan's position was quite strong: we read that Sargon took pity on him, which probably means that he could not impose

---

37. Lie, *Inscriptions of Sargon II*, 58–59, ll. 13–14; Saggs, "Nimrud Letters, Part IV," 207.

38. Van der Spek, "Struggle of King Sargon II," 58–64 (with bibliography).

39. *ARAB* 2.66.

40. Van der Spek, "Struggle of King Sargon II," 60–63 (with bibliography); Karen Radner, "How Did the Neo-Assyrian King Perceive His Land and Its Resources?," in *Rainfall and Agriculture in Northern Mesopotamia: Proceedings of the Third MOS Symposium (Leiden 1999)*, ed. Remko M. Jas, PIHANS 88 (Leiden: Nederlands Instituut voor het Nabije Oosten, 2000), 240–41.

his will on him. Possibly the town walls were pulled down in return for not destroying the city and for sparing Merodach-baladan's life. The valuables enumerated could represent the price paid for Sargon's withdrawal. The way in which Dûr-Yakin was captured was not explained in the royal inscriptions, probably because the capture was not achieved in a heroic way, but by means of negotiations.

According to the Eponym Lists, the destruction of the city occurred only in 707: "the booty of Dûr-Yakin carried off, Dûr-Yakin destroyed."[41] It seems likely that the scribes of the royal inscriptions, wanting to embellish the story of the capture of Dûr-Yakin, combined its capture in 709 with its destruction two years later, in 707: "Dûr-Yakin, the royal city, I burned with fire; its high battlements I destroyed, I devastated; its foundation platform I tore up, like a mound (left by) a flood, I made it."[42] Possibly even the destruction of the walls was not accomplished in 709, but only in 707. Then Sargon freed the citizens of Sippar, Nippur, Babylon, and Borsippa, who were imprisoned at Dûr-Yakin: "I restored to them their fields which the Sutû had seized long since, during the disturbances in the land."[43] Sargon returned the gods, which had been carried off by Merodach-baladan to Dûr-Yakin in 709, to these cities, and the regular offerings, which had stopped, he inaugurated once again. He reorganized the ancient territories of Merodach-baladan: "All of his wide land I divided from end to end, totally, and put it under my officials, the governor of Babylon and the governor of the land of Gambulu."[44] He proclaimed the remission of debts and granted exemption from the *ilku*-tax in Babylon and other cities in southern Mesopotamia.[45]

Whatever Merodach-baladan may have achieved during his twelve-year reign in Babylon, his authority evaporated as soon as he came under pressure. With almost no consideration for him, the political decisions were made separately by each tribe and city. From the Assyrian point of view, Merodach-baladan may have appeared as the king of Chaldea, but certainly not as a Babylonian. It was just the tribe of Bît-Yakin that had expanded into northern Babylonia. The empire of Merodach-baladan

---

41. SAAS 2:60.
42. *ARAB* 2.68; Frame, "New Cylinder Inscription," 72–74, ll. 5′–9′.
43. *ARAB* 2.68; Gadd, "Inscribed Prisms of Sargon II," 186–87, ll. 50–83.
44. *ARAB* 2.80.
45. SAA 17:126–27, no. 145 (restoring the privileges of Nemed-Lagudu); Lanfranchi, "Consensus to Empire," 84 (with bibliography).

would have had a long way to go to achieve Babylonian Empire status.[46] In his conquest of Babylonia, Sargon appears as a ruler both brilliant in diplomacy as well as in the battlefield. However, the mistakes of his enemies contributed in making him appear so: they lacked cohesion and coordination and were indifferent, opportunistic and selfish. Merodach-baladan survived and waited until Sargon's death to reconquer Babylonia in 703. Babylonians from cities and tribes were ready to flock to his side when he reappeared.

In fact, Sargon made a mistake because he did not take on a Babylonian name as his predecessors Tiglath-pileser III and Shalmaneser V had done; he did not create two separate names to distinguish his dual roles as king of Assyria and king of Babylonia. Instead, he took the path of direct annexation and appointed an Assyrian governor over Babylon, which could be interpreted as demeaning by the Babylonians.[47] The spirit of resistance against Assyria was embodied in the Chaldean tribes, and the populations of the great cities were divided between pro- and anti-Assyrian parties.

Dilmun

Dilmun was described in Sargon's inscriptions as an island located at "a journey of 30 bêru away in the midst of the Sea of the rising sun."[48] This sea is named "the Bitter Sea" in other inscriptions and has been identified with the Persian/Arabian Gulf.[49] Sargon liked to represent the empire that he built in its largest extension, with its farthest and most original borders for Assyrians: islands, as they had no knowledge of the seas at the beginning of their history. Thus, the western border of the Assyrian Empire was the island of Cyprus and its southern (southeastern) border was the island of Dilmun: "beginning with Iatnana (Cyprus) which is in the midst of the Sea of the setting sun, to … the shore of the Bitter Sea as far as Dilmun's border."[50] In the Cyprus stela and in the Display Inscription, the submission of the king of Dilmun, "in the midst of the Sea of the rising sun" was

---

46. Grant Frame, *Babylonia 689–627 B.C.: A Political History*, PIHANS 69 (Leiden: Nederlands Instituut voor het Nabije Oosten, 1992), 52–63; SAA 15:xxii.
47. SAA 19:xxxii–xxxiii.
48. *ARAB* 2.41, 81, 92.
49. *ARAB* 2.54, 96–99, 102.
50. *ARAB* 2.96–99; Galter, "Sargon II. und die Eroberung der Welt," 338, fig. 2.

followed by the parallel submission of seven kings of Cyprus, "in the Sea of the setting sun."[51]

But where was Dilmun located? It was often linked in Sargon's inscriptions with Bît-Yakin, which was on the shore of the Bitter Sea. Bît-Yakin was the region south of Gambulu, in the area of marshes. The configuration of this region has changed a great deal since antiquity, when the Persian/Arabian Gulf penetrated further into the mainland, probably up to the border of Bît-Yakin. This would explain why Bît-Yakin was said to be on the shore of the Bitter Sea and Sargon in Bît-Yakin to be on the seashore.[52] The distance of the island of Dilmun off the mainland coast is indicated: "Upêri, king of Dilmun, who lives, like a fish, 30 *bêru* away in the midst of the Sea of the rising sun."[53] The *bêru* was an Akkadian unit of time, the "double hour," and also a unit of distance. As the unit of distance was likely based on the unit of time, the variations in the measurement of the *bêru* could be explained on the basis of various marching speeds. Based on a value of 10.8 km for 1 *bêru*, as has most commonly been proposed, 30 *bêru* would be approximately equivalent to 324 km.[54] The question is knowing where the point of reference for calculating that distance was: the seashore facing Dilmun, the seashore of Bît-Yakin, or the heartland of Assyria. Assuming that the configuration of the Persian/Arabian Gulf was different in Sargon's time, the point of reference for the distance would correspond better to the seashore of Bît-Yakin. This would mean that the island of Dilmun was much further in the south of the Gulf, but where exactly? The problem of its exact localization is complex because, according to the period, from the third millennium on, this term probably designated various places. During the Neo-Assyrian period, several proposals for different islands of the Persian/Arabian Gulf have been made: Bahrain, Failaka in Kuwait, or Tarut in Saudi Arabia.

---

51. *ARAB* 2.70, 185; Malbran-Labat, "Inscription assyrienne," 348, 350, ll. 23–30.

52. *ARAB* 2.43, 54; Paul Sanlaville, "Considérations sur l'évolution de la basse Mésopotamie au cours des derniers millénaires," *Paléorient* 15.2 (1989): 5–27; Paul Sanlaville and Rémi Dalongeville, "L'évolution des espaces littoraux du golfe Persique et du golfe d'Oman depuis la phase finale de la transgression post-glaciaire," *Paléorient* 31/1 (2005): 10–11 (map), 19; Joannès, *Dictionnaire de la civilisation mésopotamienne*, 793 (map).

53. *ARAB* 2.41; Gadd, "Inscribed Prisms of Sargon II," 112, ll. 20–22; *PNA* 3.2:1390.

54. *CAD*, s.v. *berū*; Jeremy Black, Andrew George, and J. N. Postgate, *A Concise Dictionary of Akkadian*, SANTAG 5 (Wiesbaden: Harrassowitz, 2000), s.v. *berū(m)* III.

The identification of Dilmun with Bahrain was first proposed by Rawlinson in 1880.[55] Excavations conducted at Qalaat al-Bahrain, exhuming buildings and tombs, attested that the site was occupied in the Neo-Assyrian period.[56] Another proposal of localization is the island of Failaka. Excavations in this island, in particular at Tell Khazneh and Tell Saîd, have revealed a material culture similar to that of Bahrain, with more numerous Mesopotamian objects such as cylinder-seals and ceramics.[57] The Middle Bronze and Neo-Babylonian periods are well-attested, for example, with a stela of Nebuchadnezzar II, but the Neo-Assyrian period is only attested by some objects, and the stratigraphy is uncertain.[58] These are problems with the excavations, which does not mean that an occupation of the site during Sargon's reign is excluded. Another proposal of the localization of Dilmun is Tarut, 6 kilometers from the town of Qatif on the Saudi Arabia coastline. The excavations conducted beginning in 1968 and their fortuitous discoveries showed a continuous occupation of the site from prehistoric times to the Ottoman period, including the Neo-Assyrian period.[59] The distance given in Sargon's inscriptions—around 324 km—calculated from the ancient seashore of Bît-Yakin, does not fit either with Bahrain (around 800 km) or with Tarut (around 600 km). It corresponds to the island of Failaka. Therefore, it can be proposed as a likely hypothesis that Dilmun designated, in the reign of Sargon, the island of Failaka. A passage of Sennacherib's inscriptions, dated to a few years later, attested that the

---

55. Daniel T. Potts, "Dilmun: Where and When?," *Dilmun* 2 (1983): 15–19; Potts, *The Arabian Gulf in Antiquity* (Oxford: Oxford University Press, 1990); Geoffrey Bibby, *Looking for Dilmun* (London: Stacey International, 2001) (with bibliography).

56. Daniel T. Potts, "Revisiting the Snake Burials of the Late Dilmun Building Complex on Bahrain," *AAE* 18 (2007): 55–74 (with bibliography); Steffen Terp Laursen, *The Royal Mounts of A'ali, Bahrain: The Emergence of Kingship in Early Dilmun*, Moesgard Museum, Denmark, and BACA (forthcoming).

57. Jean-François Salles and Yves Calvet, *Failaka: Fouilles françaises 1984–1985*, TMO 12 (Lyon: Maison de l'Orient, 1986).

58. T. Howard-Carter, "Kuwait," *RlA* 6:395; Salles and Calvet, *Failaka*, 119, 126; Jean-Jacques Glassner, "Inscriptions cunéiformes de Failaka," in *Failaka: Fouilles françaises*, ed. Jean-François Salles, TMO 9 (Lyon: Maison de l'Orient, 1983), 31–50.

59. Abdullah H. Masry, *Prehistory in Northern Arabia: The Problem of Interregional Interaction* (London: Kegan Paul International, 1997), vi; Harriet Crawford, *Dilmun and its Gulf Neighbours* (Cambridge: Cambridge University Press, 1998), 38–48; P. R. S. Moorey, *Ancient Mesopotamian Materials and Industries: The Archaeological Evidence* (Winona Lake, IN: Eisenbrauns, 1999), 47–48, 88.

Assyrians had a good knowledge of Failaka and that Dilmun was Failaka. After the Assyrian king was responsible for the Euphrates flooding Babylon, carrying with it much earth, it was stated that "its earth reached unto Dilmun."[60] This is a precise designation of the muddy water that usually surrounds the island of Failaka. Even if Dilmun was not limited to the island of Failaka in antiquity, it was, from the beginning of the third millennium, an important transit point for the trade between Mesopotamia and the Indian ocean. For example, copper, wood, and precious stones came from Magan (Oman) and Melukka (Indus valley).[61]

The king of Dilmun is referred to as Upêri in all Sargon's inscriptions, except for the Tang-i Var inscription and the Nimrud Prisms, where he is called Ahundara, a likely variant of the name Hundâru, attested for a ruler of Dilmun in the reign of Ashurbanipal.[62] Gadd suggested that Upêri had made a first submission to Sargon in 709 and that Ahundara was his successor, mentioned in the latest texts of his reign.[63] There are some variants in the passages concerning Dilmun. After having heard of Sargon's "lordly might" or "of the might of Assur, Nabû (and) Marduk," the king of Dilmun himself brought his gifts to Sargon on the Bît-Yakin shoreline, or he sent his ambassador to the Assyrian king, obviously by boat.[64] The inscriptions mention "gifts," "greeting gifts," "tribute" or "tribute and gifts."[65] In some inscriptions, the king of Dilmun or his ambassador made submission to Sargon: "his ambassador, offering submission and bringing tribute (and)

---

60. *ARAB* 2.438.

61. Jean-François Salles, "La circumnavigation de l'Arabie dans l'Antiquité," in *L'Arabie et ses mers bordières: I Itinéraires et voisinages; Séminaire de recherche 1985–1986*, ed. Jean-François et al., TMO 16 (Lyon: Maison de l'Orient, 1988); Jesper Eidem and Flemming Højlund, "Trade or Diplomacy? Assyria and Dilmun in the Eighteenth Century BC," *WA* 24 (1993): 441–48; Daniel T. Potts, "Distant Shores: Ancient Near East Trade with South Asia and Northeast Africa," *CANE*, 1452–55; Himanshu Prabha Ray, *The Archaeology of Seafaring in Ancient South Asia*, CWA (Cambridge: Cambridge University Press, 2003), 85.

62. Gadd, "Inscribed Prisms of Sargon II," 194; Potts, *Arabian Gulf in Antiquity*, 335–96; Frame, "Inscription of Sargon II," 39–40, l. 27, 46; *PNA* 2.1:479.

63. Gadd, "Inscribed Prisms of Sargon II," 194.

64. *ARAB* 2.41, 70, 81; Gadd, "Inscribed Prisms of Sargon II," 192, l. 24; Frame, "Inscription of Sargon II," 39–40, l. 27; *ARAB* 2.41, 81 (he "brought"); 2.43 ("he sent his ambassador"). Other texts (2.70, 92, 185) do not give any precision ("he sent").

65. *ARAB* 2.41, 70, 81, 92, 185 ("gifts"); Frame, "Inscription of Sargon II," 39–40, l. 25 ("greeting gift"); Gadd, "Inscribed Prisms of Sargon II," 192, l. 24 ("tribute"); *ARAB* 2.43 ("tribute and gifts").

gifts, he sent to me to the Sea [of the East]."⁶⁶ In some other inscriptions, Sargon quoted Dilmun among the submitted countries: "... Bît-Yakin which is on the shore of the Bitter Sea, as far as Dilmun's border, all these I brought under my sway and set my officials over them as governors, and imposed upon them the yoke of my sovereignty."⁶⁷ The military campaign of Sargon to Bît-Yakin, on the shore of the Persian/Arabian Gulf, meant that he intended to control the trade toward the Indian Ocean, as his son Sennacherib did, after him. The king of Dilmun became a vassal of Sargon, paying tribute, but, just like Cyprus, it was difficult to control him tightly in his island refuge.

Arab Tribes

Arab presence in the Near East probably started at the beginning of the first millennium BCE.⁶⁸ The first traces of an alphabetic writing in south Arabia (modern Yemen) can be dated from around the tenth–eight century, but the first South Arabic inscriptions are only dated from the sixth century.⁶⁹ Therefore, the Arab tribes are first known from the foreign sources, mainly biblical and Assyrian. The term *Arabs* (*Aribi, Arbaia, ʿrbym*) was used in Assyrian and Babylonian records with the meaning of "bedouins," desert nomads, applied to the dwellers of the Syro-Arabian desert, North Arabia, and northern Sinai.⁷⁰ In fact, the term *Arabs* is ambiguous, having sometimes a linguistic, sometimes a geographical, and sometimes an ethnological definition. It often designated a way of life rather than an ethnic group.

The Bible opposed two different lands of Arabia: the south of the Arabian peninsula, the kingdom of Saba (*Arabia felix* of the Romans); and

---

66. *ARAB* 2.43.
67. *ARAB* 2.102.
68. Israel Ephʻal, "'Arabs' in Babylonia in the Eighth century B.C.," *JAOS* 94 (1974): 108–15; Ephʻal, *Ancient Arabs*, 91–93; Robert G. Hoyland, *Arabia and the Arabs: From the Bronze Age to the Coming of Islam* (London: Routledge, 2001); Jan Retsö, *The Arabs in Antiquity: Their History from the Assyrians to the Umayyads* (New York: Routledge, 2003); Briquel-Chatonnet, *Araméens et les premiers Arabes*, 27–34.
69. Norbert Nebes and Peter Stein, "Ancient South Arabian," in *The Ancient Languages of Syria-Palestine and Arabia*, ed. Roger D. Woodard (Cambridge: Cambridge University Press, 2008), 145–78.
70. The application of this word to the entire Arabian peninsula occurred close to the beginning of the Christian era; see Ephʻal, "'Arabs' in Babylonia," 108 and n. 1.

the desert north of Arabia. The first group descended from Ham, the evil son of Noah (Gen 10:6–7). The second group descended from Shem, and even from Abraham, as sons of Ishmael (Gen 16:1–17:25; 25:12–18). This opposition is also present in the description of Tyrian trade in the book of Ezekiel: on the one hand, the oasis of Hijaz (Dedan) and the north of Arabia (Qedar); on the other hand, Yemen, the south of Arabia (Saba) (Ezek 27:20–22). Moreover, Arabs were also presented in the Bible as people having a particular way of life, for example, in an oracle of Isaiah announcing the ruin of Babylon: "Neither shall the Arabian pitch tent there; neither shall the shepherds make their fold there. But wild beasts of the desert shall lie there" (Isa 13:20–22).

In the Assyrian inscriptions, there were three different Arabian political entities: the tribes, the kingdom of Saba, and the kingdom of Qedar. In the description of the battle of Qarqar in 853 under Shalmaneser III, a contingent of one thousand camels led by "Gindibu, the Arab" is mentioned.[71] Tiglath-pileser III received the tribute of "Zabibê, queen of Arabia."[72] The existence of walled towns with Arab names reflects the extent and intensity of Arab penetration into Babylonia in the second half of the eighth century, probably resulting from a prolonged process.[73] The language of the personal names of the Arabs known from the Assyrian and Babylonian inscriptions is close to South Arabic, but this material is too scanty to allow conclusions to be drawn concerning their ethnic origin. Two letters probably dating from the period of Sargon confirm the existence of an Arab entity in Babylonia in the eighth century. The first one mentioned an Arab raid on Sippar, probably not the fortified city, but the surrounding area.[74] The second dealt with Arab razzias in the territories of Suhi and Hindânu, in the region of the middle Euphrates.[75] Towns associated with Arabs in the inscriptions were located in the territories of Bît-Dakkuri and Bît-Amukkâni, but never in Bît-Yakin.[76] This would mean that the Arabs penetrated into western Babylonia via the main Arabian desert routes: from Wadi Sirhân via Jauf (Dûmat al-Jandal, biblical Dumah) and by the

---

71. *ARAB* 1.611.
72. *ARAB* 1.772; *PNA* 3.2:1429.
73. Eph'al, "'Arabs' in Babylonia," 111–12 (with bibliography).
74. Leroy Waterman, *Royal Correspondence of the Assyrian Empire*, vols. 1–3 (Ann Arbor: University of Michigan Press, 1930–1936), 1:58–59, no. 88.
75. Waterman, *Royal Correspondence*, 1:388–89, no. 547.
76. Eph'al, "'Arabs' in Babylonia," 113 (BM 113203).

route of Median, Hail, and Hûfa, both routes reaching the area of en-Najf. There is no evidence that the Arabs reached the region of the Persian/Arabian Gulf at that time. They were probably settled in the northern oasis and in control of trans-Arabian trade, and they occasionally became allies of the Chaldeans in their military activities.[77]

According to the Annals, Sargon confronted Arab tribes on two occasions. In 715 (year 7), the Assyrian king struck down "the tribes of Tamud, Ibâdidi, Marsîmani and Haiapâ, distant Arabs, who inhabit the desert, who know neither high nor low official, and who had not brought their tribute to any king."[78] The location of these tribes is unknown. Then Sargon deported the remnant and settled them in Samaria. In 713 (year 9), he attacked "the lands of Uiadaue, Bustis, Agazi, Ambanda, Dananu, distant provinces on the eastern Aribi border."[79] Their location has not been identified either. It is impossible to establish the kinds of relations between the Arab nomads in the desert and the settlements in Babylonia, being at differing stages of sedentary life.

Other inscriptions of Sargon mention the tribute offered by Arab kings or queens, together with that of the pharaoh: "From Piru, king of Egypt, Samsi, queen of Arabia, Itamar, the Sabean, the kings of the seacoast and the desert, I received gold, products of the mountains, precious stones, ivory, seed of the ebony, all kinds of herbs, horses and camels, as their tribute."[80] Who was Samsi, queen of Arabia? The social structures of her kingdom suggest that women enjoyed a high degree of independence and could even occupy the throne; the queens were possibly also priestesses.[81] Samsi was allied with the coalition headed by Rahianu (Rezin) of Damascus and was defeated by Tiglath-pileser III in 733 at Mount Saqurri, in the north of Jordan; among others, he seized thirty thousand camels and twenty thousand cattle.[82] To save her life, she fled to "a place of thirst, like a jenny." Apparently, she was allowed to keep her throne, under Assyrian control: "A (political) agent, I set over her." One of Samsi's successors was "Iatie, queen of the Arabs," who aided Merodach-baladan, defeated by Sennacherib in his first campaign. Teelhunu, another of her successors as

---

77. Fales, "Moving around Babylon," 97.
78. *ARAB* 2.17, 118; Gadd, "Inscribed Prisms of Sargon II," 119–20, l. 18.
79. *ARAB* 2.23.
80. *ARAB* 2.18, 55; *PNA* 2.1:587, 3.1:1085.
81. Joannès, *Dictionnaire de la civilisation mésopotamienne*, s.v. "Arabie."
82. *ARAB* 1.778, 817.

queen of the Arabs, was defeated around the end of Sennacherib's reign.[83] Samsi had the title of "queen" (*šarrat*). She ruled a kingdom that was probably a kind of tribal confederation. Its name was "the country of Arabia" (*māt Aribi*). But where was this country? Teelhunu was "queen of the Arabs," allied around 680 with Hazail "king of Qedar," who had nothing to do with Hazail, chieftain of Gambulu in 710.[84] Zabibê, listed among those who paid tribute to Tiglath-pileser III around 738, was possibly "queen of Qidri and Aribi."[85] This would mean that, at that time, the two kingdoms, Aribi (Arabia) and Qidri (Qedar), were unified and ruled by one queen; later, under Sargon and Sennacherib, they were separated and ruled by a queen and a king respectively. However, the kingdom of Qedar was not mentioned in Sargon's inscriptions.

Itamar the Sabean, who sent tribute to Sargon, did not hold the explicit title of king, but the formulation does not exclude that he was a king. Itamar was not mentioned elsewhere in Sargon's royal inscriptions. But the kingdom of Saba is well known from the Bible, with the visit of the queen of Saba (Sheba) to King Solomon at the end of the tenth century (1 Kgs 10). Saba was located in modern Yemen, rather than in Ethiopia, with Marib, which has been excavated, as its capital, high in the mountains.[86] The name Saba appears in the Bible as one of the sons of Yoktan, along with other Arabian toponyms (Gen 10:25–29).[87] The people of Saba

---

83. *ARAB* 2.259, 358; *PNA* 3.2:1322.

84. *ARAB* 2.31. On Qedar, see Ernst Axel Knauf, *Ismael Untersuchungen zur Geschichte Palästinas und Nordarabiens im 1. Jahrtausend v. Chr.*, ADPV 7 (Wiesbaden: Harrassowitz, 1985), 45.

85. *ARAB* 2.772; Ephʿal, *Ancient Arabs*, 82; Kenneth A. Kitchen, *Documentation for Ancient Arabs, Part 2: Bibliographical Catalogue of Texts* (Liverpool: Liverpool University Press, 1994), 741; Gallagher, *Sennacherib's Campaign to Judah*, 53 n. 120; Briquel-Chatonnet, *Araméens et les premiers Arabes*, 32–34; *PNA* 3.2:1429.

86. Andrey Korotayev, *Ancient Yemen: Some General Trends of Evolution of the Sabaic Language and Sabaean Culture*, JSSSup 5 (Oxford: Oxford University Press, 1995); Joseph Chelhod et al., *Arabie du Sud: histoire et civilisation, le peuple yéménite et ses racines I* (Paris: Maisonneuve & Larose, 1995); Jean-François Breton, *L'Arabie heureuse au temps de la reine de Saba, VIIIe-Ier siècle avant J.-C.*, Vie quotidienne (Paris: Hachette, 1998); Mounir Arbach, "Le royaume de Saba au Ier millénaire avant J.-C.," *DoArch* 263 (2001): 12–17; Bar Kribus, "Where Is the Land of Sheba-Arabia or Africa?," *BAR* 42.5 (2016): 26–60.

87. Gus W. van Beek, "The Land of Sheba," in *Solomon and Sheba*, ed. James B. Pritchard (London: Phaidon, 1974), 40–63; Yosef Green, "The Reign of King Solomon: Diplomatic and Economic Perspectives," *JBQ* 42.3 (2014): 153–56.

probably created a state that dominated southern Arabia, where incense, medicaments, cosmetics, and spices passed through en route to India or Africa and where women apparently enjoyed a high degree of independence. According to Josephus, the nameless queen of Saba was actually called Nikaule and ruled over Egypt and Ethiopia (*A.J.* 8.174; 158–159). Solomon's ships navigated in the Red Sea and his caravans penetrated into Arabia. He probably competed with the queen of Saba who decided to cross over 1,930 km of desert for economic and political motives. Several legends developed concerning the historical connection between the two kingdoms of Saba and Israel-Judah.

The picture of Assyrian-Arab relations under Sargon's reign is different in the official inscriptions and in the correspondence. The official inscriptions show the reaffirmation of Assyrian power in the southwestern Levant, over a group of Arab tribes already subjugated by Tiglath-pileser III. Letters spoke of troublesome movements of Arab nomads in central-southern Mesopotamia and gave a clear image of the difficulty the Assyrian king had in keeping the nomadic groups under control.[88] In order to prevent the plundering of agricultural villages, Sargon decided to create a vast reservation in southern Jezirah to keep the Arab nomads away from the settled areas. They tended to move out of bounds and to attack the sites on the riverbank of the Euphrates; they even reached the region of Nimrud.[89] There was a prohibition against selling iron to the Arabs, probably to reserve all available sources of iron directly for the Assyrian Empire.[90]

The politics of the Assyrian kings, in particular Tiglath-pileser III and Sargon, aimed to integrate the Arab tribes as much as possible, or at least to control them and to direct the caravan trade toward the Mediterranean harbors that belonged to the Assyrian Empire. Some tribes supported the anti-Assyrian rebellions and the Assyrian king was obliged to fight with them by organizing expeditions against oasis locations and pursuing them in the desert. Sargon tried to obtain the submission, trib-

---

88. F. M. Fales, "Central Syria in the Letters to Sargon II," in *Kein Land für sich allein: Studien zum Kulturkontakt in Kanaan, Israel/Palästina und Ebirnâri für Manfred Weippert zum 65. Geburtstag*, ed. Ulrich Hübner and Ernst Axel Knauf, OBO 186 (Fribourg: Presses Universitaires; Göttingen: Vandenhoeck & Ruprecht, 2002), 145–47.

89. SAA 1:74–75, nos. 82–83.

90. SAA 1:140–41, no. 179.

8. RECURRING PROBLEMS IN THE SOUTH

ute, and help of Arabian kingdoms and nonhostile tribes. For example, he entrusted the supervision of a new trade emporium on the border of the brook of Egypt (possibly Tell er-Ruqeish) to the Arab sheikh of Laban (see above); this leader of one Arab nomad group was living not far from northern Egypt. These Arab tribes probably inhabited northern Sinai. Several sources reflect the geopolitical situation in this area and the importance of the nomads as a military-logistic factor.[91] The Arab tribes of Sinai are still not well known because of the lack of inscriptions; however, several excavations provide some information.[92] The Sinai had important mineral resources, in particular copper in the southwest, next to the Wadi Nash and at Seh Nasb, and turquoises at Serabit el-Khadim; these sites, which were intensively exploited by the Egyptians, have been excavated since 2006.[93]

In short, the south of the Assyrian Empire appears to have been the most difficult region for Sargon to deal with because of its complexity and because of the recurring problems. He was obliged to wait ten years before being able to conquer Babylonia; it was a difficult task because Babylonia offered a combination of enemies: Chaldean, Aramean, and Arab tribes, Elamite allies, and anti-Assyrian Babylonians. He succeeded, but he committed the error of annexing Babylonia as an ordinary province, for which he was never forgiven; as soon as he died, the problem recurred, it was as if he had done nothing. Babylonia was the only great enemy power that Sargon conquered; others such as Egypt, Mushki, Urartu, and Elam were not. Sargon also managed to extend his domination over the multiple and moving tribal powers, which needed permanent efforts to maintain control.

---

91. Herodotus *Hist.* 2.141; Eph'al, *Ancient Arabs*, 91–93, 137–42.

92. Lina Eckenstein, *A History of Sinai* (London: Cambridge University Press, 1921); Benno Rothenberg and Yohanan Aharoni, *God's Wilderness, Discoveries in Sinai* (London: Thames & Hudson, 1961); Benno Rothenberg, *Sinai, Pharaonen, Bergleute, Pilger und Soldaten* (Bern: Kümmerly & Frey, 1979); Dominique Valbelle and Charles Bonnet, *Le Sinaï durant l'antiquité et le Moyen Age: 4000 ans d'Histoire pour un désert; actes du colloque "Sinaï" qui s'est tenu à l'UNESCO du 19 au 21 septembre 1997* (Paris: Errance, 1998).

93. Domonique Valbelle and Charles Bonnet, *Le sanctuaire d'Hathor, maîtresse de la turquoise: Sérabit el-Khadim au Moyen Empire* (Paris: Picard, 1996), 60–63 and 13 (map); Philippe Tallet, Georges Castel, and Pierre Fluzin, "Metallurgical Sites of South Sinai (Egypt) in the Pharaonic Era: New Discoveries," *Paléorient* 39 (2011): 79–89.

9
End of Reign

In 707, Sargon was at the height of his glory, power, and wealth. He had finally reconquered Babylon where he had resided for three years. The whole of his empire was pacified except for the small island of Tyre, a negligible problem as, from 709, it was isolated by the siege of Assyrian troops (see above). He had just received some excellent news: his city of Khorsabad/Dûr-Sharrukîn was completed after about ten years of colossal building work. He was preparing his return from Babylon to organize moving back and settling into his new capital and to make the preparations for its magnificent, unimaginable inauguration, a highly anticipated moment for him. He was about sixty years old, but he was carefree because his son Sennacherib, the crown prince, whom he had designated at the beginning of his reign, was helping, representing and replacing him as often as required. Moreover, he felt in better form than ever, always able to undertake a military campaign if necessary, as was the case in 705.

The Inauguration of Khorsabad/Dûr-Sharrukîn

Sargon finally possessed the city that he had wanted built in his honor. It was an old dream that was realized, maybe his main dream, and all he had to do now was to enjoy it. Khorsabad/Dûr-Sharrukîn was the capital of the world, a visual demonstration of his superhuman power, he who was the "king of the universe" (*šar kiššati*) (fig. 8). What made this city unique was the megalomaniac drive and unparalleled effort of organization behind its construction: it was a city entirely conceived and built by the king.[1] He himself claimed: "I planned and thought day and night in order to make

---

1. Parpola, "Construction of Dur-Šarrukin," 49–50; Battini, "Portes urbaines de la capitale," 41–42.

the city habitable, and to erect its shrines as abodes for the great gods, and a complex of palaces as my royal residence."[2] The foundations of the city were laid, after consulting the gods, in his fifth year (717).[3] The place chosen was a virgin land between Mount Musri and the Husur river, next to the village of Magganabba, about 16 km northeast of Nineveh. Sargon mentioned in his inscriptions that he "reimbursed the owners of the fields with silver and bronze according to the purchase documents."[4] How did he choose the location of Khorsabad? It has been proposed that he wanted to be closer to the northern and eastern borders of his empire, particularly difficult to control, and to be able to react quickly, from this strongly fortified city, in case of necessity.[5] While this reason is possible, he also chose the place for other reasons, first for practical reasons: it was easy to supply with water thanks to the proximity of the springs of Mount Musri, and a hill provided an acropolis for the city. Other reasons, more personal, were that he chose the place after much thought and because he had a soft spot for this place, as is said in his inscriptions: "following the prompting of my heart, I built a city at the foot of Mount Musri, in the plain of Nineveh, and named it Dûr-Sharrukîn (fortress of Sargon)."[6] In the pavement inscriptions of Khorsabad, besides the prompting of his heart, he said he had made his choice "at the command of gods."[7]

The historian has an exceptionally abundant amount of documentation about the city's building history: numerous royal inscriptions carved on the walls and other parts of the palaces and temples, the reliefs of the royal palace illustrating episodes of the building process, and a large number of letters (113) and other documents from the Assyrian archives.[8] While the royal inscriptions were written to glorify Sargon and thus extolled the magnificence of the city by describing it in considerable detail, the letters are mainly concerned with practical matters like the planning, organization, supervision, problems, and difficulties encountered in the execution of assigned tasks.

---

2. Fuchs, *Inschriften Sargons II*, xiv, 310, l. 31.
3. Parpola, "Construction of Dur-Šarrukin," 50; Joannès, *Dictionnaire de la civilisation mésopotamienne*, 249.
4. Fuchs, *Inschriften Sargons II*, Zyl. 51–52.
5. Joannès, *The Age of Empires*, 109–10.
6. *ARAB* 2.105.
7. *ARAB* 2.98–99, 102.
8. Parpola, "Construction of Dur-Šarrukin," 50 and nn. 14–17.

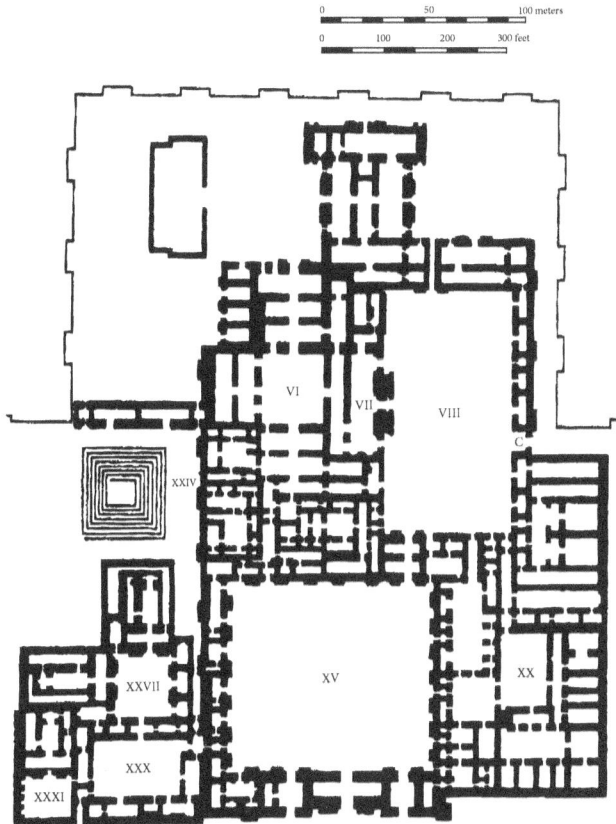

Fig. 8. Plan of the Palace of Dûr-Sharrukîn (Khorsabad). After Albenda, 1986, map 3.

Sargon named Tab-shar-Ashur, chief treasurer, eponym of the year 717, as chief coordinator and supervisor of the construction works in general and of Khorsabad in particular.[9] Moreover, twenty-six governors were explicitly associated with the works, coming from all parts of the empire; this meant that practically the whole empire was, through the governors,

---

9. Ibid., 51; Parpola, "The Assyrian Cabinet," in *Vom Alten Orient Zum Alten Testament: Festschrift für Wolfram Freiherrn von Soden zum 85. Geburtstag am 19. Juni 1993*, ed. Manfred Dietrich and Oswald Loretz, AOAT 240 (Neukirchen-Vluyn: Neukirchener Verlag, 1995), 379–401; P. Matthiae, "Subject Innovations in the Khorsabad Reliefs and Their Political Meaning," in Lanfranchi, *Leggo*, 479; May, "Administrative and Other Reforms," 81–82; *PNA* 3.2:1344–46.

committed to the realization of the project.[10] However, Sargon not only took an active interest in the project, he also directed it personally and followed the progress of the works. He felt impatient eagerness for the project to be completed as soon as possible. It can be seen from the letters, which cited about forty royal orders, that he intervened in practically all matters, from the requisition of labor to problems of material transportation, and discussions involving architectural details. The king's direct input helps to understand how the project could be completed so efficiently, for example, the following order to the governor of Nimrud, both technically precise and threatening: "700 bales of straw and 700 bundles of reeds, and each bundle no more than a donkey can carry, must be at hand in Khorsabad by the 1st day of Kislev. Should even one day pass by, you will die."[11] However, the Assyrian king could also adopt a lenient tone with relatives or friends, and a conciliatory tone when having to deal with grumbling labor.[12]

How did Sargon finance such a huge building project? First, a considerable part of the expenses was financed by loans taken from private moneylenders. The royal treasury was evidently also used by converting gold and precious stones into money, maybe weighed silver. One aim of the conquests of Sargon was to collect booty, new taxes, and tribute to contribute to covering the building expenses. However, the bulk of the labor and material for the new capital was obtained cheaply or for no cost because he built the city "with the (labor of) the enemy peoples which his hands had conquered."[13] For instance, a fragmentary letter to the king indicated that, among the workers, there were deportees from Samaria: "Concerning what the king, my lord, wrote to me: 'Provide all the Samarians in your hands with work in Khorsabad,' I subsequently sent word to the sheikhs, saying: 'Collect your carpenters and potters; let them come and direct the deportees who are in Khorsabad.'"[14] Another source of cheap labor consisted of Assyrian citizens under work obligation: they were subject to military service and also, in principle, to labor service. The only Assyrians exempt from labor service were those of the army, which included the special troops and mercenaries employed in the cav-

---

10. SAA 1:8, 62, 120–21, 185–86, nos. 4, 65, 150, 237; SAA 5:206, no. 291.
11. SAA 1:24, no. 26.
12. SAA 1:8, 14–15, 24, nos. 4, 12, 25.
13. *ARAB* 2.98–100.
14. Waterman, *Royal Correspondence*, 2:240–41, no. 1065, ll. 1–10.

alry and chariotry.[15] Concerning the specialized labor, Sargon was personally involved; the order to furnish these specialists came directly from him and not from the chief treasurer.[16] This reflected Assyria's centralized system, which concentrated all power in the king's hands to the detriment of his subordinates, even the highest officials.[17] The king's impatience was visible, for instance, when he ordered the building of boats to transport stone objects such as the bulls: "They must be finished by the beginning of the month!" In fact, the bulls could be brought across the river only once a year, in the month of Iyyar (February), when the water in the river was high enough.[18]

The city was grandiose: the area enclosed within its walls, 3 square kilometers, made it one of the largest cities in antiquity. Khorsabad was the reflection of how Sargon saw himself and wished everyone else to see him.[19] A huge artificial platform on the north side of the city supported a 7-meter-high acropolis, fortified by a wall, with temples and "palaces of ivory, maple, boxwood, mulberry, cedar, cypress, juniper, lime and pistachio-wood."[20] The massive city wall was 20 meters high and 14 meters thick; it was reinforced, at 15-meter intervals, by more than two hundred bastions. There was an unclear symbolic correspondence between the length of the city wall and the name of Sargon (see above). The two city walls and the doors were all given divine names. The internal wall was called Assur and the external Ninurta. The seven doors were also given divine names: Enlil, Anu, Ishtar, Ea, Bêlet-ilî, Shamash, and Adad.[21] There were geometrical and numerical correspondences between the different elements of the city, following a conception of the cosmos where the king was the center point, identified with Sîn and Shamash.[22] His royal palace,

---

15. J. N. Postgate, *Taxation and Conscription in the Assyrian Empire*, StPohlSM 3 (Rome: Biblical Institute Press, 1974), 90, 221; Parpola, "Construction of Dur-Šarrukin," 55; SAA 5:25–26, no. 32.

16. Parpola, "Construction of Dur-Šarrukin," 56.

17. Parpola, "Assyrian Cabinet," 379–401.

18. SAA 1:73, no. 80; Burkhard Engel, *Darstellungen von Dämoner und Tieren in assyrischen Palästen und Tempeln nach der schriftlichen Qellen* (Mönchengladbach: Hackbarth, 1987), 22–25.

19. J. E. Reade, "Ideology and Propaganda in Assyrian Art," in Larsen, *Power and Propaganda*, 342.

20. *ARAB* 2.84.

21. Joannès, *Dictionnaire de la civilisation mésopotamienne*, 249–51.

22. Battini, "Portes urbaines de la capitale," 41–55; Battini, "Des rapports géomé-

"palace without rival," following the expression used by his son Sennacherib, was the most spectacular edifice of the city on account of the magnificence of its new architecture and artistic decoration.[23] It was sitting astride the city wall, an unparalleled position, and was the largest Assyrian palace (10 hectares). With the six temples of Sîn, Shamash, Nikkal, Ea, Adad, and Ninurta, and the ziggurat that it embodied, it represented the highest point of the city. The rich decoration of the royal palace is partly preserved: most of the stone reliefs and winged bulls, but only a few remains of paintings and glazed bricks, and none of the bronze statues mentioned in the inscriptions. The temple of Nabû was connected by a stone bridge to the royal palace, and on the acropolis there were at least four residences for high officials, such as that of the king's brother, the vizier Sîn-ahu-usur. In the southeast of the city, also sitting astride the city wall, was another edifice called Palace F, identified as an "arsenal" (*ekal mâšarti*).[24]

The temples were provided with vast areas of real estate, for example, 4,000 hectares for the temple of Nabû. According to his inscriptions, Sargon also added to his project a park: "A park like unto Mount Amanus, in which were set out every tree of the Hittite-land, the plants of every mountain, I laid out by its side."[25] Seven letters referred to the saplings of trees to be planted in this park, coming from the northwestern provinces of Assyria, mostly from the Khabur region. For example, a letter from the Jezireh mentioned 2,350 bundles of apple tree saplings and 450 bundles of medlar tree saplings, almond, quince, and plum trees, transported to Khorsabad.[26] In addition to fruit trees, cedars and cypresses were planted in the park.[27] The city proper has remained largely unexcavated, but appears from some soundings to have been densely populated.[28] Even if the whole area of the city was not entirely inhabited, the hypothesis that

---

triques en architecture: Le cas de Dūr-Šarrukin," *RA* 94 (2000): 33–56; Joannès, *The Age of Empires*, 106–9.

23. *ARAB* 2.375. Victor Place, *Ninive et l'Assyrie, avec des essais de restauration par Félix Thomas*, vol. II (Paris: Imprimerie Impériale, 1867–1870), 79 and pl. 37; Loud and Altman, *Khorsabad, Part II*, 18–95; Albenda, *Palace of Sargon*.

24. See the plan of the city: Joannès, *Dictionnaire de la civilisation mésopotamienne*, 250.

25. *ARAB* 2.83.

26. SAA 1:176–77, no. 226.

27. SAA, 1:177–78, no. 227.

28. Loud and Altman, *Khorsabad, Part II*, 75; Parpola, "Construction of Dur-Šarrukin," 49–50.

presents Khorsabad as sparsely inhabited or not completely finished is probably unfounded.[29] In his new city, Sargon wished on the one hand to exalt the role of Assyrian aristocracy in the management of the empire, as is reflected in the building of high officials' residences and in its frequent representation in the reliefs of his palace.[30] On the other hand, he tried to unify the vast diversity of the peoples of his empire in the language, culture, and religion of Assyria: "Peoples of the four regions (of the world), of foreign tongue and divergent speech, dwellers of mountain and lowland … I unified them and settled them therein. Assyrians, fully competent to teach them how to fear god and the king, I dispatched to them as scribes and sheriffs."[31] Sargon evidently believed that it would lead to happy conditions being created for all his subjects. The inscriptions relating to Khorsabad evoke a kind of new golden age initiated by Sargon, the foundation of a new world order and a new Assyrian Empire.[32]

The inauguration of Khorsabad, once the city was completed, was sumptuous, a reminder of another noteworthy event: the inauguration of Nimrud by Ashurnasirpal II around 864.[33] It was also a tradition for the Sargonids when they inaugurated a new capital or a new palace: they first invited the gods, then all the people representing the empire; this inauguration was similar, for instance, to that of the new palaces of Sennacherib, Esarhaddon, and Ashurbanipal.[34] The first part of the inauguration in 707 was the settling of the gods in the temples of the new capital. Sargon choose for this transfer "a favorable month and an auspicious day."[35] According to the Eponym Lists: "on 22nd Teshrit (October), the gods of

---

29. Joannès, *Dictionnaire de la civilisation mésopotamienne*, 251.
30. Matthiae, "Subject Innovations in the Khorsabad Reliefs," 492.
31. *ARAB* 2.86.
32. Sylvie Lackenbacher, *Le palais sans rival: Le récit de la construction en Assyrie* (Paris: La découverte, 1990), 92; Sence, "Dur-Sharrukin," 441; May, "Administrative and Other Reforms," 105.
33. Luckenbill, *Annals of Sennacherib*, 98, 116; Frahm, *Einleitung in die Sanherib-Inschriften*, 42–45, 87–89; Lionel Marti, "Le banquet d'Aššurnaṣirpal II," *JA* 299 (2011): 505–20.
34. Rykle Borger, *Die Inschriften Asarhaddons Königs von Assyrien*, AfOB 9 (Graz: Weidner, 1956), 63 (Esarhaddon); Borger and Andreas Fuchs, *Beiträge zum Inschriftenwerk Assurbanipals: Die Prismenklassen A, B, C = K, D, E, F, G, H, J und T sowie andere Inschriften* (Wiesbaden: Harrassowitz, 1996), 74–75 (Ashurbanipal).
35. *ARAB* 2.74.

Khorsabad entered their temples."[36] Sargon invited the gods to a magnificent reception: "I invited Assur, father of the gods, the great lords, the gods and goddesses who abide in Assyria."[37] It seems more logical to place this divine reception as taking place when the gods were settled in the city, rather than half a year later as proposed by Parpola.[38] He gave them several rich gifts, in particular bright silver, in order to make their spirits glad. He offered before them a great number of sacrifices: sleek bullocks, fat sheep, geese, fish, birds, wine, honey, the best products of the lands that he had conquered, among others items. He offered "spotless oblations, clouds of incense, and unceasing service."[39] All the gods and goddesses of Assyria entered the city amid jubilation and feasting. Sargon described how and why he himself prayed to Assur: "For the gift of health, length of days, for the stability of my rule, I fell on my knees in adoration, I poured out my prayers before him."[40]

The first part of Khorsabad's inauguration occurred half a year before the second part, as is clearly indicated in the Eponym Lists: on the sixth of Iyyar (May).[41] In the meantime, Sargon was probably not yet officially dwelling in the new capital, when it was shaken by an earthquake. Kisir-Ashur, the governor of Khorsabad, wrote to the king: "Upon my coming from Milqia to Khorsabad, I was told that there had been an earthquake in Khorsabad on the 9th of Adar (March). Perhaps the king, my lord, now says: 'Is there any damage within the city wall?' There is [no]ne. The temples, the ziggurat, the palace, the city wall and the buildings of the city are all well; the king, my lord, can be glad."[42] Milqia was a site close to Arbela, housing the Palace of the Steppe and the New Year festival house of Ishtar of Arbela. According to Kisir-Ashur's letter, Sargon was not in Khorsabad during the earthquake. The new capital of Khorsabad was officially inaugurated on the sixth of Iyyar 706, and it was on this date that Sargon took up residence definitively in his new palace, with all his administration:

---

36. SAAS 2:60.
37. *ARAB* 2.74.
38. Parpola, "Construction of Dur-Šarrukin," 66–67.
39. *ARAB* 2.74.
40. *ARAB* 2.74, 94, 98.
41. SAAS 2:60.
42. SAA 1:101, no. 125; Parpola, "Construction of Dur-Šarrukin," 67 and n. 121; *PNA* 2.1:621–22. There was also a plague in Assyria, an inaupicious event: Grayson, *Assyrian and Babylonian Chronicles*, chr. 1, ii, ll. 4–5.

"With the princes of (all) countries, the governors of my land, scribes and superintendents, nobles, officials and elders of Assyria, I took up my abode in that palace and instituted a feast of music."[43] The banquet of Sargon was not described in detail as was that of Ashurnasirpal II. However, it was also held inside the palace, in the king's presence, with tables of four persons for certain guests, other guests remaining standing. A banquet scene was illustrated in a relief of Khorsabad and accounts of receptions are preserved in some registers.[44] The royal inscriptions are only explicit regarding the guests and their gifts to the king: "Sitting down in my palace together with rulers from the four quarters (of the world), with the governors of my land, with the princes, the eunuchs, and the elders of Assyria, I celebrated a feast, and accepted from the rulers of east and west valuable showpieces made from gold, silver, (and) all kinds of precious things befitting those palaces."[45] Sargon also added that he intended to gather these offerings in Khorsabad together with all the possessions coming from the numerous enemy countries. Concerning the guests, the comparison with the description of Ashurnasirpal II's banquet shows some similarities; they were divided into two parts, members of the empire and external guests, and they were split into four categories: Assyrians including aristocracy, the rulers of other countries, vassals or allies, the Assyrian officials of Khorsabad, and the local population who had participated in the building of the city.[46]

Sargon's major prayer to Assur was mentioned several times in his inscriptions: "May the ruler, its builder, reach and attain the old age, and (abundant) posterity, may its founder live into the distant days (of the future) … may he who dwells therein, make jubilation in health of body, joy of heart, well-being of soul; may he have abundance of luck."[47] Since

---

43. *ARAB* 2.74.

44. Albenda, *Palace of Sargon*, 116–21 and pls 116–21; R. Mattila, "Balancing the Accounts of the Royal New Year's Reception: Seven Administrative Documents from Nineveh," *SAAB* 4 (1990): 7–22; Marti, "Banquet d'Aššurnaṣirpal II," 508–9; Irene J. Winter, "The Court Banquets of Sargon II of Assyria: Commensality as a Positive Affirmation of the (Successful) Hunt and Battle," in *Not Only History: Proceedings of the Conference in Honor of Mario Liverani Held in Sapienza–Università di Roma, Dipartimento di Scienze dell'Antichità, 20–21 April 2009*, ed. Gilda Bartoloni and Maria Giovanna Biga (Winona Lake, IN: Eisenbrauns, 2016), 35–52.

45. *ARAB* 2.74, 94, 98.

46. Marti, "Banquet d'Aššurnaṣirpal II," 510.

47. *ARAB* 2.49, 89, 101.

Assur was so important for Sargon, it seems strange that he did not give the god's name either to a city gate or to a city wall. The explanation provided is the following: Assur is hidden under another divine name such as Enlil or Anu.[48] This is not entirely convincing but we have no better explanation.

The Suspicious Death of Sargon

Sargon's major prayer to Assur was not answered; he did not live happy and old in his new capital. Fate had decreed otherwise. From the sixth of Iyyar (May) 706, when he settled in Khorsabad, to the twelfth of Ab (August) 705 when he was succeeded by Sennacherib, there was less than one and a half years, even less in fact because it is unknown when he embarked on his last military expedition. The sources for the end of Sargon's reign are almost completely missing; there are only four documents. The first document is the Babylonian Chronicle, which is broken at this date, except for the following partly restored information: "[The seventeenth year, Sarg]on [marched] to Tabalu."[49] The second is the Assyrian Eponym Lists, which mentions, with some lacks, for year 705, when Nashur-bel, governor of Amidi, was eponym: "the king [ ] against Gurdî the Kulummean; the king was killed; the camp of the king of Assyria [ ]; on the 12th Ab, Sennacherib [became] king."[50] The third document is a lacunary text attributed to Sennacherib, twice mentioning Sargon's death: "the death of Sargon, [my father, who was killed in the enemy country] and who was not interred in his house"; "[Sargon my father] was killed [in the enemy country and] was not b[uried] in his house."[51] The fourth document is a badly damaged letter, relating to the death of an Assyrian king, followed by a revolt; those events could have taken place in Assur or, less probably, in Nineveh; the name of the Cimmerians is partly restored.[52] The identity of the king is uncertain: Shalmaneser V or Sargon II, and the name of the Cimmerians is

---

48. Battini, "Portes urbaines de la capitale de Sargon II," 44–45.

49. Grayson, *Assyrian and Babylonian Chronicles*, 76, chr. 1, l. 6′ (l. 8′ is missing; ll. 9–17 are too damaged to be restored).

50. SAAS 2:60.

51. Hayim Tadmor, Benno Landsberger, and Simo Parpola, "The Sin of Sargon and Sennacherib's Last Will," *SAAB* 3 (1989): 10–11, ll. 8′–9′ and 19′–20′.

52. Waterman, *Royal Correspondence*, 1:332–33, no. 473; Giovanni B. Lanfranchi, *Cimmeri: Emergenza delle élites militari iraniche nel Vicino Oriente (VIII-VII sec. a.c.)*, HANE/S 2 (Padova: Sargon, 1990), 43–45.

9. END OF REIGN

a restoration.[53] Sargon's death is not mentioned in some letters dated from year 705.[54] One thing is clear from the documents: Sargon undertook a military campaign during which he was killed.

However, it is difficult to know exactly what happened, where, and above all why. Somewhere there was apparently a rebellion against Sargon's yoke, but was it a real threat to the Assyrian Empire? Whatever the cause, the king of Assyria could have sent a military expedition to confront whoever was acting against him, led by one of his officials, as he did on other occasions, for example, against Ashdod in 711 or against Tyre in 709 (see above). But Sargon was primarily a warrior king, and he had not campaigned for several years. Khorsabad was a quiet place, inhabited by people devoted to him and without the opposition encountered in Nimrud and Babylon, but maybe the new city was too quiet for him, and he was bored with too little to do. A military expedition would have been a diverting decision.

The place where Sargon was killed has been debated, as well as the identity of his enemy. Southern Babylonia was a groundless proposition.[55] The hypothesis of Media was based on a similarity between Kulummâ and the city of Kuluman.[56] Another hypothesis was the land of the Cimmerians, $^{KUR}Gamir$, in central Transcaucasia, based on the restoration of the name "Cimmerians" in the documents.[57] The most likely hypothesis, adopted by most scholars, based on the Babylonian Chronicle, is Tabal.[58] Sargon's enemy who vanquished him in the battle was Gurdî, first erroneously read

---

53. Thompson, "Assyrian Parallel," 35–43 (Shalmaneser V); Tadmor, "Campaigns of Sargon," 37 n. 138; I. M. Diakonoff, *Urartskije pis'ma i dokumenty* (Moscow, 1963), 236 (Sargon).

54. Eckhart Frahm, "Nabû-zuqup-kēnu, das Gilgameš-epos und der Tod Sargons II," *JCS* 51 (1999): 73–90.

55. C. F. Lehmann-Haupt, "Gesichertes und Strittiges," *Klio* 16 (1920): 340.

56. Maximilian Streck, "Das Gebiet der heutigen Landschaften Armenien, Kurdistân und Westpersien nach den babylonisch-assyrischen Keilinschriften," *ZA* 15 (1900): 366; von Soden, *Herrscher im Alten Orients*, 103.

57. Ivantchik, *Cimmériens*, 53, 55; Ivantchik, "The Current State of the Cimmerian Problem," *AncCiv* 7 (2001): 307–39.

58. Arthur Ungnad, "Eponymen," *RlA* 2:435; Tadmor, "Campaigns of Sargon," 97 and n. 311; Ivantchik, *Cimmériens*, 55; Fuchs, *Inschriften Sargons II*, 464; Frahm, "Nabû-zuqup-kēnu," 75; Joannès, *Dictionnaire de la civilisation mésopotamienne*, 758; Garelli and Lemaire, *Proche-Orient Asiatique*, 116; *PNA* 3.2:1243.

Eshpai.⁵⁹ Who was this "Gurdî the Kulummean"? Several proposals have been made: he could have been a Cimmerian tribal leader, a ruler of Til-Garimme in Anatolia, a local Tabalian ruler or the same as Kurtî, king of Atunna.⁶⁰ According to a letter from Tab-sill-Esharra to Sargon, a treaty tablet from Gurdî was brought to Assur and introduced into the courtyard of the temple for the ceremonies.⁶¹ This Gurdî could have been "the Kulummean" or the ruler of Til-Garimme or another Assyrian vassal.⁶²

There is a new reading of the Eponym Lists for year 704 (eponym: Nabû-deni-epush, governor of Nineveh): "the Great(s) (marched) against the Kulummeans" (GAL-ME(Š) *ina* UGU ⌈LÚ *ku-lum-ma-a-a*⌉).⁶³ It would be expected, after Sargon's death, that Sennacherib would send his magnates in a campaign to avenge his father against the Kulummeans responsible for his death. As this campaign is not mentioned in any of the Sennacherib inscriptions, it was probably not successful. If Gurdî the Kulummean was the same as the ruler of Til-Garimme, "a city on the border of Tabal" (capital of the province of Kammanu under Sargon), it would explain that his rebellion was crushed in 695 by Sennacherib's chief eunuch.⁶⁴ Gurdî the Kulummean should probably be distinguished from Kurtî, king of Atunna, Sargon's former vassal or ally.⁶⁵ However, the ruler of Kulummâ, the ruler of Til-Garimme and the Assyrian vassal concerned by a treaty, could have been the same person.⁶⁶ In the present state of documentation, it is impossible to make any further advance in identifying the Gurdî responsible for Sargon's death.

---

59. Tadmor, "Campaigns of Sargon," 85, 97; SAA 1:70; Tadmor, Landsberger, and Parpola, "Sin of Sargon," 28–29.

60. Smith, "The Supremacy of Assyria," 59 (Cimmerian); W. Röllig, "Gurdî," *RlA* 3:703 (Til-Garimme); *PNA* 1.2:431–32 (with bibliography) (Kurtî).

61. SAA 1:70–71, no. 76.

62. *PNA* 1.2:431–32.

63. I. L. Finkel and J. E. Reade, "Assyrian Eponyms, 873–649 BC," *Or* 67 (1998): 252; Eckhart Frahm, "704 v. Chr.," *NABU* 4 (1998): 106, no. 116; Frahm, "Nabû-zuqup-kēnu," 83–84.

64. ARAB 2.290 (Gurdî's name was previously read Hidî); Luckenbill, *Annals of Sennacherib*, 62, v.4.

65. Fuchs, *Inschriften Sargons II*, 411–12; Frahm, *Einleitung in die Sanherib-Inschriften*, 8 n. 29; Sanna P. Aro, "Tabal: Zur Geschichte und materiellen Kultur des zentralanatolischen Hochplateaus von 1200 bis 600 v. Chr." (PhD diss., University of Helsinki, 1998), 140; *PNA* 3.2:1243.

66. *PNA* 1.2:431.

Events seem to have unfolded as follows: Sargon started his campaign against Tabal around early summer 705, with his well-trained army. Even though the Assyrian king did not usually take many risks when fighting, he was unfortunately killed during the battle against Gurdî, the ruler of Kulummâ. From the documents, we only know that he could not be interred in his palace as was customary for Assyrian kings: this means that for some unknown reason it was impossible to repatriate his body.[67] Several hypotheses were proposed but without sufficient basis: either his body was undiscoverable, or it had been cremated.[68] All we do know is that Sargon was killed before the Assyrian camp fell prey to the hostile troops. The fact that the king's body was not retrieved for burial and funeral cult was considered a true malediction. For example, the formula placed at the end of international treaties was a reminder of this imperative. The unburied dead became a ghost (*eṭemmu*) who came back and haunted the living people until a solution was found.[69] Sargon was considered to have met a dishonorable death. How did his son and successor Sennacherib react? It can be supposed that he tried to find his father's body and endeavored to avenge his death, maybe by the campaign of 704 against the Kulummeans. However, Sennacherib's inscriptions never mentioned his filiation (see above), and he wrote nothing and built nothing to honor Sargon's memory. The question may be asked whether he bore his father ill will because, even though he was the crown prince, he was never associated with Sargon's glorious campaigns and he was obliged to wait seventeen years before, in turn, becoming king of Assyria.

The "Sin" of Sargon

Sargon was the first and only king in the Assyrian Empire to fall on the battlefield and not to receive a burial suitable for a king. Such an ignominious death was considered an enormous tragedy and an evil omen. It was thought that Sargon had committed some sin in order for the gods to have

---

67. Contrary to an old assertion: Smith, "The Supremacy of Assyria," 59; A.T. Olmstead, *Western Asia in the Days of Sargon*, 157–58; I. M. Diakonov, *Istorija Midii: Ot drevnejshih vremen do konca IV veka do nashej jery* (Moscow, 1956), 236.

68. Tadmor, Landsberger, and Parpola, "Sin of Sargon," 28–29; Ivantchik, *Cimmériens*, 54; Joannès, *The Age of Empires*, 41; Joannès, *Dictionnaire de la civilisation mésopotamienne*, 758.

69. Joannès, *Dictionnaire de la civilisation mésopotamienne*, 773.

abandoned him so completely. His tragic death probably strengthened, from the political and religious point of view, the opponents to his Babylonian policies in Assyria. Followers of the Assyrian nationalist trend would tend to believe that it was the "sin" of Sargon that caused him to be killed and not buried in his palace.[70] There is only one document mentioning the sin of Sargon: a difficult literary text of about eighty lines on obverse and reverse (K.4730), badly damaged, plus a small additional fragment (Sm.1876).[71]

The first interpretations of this text were based on a misreading of some passages: for example, there is no relation with the motif of the unburied king in Isa 14:4–20a, and the text never mentions that Sargon's body was later recovered after much opposition for some unknown reason by the priests and buried by Sennacherib with the necessary pomp.[72] According to von Soden, the fact that the new capital of Khorsabad was given up immediately after the death of Sargon proved that its founding represented the sin of Sargon.[73] However, even if the new city was doomed as the Assyrian capital, it was not uninhabited, contrary to what has been said; there are several attestations of a governor of Khorsabad during the reigns of his successors, for example, Iddin-ahhe in 693, Nabû-belu-usur in 672, and Sharru-lu-dari in 664.[74]

The reading of the K.4730 text has been improving over the years, allowing progress in its interpretation, mainly by Tadmor, Landsberger, and Parpola, who checked the different collations and studied the photographs, and by Lambert, who discovered that fragment Sm.1876 belonged to the same tablet as K.4730.[75] After a lack of about three lines, Sennacherib identified himself, stressed his piety and his desire to submit to the will of the gods, however difficult it may be. He told the story of his father Sargon who, having offended the gods in some way, met an infamous death. He was bent on determining the nature of this offense by extispicy in order to avoid committing the same sin and having the same fate as

---

70. Tadmor, Landsberger, and Parpola, "Sin of Sargon," 28–29.

71. Hugo Winckler, *Sammlung von Keilschrifttexten II* (Leipzig: Pfeiffer, 1894), no. 52; Tadmor, Landsberger, and Parpola, "Sin of Sargon," 10–17 (with bibliography).

72. Olmstead, *Western Asia in the Days of Sargon*, 145; von Soden, *Herrscher in Alten Orients*, 103–5.

73. Von Soden, *Herrscher in Alten Orients*, 102–5.

74. SAAS 2:61; Joannès, *Dictionnaire de la civilisation mésopotamienne*, 251.

75. Tadmor, Landsberger, and Parpola, "Sin of Sargon," 5–8.

Sargon. He divided the haruspices into several groups, each group apparently giving him its answer independently.[76] The passage of his enquiry is damaged and was restored as follows: "Was it because [he honored] the gods o[f Assyria too much, placing them] above the gods of Babylonia [..., and was it because] he did not [keep] the treaty of the king of gods [that Sargon my father] was killed [in the enemy country and] not b[uried] in his house?"[77] The answer of the haruspices was unanimously positive. It can be understood that Sargon had honored his own gods at the expense of the gods of Babylonia, but the text gave no idea of the divine treaty that he violated, thus upsetting the cosmic order. This divine treaty was probably not a treaty concluded with Merodach-baladan.[78] Sennacherib wanted to know how to restore harmony and therefore repeated the extispicy; the haruspices answered that he had to honor Assur and Marduk with new statues. Having finished the new statue of Assur, he was stopped by Assyrian scribes who considered that if he made one for Marduk, he would commit the same sin as Sargon and would pay with his life.

Some scholars consider that this text, theoretically written by Sennacherib as it explicitly says, would be better dated from the reign of Esarhaddon in the year 671 or 670. Their main argument is their reading of the damaged lines 21–23 of the reverse: "As for me, after I had made the statue of Assur my lord, Assyrian scribes wrongfully prevented me from working [on the statue of Marduk] and did not let me make [the statue of Marduk, the great god], and (thus) [shortened my li]fe." They consider that this text, said to be of Sennacherib, but which mentioned his death, was logically written by his son Esarhaddon and have tried to find explanations for it: "the text is a multi-layered, skillfully contrived, almost Machiavellian composition."[79] The explanation given by Garelli seems to be better, being dictated by good sense. [80] It is more likely to consider that this text, explicitly said to be of Sennacherib, was written by

---

76. On this new type of extispicy, see Ann M. Weaver, "The 'Sin of Sargon' and Esarhaddon's Reconception of Sennacherib: A Study in Divine Will, Human Politics and Royal Ideology," *Iraq* 66 (2004): 61–65.

77. Tadmor, Landsberger, and Parpola, "Sin of Sargon," 10–11, obv., 17–20.

78. Joannès, *Dictionnaire de la civilisation mésopotamienne*, 8.

79. Tadmor, "The Campaigns of Sargon," 97; Tadmor, Landsberger, and Parpola, "Sin of Sargon," 80; Barbara Nevling Porter, *Images, Power and Politics: Figurative Aspects of Esarhaddon's Babylonian Policy*, MemPhil 208 (Philadelphia: American Philosophical Society, 1993), 2–5.

80. Paul Garelli, "Réflexions sur 'le péché de Sargon,'" in *Studi sul Vicino Oriente*

Sennacherib. The restored sentence "the Assyrian scribes... [shortened my li]fe..." (*ba-l[a?-ṭi ú-qat-tu-ú...]*)" can be understood differently: "the Assyrian scribes... [exhausted my li]fe...." It would mean that this text reflected the unceasing struggles for power between factious parties in Nineveh, nationalist and pro-Babylonian, which exhausted Sennacherib; for example, as it is mentioned, the Assyrian scribes prevented him from making a statue for Marduk. He was worried about suffering the same fate as his father: divine abandonment. As a final piece of advice to his son Esarhaddon, Sennacherib explained: "Take heed of what I have explained to you, and reconcile [the gods of Babylonia] with your gods!"[81]

What was finally considered as the "sin" (*ḫi-ṭu*, l. 10') or the "sins" (*ḫi-ṭa-a-ti*, l. 16') of Sargon? He placed the Assyrian god Assur and other Assyrian gods such as Enlil, Nabû, Sîn, Shamash, and Adad, above the Babylonian god Marduk, as can be seen from his inscriptions throughout the whole of his reign.[82] According to this text, the unfinished Marduk statue would confirm the idea that Sargon honored the Assyrian gods at the expense of those of Babylonia. However, there is something novel and contradictory in his statement that ascribed his conquest of Babylon to a command given by Marduk, the god of Babylon.[83] It is possible that there existed a prior agreement between Sargon and the Babylonian priests of Marduk who preferred to be ruled by an Assyrian rather than by a Chaldean king.[84]

However we interpret all of this, in this text Sennacherib does not appear to be the king who razed Babylon in 689. This could mean that it is to be dated earlier, at the beginning of Sennacherib's reign, when he was shocked by the ignominious death of Sargon and attempted to avoid a similar fate. For the Assyrians, the huge capital of Khorsabad remained as a testimony to the greatness of Sargon, but it was also a damned city, a reminder of the terrible fate of the king due to his incomprehensible sin or sins. It illustrated a common proverb related to tragic human fate that has spanned history: a leader who has reached the summit of his glory may be

---

Antico dedicati alla memoria di Luigi Cagni, vol. *I*, ed. Simonetta Graziani, IOUsm 61 (Naples: Istituto Universitario Orientale, 2000), 341–43.

81. Tadmor, Landsberger, and Parpola, "Sin of Sargon," 16–17, rev. ll. 26–27.

82. Ibid., 26–27 (with bibliography).

83. *ARAB* 2.31.

84. Tadmor, Landsberger, and Parpola, "Sin of Sargon," 28, 48–49; it is dubious that an agreement was concluded after the battle of Dêr.

next to his fall. As was said in ancient Rome: "The Tarpeian rock is not far from the Capitol" (*Arx Tarpeia Capitoli proxima*).[85]

---

85. Jean-Michel David, "Du *comitium* à la roche tarpéienne ... sur certains rituels d'exécution capitale sous la république, les règnes d'Auguste et de Tibère," *PEFR* 79 (1984): 131–76.

10
Chronological Synthesis of Sargon's Reign

After having scrutinized all the pertinent documents and studied in detail the specific aspects of the topic, it is now possible to proceed further toward a chronological synthesis (see the chart at the end of this chapter). It appears that Sargon's reign comprised three sequences of unequal length. From 722 to 721 BCE, he was entirely involved in repressing massive opposition in the Assyrian heartland and securing his throne. From 720 to 711, Sargon initially tried to react against the seizure of power by Merodach-baladan II in Babylonia. The indecisive character of the battle of Dêr proved to him that he was not yet ready to solve the Babylonian problem definitively. He understood that he first had to realize new conquests in order to strengthen the empire in power and resources, his main enemies being Urartu, Elam, and Phrygia. He intended to retake Babylonia, but he knew how to adapt his strategy to the circumstances by patiently waiting for the moment when he would be ready. During the third sequence of his reign from 710 to 705, it was the moment to reconquer Babylonia without difficulty and to make all his conquests profitable. Let us go into the details of these three chronological sequences, year by year, when the precise dates of the events of his reign and of his life are known. At the same time, we shall interpret the motivations of Sargon, his objectives, his strategy, his reactions, and his evolution, at each step of his reign.

722–721 BCE

In 722 BCE (accession year), Sargon, who was between forty and fifty years old, succeeded Shalmaneser V on the throne of Assyria on the twelfth of Tebet (January).[1] He was first concerned, for some unclear reasons, with

---

1. Grayson, *Assyrian and Babylonian Chronicles*, 73, chr. 1, ll. 29–31.

justifying his ascent to the throne. He was apparently not a usurper because he was a son of Tiglath-pileser III and a brother of Shalmaneser V, but he wanted to stand aloof from this dynasty.[2] He seems to have immediately met, for unknown reasons, massive opposition in the Assyrian heartland and in other parts of the empire. Therefore, he was obliged to secure his throne during his accession year (722) and his first year (721). He was actually living in Ashurnasirpal II's palace in Nimrud, which he renovated. As he was basically a warlord, he could not accept not having campaigned at the beginning of his reign, inasmuch as Merodach-baladan had seized anew the throne of Babylon. In order to obscure this period of inactivity, he had the chronology of his campaigns falsified by the scribes: his first *palû*, after his accession year (722), was not counted from his year 1 (721) but from his first campaign in year 2 (720).[3] Another result of his internal difficulties was that, for the purpose of securing the throne, he probably designated his son Sennacherib as crown prince as early as in his accession year, or in year 1.

720 BCE

Sargon's second year (720) began the second sequence of his reign: after having solved his internal problems, the first campaign was directed against Babylonia. He could not accept that Merodach-baladan, the chief of the tribal political unit of Bît-Yakin, had taken advantage of the difficulties surrounding his ascent to the throne to seize Babylon, the main traditional enemy of Assyria. Sargon's first battle occurred near Dêr, an Assyrian provincial capital, acting as a buffer state between Assyria and Elam.[4] However, he met only Humban-nikash I, king of Elam and ally of Merodach-baladan, because of the delay of the Babylonian troops, sent to his aid. The battle was apparently indecisive, but he could not accept that he was not victorious.[5] He had three immediate reactions, showing his sangfroid, pragmatism, and quality as a strategist. First he proclaimed the battle as a victory in his royal inscriptions because he could not acknowledge defeat, especially in his first campaign. Then he decided to wait patiently for the moment when he would be powerful enough to retake

---

2. *ARAB* 2.154, 177; SAA 1:43–69; *PNA* 3.2:1344–46.
3. *ARAB* 2.55; Fuchs, *Inschriften Sargons II*, 196, 344.
4. *ARAB* 2.55, 118, 137; Saggs, "Historical Texts and Fragments," 14–15, ll. 16–17.
5. Grayson, *Assyrian and Babylonian Chronicles*, 73, chr. 1, ll. 33–34.

Babylon. He understood that he first had to consolidate the Assyrian Empire by neutralizing the Elamite king, a dangerous ally of Merodach-baladan, by pacifying the turbulent states and by realizing new conquests in order to strengthen the empire in power and resources. Reinforcing the Assyrian army was also a vital necessity for achieving his objectives. His third reaction was to immediately continue his campaigns. There was another matter of great urgency: Iaûbidî, the Syrian king of Hamath had gathered an anti-Assyrian coalition, rallying Simirra, Damascus, Arpad, and Samaria.[6] The members of the coalition apparently killed some Assyrians, possibly administrators appointed by Tiglath-pileser III.[7] Sargon crushed them at the battle of Qarqar on the Orontes (probably modern Hamath).[8] He deported many people of Hamath to Assyria and, additionally, six thousand three hundred "guilty" Assyrians in Hamath, possibly his opponents. The Phoenician cities of Simirra, Damascus, and Arpad, which had been transformed into Assyrian provinces by Tiglath-pileser III in 732 BCE, were forced to submit again. Samaria had probably been seized by Shalmaneser V in 722 (autumn?), a very short time before his death.[9] Therefore Sargon proceeded to recapture Samaria after the city had participated in Iaûbidî's coalition.[10] He turned the kingdom of Israel into an Assyrian province and deported Samaria's population to several locations throughout the empire. The aim of the deportations was to intimidate, to undermine local resistance, and to acquire human resources for Assyrian projects. The deportees had to become productive as rapidly as possible by working at their old professions in their new homes. Judah did not participate in Iaûbidî's coalition, but probably received refugees from conquered Samaria.

At the same time but independently, Hanunu, king of Gaza, also took advantage of the political instability accompanying Sargon's accession to the throne to revolt against Assyria. After Samaria, Sargon marched southward against Gaza.[11] On his way, he probably captured the cities

---

6. *ARAB* 2.55.
7. Saggs, "Historical Texts and Fragments," 14, 15, ll. 17–21; Frahm, "Sculpted Slab," 46, l. 13.
8. *ARAB* 2.55; Frame, "Tell Acharneh Stela," 52, iii.6'.
9. Grayson, *Assyrian and Babylonian Chronicles*, 73, i.28.
10. *ARAB* 2.55; Saggs, "Historical Texts and Fragments," 11–20.
11. *ARAB* 2.55; Frame, "Inscription of Sargon II," 36, 40, l. 23.

of Gibbethon and Ekron.[12] He defeated Hanunu and his allies, some of them Egyptian, at Rapihu (modern Raphia). Gaza was allowed to remain an autonomous vassal state, probably because of its strategic importance, both military and commercial, at the border of Egypt. Sargon continued the Assyrian policy inaugurated by Tiglath-pileser III, maintaining diplomatic contacts with some rulers of the Delta and controlling the terminal ports of the trade routes leading from Arabia and Egypt northward.

Were Sargon's campaigns to the west in 720 only motivated by Iaûbidî's anti-Assyrian coalition and Hanunu's revolt? Just like his predecessors, he was attracted by the wealth of the western states and fascinated by the Mediterranean Sea in an attempt to make the Assyrian Empire a maritime empire. He understood that the western front was one of the most, if not the most, important part of the Assyrian Empire. He succeeded in 720 in solving most of the problems in the west, stabilizing it in order to achieve maximum profit. The campaigns of this year were extremely ambitious and covered a long distance, if he conducted them all himself. He had brilliantly succeeded in proving that he was a great conqueror, a formidable and indefatigable warlord. He started using prestige-oriented propaganda, pointing to his invincibility and superiority with the help of the gods. He delivered a simple message for the people conquered, in particular through the stelae erected along his military itineraries: never resist, be loyal and obedient, pay the tribute and taxes, and provide military assistance. He handled the different political conditions applied to the peoples with care and pragmatism: Assyrian provinces such as Arpad, Damascus, Simirra and Samaria, autonomous vassals such as Gaza. He was now free to focus on other problematic regions of his empire.

719 BCE

In year 719 (year 3), Sargon turned to the northeastern part of his empire. He knew that if he wanted to drive Merodach-baladan out of Babylon, he first had to defeat his eastern ally Humban-nikash, king of Elam. But this king was a powerful enemy, and he probably did not intend to attack him directly. Moreover, the Assyrian king first had to consider another powerful enemy: the kingdom of Urartu to the north. Between Urartu and western Iran, there were several problematic states that could ally

---

12. Albenda, *Palace of Sargon*, 109–10, 4, pl. 95 (room 5, slab 5).

alternatively with Urartu or Assyria. The pretext for intervening in this area was the call for help from Iranzû, king of Mannea.[13] This king had been a loyal vassal of Assyria for more than twenty-five years and had succeeded in preserving the unity of his kingdom. In addition to the strategic position of Mannea, Sargon appreciated the famous Mannean horses, crucially important for the Assyrian army, which he intended to strengthen. Mannea became divided into two kingdoms: one loyal to Assyria ruled by Iranzû and the other openly favoring an alliance with Urartu, headed by Mitatti. The spread of the revolt was suppressed thanks to heavy military aid from Sargon, who devastated the country of the rebels and deported them.[14] He attacked the town Pasashi (possibly Panzish), represented on a relief of his palace, in 719 or 715.[15] Unfortunately, he had to immediately solve the problem of succession upon the death of Iranzû, who had two sons. He chose to install his son Azâ on the throne of Mannea as a vassal of Assyria.[16] However, that did not solve the problem because Ullusunu, the other son, contested his brother's claim with support from the Urartian king.

718 BCE

In year 718 (year 4), Sargon was obliged to turn his attention toward a dangerous situation in the northwestern part of his empire. As in 719, he had in mind the problem of his enemy Urartu. It became a priority for him to prevent a Phrygian-Urartian alliance that, if successful, would have represented a serious threat to Assyria's northwestern borders. Midas, king of Phrygia, had a creative policy: instead of having an open conflict with Assyria, he preferred to make alliances with the various small states east of his kingdom and to encourage them to rebel against Assyria. These allies constituted a buffer zone between Phrygia and Assyria; as a result, Sargon was obliged to fight, not directly against Midas, but against Midas's allies, the Neo-Hittite states, turbulent, uncontrolled, and difficult to reach in the mountains. His strategy consisted of maintaining control over Tabal and Que in order to stop easy communication between Phrygia and Urartu. Sargon also coveted Tabal because of its natural resources such as silver,

---

13. *ARAB* 2.56.
14. *ARAB* 2.6.
15. Reade, "Sargon's Campaigns," 99.
16. *ARAB* 2.56; *PNA* 1.1:238.

alabaster, and wood, as well as its strategic position on the northern side of the Cilician Gates, where it controlled the eastern routes of the Anatolian plateau. Tabal belonged to a contested periphery, subject to the competing foreign powers of Assyria, Phrygia, and Urartu. Sargon was striving to adapt his strategy to the specificity of Tabal, which he knew from the intelligence reports. Tabal was made up of several states in competition with each other. Consequently, Sargon applied a deliberate divide and conquer strategy. His campaign in Tabal in 718 was directed against Kiakki of Shinuhtu who had decided not to pay tribute to Assyria anymore and was in intrigue with king Midas of Phrygia. Sargon defeated Kiakki and gave Shinuhtu, his royal city, to Kurtî of Atunna, a rival Tabalian state.[17] However, Kurtî was not grateful and rejoined king Midas at some moment between 718 and 713, but then again gave allegiance to Assyria.[18] This part of Anatolia was too isolated and rugged to maintain Assyrian military control (its chariotry was unusable there), so Sargon knew that conquering Tabal was not the solution. Moreover, the riches of Anatolia were far less substantial than the riches of the Levantine coast provided by the Phoenician cities and the fabulous wealth of Egypt.

717 BCE

In year 717 (year 5), Sargon was obliged to campaign again in northern Syria in order to suppress a new revolt. Pisîri, king of Carchemish, who had not participated in the anti-Assyrian coalition led by Iaûbidî in 720, was now plotting with king Midas of Phrygia and decided to revolt against Assyria.[19] Sargon defeated him, deported his population and replaced it with people of Assyria who settled in this new Assyrian province where he had an Assyrian palace built.[20] He knew that the western front of the Assyrian Empire was not definitely controlled. However, this campaign was a new opportunity for him to carry off a very rich booty, which probably inspired him with the idea of using it to build his own palace. Years 718 and 717 were quite peaceful, with only one campaign per year. He had time to imagine his building project, conceived as a visual demon-

---

17. *ARAB* 2.7, 55, 80, 92, 99, 118, 137; *PNA* 1.2:431–32.
18. *ARAB* 2.214; *PNA* 2.1:642.
19. *ARAB* 2.8, 118; Hawkins, "New Sargon Stele," 154–55, ll. 25–26.
20. Tunca, "Fragment de brique," 179–84.

stration of his superhuman power.[21] Through abundant documentation, royal inscriptions, letters, and other inscriptions, it appears that Sargon conceived the project by himself, directed it personally, and regularly monitored its progress. In 717, after much thought and "at the command of the gods," he started the project by choosing the place: Khorsabad/Dûr-Sharrukîn.[22] He was conscious that this colossal project to his glory, one of the main projects of his life, if not the major one, would require a considerable amount of wealth, a great variety of skillful craftsmen, and a very large number of workers. It meant more and more conquests, not only for proving his personal value as a warlord and for consolidating and extending his empire, but also for carrying off an abundance of booty through plundering and tribute and for obtaining free workers and craftsmen through deportations of populations.

The interventions and military clashes in the states of the north are not dated, but Sargon had two aims: to exploit the timber of these woodlands and to prepare for the confrontation with Urartu, his powerful northern enemy. The Assyrian capital Nineveh and the Urartian capital Turushpa were separated by the very high Taurus ridge and by a strip of buffer states, either kingdoms or provinces. Some of them were independent; others were under Assyrian or Urartian domination: Shubria, Amidi, Tushhan, Ukku, Kumme, the Mashennu, and Rab-Shaqe provinces.[23] Even if much of the old forest area had been greatly depleted before the Neo-Assyrian period, the Assyrians cut their wood in places claimed by the Urartians, which resulted in military clashes, as is reported in the correspondence. The cutting and transport of stones is also attested in this area. Another preoccupation of Assyrian officials on this northern frontier was gathering military intelligence about Urartu, and the Urartians did the same regarding Assyria. Sargon preferred not to annex the states located on the Urartu border, such as Ukku, because they were situated in mountainous regions that impeded effecting and maintaining direct Assyrian control and also because it would have provoked direct confrontation between Assyria and Urartu. He considered it much more valuable to keep them as buffer states. Sargon's campaigns relied heavily on the mobilization of resources from the provinces. Even if the royal inscriptions give the impression that the Assyrian king himself led nearly all the

---

21. Fuchs, *Inschriften Sargons II*, xiv, 310, l. 31.
22. *ARAB* 2.98–99, 102, 105.
23. Radner, "Between a Rock and a Hard Place," 243–64.

military expeditions, the correspondence shows that governors, who had an array of military personnel and equipment at their disposal, conducted their own expeditions, in their provinces and even in distant areas.[24]

716 BCE

The year 716 (year 6) was particularly occupied with campaigns. Sargon pretentiously claimed in the Cyprus stela that he had subjugated the people of Egypt; he never conquered any part of Egypt, even if it was an old Assyrian dream. In 716, he settled eastern populations from Zagros on the border brook of Egypt and developed international trade in this area. He decided to build a new independent trading emporium, partly populated by deportees and supervised by the Arab sheikh of Laban, a client king.[25] It has been suggested that the site of the emporium was Tell er-Ruqeish, about 20 km south of Gaza.[26] Shilkani (probably Osorkon IV), who wanted to seek help from the Assyrian king, sent him a gift of twelve great horses.[27] The texts mentioned several deportations of populations that took place in 716 and 715: from Samaria to Media, from Karalla, Allabria, and Mannea to Hamath, and from Carchemish to Assyria.

The campaigns of year 716 were concentrated in the northeast and east of the empire. The area covered by these campaigns extended between Urartu and Elam; Sargon probably had these two powerful enemies in mind. He followed an itinerary from Mannea to Media, solving on his way the problems, which apparently corresponded to a specific strategy: to control this area before confronting Urartu and Elam. In fact, Sargon was aware that Assyria was not threatened by raids coming from Zagros populations. He knew perfectly well that the polities of central Zagros and Media, ruled by city lords, were too heterogeneous to represent a serious danger.[28] He was flexible and adapted his strategy to each local situation. Contrary to what he did elsewhere, he allowed the city lords to continue to rule, even after their integration into Assyrian provinces. The difficult

---

24. SAA 5:199, no. 282.

25. Gadd, "Inscribed Prisms of Sargon II from Nimrud," *Iraq* 16 (1954): 179–80, iv.46–49.

26. E. D. Oren, "Tell er Ruqeish," *NEAEHL* 4:1293–94.

27. Gadd, "Inscribed Prisms of Sargon II," 180; Younger, "Recent Study on Sargon II," 312.

28. Lanfranchi, "Assyrian Expansion in the Zagros," 79–118.

mountain territories of the Zagros had no specific commodities that could be considered worth the heavy costs of annexation—horses from Zagros could be obtained through direct trade. Sargon's aim was to neutralize the central Zagros and Media polities in case of conflicts with Urartu or Elam and to establish important military bases there, ready to intervene, by recruiting troops locally, with horses and military aid. His campaigns of 716 in this area were in line with this strategy. First in Mannea, he captured the rebel Bag-dâti of Uishdish.[29] However, he accepted the submission of Ullusunu whom he proclaimed king of Mannea, because he understood that it was in his best interest to forgive Ullusunu's rebellion.[30]

In addition to the three already-existing Assyrian provinces of Zamua, Bît-Hamban, and Parsua, Sargon created two more provinces in this region: Kishesim and Harhar. The province of Kishesim was created after he had suppressed the revolt of Bêl-sharru-usur, the city lord of Kishesim.[31] The province of Harhar was created after he had crushed the rebellion of Kibaba, city lord of the stronghold of Harhar, or of its inhabitants, if Kibaba had already been dethroned in 719.[32] They had contacted king Taltâ of Ellipi in order to make allegiance to him, but it is unknown whether they received an answer.[33] Sargon conquered more cities and annexed them to the provinces of Harhar and Parsua. Some of them were identified as Median. When he continued further into Median territory, he received tribute from twenty-eight Median city lords.[34] In contrast with the information we have from Greek sources on a Median kingdom, in the Assyrian view Media was a conglomerate of many small independent polities, ruled by city lords, like central Zagros.

715 BCE

One year was not enough to solve the problems in Mannea, central Zagros, and Media; it required another campaign in this area in 715 (year 7). Rusâ of Urartu had confiscated twenty-two of Ullusunu's fortresses and

---

29. *ARAB* 2.10; *PNA* 1.2:251, 2.1:587–88, 3.2:1374–75.
30. *ARAB* 2.10, 56.
31. Levine, *Two Neo-Assyrian Stelae from Iran*, 38–39; *ARAB* 2.10, 56, 79, 92, 99, 183, 203.
32. *ARAB* 2.11; Radner, "Assyrian View on the Medes," 50.
33. *ARAB* 2.11.
34. Levine, *Two Neo-Assyrian Stelae from Iran*, 40–45, ii.46–70.

established Daiukku as a new leader of Mannea, ensuring his loyalty by taking his son as hostage.[35] Sargon recaptured the twenty-two fortresses taken by the Urartians and restored Ullusunu on the throne of Mannea. He defeated Telusina of Andia and seized the province of Uishdish. He received the tribute of Ianzû, king of Nairi/Hubushkia, who was forced to change sides several times, depending on the pressure exerted on him by Urartu and Assyria.[36] Maybe Sargon already had in mind his confrontation with Urartu in the near future. He encountered some problems in the Assyrian province of Bît-Hamban because Kimirra, a city of this province, revolted against Assyria. He inflicted severe punishment on it by deporting its population.[37] He manifested great severity against the revolts of cities already integrated into Assyrian provinces, such as Simirra, Damascus, Arpad, and Samaria in 720. In a bloody battle he crushed the revolt of the inhabitants of the province of Harhar by cutting off 4,000 heads of enemies and deporting 4,820 persons.[38] He annexed more cities to this province, forcing all their city lords to take oaths of loyalty to the Assyrian governor and pay tribute to Assyria.[39] Even if Sargon wanted to respect the primitively structured societies of the polities of central Zagros and Media, it seems that the creation of Assyrian provinces suffered from his decision to leave the local city lords in power, as independent vassals.

Sargon possibly also had in mind the upcoming confrontation with Urartu when he campaigned in Anatolia. He had to prevent an alliance, by making contacts impossible between two powers that were dangerous for Assyria: Phrygia and Urartu. He intended to conquer some areas between Phrygia and Urartu, such as Tabal, where he had campaigned in 718, and Que. Midas had captured some cities of Que between 718 and 715, or earlier.[40] Urik, king of Que and vassal of Assyria, moved over to the Phrygian side and also sent envoys to the king of Urartu. Sargon reconquered the cities captured by Midas and turned Que into an Assyrian province.[41] Preventing contacts between Phrygia and Urartu was not the only reason behind Sargon's annexation of Que. He wanted to exploit

---

35. *ARAB* 2.12–13.
36. *ARAB* 2.13; *PNA* 2.1:492.
37. *ARAB* 2.15.
38. *ARAB* 2.14.
39. SAA 15:xv, xxvi–xxviii.
40. Lanfranchi, "Sargon's Letter," 63.
41. *ARAB* 2.16, 18; Gadd, "Inscribed Prisms of Sargon II," 183–84, v.34–40.

the forests of Amanus and the mineral resources of the Taurus range and Anatolia. Therefore, he needed to annex Que, which controlled the accesses to the inland riches, particularly via the so-called Cilician and Amanus Gates. Moreover, he intended to use the Cilician fleets for his maritime battles. The Ionians were also interested in the strategic position of Que and had settled in some places a long time earlier. The campaign against Phrygia and the confrontation with Ionians in Que were probably two stages of a single strategy of Sargon: to relieve both Phrygian and Ionian pressure on Que, and to turn it into an Assyrian province, which happened in 715.[42] This year appears to have been crucial for the Assyrian northwestern policy.

In another unknown location of the empire, in 715 Sargon confronted some Arab tribes that had never before submitted to Assyria and deported them to Samaria, probably for diverting to that area some of the Arabian trade in which the nomad tribes played a significant role.[43] Sargon's inscriptions also mentioned the tribute offered in 715 by Arab kings or queens, together with that of the pharaoh: Piru (probably Shabaka), Samsi, queen of Arabia, and Itamar the Sabean.[44] According to a letter dated around 715, the Judean king paid tribute and sent a contingent of troops to support the Assyrian army on campaign.[45] The "kings of the seashore" who sent tribute to Sargon in 715 probably included the Phoenician kings.[46] The Assyrian king accorded great importance in particular to the acquisition of timber from Mount Lebanon for Khorsabad, as is represented in the reliefs of his new palace.

714 BCE

The year 714 (year 8) was dominated by Sargon's campaign against King Rusâ of Urartu. He seems to have considered the so-called eighth campaign as one of his major campaigns, if not the major, as can be seen from the exceptionally long and detailed Letter to Assur and from the representation of the sack of Musasir in several reliefs in his palace of Khorsabad.

---

42. *ARAB* 2.80, 92, 99, 118; Elayi and Cavigneaux, "Sargon II et les Ioniens," 64–68.
43. *ARAB* 2.17, 118; Gadd, "Inscribed Prisms of Sargon II," 119–20, l. 18.
44. *ARAB* 2.18, 55; *PNA* 2.1:587, 3.1:1085.
45. Saggs, *Nimrud Letters, 1952*, ND 2608.
46. Fuchs, *Inschriften Sargons II*, 110, l. 124.

In spite of his successive interventions in 716 and 715, Sargon had not solved the problems in the northeastern and eastern parts of his empire, and Urartu became more and more aggressive. Mitatti again ruled over Zikirtu of Mannea, in open contempt of Assyria and was making incursions into pro-Assyrian Mannean territory with Urartian military aid. The new campaign that Sargon conducted in 714 was intended first to solve the problems of Urartian incursions into Mannea, then to fight directly against Urartu. He intervened at the request of his vassal Ullusunu, king of Mannea, to drive back king Rusâ of Urartu, who had encroached on his territory.[47] Ullusunu received Sargon in his fortress of Sirdakku with all kinds of gifts and the convivial meeting ended with a banquet. Sargon had a quite different attitude toward the other Mannean king of Zikirtu, the renegade Mitatti. He defeated his troops and devastated his country. Rusâ of Urartu came promptly to his ally Mitatti's aid, but in vain. Their joint forces suffered a terrible defeat at the battle of Mount Uaush.[48] Sargon replaced Mitatti of Zikirtu with a new king, Issar-shumu-iqisha.[49] Several city lords of Gizilbunda, Namri, Sangibuti, and Bît-Abadani, and the king of Ellipi, hearing about the approach of Sargon, brought their tribute to him.[50]

From 719 to 714, war was fought neither in Assyria nor in Urartu; it was fought by proxy in Mannea and Zikirtu. In 714, Sargon decided to attack Urartu directly. He had carefully chosen the moment, thanks to his spies and intelligence reports; Urartu had encountered internal difficulties such as a revolt in its capital Turushpa and an incursion of Cimmerians in 715 or the spring of 714.[51] He had prepared his attack by neutralizing the influence of Urartu on the northwestern front, destroying Urartu's power base north and northeast of Mannea, and stabilizing central Zagros. However, Sargon knew that Urartu was a major power and that a frontal attack would have been costly, if not impossible. Urartu was not devastated because it was not his objective and because he was respectful of this outstanding foreign civilization, similar to that of Assyria on several points. Sargon's eighth campaign was a monument of his military genius: he could deviate from his original design when the situation

---

47. *ARAB* 2.149.
48. *ARAB* 2.155; SAA 5:123, no. 164.
49. *ARAB* 2.19, 56.
50. *ARAB* 2.19, 146–47.
51. SAA 5:109, no. 144; Ivantchik, *Cimmériens*, 47.

demanded, and turn the campaign so as to achieve a far greater impact than he had originally thought possible. The campaign of 714 put an end to the Assyrian-Urartian confrontation in the northeast of the empire; however, Sargon wanted to mask his failure not to have captured Rusâ, and Urartu remained for Assyria a powerful empire that it was necessary to watch. On his return march, he first went to the area of Hubushkia where he received the tribute of King Ianzû.[52] The second highlight of this campaign was the sack of Musasir. The site was a vassal of Assyria at the beginning of Sargon's reign, then it was captured by Rusâ, whether it was the holy site of the Urartian coronation or not. Sargon was angry about the behavior of King Urzana who failed to welcome him; he spoiled not only the sanctuary of god Haldi, but also the royal palace of Urzana.[53] He carried off to Assyria an enormous quantity of spoils that no doubt he used for building his new city of Khorsabad and turned Musasir into an Assyrian province. Urzana managed to be forgiven by Sargon, who reinstalled him on the throne of Musasir.[54]

713 BCE

In 713 (year 9), shortly after the withdrawal of Sargon's troops, Rusâ probably restored cultic activities in Musasir. The Assyrian king seems to have observed the progressive loss of Musasir through the eyes of his officials, who sent alarmist reports to him on the evolution of the situation.[55] Rusâ's presence on the scene continued, maybe until 708, when his successor is mentioned, contrary to Sargon's inscriptions relating his suicide just after the sack of Musasir.[56] Sargon could see that the eastern part of the empire was not definitively pacified in spite of several successive campaigns in years 716, 715, and 714. Now he had to control this part of the empire up to the powerful kingdom of Elam, ally of Merodach-baladan, which he needed to neutralize before he could reconquer Babylon. He conducted an expedition against the rebels in the Persian mountains, in particular in Karalla, receiving on his way the tributes of Ullusunu, king of Mannea,

---

52. *ARAB* 2.21, 56, 169.
53. *ARAB* 2.169, 172–76.
54. SAA 5:105–7, 110–12, nos. 136, 139, 146–47.
55. SAA 5:111–12, no. 147.
56. *ARAB* 2.183.

and Bêl-aplu-iddina, king of Allabria.[57] He crushed the revolt of Amitash-shi, brother of Ashur-lêi, and returned Karalla to the Assyrian province of Zamua.[58] Then Sargon sent his commander-in-chief to Ellipi in order to help its king Taltâ. This loyal vassal of Assyria was confronted with a revolt conducted by the whole of his land or at least by part of it. He was saved and kept his throne.[59] Sargon succeeded in maintaining good relations with Ellipi because he considered this kingdom important as a buffer state between the Assyrian provinces of Kishesim and Harhar, and the hostile kingdom of Elam. However, Elam in itself was not dangerous for Assyria, only through its alliance with Babylonia. Moreover, fighting a war against Elam would have been exhausting in the eastern Zagros, and there was also a risk that the other eastern states would become involved in the conflict. During the campaigns of 713, the Assyrian army also attacked lands on the eastern Aribi border, possibly those of Arab tribes.[60] Their location has not been identified and it is uncertain whether this action had to do with Babylonia and his project of reconquest.

In 713 Sargon was obliged to recognize that the strategy he had developed in the Tabalian states had not definitively solved the local problems. Even after his defeat in 714, Rusâ's position had not weakened in Anatolia; he always intended to extend in western Anatolia. Sargon's purpose for campaigning again in Tabal was to keep an eye on Urartu and to prevent contacts with Phrygia, but he also had its natural resources such as silver, alabaster, and wood—required in the building of Khorsabad—in view, as well as its strategic position on the northern side of the Cilician Gates, where it controlled the eastern routes to the Anatolian plateau. His policy in Tabal consisted of distributing territories and powers among the Tabalian kings to prevent any one state from becoming too strong. At the same time, he had decided to encourage Tabal proper (Bit-Purutash) in its claim for sovereignty over the other Tabalian states. He gave to Ambaris, Hullî's son, his daughter Ahat-Abisha and the dowry-land of Hilakku in order to raise him above his other vassal states in this area.[61] However, this strategy failed because Ambaris plotted with Phrygia, Urartu, and other kings of Tabal to drive the Assyrians from the region. Sargon reacted

---

57. *ARAB* 2.23–24.
58. *ARAB* 2.23.
59. *ARAB* 2.58, 212.
60. *ARAB* 2.23.
61. *ARAB* 2.25.

vigorously to the treason of Ambaris by deporting him and his family to Assyria and by transforming Tabal into an Assyrian province.[62] It was the ultimate resort when other strategies had failed. Sargon probably also went to Ashdod in 713 in order to suppress King Azuri's rebellion and to replace him with Ahî-Mîti.[63]

712 BCE

In 712 (year 10), after Sargon had solved the problems of Tabal, other problems occurred in the northwestern part of the Assyrian Empire. Tarhunazi, king of Kammanu, confused with Gunzinânu by the scribes, rebelled against him, seeking alliance with King Midas of Phrygia.[64] According to the Eponym Lists, Sargon stayed that year in Assyria and probably sent his commander-in-chief for the expedition against Kammanu.[65] However, in the Annals, he could not relate one year without campaigning himself. His reaction against Tarhun-azi was all the more violent as he had chosen and installed the rebel on the throne himself. He turned the kingdom of Kammanu into an Assyrian province and gave its capital city of Melid and its surrounding areas to Mutallu, king of the neighboring state of Kummuhu.[66] Because the kings of Kummuhu had had close relations with Assyria for a long time, Sargon put much trust in Mutallu, his ally. He seemed to have stabilized the region, with the two Assyrian provinces of Tabal and Kammanu and the allied vassal state of Kummuhu. He appears to have become more and more involved in the building of Khorsabad, explaining that at that time he had amassed in Khorsabad all kinds of ores, stones, precious stones, and goods coming from the western part of his empire.[67] This explains why he stayed in Assyria in 712, although in the Annals he pretended to have campaigned against Tarhun-azi of Melid. It was the beginning of a period where Sargon was so occupied by the building of Khorsabad that, most of the time, he sent on the military expeditions his commander-in-chief or other officers in his stead. He was probably also preparing for the reconquest of Babylon.

---

62. *ARAB* 2.55.
63. *ARAB* 2.214; SAAS 8:44, ll. 13–16.
64. *ARAB* 2.26, 60.
65. SAAS 2:47, 60.
66. *ARAB* 2.27; Fuchs, *Inschriften Sargons II*, Ann. 220–21.
67. *ARAB* 2.28.

711 BCE

In 711 (year 11), two revolts had broken out in the northwestern and western parts of the empire. The revolt of Gurgum is not clearly presented in the different sources. There were possibly two revolts and, consequently, two campaigns: the first one against king Tarhu-lara before 711 and the second in 711 against his son Mutallu who had killed his father in seizing the throne. Whatever the details may be, Sargon finally suppressed the local dynasty and turned Gurgum into an Assyrian province.[68] Having created three Assyrian provinces in central Anatolia (Tabal, Gurgum, and Kammanu) and putting his trust in Mutallu, his ally of Kummuhu, he actually controlled the whole region. Sargon sent his commander-in-chief to crush the second revolt of Ashdod. Ahî-Mîti, set on the throne by Sargon in 713, was expelled by the Ashdodites who chose Yamani as their new king, starting a new revolt.[69] In 712 Yamani had approached Hezekiah of Judah and Piru (Shabaka) for help in an anti-Assyrian coalition.[70] Sargon did not show the same clemency as he had after the first rebellion and hit hard in order to punish the insubordinate city and set an example for the neighboring Philistine cities; Ashdod was destroyed and the region's center of gravity was shifted to Ashdod-Yam, and it was turned into an Assyrian province. Yamani fled to Piru who was an opponent of Sargon.

710 BCE

710 (year 12) saw the beginning of the third and final sequence of Sargon's reign; it was a decisive year for him because it was the year in which he finally decided that he was ready to reconquer Babylon. However, according to the Eponym Lists, this action had repercussions until 707. He was clever enough to proclaim that the great Babylonian god Marduk asked him to liberate Babylon from the evil works of the Chaldean Merodach-baladan.[71] Sargon's military expedition in Babylonia can be divided into four phases. First, for a short time, he was campaigning east of the Tigris while Merodach-baladan tried to impede Assyrian activities. The second phase was characterized by alarming news reaching Babylonia about the

---

68. *ARAB* 2.29, 61; Gadd, "Inscribed Prisms of Sargon II," 183, ll. 43–44.
69. *ARAB* 2.30, 62, 193–95; Isa 20:1.
70. *ARAB* 2.195.
71. *ARAB* 2.31.

advance of Assyrian troops and by the diplomacy and secret negotiations conducted by Assyrian officers to win over tribes and cities in northern Babylonia. Following the Assyrian offers, several cities and tribes such as Sippar, Bît-Dakkûri, and Bît-Amukkâni, submitted to Sargon. He was aware that the Chaldean tribes generally viewed this war as an affair concerning only Bît-Yakin, Merodach-baladan's tribe. He did not go toward Babylon immediately but first captured the fortified Babylonian city of Dûr-Athara and created the new province of Gambulu, possibly trying to prevent Elamite military aid being sent to Merodach-baladan.[72]

In the third phase, Merodach-baladan retreated from Babylon and fled to Elam, trying without success to obtain help from king Shutruk-nahhunte II.[73] Apparently, he did not dare to fight the powerful Assyrian army, possibly because he had lost most of his forces in defending Dûr-Athara, perhaps also because he had little support from the Babylonian population. Sargon made a triumphal entry into Babylon. He became king of Babylon by seizing the hands of Marduk, sacrificed to the gods, and settled in Merodach-baladan's palace.[74] It is possible that there existed a prior agreement between him and the Babylonian priests of Marduk, who preferred to be ruled by an Assyrian king rather than a Chaldean one. After the ceremonies, Sargon probably spent the remaining year with his army in Kish.[75] However, his big mistake was to appoint an Assyrian governor over Babylon instead of taking on a Babylonian name and becoming king of Assyria and Babylonia as his predecessors Tiglath-pileser III and Shalmaneser V had done. By the expedient of the double throne, they created the impression of an autonomous Babylonian region in the face of the Assyrian Empire. The major deportation from the main Babylonian cities and the peripheral Aramean and Chaldean areas to Samaria took place in 710/709.

709 BCE

In 709 (year 13), the fourth phase of Sargon's military expedition in Babylonia took place. In the month of Iyyar (February), he departed from Babylon to pursue Merodach-baladan. The latter took refuge in Bît-Yakin,

---

72. *ARAB* 2.31.
73. *ARAB* 2.31–32, 66–71, 80, 92, 99; SAA 15:xxi.
74. *ARAB* 2.35.
75. SAAS 2:47.

which was on the shore of the Bitter Sea because, at that time, the Persian/Arabian Gulf penetrated further inland. First, Sargon gained a victory over Merodach-baladan and carried off considerable spoils. Then he besieged the fortified city of Dûr-Yakin where Merodach-baladan had taken refuge but was unable to capture it. The way in which this city was finally captured is not explained in the royal inscriptions, probably because the capture was not achieved in a heroic way but by means of negotiations. According to the Eponym Lists, the destruction of the city occurred only in 707.[76] The military campaign of Sargon to Bît-Yakin, on the seashore, meant that he intended to control, through the Persian/Arabian Gulf, the trade toward the Indian Ocean. Upêri, king of Dilmun (probably Failaka Island), brought gifts to Sargon on the seashore and became his vassal.[77] However, it would have been difficult for the Assyrian king to control him tightly in his island.

In his conquest of Babylonia, Sargon appears in his different inscriptions as a ruler both brilliant in diplomacy as well as in the battlefield. In fact, the mistakes of his enemies contributed to making him appear so. The reality was different; they lacked cohesion and coordination and were indifferent, opportunistic, and selfish. For some of the inhabitants of Babylon, Merodach-baladan was seen as a Chaldean king, but certainly not as a Babylonian, and they supported Sargon. By conquering Babylonia, Sargon had finalized his military plan, elaborated in 720 when he made a first tentative attack against the city of Dêr. However, even after the conquest of Babylonia, he had not finished the war against Elam and was obliged to reinforce the defense on the Elamite border. While he was waiting for his city of Khorsabad to be completed, he resided in Babylon from 710 to 707.

In the meantime, in 709, several expeditions were conducted by Sargon's officers or governors. The Assyrian king could not leave the problems of Que unsolved because the Cilician and Amanus Gates had to remain open for communication with northern states such as Tabal, and for exploiting the wealth of the Amanus, Taurus, and Anatolia—more and more in demand for the building of Khorsabad. The ambitions of Midas of Phrygia in this part of the empire always had to be carefully monitored. The Assyrian governor of Que, probably Ashur-sharru-usur, was assigned this mission. He made raids into Midas's kingdom three times along the

---

76. *SAAS* 2:60.
77. *ARAB* 2.41, 43.

western border of Que, a region belonging to Midas, and captured fortresses in a mountainous region, which could have been Hilakku.⁷⁸ Apparently, this defeat affected Midas, who decided to submit to Sargon and became a docile vassal from that time onward.⁷⁹

In 709, a military expedition was also conducted to the island of Cyprus. Sargon was on the one hand very interested in subjugating the island of Cyprus in order to provide a new original western frontier to his empire. On the other hand, he was too busy in his conquest of Babylon to conduct the military expedition to Cyprus himself. Therefore, he sent his officer to solve some kind of problem that had occurred and to submit the island to Assyrian tribute. The logical sequence of events was probably the following: in 709, an Assyrian military expedition was sent to Cyprus, forcing Kition to pay tribute. In the same year, this Tyrian colony revolted against King Lulî who immediately reconquered it.⁸⁰ Around 708, seven kings from the district of Ia went to Babylon and submitted to the Assyrian king, and a stela of Sargon was erected in the area of Kition.⁸¹ The Cyprian cities lost their independence and became vassals of the Assyrian Empire but, because of their insularity, they were probably not closely controlled nor forced to pay tribute with regularity.

The seizure of Tyre was briefly mentioned in a text duplicated on four cylinders found in Khorsabad and dated from 706.⁸² Sargon expressed his desire for victory, but it was not obtained, and so mentioned it only briefly, so as not to focus on his failure. The unsuccessful five-year siege of Tyre by Sargon's officer probably started in 709 and ended in 705 on Sargon's death.⁸³ Because of Lulî's action in Cyprus to reconquer Kition in 709, the Assyrian army, led by an officer of Sargon, attacked the king of Tyre, who refused to make allegiance to Assyria. According to Josephus, the Assyrians failed to capture the island of Tyre and started its blockade by cutting the supply of drinking water. This failure was unacceptable to Sargon, but he knew that the island of Tyre was impregnable; therefore his solution was to falsify his official inscriptions by turning a failure into a success.

---

78. *ARAB* 2.42.
79. *ARAB* 2.43, 71; Fuchs, *Inschriften Sargons II*, Prunk. 150–52.
80. Josephus, *A.J.* 9.283–287.
81. *ARAB* 2.44, 54, 80, 92, 99; Elayi and Cavigneaux, "Sargon II et les Ioniens," 65–66.
82. *ARAB* 2.118.
83. Elayi, *Histoire de la Phénicie*, 172–74.

This would explain the punitive expedition of his son Sennacherib against Lulî in 701 BCE.

708 BCE

In 708 (year 14), a problem occurred in Kummuhu, the last Assyrian vassal state of central Anatolia. Sargon was totally confident in his ally Mutallu, king of Kummuhu. But suddenly, for some unknown reason, Mutallu withheld tribute and tax from Assyria and allied with Argishti II, king of Urartu.[84] This was in 708 according to the Eponym Lists. Sargon sent Assyrian forces led by his officer to besiege and capture the capital city of Mutallu, who had escaped, probably to Urartu.[85] An abundance of booty was carried off to Assyria and Kummuhu was turned into an Assyrian province, the fourth in the area along with Tabal, Gurgum, and Kammanu. Sargon was busy reorganizing the province of Babylonia, mainly supervising the last stage of works to complete the building of Khorsabad. His impatience was visible in the correspondence, where he hastened his subordinates in charge of the building, imposing on them deadlines for finishing their work.[86] His direct input helps to understand how the project was accomplished so efficiently.

707 BCE

In 707 (year 15), Sargon, still in Babylon, received excellent news: his city of Khorsabad was completed after about ten years of colossal building work. He could prepare for his return from Babylon and settling into his new capital, making the preparations for its magnificent inauguration, a moment he had long awaited. The first part of the inauguration was the settling of the gods in the temples of the new capital, this happened on the twenty-second day of Teshrit (October) 707, an auspicious date chosen by Sargon.[87] He invited the gods to a magnificent reception and then they were installed in their temples. He was probably not residing in his new capital at that time, even though the Eponym Lists mentioned it before the installation of the gods, which does not seem very plausible.

---

84. *ARAB* 2.64; SAAS 2:48.
85. *ARAB* 2.41.
86. SAA 1:24, no. 26.
87. *ARAB* 2.74; SAAS 2:60.

The organization of his transfer from Babylon to Khorsabad no doubt took time, for example moving his officials and transporting all his booty.

Meanwhile, his officers were in charge of controlling his empire and conducting military expeditions as necessary. A problem occurred in the eastern part of the empire, in Ellipi, the Assyrian vassal kingdom close to Elam. In 708 or 707, Taltâ, Sargon's most loyal vassal, died, and a war of succession for the throne of Ellipi occurred between Nibê and Ashpa-bara. Nibê called on Shutruk-nahhunte king of Elam for help, who came to his rescue.[88] Ashpa-bara begged aid of Sargon, who sent seven of his officers, possibly governors of the eastern Assyrian provinces, to defeat Nibê and establish Ashpa-bara on the throne. Sargon wanted to keep Ellipi as a buffer state between Assyrian eastern provinces and the hostile kingdom of Elam. Possibly also in relation to Ellipi, three Elamite attacks are mentioned in the correspondence, one of them dated in 707.[89] Sargon had succeeded in preventing an alliance between Elam and Babylonia, which would have proved extremely dangerous for Assyria. But he never took the risk of attacking Elam anywhere other than on the borders of the Iranian plateau; consequently, he did not succeed in defeating this powerful state. The pharaoh Shabatka, who succeeded Shabaka, extradited Yamani to Sargon, bringing him into Assyria himself, as a gesture of goodwill.[90]

706 BCE

In 706 (year 16), Khorsabad was shaken by a low-intensity earthquake on the ninth of Adar (March), at a time when Sargon was not there.[91] The second part of the inauguration of the new capital took place on the sixth of Iyyar (May). It was probably at this date that Sargon officially took up residence in his new palace, with all his administration. According to tradition, he offered a banquet inside his palace, as is illustrated in a relief in Khorsabad and reported in royal inscriptions.[92] The guests were split into four categories: Assyrians including aristocracy, the rulers of other countries (vassals or allies), the Assyrian officials of Khorsabad, and the local population who had participated in the building of the city.

---

88. *ARAB* 2.47, 65.
89. *ARAB* 2.47; SAA 15:xxxiii–xxxv.
90. *ARAB* 2.63, 80.
91. SAA 1:101, no. 125.
92. Albenda, *Palace of Sargon*, 116–21 and pls. 116–21; *ARAB* 2.74, 94, 98.

It is not improbable that Hezekiah king of Judah was invited to visit the impressive new city. In his city, Sargon wished, on the one hand, to exalt the role of Assyrian aristocracy in the management of his empire as is reflected in its frequent representation in the reliefs of his palace and by high officials' residencies. On the other hand, he tried to unify the vast diversity of the people of his empire in the language, culture, and religion of Assyria, convinced that it would create happy conditions for all his subjects.[93] Sargon stayed in Assyria in 706, but his eunuch, possibly the governor of Zamua, campaigned against Karalla to crush a new revolt. After repressing Ashur-lêi's revolt in 716, Karalla had been added to the Assyrian province of Zamua.

705 BCE

In 705 (year 17), Sargon could continue to benefit from his kingship in Babylonia, from his nearly totally pacified empire (except for the island of Tyre), and from his new capital, Khorsabad. This last sequence of prosperity and happiness, where he was at the zenith of his power, was the logical outcome of so many conquests and achievements, both for his own glory and for the greatness of his empire. From the sixth of Iyyar (May) 706, when he settled in Khorsabad, to the twelfth of Ab (August) 705 when he was succeeded by Sennacherib, less than one and a half years elapsed, less in fact because he embarked on his last military expedition of unknown duration, as the sources for the end of Sargon's reign are almost totally missing. In his last major prayer to Assur, he had asked to live happy and old in his new capital; he was then about sixty years old. One thing is clear from the documents, namely, that around early summer he undertook a military campaign during which he was killed.[94] Several issues are raised: what happened, where, and why? Somewhere, there was a rebellion against Sargon's yoke, but was it a real threat to the Assyrian Empire? Why did he prefer to conduct the expedition himself rather than sending one of his officers as he did on other occasions? As Khorsabad was a quiet place, inhabited by people devoted to him and without the opposition encountered in Nimrud and Babylon, perhaps a military expedition was seen as an interesting diversion for a warrior king. The place of the campaign and

---

93. *ARAB* 2.86.
94. Grayson, *Assyrian and Babylonian Chronicles*, 76, chr. 1, l. 6′; SAAS 2:60; Tadmor, Landsberger, and Parpola, "Sin of Sargon," 10–11, ll. 8′-9′ and 19′-20′.

the identity of the enemy have been debated. The most likely hypothesis, based on the Babylonian Chronicle, is Tabal, but it is impossible to identify Gurdî the Kulummean, responsible for Sargon's death. Sargon was killed before the Assyrian camp fell prey to the hostile troops. The fact that his body was not retrieved for burial and funeral cult, following Assyrian tradition, was considered a true malediction. It was thought that Sargon had committed some sin such that the gods abandoned him so completely. The new capital of Khorsabad was immediately given up. In such a well-planned context, Sargon's ignominious death appears to be an unforeseeable and incomprehensible accident in the trajectory of his life.

Chronology of Sargon's Campaigns

Dates (BCE)	Year of Reign	Campaigns	Royal Residence
722	Accession year	Against massive opposition in heartland Assyria in 722 and 721.	Nimrud (722–711)
721	Year 1		
720	Year 2	Battle of Dêr against Humban-nikash I of Elam.	
		Victory of Qarqar against the western coalition led by Iaûbidî of Hamath; conquest of Arpad, Simirra, and Damascus.	
		Recapture of Samaria. Capture of Gibbethon and Ekron.	
		Victory of Raphia against Hanunu of Gaza and his Egyptian allies.	
719	Year 3	Against Mitatti of Zikirtu.	
		Death of Iranzû of Mannea. His son Azâ settled on the throne, contested by his second son Ullusunu.	
		Attack of Panzish in 719 or 715.	
718	Year 4	Against Kiakki of Shinuhtu, given to Kurtî of Atunna.	
717	Year 5	Against Pisîri of Carchemish. Annexation.	
		Building project of Khorsabad/Dûr-Sharrukîn.	

716	Year 6	Against Bag-dâti of Uishdish.
		Submission of Ullusunu of Mannea.
		Against Ashur-lêi of Karalla.
		Against Ittî of Allabria.
		Against Bêl-sharru-usur of Kishesim turned into an Assyrian province.
		Against Kibaba of Harhar turned into an Assyrian province.
		Conquest of more cities annexed to the provinces of Harhar and Parsua.
715	Year 7	Recapture of twenty-two Mannean fortresses and Ullusunu restored on the throne.
		Capture of Kimirra of Bît-Hamban.
		Against the province of Harhar and conquest of more cities annexed to it.
		Against Que turned into an Assyrian province.
		Against Arab tribes.
714	Year 8	Call for help of Ullusunu of Mannea.
		Victory of Mount Uaush against Mitatti of Zikirtu and Rusâ of Urartu.
		Against Urartu.
		Sack of Musasir.
713	Year 9	Against Amitashshi of Karalla.
		Against the people of Ellipi (by the commander-in-chief).
		Against Ambaris of Tabal.
		Against Azuri of Ashdod.
		Against Arab tribes.
712	Year 10	Against Tarhun-azi of Kammanu (by Sargon's officer).
		Annexation of Kammanu. Melid was given to Mutallu of Kummuhu.
711	Year 11	Two campaigns against Tarhu-lara and Mutallu of Gurgum.

10. CHRONOLOGICAL SYNTHESIS OF SARGON'S REIGN

		Annexation of Gurgum.	
		Against Yamani of Ashdod (by Sargon's officer).	
710	Year 12	Conquest of Dûr-Athara.	Babylon
		Against Merodach-baladan of Babylon. No support from his ally Shutruk-nahhunte II of Elam.	(710–707)
		Conquest of Babylonia.	
709	Year 13	Siege of Dûr-Yakin.	
		Three raids in Que in 710–709 against Phrygia and against the Ionians (by the governor of Que).	
		Submission of Cyprian kings (by Sargon's officer).	
		Siege of Tyre during five years (by Sargon's officer).	
708	Year 14	Against Mutallu of Kummuhu (by Sargon's officer). Annexation.	
707	Year 15	Destruction of Dûr-Yakin.	
		Against Nibê of Ellipi, for helping Ashpa-bara (by seven of Sargon's officers).	
		Extradition of Yamani of Ashdod by pharaoh Shabatka.	
706	Year 16	Inauguration of Khorsabad.	Khorsabad
		Against Karalla (by the governor of Zamua).	(706–705)
705	Year 17	Against Tabal.	

Conclusion
Assessment of Sargon's Reign

Let us now compare the extent of the empire that Sargon inherited in 722 and that of the empire that he left to his son and successor Sennacherib in 705.[1] In the west, in Palestine, he turned the kingdom of Israel and Ashdod into Assyrian provinces; he subjugated Gaza, Ekron, and Gibbethon. In Syria, he annexed Carchemish and turned Arpad and Damascus into Assyrian provinces again; Hamath and Til Barsip became his vassals. All the Phoenician cities were Sargon's vassals, except for Simirra, which was turned into an Assyrian province again. For the first time, he submitted seven kingdoms of Cyprus to tribute. In the northwest, Sargon gave Hilakku to Ambaris of Tabal and brought other Tabalian kings under submission. Then he turned several states into Assyrian provinces: Que, Tabal/Bit-Purutash, Gurgum, Kummuhu, and Kammanu/Melid. In the north, besides the Mashennu and Rab-Shaqe provinces, he annexed Tushhan, Amidi, and finally Kumme. Other states, which were mainly buffer states between Assyria and Urartu, such as Ukku, Mannea, Hubushkia/Nairi, and Musasir, became vassals or allies. In the east, the polities of Central Zagros were partly annexed and partly submitted to tribute, but always retained their local rulers. In addition to the three previously created provinces of Zamua, Bît-Hamban, and Parsua, Sargon created two new provinces in this area: Kishesim and Harhar, which was part of Media. Ellipi was a buffer state between Assyria and Elam and became an excellent ally of Sargon. Finally, in the south, after the reconquest of Babylonia, Sargon submitted to tribute all of southern Mesopotamia to Dûr-Yakin, together with most of the Aramean, Chaldean, and Arab tribes; he received tribute

---

1. Karen Radner, "Revolts in the Assyrian Empire: Succession Wars, Rebellions against a False King and Independence Movements," in *Revolt and Resistance in the Ancient Classical World and the Near East*, ed. John J. Collins and J. G. Manning, CHANE 85 (Leiden: Brill, 2016), 41, fig. 1.

from the kings of Dilmun and Saba and from the queen of Arabia. Therefore, quite a substantial expansion of the Neo-Assyrian Empire occurred during the seventeen years of Sargon's reign, a relatively short period. However, when Sargon was confronted with four great powers of his time: Egypt, Phrygia, Urartu, and Elam, even though he gained some momentary advantages in fighting or if he received occasional tributes, he never succeeded in conquering them.

One question is in debate: Was the Assyrian Empire that emerged after Sargon's death stable and strong, or short-lived and unstable, and why?[2] Such an ignominious death in the battlefield certainly presented an opportunity for the enemies of the Assyrians. In Babylonia, the Assyrians had to begin again; as had happened in the difficult situation of Sargon's accession in 722, Merodach-baladan reconquered Babylonia in the uncertainty of his death in 705.[3] However, Sennacherib reacted immediately, and after the victory of Kish in 704 where he put Merodach-baladan to flight, he had succeeded in reestablishing Assyrian domination over Babylonia. Even so, it still took almost his whole reign to obtain a definitive solution to the Babylonian problem. There were still confrontations with the Elamite kings, traditional allies of Babylon. He also had to face a new western anti-Assyrian coalition. In short, the Assyrian Empire bequeathed by Sargon was more stable and stronger, but it was not easy to control: Sennacherib had to face more than minor upheavals in the recently annexed areas.[4]

According to a current view, the Assyrian expansion under Sargon's reign was achieved through a total annihilation of local identities, through military confrontation, and then through deportations of populations. This picture essentially comes from Assyrian propaganda in the royal inscriptions. It is not wrong, but there is another image of Sargon, different from that of his predecessors: he did not necessarily seek to exert his domination through aggressive means. He had good relations with several external kings and ruling classes. He rewarded his loyal vassals, he was the defender of legitimate kings, promoter of good allies, and he could forgive repentant enemies. Promotions, benefits, and material advantages, both fiscal and economic, were to be gained from cooperation with the king of Assyria. Sargon aimed to obtain a consensus in

---

2. Lanfranchi, "Consensus to Empire," 81–87 (with bibliography).

3. Garelli and Lemaire, *Proche-Orient Asiatique 2*, 121; Joannès, *The Age of Empires*, 41.

4. Lanfranchi, "Consensus to Empire," 81–87.

the external aristocracies whose countries had not yet been turned into Assyrian provinces. For example, after the conquest of Babylon, he proclaimed the remission of debts and granted exemption from the *ilku*-tax in Babylon and other southern cities.[5] He removed obstacles in order to allow trade relations, even with hostile countries, for example, with the rebellious Mitatti, king of Zikirtu, who was authorized to sell horses to Assyrian representatives. Thus, several external ruling classes understood where their interests lay and became disposed to accept giving up their local independence in order to be integrated into the Assyrian Empire and to support the expansion of a supranational structure. The unification of the Near East into a supranational structure was first partially achieved by Sargon, before being completed by his successors.[6]

In addition to the noteworthy expansion of the Assyrian Empire and its political organization, Sargon's reign was characterized by many achievements, several of them being innovations, but most of them are impossible to date precisely. This Assyrian king implemented very important administrative reforms. His main purpose was to rebalance the long-established power of the offices of the main dignitaries, which sometimes restrained the power of the king. At the beginning of his rule, Sargon changed the order of the eponym officials. The traditional order, after the king, was: the "commander-in-chief" (*turtānu*), the "palace herald" (*nāgir ekalli*), the "chief cupbearer" (*rab šāqê*), the "treasurer" (*mašennu*), the "governor of the land" (*šakin māti*), and the "chief eunuch" (*rab ša rēši*). The Eponym Lists of Sargon only kept the treasurer and the governor of the land, yet under the restrictive name *šakin Libbi-āli*, "governor of the inner city," that is, Assur.[7] The treasurer changes from fifth to third place.[8] Provincial governors appeared in the same order as previously, but not at the same position after the king. However, even though most of the magnates disappeared from the Eponym Lists, they are well known from other documents and correspondence.

---

5. SAA 5:147, no. 203, r., ll. 14′–18′; 125, no. 169.
6. Lanfranchi, "Consensus to Empire," 87.
7. SAAS 2:10; Zawadzki, "Question of the King's Eponymate," 383–89; May, "Administrative and Other Reforms," 80–81. However, Taklak-ana-Bel, who was eponym in 715, was exceptionally honored in a relief of Sargon's palace for his successful siege of Kisheslu; see Albenda, *Palace of Sargon*, pl. 10.
8. SAAS 11:162.

Another important administrative change implemented by Sargon was the introduction of new offices. The commander-in-chief, who was the most powerful magnate in the reigns of the previous kings, at times even becoming a rival to the king, was split in two in 708, after the annexation of Kummuhu: the "commander of the right" (*turtān imitti*) and the "commander of the left" (*turtānu šumēli*), respectively in Kummuhu and Til Barsip.[9] Sargon intended so resolutely to break away from the old Assyrian elites that he did not mention the names of the commanders-in-chief in the royal inscriptions and even appointed a foreigner, a defector from Urartu, to this office.[10] Moreover, part of the commander-in-chief's function as head of the army was transferred to the chief eunuch who was connected with the cavalry; Sargon liked to use eunuchs in his administration and as military commanders.[11] However, even if he stripped his magnates of certain functions, the change was gradual; they were not eager to give up their power, and he still had to reckon with their influence. The most important administrative reform was the resurrection of an ancient office: the "vizier" (*sukkallu*) as the most powerful office; he gave this office to his "favorite brother" Sîn-ahu-usur.[12] In the king's absence, he led the army in the most important campaigns, and he had the unprecedented privilege of building his own residence-palace next to that of the king in Khorsabad. Sargon trusted primarily in his immediate family to limit the role of the commander-in-chief. Thus, the office of vizier served as a buffer between the king and the commander-in-chief. Sargon's trust in the support of his close family members was illustrated too by the designation of his son Sennacherib as the crown prince at the very beginning of his reign.[13] The role of the queen also seems to have changed during Sargon's reign; a letter

---

9. Fuchs, *Inschriften Sargons II*, 179, nn. 408–9.

10. SAA 1:11, no. 8. See also Radner, "Aššur-dūr-pānīya," 185–97.

11. SAAS 11:153; Dezső, "Reconstruction of the Assyrian Army of Sargon II," 122; N'Shea, "Royal Eunuchs and Elite Masculinity," 214–21; May, "Administrative and Other Reforms," 83–84 (with bibliography).

12. Zoltán Niederreiter, "L'insigne de pouvoir et le sceau du grand vizir Sîn-ah-uṣur: Les symboles personnels d'un haut-dignitaire de Sargon II," *RA* 99 (2005): 57–76; May, "Administrative and Other Reforms," 85–91 (with bibliography); May, "The Vizier and the Brother: Sargon II's Brother Sîn-aḫu-uṣur, His Involvement with the Imperial State Affairs and Territorial Affiliations of the Royal Family Members" (forthcoming).

13. *PNA* 3.1:1113–27.

probably to be ascribed to his reign mentioned the first attestation of military units belonging to the queen.[14]

Another manifestation of the redistribution of power was the rise of the scribal elite, the court scholars, initiated by Sargon and reaching its apogee during Esarhaddon's and Ashurbanipal's reigns. Even if court scholars existed before, the mass production of scholarly Neo-Assyrian texts started with Sargon. The abundance of cuneiform tablets from, and after, his reign was not occasional, but a consequence of the promotion of the scribal elite.[15] The scarcity of early Neo-Assyrian archives compared with the late Neo-Assyrian ones could be interpreted as the consequence of the reuse or destruction of the former ones in antiquity. But this was not the case: a rough counting of letters attributed to the reign of Sargon results in 1,155 letters, and in comparison, only 1,051 letters belong to the reigns of three of his successors together.[16] Library texts were different from archive texts; they were carefully copied, sometimes in several duplicates and kept for ages. Even if three libraries dating from the period before Sargon were discovered, they were clearly developed by this Assyrian king. He possibly created a new library for astronomical reports, and he invited Babylonian, Syro-Anatolian, and Egyptian scholars to the Assyrian court.[17] In addition to quantity, the change also applied to the quality of almost all kinds of texts. During Sargon's reign there was a true revolution in royal inscription writing. The texts were not only much more numerous than before, but also appeared in multiple copies. Sargon's scribes resurrected the use of clay prisms and cylinders, abandoned since the tenth century. The royal inscriptions on the back of the palace reliefs are attested for the first time at Khorsabad. Changes also occurred in the style and lexicon of royal inscriptions: for example, the multiplication of descriptive passages, the use of archaisms, neologisms, and new logograms such as AN.ŠÁR

---

14. SAA 19:160, no. 158. For a suggested earlier date, see Radner, "Shalmanassar V. in den Nimrud Letters," 101; SAAS 23:73.

15. Mikko Luukko, "The Administrative Roles of the 'Chief Scribe' and the 'Palace Scribe' in the Neo-Assyrian Period," *SAAB* 16 (2007): 227–56; May, "Administrative and Other Reforms," 92–94 (with bibliography).

16. May, "Administrative and Other Reforms," 93–94 (with bibliography).

17. Jeanette C. Fincke, "The Babylonian Texts of Nineveh: Report on the British Museum's 'Ashurbanipal Library Project,'" *AfO* 50 (2003–2004): 116–32; Fincke, "Babylonische Gelehrte am neuassyrischen Hof: Zwischen Anpassung und Individualität," in Neumann, *Krieg und Frieden im Alten Vorderasien*, 269–92; Radner, "Assyrian King and His Scholars," 221–38.

standing for Assur. Scribes created royal hymns, rituals, and epics, possibly even epics of creation (*Enūma eliš*); they translated a variety of compositions from Sumerian.

The elevation of the status of the scribal elite is demonstrated by the involvement of the scribe Nabû-zuqup-kênu and the scribes of his circle in Sargon's administrative reforms and royal ideology. For example, in 716, Nabû-zuqup-kênu introduced the concept of double and even triple dates: to the eponym dating were added the regnal years of Sargon as king of Assyria and as king of Babylonia. This innovation was not accidental; it was intended to reduce the importance of the eponym dating, which was a statement of independence for the magnates. It is clear that Nabû-zuqup-kênu used his enormous erudition to help strengthen and centralize the power of Sargon. This famous Assyrian scholar, who was possibly the astrologer accompanying the king of Assyria in his eighth campaign, was endowed with the title "illustrious and industrious."[18] In the reign of Sargon, there were connections and cooperation between important scribes of the two capitals: Nimrud and Assur.[19]

Such an enormous number of letters preserved from the reign of Sargon himself supposes that a reform of administrative correspondence was accomplished. An express service was necessary to deliver this correspondence, and it was Sargon who organized the royal post; he was the first of the Neo-Assyrian kings to arrange the imperial postal communications. This important innovation consisted of organizing a network of road stations (*bēt mardīti*) at the end of a daily riding distance (*mardītu*), where fresh mule or horse teams or camels would be awaiting the royal messenger.[20] This communication system with rapid transmission of royal messages to all ends of the empire facilitated governing it.

The reforms of the army have been discussed by several scholars adhering to different hypotheses.[21] It is not impossible that the main

---

18. Frahm, "Nabû-zuqup-kenu," 73–90; Ulla Susanne Koch, *Secrets of Extispicy: The Chapter* muttābiltu *of the Babylonian Extispicy Series and* niṣirti bārûti *Texts Mainly from Aššurbanipal's Library*, AOAT 326 (Münster: Ugarit-Verlag, 2005), 8, 85; Zoltán Niederreiter, "Le rôle des symboles figurés attribués aux membres de la Cour de Sargon II: Des emblèmes créés par des lettrés du palais au service de l'idéologie royale," *Iraq* 70 (2008): 51–86; May, "Administrative and Other Reforms," 97–98.

19. May, "Administrative and Other Reforms," 101–2.

20. Kessler, "'Royal Roads' and Other Questions," 129–36; May, "Administrative and Other Reforms," 94–95 (with bibliography).

21. May, "Administrative and Other Reforms," 79–80 (with bibliography).

changes indeed took place in Tiglath-pileser III's reign, with Sargon carrying on with the reforms of his predecessor. The army of Sargon can be reconstructed from the Nimrud Horse Lists, as well as from administrative texts and letters such as Nimrud letter 89, which gives a breakdown of the forces under the command of the governor of Zamua.[22] Assyrian warfare was developed in the reign of Sargon, and military intelligence is particularly well known from his correspondence.[23] He was by no means the first Assyrian king to conscript chariotry and cavalry from the west, particularly from the Levant, into his army. He used fully professional mercenary soldiers. According to the Horse Lists, it is quite clear that Samarian equestrian officers were employed in Sargon's army (see above).[24] It is known from the Bible that Israelites had indeed served as mercenaries at the beginning of the eighth century (2 Chr 25:6). However, it was different when they worked for their conqueror, the financial arrangements being unknown. Sargon was increasingly aware of the importance of equestrian technology and cavalry as a powerful weapon of war. Innovations such as breeds of horses, methods of harnessing, together with importing foreign experts—from Samaria and Nubia for chariotry and from Urartu for cavalry—contributed to the strengthening of the Assyrian army.

Before building Khorsabad, Sargon built and restored other edifices in the empire. When he was dwelling in Nimrud, he built a new palace, the so-called Burnt Palace, located next to the temple of Nabû (Ezida), in the southwestern part of the city.[25] He carefully described the restoration of the ancient palace of Ashurnasirpal II in order to store his booty there: "The plunder of the cities, (acquired through) the success of my weapons which I hurled against the foe, I shut up therein and filled it to bursting with luxuries"; he was probably the last king to use this palace.[26]

---

22. Postgate, "Assyrian Army in Zamua," 89–108; Postgate, "Invisible Hierarchy," 331–59; Dezsó, "Reconstruction of the Army of Sargon II," 93–140; Fuchs, "Assyria at War," 380–401.

23. H. W. F. Saggs, "Assyrian Warfare in the Sargonic Period," *Iraq* 25 (1963): 145–54; Tamás Dezsó, "Neo-Assyrian Military Intelligence," in Neumann, *Krieg und Frieden im Alten Vorderasien*, 221–35.

24. Dalley, "Foreign Chariotry," 31–48.

25. Joannès, *The Age of Empires*, 107; Joannès, *Dictionnaire de la civilisation mésopotamienne*, 438, 757; *PNA* 3.2:1244–45.

26. *ARAB* 2.138; John Malcolm Russell, *The Writing on the Wall: Studies in the Architectural Context of Late Assyrian Palace Inscriptions*, MC 9 (Winona Lake, IN: Eisenbrauns, 1999), 99.

The royal inscriptions of Sargon also testify that he restored the temples of Nabû and Marduk, the Bît-Akitu of Ishtar, and the ziggurat of Adad in Nineveh; other works of restoration were conducted at the end of his reign in Babylon (city walls) and Uruk (the Eanna temple). Other building or restoration works are mentioned in his inscriptions: in Assur (Ehursaggalkurkurra, palace of the Inner, Sîn-Shamash temple), in Harrân (Ehulhul temple), in Dêr (city walls), in Harhar, and possibly in Tabal.

The building of the new capital Khorsabad gives evidence of several innovations. The place chosen, in the middle of nowhere, was unprecedented; the other new capitals such as Nimrud or Nineveh had existed before they became capitals. Khorsabad was the first capital entirely conceived and built by an Assyrian king. For example, the number and the location of the doors in the city walls were carefully calculated following a new scheme based on a modular system.[27] The choice of the reliefs and their placement in the different sectors of the palace show important innovations compared to the traditions established in the reliefs carved in the older palaces.[28] The first innovation was representing in every hall of the palace different episodes of one individual military campaign. The second great thematic innovation of the carved reliefs was the use of hunting scenes and banquets after hunts together with military campaigns, with high personages of Assyrian aristocracy accompanying Sargon. The third innovation was the presentation of processions of large numbers of officials, a theme not used before, including the presentation of tributes or precious court fittings to the king. The king was surrounded by officials, with or without beards (eunuchs), who presumably were the most important officials of the empire.[29] Only in Khorsabad was the carved representation of Assyrian noblemen given such a prominent feature. The precise political meaning of these innovations was possibly Sargon's wish to exalt the role of Assyrian aristocracy in the composition of empire management and to celebrate visually the structural complexity of his government for the happy condition of his subjects, belonging to different lands and

---

27. Battini, "Portes urbaines de la capitale," 41–55.

28. Luc Bachelot, "La fonction politique des reliefs néo-assyriens," in *Marchands, diplomates et empereurs: Études sur la civilisation mésopotamienne offertes à Paul Garelli*, ed. Dominique Charpin and Francis Joannès (Paris: Recherche sur les Civilisations, 1991), 109–28; Matthiae, "Subject Innovations in the Khorsabad Reliefs," 477–94.

29. Parpola, "Construction of Dur-Šarrukin," 66–67.

peoples, unified by the Assyrian language, culture, and religion.³⁰ Another unusual narrative composition was the expansive scene depicting the land and sea transport of lumber, a relief some 3 m high and 14 m long.³¹ Another new type of architecture was an isolated columned building represented on a relief, situated at the edge of a small lake: it was a new-style altar with a stepped battlement at the top.³²

Sargon implemented important fiscal measures with obvious immediate advantages deriving from tax exemptions or reductions. He exempted all the temples of Assyria from paying taxes. The exemptions (*zakûtu*) were also extended to several cities. He accused his predecessor Shalmaneser V of having robbed Assur and Harrân of its traditional privileges, and he restored their exemption from taxation and their autonomy, as a kind of recompense for having supported his accession to the throne.³³ The exemption was from the *ilku*-tax, among others, as can be seen from the letter of a local official.³⁴ The main Babylonian cities such as Babylon, Nippur, and Sippar were also exempted from task work and taxes. However, the debt-remission (*andurāru*) proclaimed in Babylon was not generally welcome—as is shown by the protestation of the Babylonians.³⁵ Sargon's aim was not only to be seen as the king dispensing economic justice; he also aimed at weakening the rich owners who had invested their capital in loans. He was obviously leaning on other social groups, in particular on the powerful Babylonian clergy. Sargon also gave some privileges to other Babylonian cities: "I (re)established the freedom of Dêr, Ur, Uruk, Eridu, Larsa, Kullab, Kissik, and Nimid-laguda."³⁶ These cities, which had prestigious sanctuaries, continued to benefit from a kind of internal autonomy under Sargon's reign.

Agricultural development was important for Sargon, as is illustrated by an inscription in the temple of the storm god Adad in Khorsabad: "O Adad, … bring rain from the sky and flood from the springs, amass corn and oil in its surroundings, let your subjects graze in the meadows

---

30. Matthiae, "Subject Innovations in the Khorsabad Reliefs," 492.
31. Albenda, "Dur-Sharrukin, the Royal City," 11–12 (with bibliography).
32. Pauline Albenda, "Monument on the Hill," *NABU* 1 (2010): 12–14, no. 13.
33. *ARAB* 2.54, 99, 102; Saggs, "Historical Texts and Fragments," 14–15.
34. Waterman, *Royal Correspondence*, 1:66–67, no. 99, rev., ll. 6–8.
35. SAA 5:147, no. 203, rev., 14′-s.1; Lanfranchi, "Consensus to Empire," 86; Garelli and Lemaire, *Proche-Orient asiatique*, 138–39.
36. *ARAB* 2.54, 69, 78, 99, 102.

in plenty and abundance, strengthen the foundation of Sargon's throne (and) let his reign last for long!"[37] When a bad omen threatened the king, the country had to be ruled by a "substitute king," with the king adopting the title "farmer" and, bearing this title, carrying on his functions. This title was chosen because it reflected one of the king's supreme duties: the cultivation of land.[38] Sargon chose the combination of a fig-tree and a seeder-plough as a symbol to represent Assyria, thus stressing the importance that he attributed to agriculture and horticulture.[39] Wherever possible, he tried to convert steppe lands into arable land, as is clearly written in a prism inscription: "The well versed king, who constantly considers plans of good things and who directs his attention to the settlement of desolate steppes, to the cultivation of fallow land and to the plantation of fruit groves, contemplated causing steep rocks, from which never before green had sprouted, to produce yield."[40] The cultivation of barren land was accomplished by either the local population or deportees. Sargon had major cultivation projects in the steppe and large scale gardening plans. He supplemented rain-fed irrigation with artificial irrigation by means of wells and canals, for example, the canal between Babylon and Borsippa.[41] His interest in plants and trees is illustrated by the detailed depiction of plants in the reliefs of his palace.[42] The extensive gardens that he had built around Khorsabad and his improvement of agricultural techniques also bear witness to his keen interest in this domain. He tried to prevent natural disasters such as flooding and storms by consulting scholars who specialized in interpreting omens. Sargon distributed land among officials, temples, and soldiers, often ceding the possession rights. This land tenure was at times tax-free but sometimes entailed a duty to pay taxes, in particular on barley (*šibšu*) and straw (*nusāhē*).[43] By distributing state-owned

---

37. Fuchs, *Inschriften Sargons II*, 282, 370.

38. Radner, "How Did the Neo-Assyrian King," 233–46.

39. J. E. Reade, "The Khorsabad Glazed Bricks and Their Symbolism," in Caubet, *Khorsabad, le palais de Sargon II*, 235, 248; I. Finkel and J. E. Reade, "Assyrian Hieroglyphs," *ZA* 86 (1996): 244–68.

40. Fuchs, *Inschriften Sargons II*, 37, 292.

41. Ur, "Sennacherib's Northern Assyrian Canals," 317–20 and fig. 2.

42. Erika Bleibtreu, *Die Flora der neuassyrischen Reliefs: Eine Untersuchung zu den Orthostatenreliefs des 9.-7. Jahrhunderts v. Chr.*, WZKM/S 1 (Vienna: Institutes für Orientalistik der Universität Wien, 1980).

43. Postgate, *Taxation and Conscription*, 174–78; Paul Garelli, "Le système fiscal

land, the Assyrian king aimed to prevent the emergence of powerful independent landowners who would have endangered his absolute authority.

In every category of his achievements and innovations, the centralization and strengthening of his absolute power appears to have been one of Sargon's main concerns. He was "one of the most prestigious kings of the ancient Orient. Sargon II was the real founder of the empire, contributing decisively to ensuring its power and giving it its final character."[44] If we were to sum up his life in one sentence, it could be the following: Sargon succeeded in everything in his life, but completely failed in his death.

---

de l'empire assyrien," in *Points de vue sur la fiscalité antique*, ed. Henri van Effenterre, Études 14 (Paris: Publications de la Sorbonne, 1979), 7–18.

44. Garelli and Lemaire, *Proche-Orient Asiatique 2*, 114.

Selected Bibliography

General Works

Albenda, Pauline. *The Palace of Sargon King of Assyria: Monumental Wall Reliefs at Dur-Sharrukin, from Original Drawings Made at the Time of Their Discovery in 1843–1844 by Botta and Flandin.* Synthèse 22. Paris: Recherches sur les Civilisations, 1986.
Fuchs, Andreas. *Die Inschriften Sargons II. aus Khorsabad.* Göttingen: Cuvillier, 1993.
Lie, Arthur Gotfred. *The Inscriptions of Sargon II, King of Assyria: Part I, The Annals.* Paris: Geuthner, 1929.

Chapter 1

Battini, Laura. "Les portes urbaines de la capitale de Sargon II: Étude sur la propagande royale à travers les données archéologiques et textuelles." Pages 41–55 in *Intellectual Life in the Ancient Near East: Papers Presented at the Forty-Third Rencontre assyriologique internationale, Prague, July 1–5, 1996.* Edited by J. Prosecký. RAI 43. Prague: Oriental Institute, 1998.
Frahm, Eckhart. "Observations on the Name and Age of Sargon II and on Some Patterns of Assyrian Royal Onomastics." *NABU* 2 (2005): 46–50, no. 44.
Galter, Hannes D. "Sargon II. und die Eroberung der Welt." Pages 329–43 in *Krieg und Frieden im Alten Vorderasien: 52e Rencontre Assyriologique Internationale, International Congress of Assyriology and Near Eastern Archaeology, Münster, 17.–21. Juli 2006.* Edited by Hans Neumann, Reinhard Dittmann, Susanne Paulus, Georg Neumann, and Anais Schuster-Brandis. RAI 52; AOAT 401. Münster: Ugarit-Verlag, 2014.
Sence, Guillaume. "Dur-Sharrukin: Le portrait de Sargon II; Essai d'analyse

structuraliste des bas-reliefs du palais découvert à Khorsabad." *REA* 109 (2007): 429–47.

Chapter 2

Becking, Bob. *The Fall of Samaria: An Historical and Archaeological Study*. SHANE 4. Leiden: Brill, 1992.
Na'aman, Nadav. "The Historical Background to the Conquest of Samaria (720 BC)." *Bib* 71 (1990): 206–25.
———. "Sargon's Second *palû* according to the Khorsabad Annals." *TA* 34 (2007): 165–70.
Olmstead, Albert Ten Eyck. *Western Asia in the Days of Sargon of Assyria, 722–705 B.C.: A Study in Oriental History*. New York: Holt, 1908.
Tadmor, Hayim. "The Campaigns of Sargon II of Assur: A Chronological-Historical Study." *JCS* 12 (1958): 22–40, 77–100.
Thomas, Felix. "Sargon II., der Sohn Tiglat-pilesers III." Pages 465–70 in *Mesopotamica-Ugaritica-Biblica: Festschrift für Kurt Bergerhof*. Edited by Manfred Dietrich and Oswald Loretz. AOAT 232. Neukirchen-Vluyn: Neukirchener Verlag, 1993.
Vera Chamaza, Galo W. "Sargon II's Ascent to the Throne: The Political Situation." *SAAB* 6 (1992): 21–33.
Younger, K. Lawson. "The Fall of Samaria in Light of Recent Research." *CBQ* 61 (1999): 461–82.

Chapter 3

Dubovský, Peter. *Hezekiah and the Assyrian Spies: Reconstruction of the Neo-Assyrian Intelligence Services and Its Significance for 2 Kings 18–19*. BibOr 49. Rome: Biblical Institute Press, 2006.
Postgate, John Nicholas. "The Invisible Hierarchy: Assyrian Military and Civilian Administration in the Eighth and Seventh Centuries BC." Pages 331–60 in *The Land of Assur and the Yoke of Assur: Studies on Assyria 1971–2005*. Oxford: Oxbow, 2007.
Radner, Karen. "The Ashur-Nineveh-Arbela Triangle: Central Assyria in the Neo-Assyrian Period." Pages 321–29 in *Between the Cultures: The Central Tigris Region from the Third to the First Millennium BC*. Edited by Peter A. Miglus and Simone Mühl. HSAO 14. Heidelberg: Heidelberger Orient-Verlag, 2011.
Zawadzki, Stefan. "The Question of the King's Eponymate in the Latter Half

of the Eighth Century and the Seventh Century BC." Pages 383–89 in *Assyria 1995: Proceedings of the Tenth Anniversary Symposium of the Neo-Assyrian Text Corpus Project, Helsinki, Sept. 7–11, 1995*. Edited by Simo Parpola and Robert M. Whiting. Helsinki: Neo-Assyrian Text Corpus Project, 1997.

Chapter 4

Achenbach, Reinhard. "Jabâ und Atalja: Zwei jüdische Königstöchter am assyrischen Königshof?" *BN* 113 (2002): 29–38.
Bagg, Ariel M. "Hezekiah's Jerusalem: Nineveh in Judah?" Pages 33–39 in *From Source to History: Studies in Ancient Near Eastern Worlds and beyond Dedicated to Giovanni Battista Lanfranchi on the Occasion of His Sixty-Fifth Birthday on June 23, 2014*. Edited by Salvatore Gaspa, Alessandro Greco, Daniele Morandi Bonacossi, Simonetta Ponchia, and Robert Rollinger. AOAT 412. Münster: Ugarit-Verlag, 2014.
Berlejung, Angelika. "The Assyrians in the West: Assyrianization, Colonialism, Indifference, or Development Policy?" Pages 21–61 in *Congress Volume: Helsinki, 2010*. Edited by Martti Nissinen. VTSup 148. Leiden: Brill, 2010.
Blakely, Jeffrey A., and James W. Hardin. "Southwestern Judah in the Late Eighth Century B.C.E." *BASOR* 326 (2002): 11–64.
Dalley, Stephanie. "Recent Evidence from Assyrian Sources for Judaean History from Uzziah to Manasseh." *JSOT* 28 (2004): 387–401.
———. "Yabâ, Atalyā and the Foreign Policy of the Late Assyrian Kings." *SAAB* 12 (1998): 83–98.
Elayi, Josette. "The Phoenician Cities and the Assyrian Empire in the Time of Sargon II." *Sumer* 42 (1986): 129–32.
Eph'al, Israel. "The Samaritan(s) in the Assyrian Sources." Pages 36–45 in *Ah, Assyria…: Studies in Assyrian History and Ancient Near Eastern Historiography Presented to Hayim Tadmor*. Edited by Mordechai Cogan and Israel Eph'al. ScrHier. Jerusalem: Magnes, 1991.
Franklin, Norma. "The Room V Reliefs at Dur-Sharrukin and Sargon II's Western Campaigns." *TA* 21 (1994): 255–75.
Kahn, Dan'el. "The Inscription of Sargon II at Tang-i Var and the Chronology of Dynasty 25." *Or* 70 (2001): 1–18.
Na'aman, Nadav. "The Conquest of Yadnana according to the Inscriptions of Sargon II." Pages 357–63 in *Historiography in the Cuneiform World*.

Edited by Tvi Abush, Paul-Alain Beaulieu, John Huehnergard, Peter Machinist, and Piotr Steinkeller. RAI 45. Bethesda: CDL, 2001.

———. "Hezekiah and the Kings of Assyria." *TA* 21 (1994): 235–54.

———. "The Historical Background to the Conquest of Samaria (720 BC)." *Bib* 71 (1990): 206–25.

———. "The Number of Deportees from Samaria in the Nimrud Prisms of Sargon II." *NABU* (2000): 1.

Na'aman, Nadav, and Ran Zadok, "Assyrian Deportations to the Province of Samerina in the Light of Two Cuneiform Tablets from Tel Hadid." *TA* 27 (2000): 159–88.

Radner, Karen. "Aššur-dūr-pānīya, Statthalter von Til-Barsip unter Sargon II. von Assyrien." *BaghM* 37 (2006): 185–95.

Schoors, Anton. *Die Königreiche Israel und Juda im 8. und 7. Jahrhundert v. Chr.: Die Assyrische Krise.* BiE 5. Stuttgart: Kohlhammer, 1998.

Sweeney, Marvin A. "Sargon's Threat against Jerusalem in Isaiah 10, 27–32." *Bib* 75 (1994): 457–70.

Tetley, M. Christine. "The Date of Samaria's Fall as a Reason for Rejecting the Hypothesis of Two Conquests." *CBQ* 64 (2002): 59–77.

———. *The Reconstructed Chronology of the Divided Kingdom.* Winona Lake, IN: Eisenbrauns, 2005.

Younger, K. Lawson. "The Deportations of the Israelites." *JBL* 117 (1998): 201–27.

———. "The Fall of Samaria in Light of Recent Research." *CBQ* 61 (1999): 461–82.

———. "Recent Study on Sargon II, King of Assyria: Implications for Biblical Studies." Pages 288–329 in *Mesopotamia and the Bible: Comparative Explorations.* Edited by Mark W. Chavalas and K. Lawson Younger. JSOTSup 341. London: Sheffield Academic, 2002.

———. "The Repopulation of Samaria (2 Kings 17:24, 27–31) in Light of Recent Study." Pages 254–80 in *The Future of Biblical Archaeology: Reassessing Methodologies and Assumptions.* Edited by James K. Hoffmeier and Alan Millard. Grand Rapids: Eerdmans, 2004.

Chapter 5

Elayi, Josette, and Antoine Cavigneaux. "Sargon II et les Ioniens." *OrAnt* 18 (1979): 59–75.

Frangipane, Marcella, and Mario Liverani. "Neo-Hittite Melid: Continuity or Discontinuity?" Pages 349–71 in *Across the Border: Late Bronze-*

Iron Age Relations between Syria and Anatolia. Edited by K. Alishan Yener. ANESsup 42. Leuven: Peeters, 2013.
Galil, Gershon. "Conflicts between Assyrian Vassals." *SAAB* 6 (1992): 55–63.
Grayson, Albert Kirk. "Assyrian Expansion into Anatolia in the Sargonid Age (c. 744–650 BC)." Pages 131–35 in *The Relations between Anatolia and Mesopotamia.* Edited by H. Erkanal, V. Donbaz, and A. Uğuroğlu. RAI 34. Ankara: Türk Tarih Kurumu Basımevi, 1998.
Hawkins, John David. "Hittites and Assyrians at Melid (Malatya)." Pages 63–77 in *The Relations between Anatolia and Mesopotamia.* Edited by H. Erkanal, V. Donbaz, and A. Uğuroğlu. RAI 34. Ankara: Türk Tarih Kurumu Basımevi, 1998.
———. "The Political Geography of North Syria and South-East Anatolia in the Neo-Assyrian Period." Pages 87–101 in *Neo-Assyrian Geography*. Edited by Mario Liverani. QGS 5. Rome: Universita di Roma "La Sapienza," 1995.
Hawkins, John David, and John Nicholas Postgate. "Tribute from Tabal." *SAAB* 2 (1988): 31–40.
Lanfranchi, Giovanni Battista. "The Ideological and Political Impact of the Assyrian Imperial Expansion on the Greek World in the Eighth and Seventh Centuries BC." Pages 7–34 in *The Heirs of Assyria: Proceedings of The Opening Symposium of The Assyrian and Babylonian Intellectual Heritage Project Held in Tvärminne, Finland, October 8–11, 1998.* Edited by Sanna Aro and Robert M. Whiting. MSym 1. Helsinki: Neo-Assyrian Text Corpus Project, 2000.
———. "Sargon's Letter to Aššur-šarru-uṣur: An Interpretation." *SAAB* 2 (1988): 59–64.
Lemaire, André. "Aššur-šarru-uṣur, gouverneur de Qué." *NABU* 10 (1987): 5–6, no. 10.
Muscarella, Oscar W. "Relations between Phrygia and Assyria in the Eighth century B.C." Pages 149–57 in *The Relations between Anatolia and Mesopotamia.* Edited by H. Erkanal, V. Donbaz, and A. Uğuroğlu. RAI 34. Ankara: Türk Tarih Kurumu Basımevi, 1998.

Chapter 6

Dubovský, Peter. "Conquest and Reconquest of Muṣaṣir in the Eighth Century BCE." *SAAB* 15 (2006): 141–46.
Fales, Frederick Mario. "Evidence for West-East Contacts in the Eighth

Century BC: The Bukān Stele." Pages 131–47 in *Continuity of Empire(?): Assyria, Media, Persia*. Edited by Giovanni B. Lanfranchi, Michael Roaf, and Robert Rollinger. HANE/M 5. Padova: S.A.R.G.O.N., 2003.

Kessler, Karlheinz. "Šubria, Urartu and Aššur, Topographical Questions around the Tigris Sources." Pages 55–67 in *Neo-Assyrian Geography*. Edited by Mario Liverani. QGS 5. Rome: Universita di Roma "La Sapienza," 1995.

Kravitz, Kathryn F. "A Last-Minute Revision to Sargon's Letter to the God." *JNES* 62 (2003): 81–95.

Levine, Louis D. "Observations on Sargon's Letter to the Gods." *ErIs* 27 (2003): 111*–19*.

———. "Sargon's Eighth Campaign." Pages 135–51 in *Mountains and Lowlands: Essays in the Archaeology of Greater Mesopotamia*. Edited by Louis D. Levine and T. Cuyler Young. BMes 7. Malibu, CA: Undena, 1977.

Mayer, Walter. *Assyrien und Urartu I: Der Achte Feldzug Sargons II. im Jahr 714 v. Chr.* AOAT 395.1. Münster: Ugarit-Verlag, 2013.

Mieroop, Marc van de. "A Study in Contrast: Sargon of Assyria and Rusa of Urartu." Pages 417–34 in *Opening the Tablet Box: Near Eastern Studies in Honor of Benjamin R. Foster*. Edited by Sarah C. Melville and Alice L. Slotsky. CHANE 42. Leiden: Brill, 2010.

Muscarella, Oscar W. "The Location of Ulhu and Uiše in Sargon II's Eighth Campaign, 714 B.C." *JFA* 13 (1986): 465–75.

Parker, Bradley J. *The Mechanics of Empire: The Northern Frontier of Assyria as a Base of Imperial Dynamics*. Helsinki: Neo-Assyrian Text Corpus Project, 2001.

Radner, Karen. "Assyrians and Urartians." Pages 734–51 in *The Oxford Handbook of Ancient Anatolia, 10,000–323 B.C.E.* Edited by Sharon R. Steddman and Gregory McMahon. Oxford: Oxford University Press, 2011.

———. "Between a Rock and a Hard Place: Muṣaṣir, Kumme, Ukku and Šubria; the Buffer States between Assyria and Urarṭu." Pages 243–64 in *Biainili-Urartu: The Proceedings of The Symposium Held in Munich 12–14 October 2007*. Edited by Stephan Kroll, Claudia Gruber, Ursula Hellwag, Michael Roaf, and Paul E. Zimansky. Acta Iranica 51. Leuven: Peeters, 2012.

Reade, Julian E. "Sargon's Campaigns of 720, 716, and 715 B.C.: Evidence from the Sculptures." *JNES* 35 (1976): 95–104.

Salvini, Mirjo. "Assyrie-Urartu: guerres sans conquêtes." Pages 51–61 in

Guerre et conquête dans le Proche-Orient ancien: Actes de la table ronde du 14 novembre 1998 organisée par l'URA 1062 "Études sémitiques." Edited by Laïla Nehmé. AntSem 4. Paris: Maisonneuve, 1999.

———. "Sargon et l'Urartu." Pages 135–57 in *Khorsabad, le palais de Sargon II, roi d'Assyrie*. Edited by Annie Caubet. Paris: Documentation française, 1995.

———. "Some Historic-Geographical Problems Concerning Assyria and Urartu." Pages 43–53 in *Neo-Assyrian Geography*. Edited by Mario Liverani. QGS 5. Rome: Universita di Roma "La Sapienza," 1995.

Thureau-Dangin, François. *Une relation de la huitième campagne de Sargon (714 av. J.-C.)*. TCL 3. Paris: Geuthner, 1912.

Vera Chamaza, Galo W. "Der VIII Feldzug Sargons II. Eine Untersuchungen zu Politik und Historischer Geographie des späten 8. Jhs. v. Chr. (I)." *AMI* 27 (1994): 91–118.

Zimansky, Paul. "Urartian Geography and Sargon's Eighth Campaign." *JNES* 49 (1990): 1–21.

Chapter 7

Lanfranchi, Giovanni Battista. "The Assyrian Expansion in the Zagros and the Local Ruling Elites." Pages 79–118 in *Continuity of Empire(?): Assyria, Media, Persia*. Edited by Giovanni Battista Lanfranchi, Michael Roaf, and Robert Rollinger. HANE/M 5. Padova: S.A.R.G.O.N., 2003.

Levine, Louis D. "Geographical Studies in the Neo-Assyrian Zagros I." *Iran* 11 (1973): 1–27.

———. "Geographical Studies in the Neo-Assyrian Zagros II." *Iran* 12 (1974): 99–124.

Liverani, Mario. "The Rise and Fall of Media." Pages 1–12 in *Continuity of Empire(?): Assyria, Media, Persia*. Edited by Giovanni Battista Lanfranchi, Michael Roaf, and Robert Rollinger. HANE/M 5. Padova: S.A.R.G.O.N., 2003.

Postgate, John Nicholas. "The Assyrian Army in Zamua." *Iraq* 62 (2000): 89–108.

Postgate, John Nicholas, and Raija A. Mattila. "Il-Yada' and Sargon's Southeast Frontier." Pages 235–54 in *From the Upper Sea to the Lower Sea: Studies on the History of Assyria and Babylonia in Honour of A. K. Grayson*. Edited by Grant Frame and Linda Wilding. PIHANS 101. Leiden: Nederlands Instituut voor het Nabije Oosten, 2004.

Radner, Karen. "An Assyrian View on the Medes." Pages 37–64 in *Conti-*

nuity of Empire(?): Assyria, Media, Persia. Edited by Giovanni Battista Lanfranchi, Michael Roaf, and Robert Rollinger. HANE/M 5. Padova: S.A.R.G.O.N., 2003.

Reade, Julian E. "Iran in the Neo-Assyrian Period." Pages 31–42 in *Neo-Assyrian Geography*. Edited by Mario Liverani. QGS 5. Rome: Universita di Roma "La Sapienza," 1995.

Chapter 8

Brinkman, John A. "Elamite Military Aid to Merodach-Baladan." *JNES* 24 (1965): 161–66.

———. "Reflections on the Geography of Babylonia (1000–600 B.C.)." Pages 19–29 in *Neo-Assyrian Geography*. Edited by Mario Liverani. QGS 5. Rome: Universita di Roma "La Sapienza," 1995.

Eidem, Jesper, and Flemming Højlund. "Trade or Diplomacy? Assyria and Dilmun in the Eighteenth Century BC." *WA* 24 (1993): 441–48.

Eph'al, Israel. "'Arabs' in Babylonia in the Eighth Century B.C." *JAOS* 94 (1974): 108–15.

Fales, Frederick Mario. "Moving around Babylon: On the Aramean and Chaldean Presence in Southern Mesopotamia." Pages 91–111 in *Babylon: Wissenskultur in Orient und Okzident*. Edited by Eva Cancik-Kirschbaum, Margarete Ess, and Joachim Marzahn. Topoi 1. Berlin: de Gruyter, 2008.

Galter, Hannes D. "Sargon II. und die Eroberung der Welt." Pages 329–43 in *Krieg und Frieden im Alten Vorderasien: 52e Rencontre Assyriologique Internationale, International Congress of Assyriology and Near Eastern Archaeology, Münster, 17.–21. Juli 2006*. Edited by Hans Neumann, Reinhard Dittmann, Susanne Paulus, Georg Neumann, and Anais Schuster-Brandis. RAI 52; AOAT 401. Münster: Ugarit-Verlag, 2014.

Lanfranchi, Giovanni Battista. "Consensus to Empire: Some Aspects of Sargon II's Foreign Policy." Pages 81–87 in *Assyrien im Wandel der Zeiten*. Edited by Hartmut Waetzoldt and Harald Hauptmann. RAI 39; HSAO 6. Heidelberg: Heidelberger Orient-Verlag, 1997.

Postgate, John Nicholas, and Raija A. Mattila. "Il-Yada' and Sargon's Southeast Frontier." Pages 235–54 in *From the Upper Sea to the Lower Sea: Studies on the History of Assyria and Babylonia in Honour of A. K. Grayson*. Edited by Grant Frame and Linda Wilding. PIHANS 101. Leiden: Nederlands Instituut voor het Nabije Oosten, 2004.

Potts, Daniel T. "Dilmun: Where and When?" *Dilmun* 2 (1983): 15–19.

Spek, Robartus J. van der. "The Struggle of King Sargon II of Assyria against the Chaldean Merodach-baladan (701–708 B.C.)." *JEOL* 25 (1978): 56–66.

Chapter 9

Battini, Laura. "Des rapports géométriques en architecture: Le cas de Dūr-Šarrukin." *RA* 94 (2000): 33–56.
Frahm, Eckhart. "Nabû-zuqup-kēnu, das Gilgameš-Epos und der Tod Sargons II." *JCS* 51 (1999): 73–90.
Garelli, Paul. "Réflexions sur 'le péché de Sargon.'" Pages 341–45 in *Studi sul Vicino Oriente Antico dedicati alla memoria di Luigi Cagni*. Edited by Simonetta Graziani. Vol. 1. IOUsm 61. Naples: Istituto Universitario Orientale, 2000.
Matthiae, Paolo. "Subject Innovations in the Khorsabad Reliefs and Their Political Meaning." Pages 477–94 in *Leggo! Studies Presented to Frederick Mario Fales on the Occasion of His Sixty-Fifth Birthday*. Edited by Giovanni Battista Lanfranchi, Daniele Morandi Bonacossi, Cinzia Pappi, and Simonetta Ponchia. LAOS 2. Wiesbaden: Harrassowitz, 2012.
Parpola, Simo. "The Construction of Dur-Šarrukin in the Assyrian Royal Correspondence." Pages 47–77 in *Khorsabad, le palais de Sargon II, roi d'Assyrie*. Edited by Annie Caubet. Paris: Documentation française, 1995.
Tadmor, Hayim, Benno Landsberger, and Simo Parpola, "The Sin of Sargon and Sennacherib's Last Will." *SAAB* 3 (1989): 3–51.
Weaver, Ann M. "The 'Sin of Sargon' and Esarhaddon's Reconception of Sennacherib: A Study in Divine Will, Human Politics and Royal Ideology." *Iraq* 66 (2004): 61–66.

Conclusion

Albenda, Pauline. "Dur-Sharrukin, the Royal City of Sargon II, King of Assyria." *CSMS Bulletin* 38 (2003): 5–13.
Dalley, Stephanie. "Foreign Chariotry and Cavalry in the Armies of Tiglath-pileser III and Sargon II." *Iraq* 47 (1985): 31–48.
Dezső, Tamás. "A Reconstruction of the Army of Sargon II (721–705 BC) Based on the Nimrud Horse Lists." *SAAB* 15 (2006): 93–140.

Frahm, Eckhart. "Nabû-zuqup-kenu, das Gilgameš-Epos und der Tod Sargons II." *JCS* 51 (1999): 73–90.

Luukko, Mikko. "The Administrative Roles of the 'Chief Scribe' and the 'Palace Scribe' in the Neo-Assyrian Period." *SAAB* 16 (2007): 227–56.

May, Nathalie Naomi. "Administrative and Other Reforms of Sargon II and Tiglath-pileser III." *SAAB* 21 (2015): 79–116.

Niederreiter, Zoltán. "L'insigne de pouvoir et le sceau du grand vizir Sînah-uṣur: Les symboles personnels d'un haut-dignitaire de Sargon II." *RA* 99 (2005): 57–76.

———. "Le rôle des symboles figurés attribués aux membres de la Cour de Sargon II: Des emblèmes créés par des lettrés du palais au service de l'idéologie royale." *Iraq* 70 (2008): 51–86.

N'Shea, Omar. "Royal Eunuchs and Elite Masculinity in the Neo-Assyrian Empire." *NEA* 79 (2016): 214–21.

Radner, Karen. "Aššur-dūr-pānīya, Statthalter von Til-Barsip under Sargon II. von Assyrien." *BaghM* 37 (2006): 185–95.

———. "The Assyrian King and His Scholars: The Syro-Anatolian and the Egyptian Schools." Pages 221–38 in *Of God(s), Trees, Kings, and Scholars: Neo-Assyrian Studies in Honour of Simo Parpola*. Edited by Mikko Luukko, Saana Svärd, and Raija Mattila. StOr 106. Helsinki: Finnish Oriental Society, 2009.

Saggs, Henry William Frederick. "Assyrian Warfare in the Sargonic Period." *Iraq* 25 (1963): 145–54.

Zawadzki, Stefan. "The Question of the King's Eponymate in the Latter Half of the Eighth Century and the Seventh Century BC." Pages 383–89 in *Assyria 1995: Proceedings of the Tenth Anniversary Symposium of the Neo-Assyrian Text Corpus Project, Helsinki, Sept. 7–11, 1995*. Edited by Simo Parpola and Robert M. Whiting. Helsinki: Neo-Assyrian Text Corpus Project, 1997.

Index of Ancient Sources

Hebrew Bible/Old Testament

Genesis
- 10:6–7 — 195
- 10:25–29 — 197
- 16:1–17:25 — 195
- 25:12–18 — 195

Joshua
- 18:23 — 52

1 Kings
- 10 — 197
- 16:15 — 60

2 Kings
- 17:3–6 — 25, 46, 47, 51
- 17:24 — 52
- 18:9–11 — 25, 46, 51
- 20 — 183, 185

2 Chronicles
- 25:6 — 251

Isaiah
- 8:7–8 — 3
- 10:24–32 — 53
- 13:20–22 — 58, 195
- 14:4-20a — 214
- 20:1 — 13

Ezekiel
- 17:23 — 117
- 27:20–22 — 195

Nahum
- 1:9–11 — 39
- 1:14 — 39
- 2:4 — 39
- 3:19 — 39

Ancient Jewish Writers

Josephus, *Antiquitates Judaicae*
- 8.158–159 — 198
- 8.174 — 198
- 9.283–287 — 25, 70, 73, 75, 237 n. 80

Greco-Roman Literature

Herodotus, *Histories*
- 1.14.2 — 98 n. 60
- 1.95–106 — 164
- 2.141 — 199 n. 91
- 4.11–12 — 138

Index of Modern Authors

Abraham, Kathleen   5 n. 16, 18 n. 36, 158 n. 13, 159 n. 21, 170 n. 82
Achenbach, Reinhard   54 n. 39, 259
Aharoni, Yohanan   199 n. 92
Akdoğan, Rukiye   106 n. 105
Albenda, Pauline   6 n. 17, 7 n. 22, 7 n. 24, 11 nn. 1–2, 18 nn. 33–34, 60 n. 69, 68 n. 97, 80 n. 139, 161 n. 33, 162 n. 40, 165 n. 50, 206 n. 23, 209 n. 44, 222 n. 12, 239 n. 92, 247 n. 7, 253 nn. 31–32, 257, 265
Altaweel, Mark   37, 37 n. 15
Altman, Charles B.   206 n. 23, 206 n. 28
André-Salvini, Béatrice   145 n. 127
Arbach, Mounir   197 n. 86
Archer, Robin   36 n. 13, 50 n. 17
Aro, Sanna   102 n. 80, 212 n. 65
Arutunjan, N. V.   145 n. 127
Astour, Michael C.   107 n. 109
Avigad, Na'aman   47 n. 7
Bachelot, Luc   252 n. 28
Bagg, Ariel M.   18 n. 30, 52 n. 28, 259
Baker, H. D.   28 n. 12
Bányai, Michael   82 n. 150
Barag, Ariel M.   61 n. 72
Barnett, Richard D.   66 n. 90
Barstad, Hans M.   39 n. 20
Batiuk, Stephen   64 n. 81
Battini, Laura   12 n. 7, 205 n. 22, 210 n. 48, 252 n. 27, 257, 265
Baurain, Claude   72 n. 107
Becking, Bob   26 n. 4, 49 n. 11, 51 n. 21, 52 n. 24, 258
Beek, Gus W. van   197 n. 87
Berlejung, Angelika   83 n. 154, 259
Bibby, Geoffrey   192 n. 55
Binandeh, Ali   130 n. 67
Bing, John   91 n. 28
Black, Jeremy   191 n. 54
Blakely, Jeffrey A.   17 n. 29, 56 n. 46, 58 n. 55, 259
Bleibtreu, Erika   254 n. 42
Bonatz, Dominik   17 n. 30
Bonnet, Charles   199 nn. 92–93
Borger, Rykle   207 n. 34
Botta, Paul Émile   6 n. 17, 7, 59
Bottéro, Jean   4, 4 n. 15
Botto, Massimo   67 n. 92
Brannon, Barbara   79 n. 135
Breton, Jean-François   197 n. 86
Briant, Pierre   164 n. 47
Brinkman, John A.   25 n. 2, 95 n. 48, 179 n. 2, 180 n. 6, 181 n. 12, 182 n. 14, 183 n. 18, 264
Briquel-Chatonnet, Françoise   179 n. 3, 194 n. 68, 197 n. 85
Bron, François   93 n. 39
Brown, S.   164 n. 46
Bryce, Trevor   91 n. 30, 99 n. 63
Bunsen, Christian Karl Josias von   2 n. 6
Calvet, Yves   192 nn. 57–58
Çambel, Halet   93 n. 39
Cannavo, Anna   74 n. 113
Carey, Brian T.   19 n. 41
Casabonne, Olivier   91 n. 28
Castel, Georges   199 n. 93
Castellino, Giorgio Raffaele   5 n. 16, 172 n. 92

Caubet, Annie   7 n. 22, 42 n. 32, 138 n. 96
Cavigneaux, Antoine   59 n. 58, 59 n. 60, 69 n. 100, 75 n. 118, 93 n. 40, 95 nn. 50–51, 96 n. 53, 97 n. 58, 229 n. 42, 237 n. 81, 260
Chelhod, Joseph   197 n. 86
Chevalier, Nicole   7 n. 21
Çilingiroğlu, Alton   119 n. 17
Cole, Steven W.   179 n. 5
Collins, Billie Jean   1 n. 2
Collombier, Anne-Marie   72 n. 108
Cooper, Jerrold S.   14 n. 16
Crawford, Harriet   192 n. 59
Crowfoot, G. M.   47 nn. 8–9
Crowfoot, J. W.   47 nn. 8–9
Dalley, Stephanie   28 n. 13, 50 n. 17, 51 n. 22, 54 n. 39, 63 n. 75, 251 n. 24, 259, 265
Dalongeville, Rémi   191 n. 52
David, Jean-Michel   217 n. 85
Dereser, Christian   79 n. 135
Deshayes, Jean   93 n. 39
Desideri, Paolo   91 n. 28
Dever, William G.   85 n. 1
Dezső, Tamás   36 n. 13, 117 n. 7, 248 n. 11, 251 nn. 22–23, 265
Diakonoff, Igor Mikhailovich   4 n. 12, 117 n. 3, 211 n. 53, 213 n. 67
Dietrich, Manfred   13 n. 11
Dodson, Aidan   79 n. 134
Dolce, Rita   18 n. 31
Donbaz, V.   103 n. 87
Donner, Herbert   27 nn. 7–8, 29 n. 22
Dothan, Moshe   59 n. 63
Driel, G. van   39 n. 20
Dubovský, Peter   19 n. 40, 43 n. 35, 150 n. 146, 151 n. 148, 258, 261
Eckenstein, Lina   199 n. 92
Edzard, Dietz Otto   14 n. 14
Eidem, Jesper   193 n. 61, 264
Elayi, Alain G.   63 n. 77, 67 n. 92, 68 n. 98
Elayi, Josette   8 n. 25, 26 n. 3, 32 n. 30, 59 n. 58, 59 n. 60, 63 n. 77, 67 n. 92, 68 nn. 95–96, 68 n. 98, 69 n. 100, 69 n. 102, 69 nn. 104–105, 75 n. 118, 75 n. 120, 77 n. 125, 78 n. 130, 92 n. 37, 93 n. 40, 94 n. 47, 95 nn. 50–51, 96 n. 53, 97 n. 58, 229 n. 42, 237 n. 81, 237 n. 83, 259, 260
Engel, Burkhard   205 n. 18
Eph'al, Israel   51 n. 21, 51 n. 24, 130 n. 68, 194 n. 68, 194 n. 70, 195 n. 73, 195 n. 76, 197 n. 85, 199 n. 91, 259, 264
Erkanal, H.   85 n. 1, 90 n. 26, 112 n. 134, 261
Erzen, A.   91 n. 28
Fales, Frederick Mario   3 n. 11, 21 n. 44, 92 n. 36, 130 n. 69, 134 n. 83, 177 n. 1, 179 n. 2, 181 n. 11, 196 n. 77, 198 n. 88, 261, 264
Fantalkin, Alexander   57 n. 49, 60 n. 65, 94 n. 47
Farber, Walter   67 n. 92
Fielder, G.   87 nn. 2–3, 87 n. 6
Fincke, Jeannette C.   249 n. 17
Finkel, I. L.   212 n. 63, 254 n. 39
Finkelstein, Israel   52 n. 28, 60 n. 65
Fluzin, Pierre   199 n. 93
Forsberg, Stig   46 n. 6
Foster, Benjamin R.   18 n. 35, 20 n. 45
Frahm, Eckardt   12 n. 7, 13 nn. 8–9, 13 n. 12, 14 n. 15, 29 nn. 19–20, 50 n. 14, 62 n. 73, 63 nn. 75–76, 207 n. 33, 211 n. 54, 211 n. 58, 212 n. 63, 212 n. 65, 221 n. 7, 250 n. 18, 257, 265, 266
Frame, Grant   5 n. 6, 21 n. 45, 48 nn. 8–9, 55 n. 43, 59 n. 62, 64 n. 79, 64 n. 82, 66 nn. 88–89, 67 n. 91, 74 n. 113, 75 n. 120, 82 n. 151, 102 n. 79, 105 n. 99, 108 n. 112, 110 n. 126, 111 n. 128, 144 n. 123, 158 n. 13, 159 n. 19, 161, 161 n. 35, 169 n. 71, 181 n. 8, 183 n. 17, 186 n. 31, 189 n. 42, 190 n. 46, 193 nn. 62–65, 221 n. 8, 221 n. 11
Frangipane, Marcella   110 n. 123, 110 n. 125, 112 n. 135, 112 n. 137, 260
Franklin, Norma   48 n. 9, 57 n. 49, 60 n. 69, 80 n. 139, 259

French, Elizabeth 91 n. 28
Fuchs, Andreas 5 n. 16, 9 n. 26, 12 n. 4, 12 n. 6, 13, 13 nn. 8–9, 15 n. 22, 16 n. 23, 16 n. 26, 19 nn. 40–41, 20 n. 42, 21 n. 43, 21 n. 46, 23 n. 52, 31 nn. 27–29, 36 n. 13, 48 n. 10, 50 n. 16, 51 n. 18, 52 n. 24, 55 n. 42, 57 n. 50, 57 n. 52, 63 n. 74, 64 n. 78, 64 n. 82, 65 nn. 85–86, 66 n. 88, 67 n. 94, 69 n. 99, 75 n. 120, 76 nn. 123–124, 79 n. 136, 90 n. 23, 92 n. 33, 96 nn. 57–58, 101 n. 75, 105 n. 96, 105 n. 100, 106 n. 105, 108 n. 112, 108 n. 115, 109 n. 120, 110 n. 126, 111 n. 128, 115 n. 1, 144 n. 123, 149 n. 139, 156 n. 6, 167 n. 59, 167 n. 61, 169 n. 72, 183 n. 16, 202 n. 2, 202 n. 4, 207 n. 34, 211 n. 58, 212 n. 65, 220 n. 3, 225 n. 21, 229 n. 46, 233 n. 66, 237 n. 79, 248 n. 9, 251 n. 22, 254 n. 37, 254 n. 40, 257
Gadd, Cyril John 5 n. 16, 48 n. 10, 50 n. 16, 51 n. 18, 51 n. 23, 56 n. 47, 63 n. 74, 66 n. 88, 73 n. 111, 81 n. 144, 90 n. 24, 93 n. 42, 95 n. 49, 96 n. 56, 102 n. 79, 105 n. 99, 105 nn. 102–103, 106, 111 n. 129, 181 n. 9, 189 n. 43, 191 n. 53, 193 nn. 62–65, 196 n. 78, 226 n. 25, 226 n. 27, 228 n. 41, 229 n. 43, 234 n. 68
Galil, Gershon 46 n. 3, 49 n. 11, 53 n. 31, 101 nn. 72–73, 104 n. 93, 261
Gallagher, William R. 54 n. 36, 197 n. 85
Galter, Hannes D. 14 n. 17, 16 n. 24, 190 n. 50, 257, 264
Garelli, Paul 2 n. 6, 32 n. 30, 33 n. 2, 46 n. 3, 53 n. 29, 93 n. 39, 171 n. 85, 211 n. 58, 215, 215 n. 80, 246 n. 3, 253 n. 35, 254 n. 43, 255 n. 44, 265
Garstang, John 109 n. 120
George, Andrew 191 n. 54
Gibson, J.C.L. 104 n. 93
Gibson, MacGuire 104 n. 93, 167 n. 57
Gillmann, Nicolas 149 n. 142

Gitin, Seymour 85 n. 1
Gjerstad, Einar 77 n. 125
Glassner, Jean-Jacques 1 n. 4, 27 n. 8, 29 n. 20, 192 n. 58
Gordon, Robert P. 39 n. 20
Grayson, Albert Kirk 2 n. 5, 14 n. 16, 15 n. 19, 25 n. 1, 46 n. 4, 85 n. 1, 103 n. 84, 136 n. 91, 171 n. 86, 172 n. 93, 173 n. 97, 183 n. 15, 187 n. 32, 208 n. 42, 210 n. 49, 219 n. 1, 220 n. 5, 221 n. 9, 240 n. 94, 261
Green, Alberto R. W. 46 n. 2
Green, Yosef 197 n. 87
Grimal, Nicolas-Christophe 79 n. 133
Grosz, Katarzyna 41 n. 28
Gurney, O. R. 109 n. 120
Hallo, William W. 31 n. 27
Hardin, James W. 17 n. 29, 56 n. 46, 58 n. 55
Hassanzadeh, Yousef 130 n. 67
Hawkins, John David 5 n. 16, 27 n. 11, 59 n. 57, 64 n. 80, 64 nn. 82–83, 77 n. 124, 77 n. 127, 98 n. 63, 99 n. 66, 100 n. 69, 100 n. 70, 101 n. 72, 102 n. 81, 104 n. 87, 104 nn. 89–90, 106 n. 104, 107 nn. 107–108, 109 n. 120, 110 nn. 121–22, 112 n. 134, 165 n. 51, 224 n. 19, 261
Hayes, John H. 49 n. 11
Heimpel, Wolfgang 14 n. 16
Helm, P. R. 95 n. 48, 164 n. 48
Højlund, Flemming 193 n. 61, 264
Hooker, Paul K. 55 n. 40, 55 n. 43
Hornung, Erik 46 n. 2, 79 n. 133
Howard-Carter, T. 192 n. 58
Hoyland, Robert G. 194 n. 68
Hrouda, Bartel 171 n. 88
Hughes, Jeremy 49 n. 11
Hurowitz, Victor A. 134 n. 83
Iacovou, Maria 72 n. 108
Ivantchik, Askold I. 138 nn. 98–101, 211 nn. 57–58, 230 n. 51
Jasink, Anna M. 91 n. 28
Joannès, Francis 7 n. 22, 34 n. 3, 37 n. 14, 37 n. 18, 41 n. 25, 41 n.

27, 42 n. 30, 136 nn. 92–93, 171 n. 84, 177 n. 1, 182 n. 14, 183 n. 18, 191 n. 52, 196 n. 81, 202 n. 5, 205 nn. 21–22, 206 n. 24, 207 n. 29, 211 n. 58, 213 nn. 68–69, 214 n. 74, 246 n. 3, 251 n. 25
Kahn, Dan'el   80 n. 137, 80 n. 140, 81 n. 146, 82, 82 n. 152, 259
Kalaç, Mustafa   100 n. 69, 107 n. 107
Kanzaq, Rasoul Bashash   130 n. 68
Kapera, Zdzislaw Jan   5 n. 16, 60 n. 66
Kaplan, Jacob   60 n. 65
Karageorghis, Vassos   72 n. 107
Kargar, Bahman   130 n. 67
Kashkai, S. M.   117 n. 3
Kenyon, Kathleen M.   47 nn. 8–9
Kessler, Karlheinz   43 n. 36, 67 n. 91, 115 n. 2, 117 n. 6, 117 n. 8, 120 n. 18, 121 n. 25, 127 n. 49, 129 n. 62, 250 n. 20, 262
King, L. W.   68 n. 95, 96 n. 53, 137 n. 93
Kitchen, Kenneth A.   56 n. 45, 79 n. 133, 197 n. 85
Klein, Jacob   5 n. 16, 18 n. 36, 158 n. 13, 159 n. 21, 170 n. 82
Knauf, Ernst Axel   197 n. 84
Koch, Ulla Susanne   250 n. 18
Korotayev, Andrey   197 n. 86
Kossian, Aram V.   87 n. 5
Krauss, Rolf   46 n. 2, 79 n. 133
Kravitz, Kathryn F.   134 n. 83, 139 n. 102, 142 n. 114, 143 nn. 118–19, 147 nn. 134–35, 262
Kreppner, F. Janosch   16 n. 24, 146 n. 131
Kribus, Bar   197 n. 86
Kroll, Stephan   143 n. 119
Kuan, Jeffrey K.   49 n. 11
Kühne, Hartmut   41 n. 26
Labat, René   33 n. 1
Lackenbacher, Sylvie   207 n. 32
Lambert, W. G.   64 n. 80, 214
Landsberger, Benno   210 n. 51, 213 n. 68, 214, 214 n. 71, 214 n. 75, 215 n. 77, 215 n. 79, 216 nn. 81–82, 216 n. 84, 240 n. 94, 265

Lanfranchi, Giovanni Battista   89 n. 17, 92 n. 34, 92 n. 38, 93 n. 40, 95 n. 48, 97, 97 n. 59, 98 n. 62, 108 n. 112, 130 n. 69, 144 n. 124, 151, 155 n. 5, 157 n. 7, 157 n. 9, 160 n. 23, 162 n. 37, 189 n. 45, 203 n. 9, 210 n. 52, 226 n. 28, 228 n. 40, 246 n. 2, 246 n. 4, 247 n. 6, 253 n. 35, 261, 263, 264
Lauinger, Jacob   64 n. 81
Laursen, Steffen Terp   192 n. 56
Laxer, James   2, 3 n. 8
Lehmann-Haupt, C. F.   211 n. 55
Leick, Gwendolyn   173 n. 96
Lemaire, André   46 n. 3, 53 n. 29, 57 n. 48, 93 n. 39, 94 n. 44, 130 n. 68, 171 n. 85, 211 n. 58, 246 n. 3, 253 n. 35, 255 n. 44, 261
Levine, Louis D.   5 n. 16, 104 n. 88, 134 n. 83, 139, 139 n. 105, 144 n. 124, 151 n. 150, 152 n. 152, 153 n. 1, 159 n. 14, 161 n. 31, 161 n. 34, 166 n. 56, 167 n. 60, 172 n. 90, 189 n. 45, 227 n. 31, 227 n. 34, 262, 263
Lewis, Brian   14 n. 16
Lewis, Theodore J.   17 n. 30, 19 n. 39
Lie, Arthur Gotfred   5 n. 6, 21 nn. 47–48, 67 n. 94, 89 n. 15, 90 nn. 21–22, 94 n. 46, 188 n. 37, 257
Linder, Elisha   68 n. 97
Lipiński, Edward   63 n. 75, 65 n. 84, 65 n. 86, 66 n. 88, 93 n. 39, 98 n. 62, 179 n. 2
Liverani, Mario   1 n. 4, 33 n. 1, 46 n. 1, 77 n. 128, 83 n. 153, 100 n. 69, 110 nn. 124–25, 112 n. 135, 115 n. 2, 144 n. 124, 155 n. 2, 164 n. 47, 164 n. 49, 168 n. 68, 180 n. 6, 260, 263
Loud, Gordon   206 n. 23, 20 n. 28
Luckenbill, Daniel David   69 n. 103, 74 n. 115, 123 n. 31, 181 n. 10, 207 n. 33, 212 n. 64
Luukko, Mikko   249 n. 15, 266
Lyon, David Gordon   5 n. 16
MacGinnis, John   51 n. 19, 120 n. 22
Machinist, Peter   54 n. 39, 182 n. 14

Malbran-Labat, Florence   74 n. 113, 77 nn. 126–27, 77 n. 129, 191 n. 51
Mallowan, Max E. L.   39 n. 19
Marf, Dlshad   146 n. 131
Marriott, John   36 n. 13, 135 n. 84
Marti, Lionel   207 n. 33, 209 n. 44, 209 n. 46
Masry, Abdullah H.   192 n. 59
Matney, Timothy   120 n. 22
Matthiae, Paolo   203 n. 9, 207 n. 30, 252 n. 28, 253 n. 30, 265
Mattila, Raija   44 n. 41, 172 n. 89, 172 n. 91, 185 n. 26, 209 n. 44
May, Nathalie Naomi   6 n. 18, 14 n. 17, 27 n. 9, 28 n. 15, 58 n. 55, 134 n. 83, 203 n. 9, 207 n. 32, 247 n. 7, 248 nn. 11–12, 249 nn. 15–16, 250 nn. 18–21, 266
Mayer, Walter   13 n. 13, 262
McKenzie, Steven L.   49 n. 12
Meissner, Bruno   27 n. 8
Mellink, Machteld   106 n. 106
Melville, Sarah C.   99 n. 64, 99 nn. 66–67, 100 n. 69, 101 n. 75, 102 n. 78, 102 n. 81, 103 n. 86
Merrillees, Robert S.   72 n. 107
Miroop, Marc van de   12 n. 3, 15 n. 20, 141 n. 111, 142 nn. 115–16, 262
Mollasalehi, H.   130 n. 67
Moorey, P. R. S.   192 n. 59
Müller-Karpe, Andreas   112 n. 136
Muscarella, Oscar W.   90 n. 26, 140 n. 107, 261, 262
Na'aman, Nadav   26 n. 4, 31 n. 27, 45 n. 1, 46 n. 2, 46 nn. 5–6, 48 n. 11, 51 n. 18, 52 nn. 25–29, 53 n. 31, 54 n. 35, 56 n. 45, 60 n. 68, 61 n. 70, 66 n. 88, 74 n. 112, 75 n. 119, 82 n. 151, 158 n. 11, 258, 259, 260
Nebes, Norbert   194 n. 69
Neumann, Hans   249 n. 17, 251 n. 23
Niederreiter, Zoltán   248 n. 12, 250 n. 18, 266
Nováček, Karel   40 n. 22
Novotny, J. R.   13 n. 11

N'Shea, Omar   35 n. 10, 248 n. 11, 266
Oded, Bustenay   42 n. 33, 51 n. 20
Olmstead, Albert Ten Eyck   27 n. 8, 30, 30 n. 24, 49 n. 11, 161 n. 30, 213 n. 67, 214 n. 72, 258
Oppenheim, A. Leo   134 n. 83, 147 n. 132, 151 n. 147
Oren, E. D.   56, 56 n. 48, 226 n. 26
Parker, Bradley J.   6 n. 18, 115 n. 2, 118 n. 10, 118 nn. 12–13, 119 n. 15, 120 n. 20, 121 n. 24, 122 n. 27, 122 n. 29, 124 n. 38, 126 n. 44, 126 n. 46, 127 n. 49, 127 n. 51, 128 n. 57, 129 nn. 61–62, 262
Parpola, Simo   36 n. 12, 42 n. 32, 43 n. 36, 44 n. 41, 54 n. 39, 59 n. 58, 83 n. 153, 85 n. 1, 89, 109 n. 120, 127 n. 48, 148 n. 138, 184, 201 n. 1, 202 n. 3, 202 nn. 8–9, 205 nn. 15–17, 206 n. 28, 208, 208 n. 38, 208 n. 42, 210 n. 51, 213 n. 68, 214, 214 n. 71, 214 n. 75, 215 n. 77, 215 n. 79, 216 nn. 81–82, 216 n. 84, 240 n. 94, 252 n. 29, 265
Payraudeau, Frédéric   80 n. 140, 82 n. 150
Pearce, Laurie E.   6 n. 20, 12 n. 7
Peker, Hasan   66 n. 87
Piotrovskij, Boris B.   151 n. 151
Place, Victor   7, 206 n. 23
Ponchia, Simonetta   33 n. 2
Porter, Barbara Nevling   74 n. 113, 79 n. 134, 215 n. 79
Porter, Robert M.   77 n. 128, 105 nn. 96–97, 109 n. 120, 123 n. 33
Postgate, John Nicholas   2 n. 6, 20 n. 43, 34 n. 4, 36 n. 13, 43 n. 37, 50 n. 17, 89 n. 13, 99 n. 66, 102 n. 81, 160 n. 28, 172 n. 89, 172 n. 91, 185 n. 26, 191 n. 54, 205 n. 15, 251 n. 22, 254 n. 43, 258, 261, 263, 264
Potts, Daniel T.   192 nn. 55–56, 193 nn. 61–62, 264
Prabha Ray, Himanshu   193 n. 61
Priese, Karl-Heinz   79 n. 134
Radner, Karen   5 n. 16, 25 n. 2, 28 n. 12, 29 n. 20, 33 n. 1, 34 n. 4, 35 n. 11,

INDEX OF MODERN AUTHORS 273

36 n. 13, 37 nn. 16–17, 39 n. 19, 40, 40 nn. 22–24, 42 n. 31, 42 n. 33, 43 n. 36, 43 n. 38, 43 n. 1, 59 n. 58, 64 n. 82, 67 n. 91, 69 n. 99, 72 n. 107, 74 n. 113, 77 nn. 126–28, 78 n. 132, 107 n. 110, 108, 108 n. 114, 109 nn. 118–19, 112 n. 136, 115 nn. 1–2, 117 n. 5, 117 nn. 7–8, 122 n. 28, 122 n. 30, 123 n. 32, 124 n. 36, 126 n. 45, 130 n. 66, 135 n. 84, 136 n. 92, 138 n. 95, 144 n. 126, 145 n. 128, 146 nn. 130–131, 149 n. 142, 152 n. 152, 162 n. 37, 162 n. 41, 166 n. 53, 167 n. 57, 168 n. 64, 168 n. 66, 168 nn. 69–70, 188 n. 40, 225 n. 23, 227 n. 32, 244 n. 1, 248 n. 11, 249 n. 14, 249 n. 17, 254 n. 38, 258, 260, 262, 263, 266
Rainey, Anson F. 57 n. 48
Reade, Julian E. 48 n. 9, 49 n. 11, 132 n. 76, 149 n. 142, 155 n. 2, 155 n. 4, 159 n. 15, 170 n. 83, 205 n. 19, 212 n. 63, 223 n. 15, 254 n. 39, 262, 264
Redford, Donald B. 82 n. 150
Reich, Ronny 57 n. 48
Renger, Johannes 73 n. 110
Retsö, Jan 194 n. 68
Reyes, A. T. 72 n. 107
Rezvani, H. 130 n. 67
Riis, P. J. 59 n. 58
Roaf, Michael 143 n. 119, 166 n. 54
Röllig, W. 96 n. 53, 104 n. 89, 212 n. 60
Rollinger, Robert 92 n. 36, 95 n. 48, 95 n. 50, 98 n. 61
Roth, Martha 29 n. 18
Rothenberg, Benno 199 n. 92
Roustaei, K. 130 n. 67
Russell, John Malcom 251 n. 26
Saggs, Henry William Frederick 5 n. 16, 26 n. 5, 29 n. 21, 48 n. 10, 54 nn. 36–37, 62 n. 73, 70 n. 106, 89 n. 13, 92 n. 36, 93 n. 40, 172 n. 92, 181 n. 13, 188 n. 37, 220 n. 4, 221 n. 7, 221 n. 10, 229 n. 45, 251 n. 23, 253 n. 33, 266
Salles, Jean-François 192 nn. 57–58, 193 n. 61

Salvini, Mirjo 136 n. 92, 137 n. 94, 138 nn. 96–97, 139 nn. 105–7, 140 nn. 109–10, 144 n. 124, 145 n. 127, 262
Sancisi-Weerdenburg, Hélène 164 n. 48
Sanlaville, Paul 191 n. 52
Sano, Katsuji 16 n. 24
Sazonov, Vladimir 21 n. 45
Schmökel, Harmut 27 n. 7
Schoors, Anton 260
Scurlock, Jo Ann 164 n. 46
Sence, Guillaume 11 n. 2, 29 n. 20, 207 n. 32, 257
Seux, Marie Joseph 1 n. 3
Shavit, Alon 56 n. 48
Singer-Avitz, Lily 60 n. 65
Smith, Sidney 23 n. 53, 212 n. 60, 213 n. 67
Soden, Wolfram von 12 n. 7, 27 n. 8, 211 n. 56, 214, 214 nn. 72–73
Soysal, Oguz 87 n. 3
Spalinger, Anthony 82 n. 150
Spek, Robartus J. van der 186 n. 31, 188 n. 38, 188 n. 40, 265
Squitieri, Andrea 146 n. 131
Stein, Peter 194 n. 69
Steiner, Gerd 26 n. 4
Stern, Ephraim 45 n. 1, 52 n. 27
Streck, Maximilian 211 n. 56
Sweeney, Marvin A. 53 nn. 33–34, 56 n. 45, 260
Sznycer, Maurice 93 n. 39
Tadmor, Hayim 5 n. 16, 30 n. 25, 30, 49 n. 11, 50 n. 13, 53 n. 34, 55 n. 41, 56 n. 45, 56 n. 47, 57 n. 51, 58, 58 nn. 55–56, 59 n. 58, 60 n. 66, 77 n. 127, 81, 81 n. 145, 148 n. 138, 159 n. 14, 171 n. 87, 210 n. 51, 211 n. 53, 211 n. 58, 212 n. 59, 213 n. 68, 214, 214 nn. 70–71, 215 n. 77, 215 n. 79, 216 nn. 81–82, 216 n. 84, 240 n. 94, 258, 265
Tallet, Philippe 199 n. 93
Tallqvist, Knut Leonard 15 n. 18
Tavernier, Jan 173 n. 96
Tetley, M. Christine 46 n. 3, 49 nn. 11–12, 260

Thiele, Edwin R. 49 n. 11
Thomas, Felix 27 n. 10, 258
Thompson, R. Campbell 28 n. 14, 108 n. 117, 211 n. 53
Thureau-Dangin, François 5 n. 16, 134 n. 83, 145 n. 129, 263
Tsetskhladze, Gocha R. 87 n. 2
Tunca, Onhan 66 n. 90, 224 n. 20
Ungnad, Arthur 31 n. 28, 211 n. 58
Ur, Jason A. 42 n. 34, 254 n. 41
Valbelle, Dominique 199 nn. 92–93
Vallat, François 171 n. 84, 173 n. 96
Vera Chamaza, Galo W. 13, 13 n. 13, 26 nn. 4–5, 28 nn. 15–16, 29 n. 22, 145 n. 127, 258, 263
Villard, Pierre 1 n. 3, 19 n. 40
Wagner, Jörg 106 n. 106
Warburton, David 46 n. 2, 79 n. 133
Wartke, Ralf-Bernhard 145 n. 129
Waterman, Leroy 195 nn. 74–75, 204 n. 14, 210 n. 52, 253 n. 34
Weaver, Ann M. 215 n. 76, 265
Weidner, Ernst Friedrich 15, 20, 28 n. 16, 30 n. 25
Weippert, Manfred 103 n. 87
Weissbach, Franz Heinrich 5 n. 16, 26 n. 6
Westenholz, Aage 1 n. 1
Westenholz, Joan Goodnick 1 n. 1, 14 n. 16
Wilcke, Claus 39 n. 20
Wilson, Karen L. 7 n. 22
Winckler, Hugo 5 n. 16, 18 n. 38, 46 n. 5, 48 n. 11, 53 n. 32, 58 n. 57, 59 n. 59, 69 n. 101, 95 n. 51, 214 n. 71, 214 n. 75
Winter, Irène 77 n. 128, 209 n. 44
Wittke, Anne-Marie 97 n. 2, 87 n. 7
Woolley, Leonard 66 n. 90
Yamada, Shigeo 99 n. 65
Young, T. Cuyler 139 n. 105
Younger, K. Lawson 26 n. 4, 49 n. 11, 51 n. 20, 51 nn. 22–23, 52 n. 24, 52 n. 27, 53 n. 34, 54 n. 38, 59 n. 63, 61 n. 70, 98 n. 62, 226 n. 27, 258, 260
Yurco, Frank 82 n. 150
Zadok, Ran 52 nn. 26–27, 54 n. 39, 60 n. 68, 260
Zawadzki, Stefan 44 n. 41, 247 n. 7, 258, 266
Zimansky, Paul E. 139 nn. 103–4, 140 n. 107, 144 n. 124, 147 n. 132, 152 n. 152, 263

Index of Personal Names

Abibaal, king of Tyre (before 970)   73
Abraham, biblical patriarch   195
Adâ, ruler of Shurda   159
Adad-issêa, governor of Zamua   160
Adad-narari II, king of Assyria (911–891)   124, 172
Adad-narari III, king of Assyria (810–783)   37, 103–4, 107
Adapu, mythical sage   16
Ahat-Abisha, Sargon's daughter   102, 232
Ahaz, king of Judah (ca. 735–719)   52
Ahî-Mîti, king of Ashdod   57–58, 233–34
Ahundara, king presumably of Dilmun   193
Alexander Polyhistor, Greek scholar, enslaved by the Romans (first century BCE)   70
Alexander III the Great, king of Macedonia (336–323)   2, 19
Ambaris, king of Tabal   89, 91, 98 n. 63, 101–3, 232–33, 242, 245
Amitashshi, ruler of Karalla, brother of Ashur-lêi   18, 159, 169, 232, 242
Argishti I, king of Urartu (787–766)   110, 137
Argishti II, king of Urartu (713–679)   108, 125–26, 149, 151, 238
Ariazâ, co-ruler of Kumme   124
Ariye, king of Kumme   124–25
Ashîpâ, governor in northern part of the empire, possibly of Tushhan   118, 120–22
Ashpa-bara, king of Ellipi   170, 170 n. 82, 239, 243

Ashurbanipal, king of Assyria (668–627)   3, 23, 40, 51, 74, 76, 78, 128–29, 136, 174, 207, 207 n. 34, 249
Ashur-bêlu-usur, governor of Kishesim or Parsua   162
Ashur-dûr-pânîya, treasurer and governor of the Mashennu province   129
Ashur-lêi, city lord of Karalla   133, 158–59, 232, 240, 242
Ashur-nâdin-shumi, king of Babylon (699–694)   28–29
Ashur-rêsûwa, royal delegate of Kumme, reporting on Urartian activities   123, 125, 138, 150
Ashur-sharru-usur, governor of Que   88–89, 92–94, 101, 236
Ashurnasirpal II, king of Assyria (883–859)   1, 3, 7, 11, 17, 38, 107, 160, 207, 209, 220, 251
Assur-narari V, king of Assyria (754–745)   137
Astyages, Median king (ca. 584–550)   164
Atalia, wife of Sargon II   28, 54
Awarikku. See Urik
Azâ, king of Mannea (719–716)   133, 223, 241
Azitawada, king of the Danunians (Adana), vassal of Urik (last part of the eighth century BCE)   93
Azuri, king of Ashdod   57–58, 233, 242
Bag-dâti, Mannean governor of Uishdish   18, 133, 133 n. 80, 227, 242
Bakenrenef, ruler of Saïs   58, 81

Banîtu, queen of Assyria, wife of Shalmaneser V 28
Bar-rakib, king of Samal (ca. 733–713/1) 98
Bazia, crown prince of Ukku 123
Bêl-aplu-iddina, ruler of Allabria in western Iran 158, 232
Bêl-dîni, governor of Damascus 41
Bêl-sharru-usur, city lord of Kishesim in western Iran 161, 227, 242
Berossos, Babylonian priest (end of fourth century BCE) 95
Bochoris. See Bakenrenef
Cyrus II, king of Anshan, then of Persian Empire (549–530) 164
Daiukku, Mannean governor 64, 133, 228
Daltâ. See Taltâ
David, king of Israel and Judah (ca. 1010–970) 69
Deioces, founder of the Median Empire 164
Elulaios. See Lulî
Erîba-Marduk, Chaldean chief, king of Babylon (769–761) 183
Esarhaddon, king of Assyria (680–669) 3, 17, 74, 76, 90, 112, 117, 136, 164, 207, 207 n. 34, 215–16, 249
Ezekiel, biblical prophet 117, 195
Gabbu-ana-Ashur, high official, possibly palace herald 150
Gindibu, Arabian ruler under the reign of Shalmaneser III 195
Gunzinânu, king of Kammanu with its capital Melid 30, 111–12, 233
Gurdî, ruler of Kulummâ in Anatolia 103, 210–12, 212 n. 64, 213, 241
Gurdî, ruler of Til-Garimme 212
Gûsh, founder of Bît-Agusi ca. 890 65
Hallushu-inshushinak, king of Elam (699–693) 175
Ham, son of Noah 195
Hanunu, king of Gaza 55, 61, 79–80, 221–22, 241
Hattushili. See Qatazili

Hazail, king of Qedar around 680 197
Hazail, chieftain of Gambulu in 710 197
Herodotus, Greek historian (fifth century BCE) 98 n. 60, 138, 164, 199 n. 91
Hezekiah, king of Judah (719–699) 46, 53, 54, 60, 185, 234, 240
Hiram I, king of Tyre (ca. 970–936) 73
Homer, Greek mythical poet, associated with the author of the *Iliad* and the *Odyssey* 72
Hoshea, king of Israel (ca. 731–722) 46, 49–50
Hullî, king of Tabal 30, 99, 101, 232
Hullû. See Hullî
Humban-nikash I, king of Elam (743–717) 30–31, 171–73, 184, 220, 222, 241
Hundâru. See Ahundara
Hu-Teshub, ruler of Shubria, Assyrian vassal 118
Iabâ, Assyrian queen, wife of Tiglath-pileser III 28, 54
Ianzû, king of Hubushkia/Nairi, Assyrian vassal 143–44, 228, 231
Iatie, queen of the Arabs in the reign of Sennacherib 196
Iaûbidî, rebel leader in Hamath 18, 48–50, 55, 61–65, 67, 221–22, 224, 241
Iddin-ahhe, governor of Simirra, eponym in 688 67
Iddin-ahhe, governor of Khorsabad, eponym in 693 214
Idibi-ilu, Arab sheikh at the border of Egypt in the reign of Tiglath-pileser III 83
Il-Iada, possibly an Aramean sheikh described as governor of Dêr 172, 185–87
Ilu-bidi. See Iaûbidî
Iranzû, king of Mannea 131–33, 135, 223, 241
Irhulena, king of Hamath in the reign of Shalmaneser III 65
Isaiah, biblical prophet 3, 54 n. 39, 58, 185, 195, 214
Ishmael, son of Abraham 195

Ishpuini, king of Urartu (ca. 825–810) 137, 145
Issar-shumu-iqisha, provincial officer, active in the northeast of the empire 135, 230
Itamar, ruler of Saba, possibly king 80, 196–97, 229
Ittî, city lord of Allabria in the Zagros mountains 64, 133, 158, 242
Ittobaal I, king of Tyre (ca. 888–856) 69
Jeroboam, king of Israel (ca. 931–910) 3
Jonah, biblical prophet 39
Josephus, Jewish historian (first century CE) 25, 69–71, 73, 75, 237, 237 n. 80
Karakku, Median city lord of Uriakku 168
Khilaruata, king of Melid in the first half of the eighth century BCE 110
Kiakki, king of Shinuhtu in Tabal 89, 100, 102, 224, 241
Kibaba, city lord of Harhar 162, 227, 242
Kikki, son of Tuatti, ruler of Tabal in the reign of Shalmaneser III 99
Kirua, ruler of Hilakku in the reign of Sennacherib 95
Kisir-Ashur, governor of Khorsabad 208
Kiyakiya. *See* Kiakki
Kunzinânu. *See* Gunzinânu
Kurtî, king of Atunna in Tabal 100, 102–3, 212, 212 n. 60, 224, 241
Kushkâiu, individual in charge of a town, possibly in Zamua 160
Kushtashpi, king of Kummuhu in the reign of Tiglath-pileser III 107
Kuzi-Teshub, king of Carchemish in the ninth century BCE 110
Laramas I, dynastic founder in Gurgum 105
Liphur-Bêl, governor of Amidi 120
Lulî, king of Tyre (ca. 728–695) 69–70, 71–73, 75, 78, 237
Manethon, Egyptian priest, writer in Greek (third century BCE) 81

Maniye, king of Ukku in the reign of Sennacherib and possibly earlier 123
Mannu-kî-Nînua, governor of Harhar 163
Marduk-apla-iddina. *See* Merodach-baladan II
Marduk-balâssu-iqbi, king of Babylon (ca. 818–813) 185
Marduk-sharrani, Assyrian official in Babylonia 186
Marduk-zâkir-shumi I, king of Babylon (854–819) 182
Mattan II, king of Tyre (ca. 729) 69
Mattî. *See* Kurtî
Menander of Pergamon, Greek author (second century BCE) 70
Merodach-baladan II, king of Babylon (721–710, 703) 30, 45, 94, 171–74, 181, 183–90, 196, 215, 219–22, 231, 234–36, 243, 246
Midas, king of Phrygia (ca. 738–695) 87–94, 96–98, 100–102, 105, 111, 113, 223–24, 228, 233, 236–37
Minua, king of Urartu (805–788) 117, 137, 145
Mitâ. *See* Midas
Mitatti, king of Zikirtu, in western Iran 131–32, 134–35, 139, 223, 230, 241–42, 247
Mugallu, ruler of Melid 112
Mutallu, king of Gurgum 105–6, 234, 242
Mutallu, king of Kummuhu 105, 108, 112, 233–34, 238, 242–43
Muwatalis. *See* Mutallu of Gurgum
Muwattalli, Hittite king 105
Nabopolassar, king of Babylon (626–605) 136
Nabû-ahu-usur, royal bodyguard active in Zamua 160
Nabû-bêlu-kain, governor of Harhar 44, 163
Nabû-belu-usur, governor of Khorsabad, eponym in 672 214

Nabû-damqi-ilâni, individual stationed at Sagbat 174
Nabû-deni-epush, governor of Nineveh, eponym in 704 212
Nabû-hamâtûa, royal official, possibly deputy governor of the province of Zamua 160
Nabû-mukîn-zêri, chief of the Chaldean tribe of Bît-Amukkâni 182–83
Nabû-nâsir, king of Babylon (747–734) 182
Nabû-rêmanni, governor of Parsua 162
Nabû-shallimshunu, royal scribe 134
Nabû-shuma-ukîn II, rebellious candidate to throne of Babylon (732) 182
Nabû-zuqup-kênu, scribe from Nimrud 250
Nadi-ilu, chief cupbearer 129
Naram-Sîn, Assyrian king (early second millennium) 1
Nashur-bel, governor of Amidi, eponym in 705 210
Nebuchadnezzar II, king of Babylon (604–562) 109, 192
Nibê, king of Ellipi 170, 174, 239, 243
Nikaule, queen of Saba; ruled Egypt and Ethiopia according to Josephus 198
Noah, biblical hero of the deluge 136, 195
Omri: king of Israel (ca. 885–874) 45
Osorkon IV, pharaoh, probably of the Twenty-Third Dynasty 46, 79–81, 226
Padi, local ruler of Ekron 61 n. 70
Palalam. See Laramas I
Panamuwa II, king of Samal (ca. 740–733) 104
Peqah, king of Israel (ca. 740–732) 46
Phidias, Athenian sculptor (fifth century BCE) 4
Piankhy, pharaoh of the Twenty-Fifth Dynasty 79–80
Piru. See Shabaka
Pisîri, king of Carchemish (ca. 738–717) 66, 88–89, 224, 241

Piye. See Piankhy
Pulû. See Tiglath-pileser III
Qatazili, king of Kummuhu 107
Qurdi-ashur-lâmur, Assyrian official, possibly settled at Ushu 69, 92
Rahianu, king of Damascus (ca. 750–732) 65, 196
Rametî, Median city lord of Uriakku 168
Rêû, commander-in-chief in Egypt 55, 79, 80
Rezin. See Rahianu
Rusâ I, king of Urartu (730–714) 17, 20–21, 90, 102, 132–33, 135, 138–39, 141–51, 158, 227, 229–32, 242
Rusâ II, king of Urartu (678–654) 151
Sama, a Samarian deportee 51
Samsi, queen of the Arabs 80, 196–97, 229
Samsî-Addu, king of Ekallâtum (1807–1776) 1
Saninu (?), Elamite commander of the fortress of Samuna 173
Sarduri II, king of Urartu (765–733) 107, 110, 137, 149
Sargon I, king of Assyria (ca. 1920–1881) 4
Sargon II, king of Assyria (722–705)
Sargon of Akkad/Agade, king of Assyria (ca. 2335–2279) 1, 4, 4 n. 14, 14, 23, 27
Sennacherib, king of Assyria (704–681) 3, 11, 13 n. 10, 19, 23, 27, 29, 36, 39, 43, 52–53, 61, 69, 71, 74–75, 95–97, 112, 122–23, 131, 138, 170, 174, 181, 192, 194, 196–97, 201, 206–7, 210, 212–16, 220, 238, 240, 246, 248
Sha-Ashur-dubbu, governor of Tushhan, eponym in 707 118, 120, 121
Shabaka, pharaoh (ca. 720–707/6) 80, 81, 82, 196, 229, 234, 239
Shabatka, pharaoh (accession year, ca. 707/6) 81, 82, 82 n. 151, 239, 243
Shalmaneser I, king of Assyria (1273–1244) 145

INDEX OF PERSONAL NAMES 279

Shalmaneser III, king of Assyria (858–824)   65, 68, 91, 99, 107, 109–10, 117, 139, 164, 166, 182, 195
Shalmaneser IV, king of Assyria (782–773)   103, 104, 107
Shalmaneser V, king of Assyria (726–722)   3, 15, 25–28, 28 n. 12, 29, 29 n. 20, 30–32, 46–47, 49–51, 61, 70–71, 97, 101, 104, 170, 172, 183, 190, 210, 211 n. 53, 219–21, 235, 253
Shamshi Adad I. *See* Samsî-Addu
Shamshi Adad V, king of Assyria (823–811)   182
Sharru-êmuranni, governor of Zamua, eponym in 712   44, 160, 187
Sharru-lu-dari, governor of Khorsabad, eponym in 664   214
Shem, son of Noah   195
Shêp-sharri, city lord of Shurgadia in the province of Parsua   159
Shilkani, pharaoh, possibly the same as Osorkon IV   80–81, 226
Shilta, ghost king of Tyre   75
Shulmu-bêli, Assyrian deputy, responsible in Musasir   150
Shuppiluliuma. *See* Ushpilulume
Shutruk-nahhunte II, king of Elam (717–699)   170, 173–74, 187, 235, 239, 243
Shutur-nahhunte, king of Elam (ca. 645–620)   173
Sîn-ahu-usur, vizier, "favorite brother" of Sargon II   27, 206
Singamshibu (?), commander of the fortress of Bâb-dûri   173
So. *See* Osorkon IV
Solomon, king of Israel and Judah (ca. 970–931)   197–98
Tab-shar-Ashur, chief treasurer, governor of the Mashennu province, eponym in 717   127–29, 132, 203
Tab-sill-Esharra, governor of Assur, eponym in 716   212
Taklak-ana-Bel, governor of Nasibina, eponym in 715   247 n. 7

Taltâ, king of Ellipi (737–713)   162, 169, 170, 175, 227, 232, 239
Tarhu-lara, king of Gurgum (ca. 742–711)   104–6, 234, 242
Tarhun-azi, man of Melid, successor of king Gunzinânu   30, 105, 111–12, 233, 242
Teelhunu, queen of the Arabs in the reign of Sennacherib   196, 197
Tefnakht, pharaoh (ca. 736–729)   79, 81
Telusina, ruler of Andia   133, 228
Tiglath-pileser I, king of Assyria (1114–1076)   87, 145, 179
Tiglath-pileser III, king of Assyria (744–727)   2–3, 13, 19, 25, 27–28, 32, 36, 42–43, 45, 50–52, 55–56, 61–62, 65, 67, 69–70, 79, 83, 88, 91–92, 97–99, 101–4, 107, 110, 119–20, 122, 126, 130, 137, 155, 157, 160, 166, 170, 172, 179–83, 190, 195–96, 198, 220–22, 235, 251
Tuatti, ruler of Tabal in the reign of Shalmaneser III   99
Tukultî-Ninurta I, king of Assyria (1243–1207)   38
Uassurme, ruler of Tabal in the reign of Tiglath-pileser III   101
Ullusunu, Mannean ruler   133, 135–36, 158, 223, 227–28, 230–31, 241–42
Ulûlâyu, see Shalmaneser V
Upêri, king of Dilmun   77, 191, 193, 236
Uppite, Median city lord of Uriakku   168
Urik, king of Que (last part of the eighth century BCE)   88, 91–93, 97, 228
Urikki. *See* Urik
Urpalâ, king of Tuhana in Tabal   101
Ursâ. *See* Rusâ
Ur-Zababa, governor of Kish   14
Urzana, king of Musasir   145–51, 231
Ushpilulume, ruler of Kummuhu in the reign of Adad-narari III   107
Warpalawas. *See* Urpalâ
Yamani, king of Ashdod   53, 58–59, 81–82, 234, 239, 243
Yoktan, second son of Eber   197

Zabibê, queen of the Arabs in the reign of Tiglath-pileser III 195
Zalâ, city lord of Kitpatai in Gizilbunda, in central Zagros 159
Zimredda, king of Sidon (ca. 1360–1330) 71
Zimri-Lim, king of Mari (ca. 1782–1759) 124
Zîzî, city lord of Appatar in Gizilbunda, in central Zagros 159